Media Choice

This timely collection represents the next generation of research in media psychology, bridging selective exposure to a larger framework of choice in media usage. Considering the myriad media options available, this work seeks to answer such questions as: What mechanisms guide an individual's exposure to/choice of media? How can researchers model them?

Editor Tilo Hartmann provides a thorough overview of various perspectives on media choice, offering a foundation to stimulate new research initiatives. Contributors to the work include top-notch scholars from the United States and Europe, representing the current state of research in this area.

This volume will be of great interest to scholars utilizing a psychological approach to media study, and it will be relevant to researchers seeking a state-of-the-art overview about the field or who are interested in a systematized look at the research conducted in the past.

Tilo Hartmann, Ph.D., is an Assistant Professor in the Department of Communication Science at the VU University, Amsterdam. Previous affiliations include positions at the Hanover University of Music and Drama, the University of Southern California, the University of Erfurt, the Institute of Mass Communication and Media Research, and the University of Zurich. His research interests focus on media use, in particular selective exposure, reception, and effects.

Media Choice

A Theoretical and Empirical Overview

Edited by Tilo Hartmann

Routledge
Taylor & Francis Group

NEW YORK AND LONDON

First published 2009
by Routledge
270 Madison Ave, New York, NY 10016

Simultaneously published in the UK
by Routledge
2 Park Square, Milton Park, Abingdon, Oxon OX14 4RN

Routledge is an imprint of the Taylor & Francis Group, an informa business

Typeset in Galliard by Wearset Ltd, Boldon, Tyne and Wear
Printed and bound in the United States of America on acid-
free paper by Sheridan Books, Inc.

Library of Congress Cataloging-in-Publication Data
Media choice : a theoretical and empirical overview/[edited]
by Tilo Hartmann.
p. cm.

1. Mass media–Social aspects. 2. Mass media–Psychological
aspects. 3. Choice (Psychology) I. Hartmann, Tilo.
HM1206.M3894 2008
306.4'6--dc22
2008027006

ISBN10: 0-415-96456-3 (hbk)
ISBN10: 0-415-96458-X (pbk)
ISBN10: 0-203-93865-8 (ebk)

ISBN13: 978-0-415-96456-2 (hbk)
ISBN13: 978-0-415-96458-6 (pbk)
ISBN13: 978-0-203-93865-2 (ebk)

Contents

Figures

Tables

Contributors

Helena Bilandzic, Ph.D., Assistant Professor at the University of Erfurt in Germany. Research interests include media use, cultivation, narrative persuasion, qualitative and quantitative methodology.

Tabea Böcking, Ph.D., Assistant Professor at the Ludwig-Maximilians-University Munich. Interests include framing research, search engines and new media, media choice, and methodological issues.

Alan R. Dennis, Professor of Information Systems. Holds the John T. Chambers Chair of Internet Systems in the Kelley School of Business at Indiana University. His research interests include team collaboration, knowledge management, and the Internet.

Wolfgang Donsbach, Professor of Communication and founding director of the Department of Communication at Dresden University of Technology, Germany. He has taught at the universities of Dortmund, Mainz and Berlin in Germany, and was a visiting professor at Syracuse University (USA), University of Navarra (Spain), and Harvard University. He has been president of the World Association for Public Opinion Research (1995–1996) and the International Communication Association (2004–2005). Donsbach has been managing editor of the *International Journal of Public Opinion Research* between 1999 and 2007. His main research interests are in journalism, political communication, and exposure to communication.

Andreas Fahr, Dr. rer. pol., Assitant Professor at the Ludwig-Maximilians-University Munich. Scholarship focuses on mass communication, mainly from a media psychological perspective. Interests include media choice, media use, psychophysiology, entertainment, advertising, and methodological issues.

Robert M. Fuller, Ph.D., Assistant Professor at the University of Tennessee, USA. Interests include the use of collaborative technologies and virtual team performance, participation and individual use of communication technologies, and the improvement of requirements elicitation through the use of semi-structured communication techniques.

Mirta Galesic, Ph.D., Research Scientist at the Max Planck Institute for Human Development, Center for Adaptive Behavior and Cognition, Berlin, Germany. Research interests include judgment and decision making, risk communication, and survey methodology.

Gerd Gigerenzer, Director, Max Planck Institute for Human Development and Head of the Harding Center for Risk Literacy. Research interests include models of bounded rationality, social intelligence, heuristics of scientific discovery, and the philosophy, history, and methodology of the social sciences.

Tilo Hartmann, Ph.D., Assistant Professor in the Department of Communication Science at the VU University, Amsterdam. Research interests focus on media use, in particular selective exposure, reception, and effects.

Matthias R. Hastall, M.A., doctoral candidate and lecturer at the University of Erfurt, Germany. His interests include selective exposure research, health communication, and the role of individual differences in media behavior.

Marina Krcmar, Ph.D., Associate Professor at the Department of Communication at Wake Forest University. Her research focuses on the role of media in the lives of children and adolescents.

Cees M. Koolstra, Ph.D., Associate Professor at the VU University, Amsterdam. His research interests concern theoretical and methodological approaches to media use and effects, particularly in respect to television and other audiovisual media.

Robert LaRose, Ph.D., University of Southern California, 1979, Professor in the Department of Telecommunication, Information Studies, and Media, Michigan State University. His interests are the uses and effects of new media.

Julian N. Marewski, Post doctoral research fellow at the Max Planck Institute for Human Development, Center for Adaptive Behavior and Cognition, Berlin, Germany. Research interests include judgment and decision making, memory, computer modeling, and methodology.

Teresa K. Naab, M.A. in Media Management, research assistant at University for Music and Drama, Department for Journalism and Communication Studies, Hanover/Germany. Her main interests are audience research (especially routine and ritual media use) and issues of press freedom and freedom of opinion.

Mary Beth Oliver, Ph.D., Professor of Media Studies and Communications at Penn State University. Interests include media and emotion, media and cognition, psychology of entertainment, and social cognition.

Ute Ritterfeld, Professor for Media Psychology, co-founder and director of interdisciplinary research at the Center for Advanced Media Research Amsterdam (CAMeRA), VU University Amsterdam. Research interests include health communication, serious games, and developmental perspectives.

Helmut Scherer, Professor of Communication Research of the Department of Journalism and Communication Research of the Hanover University of Music and Drama. Helmut Scherer's major research areas are media reception, public opinion and political communication.

Yuliya Strizhakova, Ph.D., University of Connecticut, Assistant Professor of Marketing, Michigan Technological University. Her research interest include cognitive and emotional motives of media use and other leisure choices, branding, and advertising.

Joseph S. Valacich, Hubman Distinguished Professor of MIS at Washington State University. His primary research interests include technology-mediated collaboration, human–computer interaction, mobile and emerging technologies, e-business, and distance education. He is a prolific researcher, with more than 70 publications in numerous prestigious journals including *MIS Quarterly, Information Systems Research, Management Science, Academy of Management Journal, Communications of the ACM, Decision Science, Journal of MIS, Journal of Applied Psychology, Organizational Behavior and Human Decision Processes*, and many others.

Thilo von Pape, Ph.D., Postdoctoral Fellow in Mass Communication at the Centre de Recherche sur les Médiations (CREM) at the Paul-Verlaine University of Metz, France. His main research interests lie in the fields of diffusion and appropriation of new information and communication technologies and in the reception of persuasive communication.

Peter Vorderer, Professor of Communication Science at VU University, Amsterdam and Scientific Director of Center for Advanced Media Research, Amsterdam (CAMeRA). Editor of *Media Psychology*. Research interests include exposure and responses to communication content, (interactive) entertainment theory and research, video games and new technologies.

James G. Webster, Ph.D., Professor of Communication Studies at Northwestern University. His research interests include audience measurement, media industries, and understanding patterns of digital media consumption.

Jens Wolling, Professor for Communication Research and Political Communication at the TU Ilmenau. Interests include research on media use, media effects, political communication, online research and media quality.

Preface

This book provides an overview of established and evolving approaches about media choice, i.e., why and how people turn to the media. The endeavor to provide such an overview is closely linked to the ultimate goal to support theory-building on media choice, in communication science and other disciplines in the social sciences. In the past, studies on media choice often followed applied questions instead of working towards conceptual models or theories. This book builds on the hope that the field undergoes a change. In the recent past, new ideas about media choice evolved that now promise to enter a fruitful competition with existing approaches that already stood on solid theoretical grounds. To pick up two chapters of the current volume, cognitive-dissonance-based media choices now have a new neighbor, fast-and-frugal media choices.

Whereas media research currently benefits from a growing number of handbooks and synopses about media effects, similar overviews about media choice are rare, if they exist at all. When I started to elaborate the idea of editing an overview about media choice, the only similar book that came to my mind was *Selective Exposure to Communication*, by Dolf Zillmann and Jennings Bryant (1985). Now being a classic in the field, that book was published in 1985. Since then, research on media choice evolved, older approaches changed, new plantlets started to grow (some of them not until the current volume). It therefore seems timely to publish a new overview about conceptualizations of media choice. Most fortunately, many scholars that made important and exciting contributions to the field in the past agreed to contribute to this enterprise.

It needs to be noted that the current book is not a *handbook* on media choice. It focuses on theory, i.e., models, conceptualizations, approaches towards media choice. Empirical research is certainly reviewed as well, as it is key to theoretical substance. But the book neither includes an overview about methods and measures of media choice, nor does it fully reflect the breadth of non-academic practices of audience research. The aim of the current book is to present a balanced *selection* of *conceptualizations* of media choice (a general introduction to the term "media choice" is given in the first chapter). Some chapters describe the status quo of established approaches like cognitive dissonance or affect-dependent media choices, other chapters introduce more recent ideas and approaches like social cognitive theory of media selection. Further, some chapters focus on media choice in general, others highlight a certain aspect in the process (like the consideration of costs), or stress a specific type of media choice (e.g., zapping).

The book was developed with two groups of people in mind. First, the current collection of chapters may be of use for scholars and researchers from various disciplines that are interested in media choice. That includes both experts and people who are new to the field, whether they seek an update of existing theories and new approaches or are simply interested in an inter-disciplinary view on the topic. Graduate students and master students, again across disciplines, who are interested in media choice may also be part of this group. As the book aims to provide an overview about the field, it may also be a good source in classes on media choice, particularly if read together with a book that takes a more applied perspective, like the excellent *Ratings Analysis: The Theory and Practice of Audience Research* by James Webster and colleagues (2006).

A second group of people who I had in mind when editing this book are practitioners, i.e. experts in commercial audience research who share an interest in scientific perspectives on media choice. Whereas the book takes a rather academic perspective and does not explicitly connect academic and commercial perspectives, the presented issues still intuitively connect to applied questions followed by audience researchers. Several chapters discuss habitual—or even compulsive—versus intentional media choices, for example, which tells about the boundaries of rating forecasts or audience analyses that implicitly assume that people's actions are solely based on what they prefer.

References

Webster, J., Phalen, P. F., & Lichty, L. W. (2006). *Ratings Analysis: The Theory and Practice of Audience Research* (3rd ed.). Mahwah, NJ: Lawrence Erlbaum Associates.

Zillmann, D. & Bryant, J. (1985). (Eds.). *Selective Exposure to Communication.* Hillsdale, NJ: Lawrence Erlbaum.

Chapter 1

A Brief Introduction to Media Choice

Tilo Hartmann

This book provides fresh insights into established and evolving theoretical and empirical perspectives on media choice. Today, media play an essential role in our daily activities: in the workplace, we use the computer, write emails and letters, and make phone calls; during our leisure time, we watch television, surf the Web, listen to the MP3-player, go to the movies, play video games, and read the newspaper or magazines. Every day, we choose from an abundance of available media technologies and different content to pursue our goals—sometimes mindlessly and automatically, sometimes via a reflective and well-planned approach (cf., Sloman, 2002; Smith & deCoster, 2002; Strack & Deutsch, 2004).

The aim of this volume is to provide an overview of recent developments in the modeling and explaining of media choices, seeking to answer the question of why and how people choose media. A recent rush of books has sought to provide overviews on users' experiences during media exposure or media effects (Bryant & Oliver, in press; Berger, Roloff, & Roskos-Ewoldsen, in press; Nabi & Oliver, in press; Bryant & Vorderer, 2006; Preiss, Gayle, Burrell, Allen, & Bryant, 2006), yet the only book written with a similar goal to that of the present volume was the classic *Selective Exposure to Communication*, edited by Dolf Zillmann and Jennings Bryant and published in 1985. Since this time, major developments have emerged within the main lines of research into media choice, including mood-management theory (Oliver, this volume), information-seeking (Hastall, this volume), uses-and-gratifications research (Krcmar & Strizhakova, this volume; Rubin, 2002), and selective exposure based on avoidance of cognitive dissonance (Donsbach, this volume). New, alternative approaches have also entered the field, some of which follow well-established psychological theories (e.g., LaRose, this volume; Hartmann, this volume), whereas others dwell on more specific mechanisms in conceptualizing media choice (e.g., Koolstra, Ritterfeld, & Vorderer, this volume; Fahr & Boecking, this volume; Wolling, this volume). With more than 20 years having passed since the publication of *Selective Exposure to Communication*, it is timely to provide an up-to-date overview of the field.

The current volume pursues this endeavor, with special attention devoted to new and emerging approaches toward media choice.

What is Media Choice About?

In its broadest sense, the term "media choice" captures all of the macro- and micro-level factors that determine a person's actual exposure to mediated content or a person's deselection of mediated content (cf. van den Bulck, 2006; the term "selective exposure" (Zillmann & Bryant, 1985b) has a similar definition). The term should not be reduced in scope to people's deliberate or reflected decisions to use or not to use mediated content (see Hartmann, this volume); rather, it entails all of the processes necessary to describe and explain why a person came into contact with, or indeed refrained from coming into contact with, mediated content. In turn, the expressions "to come into contact" and "exposure" imply that a person's behavior was directed in at least a rudimentary manner towards perceiving (or not perceiving) mediated content. Thus, media choice—whether performed deliberately or mindlessly and whether based on reasoned grounds or highly automatic processes (Strack & Deutsch, 2004; Strack, Werth, & Deutsch, 2006)—is always affected by an inner drive or impulse (Biocca, 1988; Hearn, 1989; Levy & Windahl, 1985). Accordingly, media choice entails a broad range of different ways to turn toward or away from the media: not only obvious choices such as intentional exposure to the media (Blumler, 1979), but also habitual and even addictive media choices (LaRose, this volume) that may be largely determined by the environment but still regulated by the user if s/he is able to invest sufficient willpower (Baumeister, Sparks, Stillman, & Vohs, 2008). However, the term does not include exposure to media content that is determined solely by environmental factors, without any chance for moderation by the individual user.

Analyzing Media Choice

Research into media choice seeks to illuminate *why* and *how* people come to use or reject mediated content. Such research also analyzes why and how people develop, pursue, regulate, and implement a drive to approach or avoid mediated content. The *why* and *how* aspects are closely linked: if researchers succeed in *describing* how media choice works (i.e., succeed in capturing all individual and environmental processes involved in media choice), they will also arrive at reasons or determinants that *explain* why people turn to the media.

From an analytical perspective, descriptions and explanations of media choice focus on aspects at either the *micro* or *macro* levels. The macro level reflects both societal (e.g., cultural aspects) and structural aspects of the media system (cf. Webster, this volume) that affect media choice, whereas the micro level entails primarily (socio)-psychological aspects (e.g., Dennis, Fuller, & Valacich, this volume; LaRose, this volume; Oliver, this volume; Marewski, Galesic, & Gigerenzer, this volume). In a similar fashion, media choice itself can be described on either the level of social aggregates (e.g., "audiences;" Webster, 2006; Webster, Phalen, & Lichty, 2006) or the level of the individual (e.g., Rubin, 2002). Furthermore, media choice can be analyzed as *a single-act behavior* (e.g., in experimental research; Zillmann & Bryant, 1985c) or as a *repetitive behavior* (intensity or frequency of use; e.g., Dimmick, Ramirez, Wang, & Lin, 2007).

In modeling media choice, it may be helpful to distinguish in an analytical sense between proximate and distant explanatory factors. *Proximate factors* are those causal factors that immediately precede the selection or deselection of mediated content. Depending on the selected model, such factors exert a direct causal effect on exposure behavior (although this does not necessarily require that they belong to the motor and sensory behavior of an individual that initiates or stops exposure). Proximate factors are typically situational and may change dynamically; emotions are a typical example of a proximate factor in media choice. People may feel bored, for example, and therefore turn to exciting media fare (Zillmann, 2000).

In contrast, *distant factors* are mediated or moderated by proximate factors, commonly capturing more stable and enduring aspects than proximate factors. Personality characteristics are typical examples of distant factors in media choice: certain persons may be more prone to feelings of boredom than others, for example, and therefore have a tendency to switch on exciting media fare (Kestenbaum & Weinstein, 1985). The relationship between proneness to boredom and media choice, however, may be mediated entirely by actually felt states of boredom. Next to personality traits (e.g., Finn, 1997), other typical examples of distant factors are components of the media structure (Webster, this volume), people's age (Mares & Woodard, 2006; Rubin & Rubin, 1982), and gender (Knobloch-Westerwick, 2007).

Meta-theoretical Perspectives

In meta-theoretical hindsight, conceptualizations of media choice can be distinguished according to their implicit model of man. Three main perspectives can be recognized among those that have dominated past research into media choice. Each perspective models media choice based on a specific model of man. The premises inherent in each model have a strong effect on the way that media choice is ultimately conceptualized.

First, a *neo-behaviorist model* of man underlies those studies based on the theory of affect-dependent stimulus arrangement (Zillmann & Bryant, 1985c) or mood-management theory (Zillmann, 1988; Zillmann, 2000; Oliver, 2003; Oliver, this volume). The original formulation of this perspective (Zillmann & Bryant, 1985c) dwells on the behaviorist thoughts of

Skinner (1969) and Thorndike (1932). Accordingly, human beings are considered complex machines that learn via operant conditioning: people initially choose media in a random manner, but their choice moves away from random selection due to positive and negative reinforcement, which "stamps in the preference" (p. 159). Consequently, "consistent with reinforcement theory generally [...], it is assumed that individuals execute choices rather 'mindlessly', that is, without awareness of choice criteria and without deliberate considerations of desirable effects" (Zillmann & Bryant, 1985b, p. 16). Later conceptualizations of related approaches redeemed this radical behaviorist direction. For example, in an attempt to extend mood-management theory to choices of media that are not immediately rewarding, Zillmann (2000) concedes that "mood-impacting behavior choices are bound to engage anticipatory evaluation" (p. 9) and that "gratifications may be critically evaluated and their desirability determined" (p. 13).

A second group of studies analyzed media choice via selective exposure theory (Hastall, this volume), with a strong emphasis on cognitive consonance and dissonance as a mechanism underlying media choice (Donsbach, this volume; D'Allessio & Allen, 2006; Smith, Fabrigar, & Norris, 2008). In this case, the underlying model of man is based on the metaphor of *human beings as a computer* (Erb, 1997, p. 161): media users are primarily considered processors of information, and media choice is thought to focus on information. Accordingly, computational capabilities, consistencies and inconsistencies, and limited resources with which to process information are thought to be the key factors in media choice. A similar model of man is apparent in decision theory, which can also be linked to media choice (Marewski et al., this volume). Simon (1990, p. 7), for example, regards "human [...] behavior [to be] shaped by a scissors whose two blades are the structure of task environments and the computational capabilities of the actor."

A third group of studies may be categorized as *action-theoretical* research. Such studies conceive of human beings as somewhat self-determined and principally autonomous agents. In contrast to a behaviorist approach, "this perspective suggests a different analytic sequence, one that begins with the organism rather than the stimulus. [...] The sequence would be O-S-O-R" (Deci & Ryan, 1985, p. 151). Human behavior is thought to rest on people's subjective cognitive representation of their environment and their ability to anticipate future situations. Accordingly, related studies tend to focus on conscious and explicit determinants of media choice. Although not always explicitly outlined, such a model of man is most apparent within uses-and-gratifications research (Krcmar & Strizhakova, this volume; Rubin, 2002), which stresses that users may actively choose media over other alternatives based on anticipated gratifications (Biocca, 1988).

Recent developments in psychology suppose an *integrated* model of man that combines both deliberate and conscious determinants of human behavior (as traditionally outlined in action-theory), and more mindless and impulsive mechanisms of behavior (as traditionally outlined in behaviorism) (Baumeister et al., 2008; Strack & Deutsch, 2004; Smith & DeCoster, 2000). For example, the reflective–impulsive model proposed by Strack and Deutsch (2004; see also Strack, Werth, & Deutsch, 2006) suggests that behavior is affected by two intertwined routes. Behavior can build on a reflective system, i.e., on "a decision that is based on the evaluation of a future state and an assessment of the likelihood with which the state will be reached through this behavior" (reflective system; p. 209). Behavior may depend on the reflective system, especially if the behavioral outcome is important and if ample time and resources are available in planning the behavior. However, if the environment offers highly seductive options that are "within reach" (e.g., a tasty cake or a hilarious comedy), or if the motivation to plan the behavior is low or time pressures and other urges leave no opportunity for thoughtful elaborations (cf. Baumeister et al., 2008), behavior is more likely to occur "through the mere spread of activation to behavioral schemata" (impulsive system; Strack et al., 2006, p. 209).

Both the reflective and impulsive systems are strongly interconnected, and may on occasion even override one another. Immediate urges from the impulsive system can override deliberate action plans developed via the reflective system. For example, users may not be able to resist the immediate appeal of certain media offerings, even if they intended not to use them. However, via self-regulation and the allocation of willpower (see Baumeister et al., 2008), the reflective system may be able to suppress urges arising from the impulsive system. For example, users may be able to withstand inner urges to turn to certain media offerings.

Such an integrated model of man as the one outlined above may not only help to overcome past discussions about the passive or active media user (Biocca, 1988). It may also help to bridge the gap between prominent lines of research (e.g., mood-management theory and the uses-and-gratifications approach) that strongly differ in the way that they understand media choice as human behavior.

The Object of Choice

On a phenomenological level, media choices can be further distinguished according to the *unit* or *object* of choice (Donsbach, 1989; Levy & Windahl, 1985). From the perspective of decision theory, users choose among mentally represented options. Depending on exactly what the users mentally represent, they may aim to turn toward or away from (1) the media in general (unspecific media choice; Doll & Hasebrink, 1989), (2) different media technologies, (3) media content presented by a certain technology (specific media choice; Perse, 1990; zapping, Bilandzic, this volume), or (4) certain aspects of the media content (e.g., selective attention paid to characters, objects, information, etc.).

The way in which people pursue decisions is affected by the number of options available and the level of detail and natural characteristics of the options (e.g., costs; Scherer & Naab, this volume). The modeled unit of media choice may therefore shape the overall conceptualization. For example, a model of users' selective attention towards characters in movies may stress different psychological mechanisms to those emphasized in a model that aims to explain and predict people's choice of media technology (see von Pape, this volume; Dennis et al., this volume).

In a similar fashion, media choice can take place in different *situations* or *contexts*. A given model may aim to analyze media choice that takes place in a certain context. For example, people turn to the media in both working environments and during leisure time, and these contexts are characterized by systematic differences (Shivers, 1979; Stebbins, 1997). The working environment is characterized by external pressures and task affordances, for example, whereas leisure time provides greater opportunities for self-determined activities (Shivers, 1979). Consequently, a model of media choice in the workplace would focus more on the functional utilities of media, extrinsic rewards, and social pressures (Dennis et al., this volume), whereas a model of media choice during leisure time would emphasize people's seeking of pleasure-based gratifications and the intrinsic rewards of the media (Oliver, this volume).

Conclusion

This chapter, in introducing the present volume, provided a brief outline of the term "media choice." Researchers who analyze media choice aim to predict and explain why and how people turn to (or away from) the media. In addition to continuously developing, well-established approaches such as uses-and-gratifications, mood-management theory, and dissonance-based media choices, the field has recently been enriched by new and emerging models of media choice. Together, the established and emerging conceptualizations represent a colorful bouquet of ideas that dwell on different models of man, vary in the way that they stress proximate, distant, and micro- or macro-level factors of media choice, and differ in the type of conceptualized media choice. The current volume aims to provide a comprehensive overview of the variety of existing conceptualizations of media choice. This goal is tied to the hope that the field will continue to grow and blossom, and that this book may help to stimulate this development.

References

Baumeister, R. F., Sparks, E. A., Stillman, T. F., & Vohs, K. D. (2008). Free will in consumer behavior: Self-control, ego depletion, and choice. *Journal of Consumer Psychology*, 18, 4–13.

Berger, C., Roloff, M., & Roskos-Ewoldsen, D. (Eds.). (in press). *Handbook of Communication Science* (2nd edition). London: Sage.

Biocca, F. A. (1988). Opposing conceptions of the audience: The active and passive hemispheres of mass communication theory. In J. A. Anderson (Ed.), *Communication Yearbook 11* (pp. 51–79). London: Sage.

Blumler, J. (1979). The role of theory in uses and gratifications studies. *Communication Research*, 6, 9–36.

Bryant, J. & Oliver, M. B. (Eds.). (in press). *Media Effects: Advances in Theory and Research*. New York: Routledge.

Bryant, J. & Vorderer, P. (Eds.). (2006). *Psychology of Entertainment*. Mahwah, NJ: Lawrence Erlbaum Associates.

D'Alessio, D. & Allen, M. (2006). The selective exposure hypothesis and media choice processes. In R. W. Preiss, B. M. Gayle, N. Burrell, M. Allen, & J. Bryant (Eds.). *Mass Media Effects Research: Advances Through Meta-analysis* (pp. 103–118). Mahwah, NJ: Lawrence Erlbaum Associates.

Deci, E. L. & Ryan, R. M. (1985). *Intrinsic Motivation and Self-Determination in Human Behavior*. New York: Plenum.

Dimmick, J., Ramirez, A., Wang, T., & Lin, S.-F. (2007). Extending society: The role of personal networks and gratification-utilities in the use of interactive communication media. *New Media & Society*, 9(5), 795–810.

Doll, J. & Hasebrink, U. (1989). Zum Einfluß von Einstellungen auf die Auswahl von Fernsehsendungen. In J. Groebel & P. Winterhoff-Spurk (Eds.), *Empirische Medienpsychologie* (pp. 45–63). München: PVU.

Donsbach, W. (1989). Selektive Zuwendung zu Medieninhalten. In M. Kaase & W. Schulz (Eds.), *Massenkommunikation. Theorien, Methoden, Befunde* (pp. 392–405). Opladen: Westdeutscher Verlag.

Erb, E. (1997). Gegenstand- und Problemkonstituierung: Subjektmodelle (in) der Psychologie. In N. Groeben (Ed.), *Zur Programmatik einer sozialwissenschaftlichen Psychologie* (pp. 139–240). Münster: Aschendorff.

Finn, S. (1997). Origins of media exposure: Linking personality traits to TV, radio, print, and film use. *Communication Research*, 24, 507–529.

Hearn, G. (1989). Active and passive conceptions of the television audience: Effects of a change in viewing routine. *Human Relations*, 42(10), 857–875.

Kestenbaum, G. & Weinstein, L. (1985). Personality, psychopathology and development issues in male adolescent video game use. *Journal of American Academy of Child Psychiatry*, 24, 329–333.

Knobloch-Westerwick, S. (2007). Gender differences in mood management and mood adjustment. *Journal of Broadcasting and Electronic Media*, 51, 73–92.

Levy, M. R. & Windahl, S. (1985). The concept of audience activity. In K. E. Rosengren, L. A. Wenner, & P. Palmgreen (Eds.), *Media Gratifications Research: Current Perspectives* (pp. 109–122). Beverly Hills: Sage.

Mares, M. L. & Woodard, E. (2006). In search of the older audience. *Journal of Broadcasting & Electronic Media*, 50, 595–614.

Nabi, R. & Oliver, M. B. (Eds.). (in press). *Handbook of Media Effects*. London: Sage.

Oliver, M. B. (2003). Mood management and selective exposure theory. In J. Bryant, D. R. Roskos-Ewoldsen, & J. Cantor (Eds.), *Communication and Emotion: Essays in Honor of Dolf Zillmann* (pp. 85–106). Mahwah, NJ: Erlbaum.

Perse, E. (1990). Audience activity and involvement in the newer media environment. *Communication Research*, 17(5), 675–697.

Preiss, R. W., Gayle, B. M., Burrell, N., Allen, M., & Bryant, J. (2006). *Mass Media Effects Research: Advances Through Meta-Analysis*. London: Lawrence Erlbaum Associates.

Rubin, A. M. (2002). The uses and gratifications perspective of media effects. In J. Bryant & D. Zillmann (Eds.), *Media Effects: Advances in Theory and Research* (pp. 525–548). Mahwah, NY: Lawrence Erlbaum Associates.

Rubin, A. M. & Rubin, R. B. (1982). Contextual age and television use. *Human Communication Research*, 8, 228–244.

Shivers, J. S. (1979). The origin of man, culture, and leisure. In H. Ibrahim & J. S. Shivers (Eds.), *Leisure: Emergence and Expansion* (S. 3–44). Los Alamitos: Hwong Publishing.

Simon, H. A. (1990). Invariants of human behaviour. *Annual Review of Psychology*, 41, 1–19.

Skinner, B. F. (1969). *Contingencies of Reinforcement: A Theoretical Analysis*. New York: Appleton-Century-Crofts.

Sloman, S. S. (2002). Two systems of reasoning. In T. Gilovich, D. Griffin, & D. Kahneman (Eds.), *Heuristics and Biases: The Psychology of Intuitive Judgement* (pp. 370–396). New York: Cambridge University Press.

Smith, E. R. & DeCoster, J. (2000). Dual process models in social and cognitive psychology: Conceptual integration and links to underlying memory systems. *Personality and Social Psychology Review*, 4, 108–131.

Smith, S. M., Fabrigar, L. R., & Norris, M. E. (2008). Reflecting on six decades of selective exposure research: Progress, challenges, and opportunities. *Social and Personality Psychology Compass*, 2(1), 464–493.

Stebbins, R. A. (1997). Casual leisure: A conceptual statement. *Leisure Studies, 16*, 17–25.

Strack, F. & Deutsch, R. (2004). Reflective and impulsive determinants of social behavior. *Personality and Social Psychology Review*, 8(3), 220–247.

Strack, F., Werth, L., & Deutsch, R. (2006). Reflective and impulsive determinants of consumer behavior. *Journal of Consumer Psychology*, 16(3), 205–216.

Thorndike, E. L. (1932). *The Fundamentals of Learning*. New York: Columbia University.

Van den Bulck, J. (2006). Television news avoidance: Exploratory results from a one-year follow-up study. *Journal of Broadcasting and Electronic Media*, 50(2), 231–252.

Webster, J. (2006). Audience flow past and present: Television inheritance effects reconsidered. *Journal of Broadcasting and Electronic Media*, 50(2), 323–337.

Webster, J., Phalen, P. & Lichty, L. (2006). *Ratings Analysis: The Theory and Practice of Audience Research* (3rd edition). Mahwah, NJ: Erlbaum.

Zillmann, D. (1988). Mood management: Using entertainment to full advantage. In L. Donohew, H. E. Sypher, & E. T. Higgins (Eds.), *Communication, Social Cognition, and Affect* (pp. 147–171). Hillsdale, NJ: Lawrence Erlbaum.

Zillmann, D. (2000). Mood management in the context of selective exposure theory. In M. E. Roloff (Hrsg.), *Communication Yearbook 23* (S. 103–123). Thousand Oaks, CA: Sage.

Zillmann, D. & Bryant, J. (Eds.). (1985). *Selective Exposure to Communication.* Mahwah, NY: Lawrence Erlbaum Associates.

Zillmann, D. & Bryant, J. (1985b). Selective-exposure phenomena. In D. Zillmann & J. Bryant (Eds.), *Selective Exposure to Communication* (pp. 1–10). Mahwah, NY: Lawrence Erlbaum Associates.

Zillmann, D. & Bryant, J. (1985c). Affect, mood, and emotion as determinants of selective exposure. In D. Zillmann & J. Bryant (Eds.), *Selective Exposure to Communication* (pp. 157–190). Hillsdale, NJ: Erlbaum.

Chapter 2

Social Cognitive Theories of Media Selection

Robert LaRose

The Social Cognitive Perspective

Social Cognitive Theory (SCT, Bandura, 1989) is perhaps best known in the annals of communication research in its prior incarnation as Social Learning Theory (Bandura, 1977). Social Learning Theory was a seminal theory of the effects of the media, particularly the effects of television on children. The famous "Bobo doll studies" (Bandura, 1965), in which young children were taught to attack inflatable plastic clowns ("Bobo" dolls) by observing models punish the inflatable toys on film, are a staple in textbook accounts of mass media effects and continue to inform media effects studies (e.g., Anderson & Dill, 2000; Huesmann, Moise-Titus, Podolski, & Eron, 2003). In particular, the process of observational learning was an important advance in our understanding of media effects, describing how visual media could teach, reinforce, and prompt behaviors portrayed on the screen. The present chapter examines how SCT can explain media selection behavior that determines what media consumers choose to see on their screens rather than the behavioral effects of those selections.

SCT is described by reciprocal, causal relationships among the environment, individuals, and their behaviors (Bandura, 1989). Humans have emergent interactive agency, meaning that they are neither completely autonomous from their environment nor totally subservient to environmental influences. Rather, the triadic causal mechanism is mediated by the human capacity to transform sensory experiences into symbolic cognitive models, or schemas, that guide human actions. Cognitive schemas arise both from direct, first person experiences (enactive learning) and the vicarious experiences of others (observational learning). Both mechanisms impact behavior in the same basic way, by influencing judgments of the likely consequences of a behavior, or outcome expectations (Bandura, 1986, p. 391). The degree to which an outcome is contingent upon enacting a particular behavior is what endows expected outcome expectations with their motivational power.

As such, SCT has been characterized (in Eccles & Wigfield, 2002) as an expectancy theory. In addition to expectations about outcomes, behavior is also guided by expectations regarding one's own personal capabilities to perform a behavior successfully to achieve those outcomes, the concept of self-efficacy. In contrast, other expectancy-value theories also consider the relative values of outcomes and the costs and trade-offs associated with the choices people make. Still, SCT's self-regulatory mechanism incorporates many of the features of expectancy value theories, such as comparisons to values and long-term goals, even if they have not been the primary focus of SCT-inspired media research to date.

Even while rejecting the radical behaviorist position (e.g., Skinner, 1938) that inner thought processes are irrelevant to understanding human behavior, SCT draws upon key tenets of behaviorism. For example, behaviors that are positively reinforced are more likely to be enacted than those that are punished. However, social cognitive theory adds subjective mental processes that behaviorists disdain. This distinction accounts for the possibility of forethought and planning.

Key SCT mechanisms find support in behavioral neuroscience (Berridge, 2004; Poldrack, Sabb, Foerde, Tom, Asarnow, Bookheimer, et al., 2005; Yin & Knowlton, 2006). For example, humans (but also lab animals) respond to what the neuroscientists call anticipatory motivations or predictive cues and what SCT terms "forethought." In addition to instrumental learning, modern behavioral neuroscience also recognizes cognitive inferences about goal directedness, goal expectation, affective responses to goal attainment, and cognitive expectancy, neurological processes that account for the motivational influence of outcome expectations.

The SCT concept of outcome expectations shares with decision theory the assumption that people make choices based on the predicted consequences of their choices (Hsee & Hastie, 2006). However, the so-called "prediction biases" that interest decision analysts are of little consequence in SCT, since there is no underlying assumption of rational choice, only that the outcome expectations of the individual, whether accurate or inaccurate, are what determine behavior. Correction of these biases (e.g., the projection bias that leads shoppers to buy more food when shopping hungry) would presumably restore effective self-regulation as understood in SCT. Decision analysis recognizes impulsivity, which might be defined as deficient self-regulation in socio-cognitive terms. The "lay rationalism," "medium maximization," and other rule-based decision biases that consumers utilize to control impulsivity may be understood as personal standards (if sometimes defective ones) within the self-regulatory mechanism. Thus, decision analysis may be interpreted within the SCT mechanism of self-regulation.

A Socio-cognitive Theory of Media Selection

Since SCT purports to be a general theory of human behavior, it may be applied to the many dimensions of media selection behavior. These include the initial adoption of media channels and media forms; selection of content within those options; continuing active media selection behavior; habitual selection of media; the development of dysfunctional, "problematic" or even "addictive" media behavior; and also the discontinuance of media behaviors that were previously selected. In so doing, the tradition of social learning theory in media research is stood on its head: Media consumption behavior becomes the effect, or dependent variable, of interest rather than the cause of downstream behavioral effects.

Media behavior may be explained in SCT terms through the interplay of humans' basic capabilities to use symbols, exercise forethought, learn through vicarious experience, and to reflect upon and regulate their behavior (Bandura, 1986). Symbolic representations of the expected outcomes of media selections develop either through direct personal experience with the media or vicariously through observations of the experiences of others, representations that are organized in neural codes that facilitate forethought about the desirability of carrying out future media behaviors. The human capability of self-reflection makes it possible for individuals to analyze their experience with the media and also to modify their thought processes to respond better to the media alternatives available to them. Self-efficacy judgments about personal capabilities to use and benefit from media consumption are a particularly meaningful form of self-reflection that guide individuals to decide which forms of consumption to undertake or maintain. The self-regulation capability means that humans can generate reinforcement for their media behaviors in response to self-reflection and are thus not necessarily driven by media stimuli. Thus, the enactment of media behaviors may be understood through outcome expectations, self-efficacy beliefs, and self-regulation.

Outcome Expectations

Outcome expectations provide the motivation for enacting behavior, including both positive outcomes that provide direct incentives and negative outcomes that offer disincentives for performing a behavior. Outcome expectations are of two basic types: biological and cognitive. There are biologically based primary incentives such as food, drink, and physical contact. Humans also respond to a variety of cognitive motivators including monetary, social, status, novel sensory stimuli, and enjoyable activity incentives (Bandura, 1986, p. 232). Humans can provide their own self-reactive incentives to adjust their internal psychological states, such as by relieving boredom or pursuing pleasure. Outcome expectations are formed through observational learning or enactive learning.

Observational learning describes how outcome expectations are formed by the observation of the behavior of others, through vicarious experience of the behavioral outcomes achieved by others rather than from the outcomes of one's own actions. In the "Bobo doll studies" when preschool children observed films of adult models being rewarded with candy and words of praise for punishing an inflatable doll they were likely to inflict punishment on inflatable dolls themselves when placed in real world playrooms equipped with identical dolls by the researchers. Similarly, when the film model was shown being spanked and verbally upbraided for aggressive behavior then the children who observed the demonstration were unlikely to be aggressive in their own play. A notable finding of the early studies was that even children who observed no reward or punishment were also likely to engage in aggressive play (Bandura, 1965). This suggested the power of a glamorous medium such as television to reinforce a behavior even when the rewards were not explicitly demonstrated.

Turning to an example from the domain of media selection behavior, observational learning explains the adoption of new media technologies. As they entered the work force, the preschoolers of 1965 may have observed peers of theirs working with spreadsheet programs on early personal computers. This may had led them to expect that if they bought an Apple II with the Visicalc spreadsheet they, too, could perform their work and manage their personal finances more efficiently, leading to financial benefits for themselves, an example of an outcome expectation involving an economic incentive. Expecting that outcome, they performed the behavior of purchasing their own personal computer. But they may also have observed the balkiness of early computer technology and so could have been deterred by a negative instance of an "enjoyable activity" incentive. Observational learning does not necessarily require direct visual observation. In this example "water cooler talk" about the innovation, press accounts of the merits of early personal computers, or movies featuring personal computer users could also affect outcome expectations. Thus, SCT can explain a key component of the diffusion of innovation process, the observation of the relative advantages of new media (Bandura, 2001; Rogers, 1995).

Likewise, direct personal experience with the consequences of one's own actions also affect outcome expectations, the process of enactive learning. Imagine what may have happened to the Stanford preschoolers upon return to their own playrooms at home. Did their parents send them to bed without supper for assaulting their toys (or their siblings) or promise food treats for "playing nice?" The application of those primary (food) incentives would also affect the outcome expectations of the preschoolers with respect to future violent play. Through this example the causal relationship between outcome expectations and behavior can be seen to be reciprocal: the expectation of a reward led the children to abuse their toys but the performance of the behavior led to the modification of those initial expectations.

Enactive learning explains ongoing media selections and the evolution of our tastes in media over time. Consider the process of movie selection. Moviegoers have prior experience with the stars and the genre that affect their outcome expectations. They have enjoyed prior movies starring George

Clooney and so expect his next opus to be entertaining, an enjoyable activity incentive for moviegoing behavior. But, they may be put off by negative reviews of the film (an instance of observational learning) or by the belief that their dates do not enjoy George's movies, resulting in an expected negative social outcome. And, if the current film fails to deliver as expected, they may modify their expectations of future George Clooney movies.

Self-efficacy

Self-efficacy is the belief in "one's capabilities to organize and execute a course of action required to produce given attainments" (Bandura, 1997, p. 3). Self-efficacy helps to determine the tasks that individuals are willing to undertake and those they are not. Even prior to performing a behavior for the first time individuals may form beliefs about their capability to enact it. Those with high levels of self-efficacy are likely to attempt a novel behavior while those with low self-efficacy are unlikely to. Those with high self-efficacy persist in the performance of difficult behaviors while those with low self-efficacy are more likely to be discouraged in the face of challenges.

Self-efficacy is distinguishable from self-esteem, which is a general belief in one's self-worth (Bandura, 1986). Individuals with high levels of self-esteem may still regard themselves to have low self-efficacy with respect to specific tasks. Similarly, those with low overall levels of self-esteem might nonetheless feel themselves capable of performing a specific task. Self-efficacy is also distinguishable from objective levels of skill. Even those with prior levels of experience with a behavior or who have been trained to perform it may still have low confidence in their ability to repeat a difficult or seldom-used behavior. Once again, causation is reciprocal. Successful performance of a behavior generally enhances self-efficacy while unsuccessful performance may lessen it. Anxiety, observation of successful models of behavior, and verbal persuasion also affect self-efficacy (Bandura, 1997).

The self-efficacy mechanism obviously affects new media choices that require high levels of preparation or skill on the part of their users, including computers (Compeau, Higgins, & Huff, 1999; Hill, Smith, & Mann, 1987, Igbaria & Iivari, 1995), the Internet (Eastin & LaRose, 2000; Hsu & Chiu, 2004), and video games (Klimmt & Hartmann, 2006; Lee & LaRose, 2007). However, many conventional media selections also challenge their consumers with tasks that they may perceive to be beyond their ability. For example, a college freshman confronted with a calculus book or a semi-literate person confronted with the front page of the *New York Times* may have self-efficacy deficits that deter those media choices. Or, moviegoers who cover their eyes during a horror show dramatically express their lack of self-efficacy in handling the intense emotions that the horror sequences evoke.

Self-regulation

Self-regulation is the exercise of self-directedness and forethought that accounts for the human ability to engage in long-range planning in pursuit of distant goals. It has three subfunctions: self-observation, judgmental process, and self-reaction (Bandura, 1991). Individuals engage in self-observation when they monitor their own behavior to provide diagnostic information about the impact of that behavior on themselves, others, and the environment. Self-observations are compared to personal, social, normative, or collective standards through the judgmental process, standards that may be taught directly by parents or social institutions or inferred from observation of models.

Finally, self-reaction aligns the self-observed pattern of behavior with relevant standards. Individuals are motivated to apply their own rewards or punishments in an effort to modify behavior to conform with their standards. Alternatively, if they find their behavior to be consistent with the relevant standards the behavior is likely to be maintained. The motivation for self-reactive influence arises from self-evaluations that have inherent incentive value in that positive self-evaluations resulting from living up to one's standards of performance are gratifying while negative self-evaluations resulting from failure are aversive. But also, most individuals set goals for themselves that are defined by standards of conduct that are within the scope of their capabilities and yet embody a slightly higher level of performance than they currently exhibit. Therefore, the external rewards that are associated with improvements in performance also reinforce the specific behaviors in question and bolster the individual's self-reactive capabilities. However, self-reactive influence is diminished if the cause of behavior is attributed to external forces, if the behavior itself is not valued, or if self-regulation is disengaged through defensive rationalizations (e.g., moral justifications, euphemistic labeling, displacement of responsibility).

Understanding Media Behavior

Media behavior is thus determined by the mutual influence of and interactions among outcome expectations, self-efficacy beliefs, and self-regulation. For example, self-efficacy beliefs help determine which outcomes it may be reasonable to expect from using the Internet. A novice user may not reasonably expect to obtain social support from visiting a social networking site but subsequent direct (enactive) experience or the observations of other users might modify both the relevant outcome expectations and self-efficacy beliefs.

Self-regulation plays a central role in SCT. The self-regulation mechanism might either constrain or facilitate media selections. For example, if Internet users notice that they are spending so much time responding to e-mail that important work tasks are being neglected they are engaging in self-observation of their behavior and also comparing it to personal standards of task effectiveness. They might then intervene in their daily routines to restore self-control, such as by delaying their morning coffee break until e-mail is completed. They might also compare their behavior against perceived social norms, such as when a significant other criticizes them for spending too much time playing the *World of Warcraft* online game and delaying dinner. Judgmental process involving moral norms is activated when individuals decide, for example, to refrain from downloading music files because of moral strictures against stealing the property of others.

However, the self-regulation system is not deterministic in itself and acts in conjunction with other SCT mechanisms, so that it is not very productive to consider isolated hypotheses that explore, for example, the relationship between the observance of moral norms and media selections. To illustrate, illegal downloading of music from the Internet was determined by moral rationalizations (e.g., "everyone is doing it") but only acting through deficient self-regulation acting in conjunction with expected economic, social, and novelty outcomes (LaRose & Kim, 2007).

Under some conditions self-regulation may lead to increased media consumption, notably when media are selected to relieve dysphoric emotional states. Media consumption to manage moods is well established (Zillmann & Bryant, 1985; Oliver, this volume). When TV viewers tune in their favorite show or go "channel surfing" for comedy to cheer themselves up they are engaging in self-reactive influence after observing themselves to be "bored" and judging the level of boredom to be sufficient to seek diversion to remediate that dysphoric condition. They may also select media in response to comparisons with lax standards for media behavior, such as through descriptive norms that assure them that their viewing is within the bounds of the four hours a day of TV viewing that is "normal" for U.S. adults. However, when self-regulation is ineffective, viewing behavior might also be cued directly in response to dysphoric moods, below the level of awareness implied by conscious consideration of outcome expectations (Verplanken & Wood, 2006), a phenomenon which has also been explored through recent developments in the SCT explanation of media selection.

Recent Developments in Socio-cognitive Media Selection

The concept of deficient self-regulation was introduced in the media studies literature (LaRose, Mastro, & Eastin, 2001) to describe a state in which self-regulatory processes become impaired and self-control over media use is diminished. That is, individuals may cease to pay conscious attention to their behavior and its impact on themselves, others, or the environment, a failure of self-observation. Or, they may fail to judge their behaviors against relevant personal or social standards or judge themselves against lax standards. Finally, even when individuals observe that behavior is inconsistent with relevant standards they may fail to apply appropriate self-corrective measures, a failure of self-reaction.

Thus, the self-regulatory mechanism of SCT helps us understand the formation, maintenance, and disruption of media habits. Media habits may be defined (LaRose, 2004) as situation-media behavior sequences that are or have become automatic, so that they occur without self-instruction (after Triandis, 1980, p. 204). TV viewers may initially formulate a well-reasoned decision to make Wednesday their "TV night" based on the selection of entertaining shows on the schedule. Over time, weekly viewing may become a habit, independent of the merits of any particular Wednesday programs. In terms of the self-regulatory mechanism this means that the outcomes of viewing that they actively considered at one point in time were no longer present in their conscious minds as their media selection became automatic. Rather, whenever Wednesday night rolls around that provides the environmental cue to engage in viewing behavior, even if some of the subsequent Wednesday programs fail to match the first ones. In other words, they suspend self-observation of their viewing behavior, or fail to judge it compared to their standards of "good television" or "wasting too much time on TV," and repeat a behavior without applying self-reactive influence to modify the pattern.

Current accounts of habits from social psychology (Aarts & Dijksterhuis, 2000; Wood & Neal, 2007) and from neurophysiology (Yin & Knowlton, 2006) generally support the above SCT-grounded explanation. However, shortly we will see that LaRose and colleagues have uncovered two dimensions of deficient self-regulation that usually, but not always (e.g., Diddi & LaRose, 2006; LaRose & Jung, 2007), emerge in their data. On a theoretical level these can be identified with the various dimensions of automatic behavior (lack of awareness, lack of attention, lack of intentionality, and lack of controllability, Bargh, Gollwitzer, Chai, Barndollar, & Troschel, 2001). LaRose and colleagues have associated the habit construct with lack of awareness and attention (e.g. performing a behavior without thinking, as a matter of habit, or as part of a routine) that are failures of self-observation and judgmental process. They reserve the term deficient self-regulation for media behaviors that lack controllability (e.g., trying unsuccessfully to discontinue a behavior or maintaining it despite negative consequences), a failure of self-reaction. These qualities are united in conceptual and operational definitions of habits as mental constructs (Verplanken & Orbell, 2003), although recent research suggests they might be separate dimensions that could co-occur in a variety of combinations (Saling & Phillips, 2007).

Habits change when goals change (Aarts & Dijksterhuis, 2000) or when the context of the behavior changes (Wood, Tam, & Witt, 2005). In the lexicon of the SCT self-regulatory mechanism, changing goals force us to attend to our behavior and judge it against new standards while a change in context is likely to make us more observant of our behavior under new conditions. Social norms may also impact habits by restoring effective self-regulation through the judgmental process (LaRose & Kim, 2007). So, a Wednesday night viewing habit might change if spouses exhort the viewers that they are not spending enough quality time with their families (establishing a new goal) or if the spouses cease to share Wednesday evenings in front of the TV (a new social context). Or, viewers may come to the realization that spending so much time on popular entertainment is morally wrong or inconsistent with their self-image, invoking personal standards.

Deficient self-regulation may also explain the development of problematic forms of media consumption, sometimes called media addictions (Kubey & Csikszentmihalyi, 2002). LaRose, Lin, and Eastin (2003) theorized that media behavior progresses from habitual to problematic when media consumption becomes a primary means of relieving dysphoric moods. Media consumption may then become a conditioned response to dysphoria as the cues associated with a habitual media consumption pattern (e.g. the sight of one's video game console) become sensitized and trigger the behavior below the level of controlled thought (Thalemann, Wölfling, & Güsser, 2007). A pattern of mounting usage follows as self-regulatory mechanisms fail. Excessive usage causes problems in the real world in the form of neglected families and reduced productivity at school or work, leading to more dysphoria, and then to yet more media usage to dispel it. Since depression inhibits effective self-regulation (Bandura, 1999), a downward spiral can result that in rare cases ends in major life crises—divorce, flunking out of school, losing one's job, etc. However, self-regulation usually intervenes well short of that, else nearly everyone would be a media "addict."

Socio-cognitive Media Selection Research

SCT and its component mechanisms enjoy strong empirical support across a wide variety of behavioral domains (Bandura, 1986; 1997). Empirical evidence for socio-cognitive models of media selection comes primarily from cross-sectional studies of media usage conducted by myself and my colleagues using structural equation modeling analyses. These build upon causal relationships established in other domains of human behavior.

The SCT model of media attendance is shown in Figure 2.1 (LaRose & Eastin, 2004). Forty-two percent of the variance in Internet usage, at the right, was predicted by expected outcomes, Internet self-efficacy, habit strength, and deficient self-regulation. In turn, habit strength was predicted by expected outcomes and deficient self-regulation. The relationship between expected outcomes and habit strength is seen as an indication that while behavior may initially be performed in response to actively considered outcome expectations, repeated behavior gradually becomes automatic as control is passed from the cortex to the cerebrum (Yin & Knowlton, 2006) and individuals become less aware of their behavior and less attentive to its conformance to relevant behavioral standards. For example, one's initial exposure to a new online game may be governed by controlled thought about the reviews one has read (an instance of observational learning) or one's personal experience with similar games (enactive learning). Expected outcomes reflect the six dimensions of incentives proposed by SCT: Novel sensory, social, enjoyable activity, monetary, self-reactive, and status outcomes. In our example, the expectation that the new game will be an enjoyable activity, treat us to a novel game play experience, give us something to talk about in online gamer forums (a social outcome), or simply relieve our boredom (a self-reactive outcome) might be among the outcomes actively considered. However, if after repeated play the game becomes one of our favorites our nervous system passes control from the cortex to the cerebellum so we can devote our scarce cognitive resources to other tasks and automatically start playing whenever we set eyes on our game machine.

In the model, both habit strength and usage are predicted by deficient self-regulation. Deficient self-regulation may affect any of the three subprocesses identified earlier but, empirically, deficient self-regulation has been associated with a failure of self-reaction, indicating a failure to exercise self-control by applying self-generated reinforcement to modify behavior. This lapse bolsters habit strength since, in the absence of effective self-reaction, habitual behavior remains under the control of automatic processes. For example, after we become "hooked" on our new game we might cheerfully acknowledge, if you asked us, that we can't seem to do anything else with our spare time but might also add that the thought of doing anything else never occurs to us. However, the relationship between defective self-regulation and behavior is not completely mediated by habit strength, when defined as a failure of self-observation and judgmental process, since there are instances in which we become intensely aware of an uncontrolled behavior. If our significant other threatens to dissolve our relationship over incessant game play that we feel powerless to stop, we may become intensely self-observant and self-judgmental but still fail apply appropriate self-reinforcements to modify our behavior because we have fallen into the downward spiral of mounting usage described previously.

How can it be that individuals continue media behaviors that they wish to stop, perhaps even those which are self-destructive? The socio-cognitive explanation of "problematic" or "addictive" media behavior argues that self-regulation becomes deficient and habits gain strength especially when media are used to relieve dysphoric states through the pursuit of self-reactive incentives. LaRose et al. (2003) found that depression contributed both to self-reactive outcome expectations and to deficient self-regulation. In reference to the model shown in Figure 2.1, depression was added as an exogenous variable that preceded these two mediating variables. Depression is thus thought to cause individuals to seek media that will relieve dysphoria (cf. Zill-mann & Bryant, 1985), such as logging in to an online video game in hopes of dispelling a somber mood. Having nothing else to do is also an unpleasurable state that might prompt the quest for self-reactive media outcomes (Henning & Vorderer, 2001). Loneliness and anxiety are yet other dysphoric moods that lead media consumers to seek self-reactive outcomes. But depression plays a special role in that it impairs self-regulation by causing individuals to slight their attempts at self-regulation and thereby diminish their impact (Bandura, 1999). So, a depressed "game addict" who succeeds in ending play "in time for bed" on one occasion would be less likely to expect future success at restoring self-control than a happy player. The resulting negative self-evaluation might fail to motivate future attempts at self-regulation.

To obtain the outcomes they expect, users must first obtain confidence in using the medium to achieve desirable attainments, reflected by the link from self-efficacy to expected outcomes. Prior experience with the Internet builds self-efficacy levels through a process of progressive mastery in which we learn from our mistakes (Bandura, 1997). We gradually learn what information sources we can trust on the Internet and which ones we cannot, for example. Confidence in our ability to obtain useful information online in turn encourages us to use the Internet more and more to seek information, reflected in the direct link from self-efficacy to usage. Since novel sensory outcomes reflect the search for useful information that may require some special skills in implement-ing searches, a direct link between self-efficacy and novel stimuli outcomes was justified.

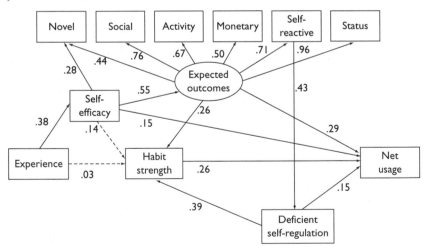

Figure 2.1 Path analysis of social cognitive model of internet usage (LaRose & Eastin, 2004).

Note
Significant path coefficients are indicated by solid lines, $p < .05$ $\chi^2 = 62.3$; df = 34; CFI = .994; RMSEA = .071.

The key elements of the SCT model of media attendance have been verified in subsequent studies of music downloading behavior (LaRose, Lai, Lange, Love, & Wu, 2005; LaRose & Kim, 2007), video game usage (Lee & LaRose, 2007) and the selection of news sources (Diddi & LaRose, 2006). The relationships among self-efficacy, expected outcomes, and computer usage were also found by Compeau et al. (1999). Lam and Lee (2006) confirmed the same relationships in a longitudinal study of elderly Internet users in Hong Kong. The possibility of a reciprocal causal relationship between media selection and expected outcomes was confirmed in a path analysis of Internet usage (Eastin & LaRose, 2000). The effect of self-regulation on media consumption behavior has been confirmed (Robinson & Borzekowski, 2006) through an experimental test of a grade school television reduction intervention (called SMART) based on Bandura's (1991) theory of self-regulation. At the same time that LaRose and colleagues were developing measures of deficient self-regulation a parallel measure of habit strength, the Self-Report Habit Index (SRHI) was also being developed (Verplanken & Orbell, 2003). Newell (2003) found that the SRHI was directly related to consumption of television and three specific Internet applications (r = .39–.55). Verplanken and Orbell found high correlations between the SRHI and viewership of a television soap opera (r = .74) and music listenership (r =.65).

The relationship between self-efficacy and media usage has received the most attention but has not enjoyed entirely consistent empirical support. The predicted positive relationship between self-efficacy and behavior has been observed in numerous media-related studies involving computers (Compeau, Higgins, & Huff, 1999; Hill, Smith, & Mann, 1987; Igbaria & Iivari, 1995), the Internet (Eastin & LaRose, 2000; Hsu & Chiu, 2004; LaRose & Eastin, 2004; LaRose, Lin, & Eastin, 2003), and conventional mass media (Hofstetter, Zuniga, & Dozier, 2001). However, the effects of self-efficacy on media consumption behavior decline with practice as users in a population become more familiar with media, an effect observed both within time-series studies (Venkatesh, Morris, Davis, & Davis, 2003) and across cross-sectional studies of similar populations completed at different points in time (e.g., Eastin & LaRose, 2000 compared to LaRose et al. 2003). Ceiling effects on self-efficacy measures are a partial explanation, but self-efficacy may be generally elevated to the point that it no longer predicts media behavior as entire populations (e.g., college students) become adept in their use of new media. The direction of the relationship of self-efficacy to behavior relationship reversed in a study of favorite Internet activities (LaRose et al., 2008). It may be that highly self-efficacious media consumers learn how to use their favorite media forms so efficiently that the level of use diminishes. In the case of video games, high self-efficacy may also indicate that the activity is no longer challenging, leading to diminished play (Klimmt & Hartmann, 2006; Lee & LaRose, 2007).

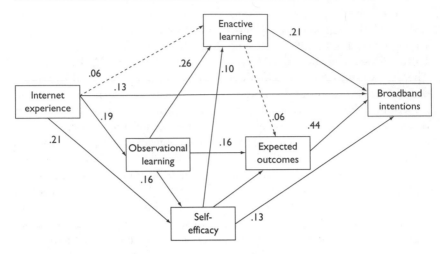

Figure 2.2 Socio-cognitive model of broadband adoption (LaRose et al., 2007).

Note
Significant path coefficients are indicated by solid lines, $p < .05$; $\chi^2 = 1.6$; df = 2; CFI = 1.00; RMSEA = .000.

The SCT approach to the adoption of media innovations was partially confirmed in a study of broadband Internet adoption in rural America (LaRose, Gregg, Strover, Straubhaar, & Carpenter, 2007). Self-efficacy was once again a predictor of expected outcomes and intentions to use a broadband connection in the future, which were also predicted from prior Internet experience, enactive learning and expected outcomes. Observational learning causally followed prior experience but preceded enactive learning. The paths between enactive learning and Internet experience and expected outcomes were not significant, perhaps due to reliability problems associated with the a single-item measure of enactive learning that was used (see Figure 2.2).

Rival Paradigms

Socio-cognitive theories of media selection have parallels in Diffusion of Innovations (DOI, Rogers, 1995; von Pape, this volume), Uses and Gratifications (UGs, Palmgreen, Wenner, & Rosengren, 1985), and the Theory of Planned Behavior (TPB, Ajzen, 1991). Here we examine the relative merits of these four paradigms as applied to media selection behavior.

Compared to Diffusion of Innovation

As a model of initial media adoption, SCT was at one point well integrated into the DOI paradigm (Rogers, 1995). Specifically, the diffusion process was described as an instance of observational learning in which the relative advantages of new media could be learned by observing the experiences of previous adopters (Bandura, 2001). However, all five attributes of innovations thought to promote their adoption—relative advantage, complexity, trialability, observability, and compatibility—have socio-cognitive parallels. For example, the relative advantage of a new medium might be understood as the outcome expectations associated with its adoption. Trialability, or the ease with which the merits of an innovation can be sampled on a trial basis, is aligned with enactive learning, while observability parallels observational learning. Complexity parallels the self-efficacy construct. Compatibility may be understood in terms of the self-regulatory mechanism of judgmental process: comparing behavior to personal and social norms.

Defining innovation attributes in socio-cognitive terms potentially overcomes one of the enduring criticisms of the DOI paradigm, that it is technologically deterministic. In SCT it is the perception of one's future use of the innovation, rather than its objective technological attributes, that determines adoption behavior. Socio-cognitive concepts can integrate disparate phenomenon that have accreted to the diffusion paradigm over the years. For example, innovation clusters—the tendency to adopt innovations like broadband Internet that are similar to past innovations such as dial up Internet (Rogers, 1986)—might be explained in terms of the self-efficacy gained through experience with similar, past innovations. The critical mass phenomenon, in which the adoption of interactive media like email is driven by the number of other users, might be understood as a social outcome expectation. By reconceptualizing relative advantage in terms of the benefits perceived by potential adopters, the re-invention process can be understood, such as the re-purposing of an instrument of nuclear annihilation (Arpanet) as an entertainment and communication medium (the Internet). Finally, SCT offers a causal ordering among innovation attributes, as described above (LaRose et al., 2007).

Compared to Uses and Gratifications

The social cognitive theory of UGs (LaRose & Eastin, 2004) was conceived to improve upon the UGs paradigm (see Scherer, this volume; Krcmar & Strizhakova, this volume) by refining the core gratifications construct and adding self-efficacy and self-regulatory mechanisms. Like SCT, UGs theory posits an active thought process in which media are selected through reflection on the relative merits of media alternatives along multiple dimensions. Within UGs, these dimensions are though to be related to needs while in SCT they are expected outcomes of behavior related to the six dimensions of incentives discussed previously.

Thus, expected outcomes in SCT parallel gratifications in UGs in that both are multidimensional constructs of media perceptions that are thought to determine media selection behavior. However, neither gratifications sought (GS), nor gratifications obtained (GO), nor the arithmetic difference between them (GS–GO) are identical to expected outcomes. For example, a viewer might *seek* an exciting hour's entertainment by tuning in a favorite television show but only realistically *expect* it to be mildly entertaining. Our viewer might be disappointed to find a rerun and thus *obtain* no entertainment at all but that may or may not dramatically affect future expectations. That is because a single negative instance might be easily rationalized and, after a behavior becomes habitual, individuals respond only to the long-run average of the outcomes they experience (Yin & Knowlton, 2006). Or, observational learning experiences, such as the reviews published in the newspaper, might bolster outcome expectations. When forming the plan to tune in again, SCT argues that it is what the viewer expects going forward, as opposed to what they sought or obtained in the past, that determines behavior. Studies involving prospective measures of outcomes provide better predictions of media behavior than those using conventional UGs measures (LaRose & Eastin, 2004) and the SCT account of outcome expectations is now confirmed by neurological research (Yin & Knowlton, 2006).

SCT also offers *a priori* categories of incentives (social, status, novel sensory, enjoyable activity, economic, and self-reactive) while UGs researchers derive their gratification dimensions *de novo* in each study through exploratory factor analysis. However, since the lists of gratifications used in many UGs studies trace back to a study of television viewing among British school children in the early 1970s (Greenberg, 1974), motivators of media selection that were beyond the ken of British school children (e.g., social status incentives) or beyond the capabilities of early 1970s British television (e.g., the attainment of economic outcomes) were quite naturally overlooked (LaRose, 2004).

Also beginning with Greenberg (1974), measures of habit strength (e.g., I watch TV "because it's a habit") were treated analytically as gratifications. Despite later efforts (Palmgreen, et al., 1985, p. 17) to conceptualize habit as a separate variable this practice continues unto this day in studies of the uses and gratifications of the Internet (e.g., Papacharissi & Rubin, 2000). A distinction made between instrumental and ritual uses of media (Rubin, 1984) was an attempt to explain the contradiction between purposeful media selection processes (instrumental) and more or less habitual ones (ritual) but failed to resolve the inherent contradiction between ritual uses and the active selection processes said to underpin UGs (LaRose, 2004). Thus, the addition of self-regulation and its deficiencies (LaRose & Eastin, 2004) revives an earlier model of media selection in the UGs tradition.

Finally, SCT proposes a new variable not found in UGs, self-efficacy. Belief in one's ability to successfully complete a media behavior to produce an attainment is an important addition to our understanding of the consumption of complex new media such as the Internet. However, readers who put down a book because it is "too deep" may also have media self-efficacy issues.

Compared to Theory of Planned Behavior

A close parallel to the outcome expectations construct is also found in the Theory of Planned Behavior (TPB), in behavioral beliefs, or "beliefs that link a behavior to a certain outcome or other attributes such as cost" (Ajzen, 1991, p. 191). In TPB, behavioral beliefs are a component of attitudes toward the behavior, formulated operationally by multiplying the strength of belief in the occurrence of a particular outcome by the corresponding evaluation of that outcome, summed across all of the modal salient beliefs held by a particular population (Hartmann, this volume). As applied in media studies (e.g. by LaRose & Eastin, 2004), SCT measures of expected outcomes are an additive index of beliefs about the outcomes of behavior without the evaluation component, an inferior approach since individuals may vary in their evaluation of outcomes as well as the likelihood of their occurrence. However, SCT researchers can account for negative outcomes by creating a separate additive index of negative outcome expectations (LaRose, 1992) that explains additional variance in behavior. TPB likely produces superior predictions in instances where outcome expectations (e.g., being always reachable via cell phone) are perceived as positive outcomes by some respondents but negative outcomes by others.

A further area of intersection is between self-efficacy and perceived behavioral control. Ajzen (1991, p. 184) adopted Bandura's definition of self-efficacy as the conceptual definition of perceived behavioral control. However, operational definitions of perceived behavioral control focus on control beliefs about "the presence or absence of requisite resources or opportunities, weighted by their perceived power to interfere with the behavior" (Ajzen, 1991, p. 196) with the latter defined in terms of the ease or difficulty of overcoming them. A person's intention to view a forthcoming political debate might illustrate the distinction. The belief that one's work schedule will interfere with viewing the debate is a relevant control belief, but its power to interfere with the behavior might be minimal if the viewer can easily use her TiVO to record the program. However, the viewing intention may also be affected by the viewer's beliefs about her ability to understand the debate to a degree that will inform her voting decision, a self-efficacy belief. Thus, while perceived behavioral control refers to one's ability to control a behavior, self-efficacy refers more to the perceived ability to execute the behavior to obtain desired outcomes, independent of the external barriers (such as the broadcast schedule). One might also have low perceived behavioral control but high self-efficacy with respect to the same behavior, such as playing one's favorite video game on one's wedding anniversary. The relationship between the two constructs remains controversial (Ajzen, 2002a) and there is considerable empirical evidence from beyond the media consumption domain that supports the position that the two are complementary rather than competing concepts (Norman & Hoyle, 2004).

Perceived social norms, or "perceived social pressure to perform or not perform a behavior" (Ajzen, 1991, p. 188), also have an SCT parallel in the judgmental process component of self-regulation. Proposed additions to TPB including self-image and moral norms (Conner & Armitage, 1998) may also be understood through this mechanism since judgmental process covers individual, social, and collective norms. But, while these normative constructs are assumed to be directly related to behavioral intentions by TPB researchers, SCT posits an indirect relationship. If norms are to have any impact on behavior, individuals must not only be aware of them but also apply self-reaction to their own behavior, such as offering themselves rewards for moderating excessive media consumption or indulging feelings of guilt about them when norms for media consumption are violated.

A further precondition for normative influence is that individuals be attentive to their own behavior, through self-observation. An online game player may be aware that his parents want him to reduce his play time, a perceived social norm. However, if the player is inattentive to the amount of time he spends playing (a failure of self-observation) or fails to internally generate rewards for reduced game play (a failure of self-reaction) then the norm is unlikely to have an effect on behavior. Thus, norms act through self-regulation and deficient self-regulation may mediate their impact on behavioral intentions. LaRose and Kim (2007) found preliminary evidence of this relationship in a study of music downloading among college students in which the SCT and TPB models of normative influence were compared.

Deficient self-regulation is related to habit strength (LaRose & Eastin, 2004), a controversial subject in the annals of TPB. Numerous studies show that habit strength, usually defined as the frequency of past behavior, is related to behavioral intentions and to the performance of behavior (Conner & Armitage, 1998). However, the chief proponent of TPB has argued that there is no logical reason for past behavior to affect future behavior, at least not after the impact of past performance on attitudes is accounted for (Ajzen, 2002b). Ajzen argued that studies finding a significant effect for habit strength demonstrated the insufficiency of the variables that the researchers employed to explain behavior. And, after all, TPB is a theory of *planned* behavior while habitual behavior is thought to be automatic and thus unplanned. So, the addition of deficient self-regulation points to an explanation of media selection that includes both actively and automatically selected media. Recent neurological research (Saling & Phillips, 2007) indicates that automaticity results not from processing conscious thoughts (e.g., attitudes and perceived social norms related to TV viewing) more quickly but rather from completely reorganizing the cognitive task (e.g., so that sight of the TV triggers the behavior). The SRHI is a measure of habit strength that parallels deficient self-regulation and has been shown to explain behavior independent of the effects of behavioral intentions and other standard components of the TPB model (Verplanken, 2006).

Summary and Conclusion

Thus, SCT offers an explanation of a wide range of media selection behaviors, beginning with the initial choice of new media channels and content, continuing with daily media choices, the development of media habits, and problematic media use. Recent research provides preliminary evidence of its superiority to one of the leading paradigms of media choice, UGs, and it also fills important conceptual gaps in TPB.

SCT holds the promise of an integrated theory of media that encompasses both conscious and nonconscious processes governing media selection and the effects of those choices. The potential contributions of SCT to an integrative theory are the self-efficacy construct, the self-regulatory mechanism, and observational learning. While TPB and UGs offer suitable rival paradigms on which to build a comprehensive theory of media selection, SCT holds the unique distinction of offering an integrated approach to understanding both exposure to the media and the effects of that exposure on audiences. LaRose, Eastin, and Gregg (2001) examined the effects of the Internet on psychological well-being through a model that worked from SCT explanations of exposure to media effects.

An important limitation of the present SCT research corpus related to media selection is its cross-sectional nature. Key relationships, such as that between deficient self-regulation and habit strength, while theoretically justifiable, have not been experimentally verified and so the direction of causation is still speculative. Indeed, the direction of causation is a problematic issue throughout SCT since many of the causal relationships are reciprocal in nature. For example, self-efficacy and expected outcomes predict behavior, but experience with a behavior also affects self-efficacy (through a process of progressive mastery) and expected outcomes (through the mechanism of enactive learning). Likewise, strong media habits may diminish self-regulation as much as deficient self-regulation may lead to strong habits.

A Research Agenda

So, experimental and time series studies are required to further explore socio-cognitive models of media selection. This is a particularly salient need in examining the relationships among expected outcomes, habit strength, deficient self-regulation, and behavior since these have been introduced through the communication research literature without the supporting evidence that is available from other domains for other elements of SCT. The relationship between habit strength and deficient self-regulation should be further explored since these variables overlap somewhat both conceptually and empirically.

Self-efficacy is a multidimensional construct worthy of further attention by media researchers. While confidence in one's ability to, say, watch television may seem a trivial issue, coping self-efficacy in relation to overcoming the obstacles to watch a favorite show might sharpen the predictiveness of perceived behavioral control. Belief in one's ability to obtain important outcomes, such as an informed decision about political candidates, from media exposure is another example of a potentially highly consequential self-efficacy belief.

By further exploring self-regulation, SCT might explain the role of social norms by considering possible moderating effects of self-observation, judgmental process and self-reaction. Further research inspired by action control paradigms (Sniehotta, Scholz, & Schwarzer, 2005) and decision theory (Hsee & Hastie, 2006) could specify conditions under which individuals can be made mindful of problematic media behavior and of self-reaction strategies for behavioral control. While it is difficult to disrupt well-established consumer habits (Verplanken & Wood, 2006), interventions that target habits in their formative stage (e.g., Robinson & Borzekowski, 2006) hold promise. But also, there are some media behaviors such as news reading and book reading that we as a society may wish to make even more habit-forming. The construction and destruction of media habits is of practical value in media industries. A further understanding of how repeated media choices become habitual (Wood & Neal, 2007) and automatic (Bargh et al. 2001) is another avenue for further exploration.

References

Aarts, H. & Dijksterhuis, A. (2000). Habits as knowledge structures: Automaticity in goal-directed behavior. *Journal of Personality and Social Psychology, 78*, 53–63.

Anderson, C. A. & Dill, K. E. (2000). Video games and aggressive thoughts, feelings, and behavior in the laboratory and in life. *Journal of Personality and Social Psychology, 78*, 772–790.

Ajzen, I. (1991). The theory of planned behavior. *Organizational Behavior and Human Decision Processes, 50*, 179–211.

Ajzen, I. (2002a). Perceived behavioral control, self-efficacy, locus of control, and the Theory of Planned Behavior. *Journal of Applied Social Psychology, 32*, 665–683.

Ajzen, I. (2002b). Residual effects of past on later behavior: Habituation and reasoned action perspectives. *Personality and Social Psychology Review, 6*, 107–122.

Bandura, A. (1965). Influence of models' reinforcement contingencies on the acquisition of imitative responses. *Journal of Personality and Social Psychology, 1*, 589–595.

Bandura, A. (1977). *Social Learning Theory*. Englewood Cliffs, NJ: Prentice Hall.

Bandura, A. (1986). *Social Foundations of Thought and Action: A Social Cognitive Theory*. Englewood Cliffs, NJ: Prentice Hall.

Bandura, A. (1989). Human agency in social cognitive theory. *American Psychologist, 77*, 122–147.

Bandura, A. (1991). Social cognitive theory of self-regulation. *Organizational Behavior and Human Decision Processes, 50*, 248–287.

Bandura, A. (1997). *Self-efficacy: The Exercise of Control*. New York: W. H. Freeman.

Bandura, A. (1999). A sociocognitive analysis of substance abuse: An agentic perspective. *Psychological Science,10*, 214–217.

Bandura, A. (2001). Social cognitive theory of mass communication. *Media Psychology, 3*, 265–299.

Bargh, J. A., Gollwitzer, P. M., Chai, A., Barndollar, K., & Troschel, R. (2001). The automated will: Nonconscious activation and pursuit of behavioral goals. *Journal of Personality and Social Psychology, 81*, 1014–1027.

Berridge, K. C. (2004). Motivation concepts in behavioral neuroscience. *Physiology and Behavior, 81*, 179–209.

Compeau, D., Higgins, C. A., & Huff, S. (1999). Social cognitive theory and individual reactions to computing technology: A longitudinal study. *MIS Quarterly, 23*, 145–158.

Conner, M. & Armitage, C. (1998). The theory of planned behavior: A review and avenues for future research. *Journal of Applied Social Psychology, 28*, 1429–1464.

Diddi, A. & LaRose, R. (2006). Getting hooked on news: Uses and gratifications and the formation of news habits among college students in an internet environment. *Journal of Broadcasting and Electronic Media, 50*, 193–210.

Eastin, M. S. & LaRose, R. (2000). Internet self-efficacy and the psychology of the digital divide. *Journal of Computer Mediated Communication, 6*(1). Online. Retrieved September 30, 2001 from: www.asusc.org/jcmc/vol6/issue1/eastin. html.

Eccles, J. S. & Wigfield, A. (2002). Motivational beliefs, values, and goals. *Annual Review of Psychology, 53*, 109–132.

Greenberg, B. S. (1974). Gratifications of television viewing and their correlates for British children. In J. Blumler & E. Katz (Eds.), *The Uses of Mass Communication*. Beverly Hills, CA: Sage.

Henning, B. & Vorderer, P. (2001). Psychological escapism: Predicting the amount of television viewing by need for cognition. *Journal of Communication, 51*, 100–120.

Hill, T., Smith, N. D., & Mann, M. F. (1987). Role of efficacy expectations in predicting the decision to use advanced technologies: The case of computers. *Journal of Applied Psychology, 72*, 307–313.

Hofstetter, C. R., Zuniga, S., & Dozier, D. M. (2001). Media self-efficacy: Validation of a new concept. *Mass Communication and Society, 4*, 61–78.

Hsee, C. K. & Hastie, R. (2006). Decision and experience: Why don't we choose what makes us happy? *Trends in Cognitive Sciences, 10*, 31–37.

Hsu, M. H. & Chiu, C.-M. (2004). Internet self-efficacy and electronic service acceptance. *Decision Support Systems, 38*, 369–381.

Huesmann, L. R., Moise-Titus, J., Podolski, C., & Eron, L. D. (2003) Longitudinal relations between children's exposure to TV violence and their aggressive and violent behavior in young adulthood: 1977–1992. *Developmental Psychology, 39*, 201–221.

Igbaria, M. & Iivari, J. (1995). The effects of self-efficacy on computer usage. *Omega, 23*, 587–605.

Klimmt, C. & Hartmann, T. (2006). Effectance, self-efficacy, and the motivation to play video games. In P. Vorderer & J. Bryant (Eds.), *Playing Video Games: Motives, Responses, and Consequences* (pp. 132–145). Mahwah: Lawrence Erlbaum Associates.

Kubey, R. & Csikszentmihalyi, M. (2002). Television addiction is no mere metaphor. *Scientific American, 286*, 74–81.

Lam, J. C. Y. & Lee, M. K. O. (2006). Digital inclusiveness—longitudinal study of internet adoption by older adults. *Journal of Management Information Systems, 22,* 177–206.

LaRose, R. (1992). Telephone apprehension: Definition, measurement and validity issues. Paper presented to the International Communication Association, Miami, Florida, May.

LaRose, R. (2004). Cyber compulsions: Media habits, media addictions and the Internet. In P. Lee, L. Leung & C. So (Eds.), *Impact and Issues in New Media: Toward Intelligent Societies.* Cresskill, NJ: Hampton Press.

LaRose, R. & Eastin, M. S. (2004). A social cognitive theory of internet uses and gratifications: Toward a new model of media attendance. *Journal of Broadcasting and Electronic Media, 48,* 358–377.

LaRose, R. & Kim, J. (2007). Share, steal, or buy? A social cognitive perspective of music downloading. *Cyberpsychology & Behavior, 10*(2), 267–277.

LaRose, R., Eastin, M. S., & Gregg, J. (2001). Reformulating the Internet paradox: Social cognitive explanations of Internet use and depression. *Journal of Online Behavior, 1* (2). Online. Retrieved September 30, 2001 from: www.behavior.net/JOB/v1n2/paradox.htmlLarose 2001.

LaRose, R., Gregg, J., Strover, S., Straubhaar, J., & Carpenter, S. (2007). Closing the rural broadband gap: Promoting adoption of the Internet in rural America. *Telecommunication Policy, 31,* 359–373.

LaRose, R., Kim, J., & Peng, W. (2008). The problem of problematic Internet use: Antisocial disease, dangerous habit, or just one of our favorites? Submitted for publication.

LaRose, R., Lai, Y. J., Lange, R., Love, B., & Wu, Y. H. (2005). Sharing or piracy? An exploration of downloading behavior. *Journal of Computer-Mediated Communication, 11*(1).

LaRose, R., Lin, C. A., & Eastin, M. S. (2003). Unregulated internet usage: Addiction, habit, or deficient self-regulation? *Media Psychology, 5,* 225–253.

LaRose, R., Mastro, D., & Eastin, M. S. (2001). Understanding internet usage—a social-cognitive approach to uses and gratifications. *Social Science Computer Review, 19,* 395–413.

Lee, D.W. & LaRose, R. (2007). A socio-cognitive model of video game usage. *Journal of Broadcasting and Electronic Media, 51,* 632–650.

Newell, J. (2003). The role of habit in the selection of electronic media. Unpublished doctoral dissertation, Michigan State University.

Norman, P. & Hoyle, S. (2004). The theory of planned behavior and breast self-examination: Distinguishing between perceived control and self-efficacy. *Journal of Applied Social Psychology, 34,* 694–708.

Palmgreen, P., Wenner, L., & Rosengren, K. (1985). Uses and gratifications research: The past ten years. In K. Rosengren, L. Wenner, & P. Palmgreen (Eds.), *Media Gratifications Research* (pp. 11–37). Beverly Hills, CA: Sage Publications.

Papacharissi, Z. & Rubin, A. M. (2000). Predictors of Internet usage. *Journal of Broadcasting and Electronic Media, 44,* 175–196.

Poldrack, R. A., Sabb, F. W., Foerde, K., Tom, S. M., Asarnow, R. F., Bookheimer, S. Y., et al. (2005). The neural correlates of motor skill automaticity. *Journal Of Neuroscience, 25,* 5356–5364.

Robinson, T. N. & Borzekowski, D. L. G. (2006). Effects of the SMART classroom curriculum to reduce child and family screen time. *Journal of Communication, 56,* 1–26.

Rogers, E. M. (1986). *Communication Technology.* New York: Free Press.

Rogers, E. M. (1995). *Diffusion of Innovations.* 4th edition. New York: Free Press.

Rubin, A. M. (1984). Ritualized and instrumental television viewing. *Journal of Communication, 34,* 67–77.

Saling, L. L. & Phillips, J. G. (2007). Automatic behaviour: Efficient not mindless. *Brain Research Bulletin, 73,* 1–20.

Skinner, B. F. (1938). *The Behavior of Organisms.* New York: Appleton-Century-Crofts.

Sniehotta, F. F., Scholz, U., & Schwarzer, R. (2005). Bridging the intention–behaviour gap: Planning, self-efficacy, and action control in the adoption and maintenance of physical exercise. *Psychology and Health, 20,* 143–160.

Thalemann, R., Wölfling, K., & Güsser, S. M. (2007). Specific cue-reactivity on computer game related cues in excessive gamers. *Behavioral Neuroscience, 121,* 614–618.

Triandis, H. C. (1980). Values, attitudes and interpersonal behavior. In *Nebraska Symposium on Motivation. Volume 37* (pp. 195–259). Lincoln: University of Nebraska Press.

Venkatesh, V., Morris, M. G., Davis, G. B., & Davis, F. D. (2003). User acceptance of information technology: Toward a unified view. *MIS Quarterly, 27,* 425–478.

Verplanken, B. (2006). Beyond frequency: Habit as mental construct. *British Journal of Social Psychology, 45,* 639–656.

Verplanken, B. & Orbell, S. (2003). Reflections on past behavior: A self-report index of habit strength. *Journal of Applied Social Psychology, 33,* 1313–1330.

Verplanken, B. & Wood, W. (2006). Interventions to break and create consumer habits. *Journal of Public Policy & Marketing, 25,* 90–103.

Wood, W. & Neal, D. T. (2007). A new look at habits and the habit–goal interface. *Psychological Review, 114,* 843–863.

Wood, W., Tam, L., & Witt, M. G. (2005). Changing circumstances, disrupting habits. *Journal of Personality and Social Psychology, 88,* 918–933.

Yin, H. H. & Knowlton, B. J. (2006). The role of the basal ganglia in habit formation. *Nature Reviews Neuroscience, 7,* 464–476.

Zilllman, D. & Bryant, J. (1985). Affect, mood and emotion as determinants of selective media exposure. In D. Zillmann & J. Bryant (Eds.), *Selective exposure to communication* (pp. 157–190). Hillsale, NJ: Lawrence Erlbaum.

Chapter 3

Action Theory, Theory of Planned Behavior and Media Choice

Tilo Hartmann

Action theory regards people as decision-makers who follow intentions and voluntarily pursue their goals (Eccles & Wigfield, 2002). According to this theory, people may be affected by environmental and inner pressures and affordances, but ultimately behavior is guided by reflective, higher-order cognitive processes (Smith & DeCoster, 2000; Westerick, Renckstorf, Lammers, & Wester, 2006). People's higher-order cognitive processing responds to immediate "forces" such as internal drives or external pressures, but is not considered to be fully determined by them. Accordingly, action theory underlines the capability of people to cognitively ponder their environment and to run projections regarding various outcomes before they choose an option and undertake an action. A full explanation of media choice from the perspective of action theory involves the following four components: (1) it stresses users' decision-making (Frisch & Clemen, 1994; Marewski, Galesic, & Gigerenzer, this volume), which may include a likelihood-estimation and evaluation of possible rewards and costs (c.f., Eccles & Wigfield, 2002); (2) it highlights the way in which intentions are developed within the decision process; (3) it explicates how an intention is eventually implemented and shielded against competing action plans (Gollwitzer, 1990; Heckhausen & Beckmann, 1990); and (4) it thus tells how intentions result in actual behavior (Sheeran, Webb, & Gollwitzer, 2005).

A specific theoretical framework, which originated in social psychology and strongly builds on action-theoretical ideas, is the Theory of Planned Behavior (TOPB; Ajzen, 1988, 1991; see Ajzen & Fishbein, 2005, for an excellent summary; see for reviews, Armitage & Conner, 2001; Hagger, Chatzisarantis, & Biddle, 2002; Conner & Armitage, 1998; Sutton, 1998). TOPB can be understood as an extension of its precursor, the Theory of Reasoned Action (TRA; Ajzen & Fishbein, 1980; Fishbein & Ajzen, 1975; for a comparison of TRA and TOPB, see Madden, Ellen, & Ajzen, 1992). The scope of TOPB is—as already suggested by the labels "planned behavior" and "reasoned action"—predicting and explaining human behavior that is based on motivational choices and intentions.

This chapter discusses an application of TOPB to media choice. The first section introduces the theory, defines the core scope of the theory, and discusses the potential boundaries of the scope. The second section reviews existing applications of TOPB to the realm of media choice, and the third section concludes the chapter with a review of the potential of TOPB to inspire research on media choice via discussing initial steps towards a theory of planned media choice.

General Assumptions of the Theory of Planned Behavior

TOPB is considered a general framework in which to explain and predict behavior that is, at least to a certain degree, under *volitional control* (Ajzen, 1991) and as such depends on a person's free will. The model does not predict behavior that is either completely determined by external forces or pressures (e.g., experiencing an accident) or that is under the complete command of autonomous mechanisms (e.g., getting ill, sneezing, compulsive behavior). TOPB explains behavior as an observable action (e.g., watching) defined by a specific situation (e.g., in the living room), linked to a specific target (e.g., the television) and restricted to a certain episode (e.g., within the next 14 days). The behavior may also occur repeatedly across similar situations (compound behavior; e.g., frequency of television use in the living room over the next 14 days).

According to TOPB, behavior is determined by the interaction (Ajzen, 1991, p. 188) of an *intention* (which indicates "how hard people are willing to try" (p. 181)) and the degree of *actual control* exerted over the behavior (p. 183). Behavior that is at least to certain a degree under volitional control will be performed if people really want to perform it and if they have the resources and abilities to do so. If the behavior is solely under volitional control (i.e., does not require any specific efforts, skills, or resources), its performance would depend entirely on one's intention.

According to TOPB, a person's *intention* to carry out a behavior builds on his/her motivational disposition, which entails three factors: (1) a favorable attitude toward the behavior (i.e., evaluating the behavior as good, healthy, worthwhile, valuable, etc.), (2) subjective norms (i.e., believing that important others will approve of conducting the behavior and even carry it out themselves), and (3) a perceived behavioral control over the behavior (i.e., believing that it is generally possible to carry out the behavior, and that one is able to carry it out; cf. Figure 3.1).

Each of these three factors (methodologically addressed as "direct measures") is thought to be a function of a specific set of people's expectancies and evaluations of *salient* outcomes or attributes (including costs) that people associate with a behavior (cf. "expectancy-value estimations," Eccles & Wigfield, 2002, p. 118; Marewski et al., this volume; Wolling, this volume; methodologically addressed as "indirect measures"). People's *attitude*

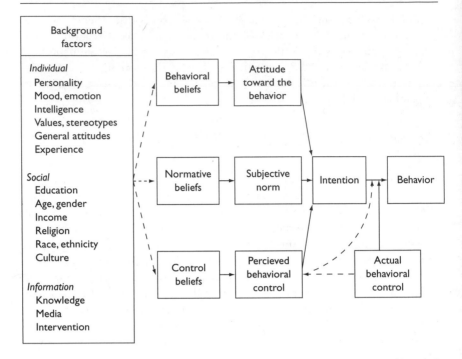

Figure 3.1 The theories of reasoned action and planned behavior (Ajzen & Fishbein, 2005, p. 194).

towards a behavior is a function of how likely they deem different outcomes associated with the behavior, and how desirable they find these outcomes (behavioral beliefs): people develop a favorable attitude towards the behavior if they perceive the outcomes to be both highly likely and desirable. People's *subjective norms* build on their beliefs about the normative expectations of relevant others and the motivation to comply with these expectations (normative beliefs). Subjective norms have a positive influence on behavior if people think that relevant others (friends, parents, classmates, etc.) appreciate the behavior or even pursue it themselves, and if people are at the same time willing to comply to their social surrounding.

It is commonly the case that behavior not only depends on people's will, but also on favorable external circumstances. The last of the three determinants outlined above, *perceived behavioral control*, therefore builds on the factors that people think may facilitate or impede the behavior, as well as the presumed power of these factors (control beliefs). Following TOPB, behavioral control is high if people consider it possible for them to carry out the behavior (cf. "self-efficacy," Bandura, 1997); that is, behavioral control is high if people think the expected circumstances will ease the behavior and/ or if people believe they are capable of overcoming circumstances that they expect to impede the behavior. A person may believe, for example, that playing a multiplayer video game ultimately depends on the circumstance that another player is available. Accordingly, the perceived control regarding the playing of a multiplayer game will be low if the person believes that no other player will be present.

At the Borders of TOBP: Automatic Behavior Under Volitional Control

Behavior is often elicited in a spontaneous, impulsive manner. Such behavior is said to be triggered *automatically* by environmental stimuli (Bargh & Barndollar, 1996). Automatic behavior is usually carried out in a mindless fashion; i.e., without conscious reflection. Media choices are also commonly automatic (Jaeckel, 1992; LaRose, this volume; Marewski et al., this volume). For example, after a hard day's work a tired person may become aware of the television set and feel an immediate drive to switch it on (cf. Fazio, 1990). She/he may pursue this "decision" with little reflection, switching on the TV somewhat mindlessly. If such automatic behavior reflects the fact that the person has successfully carried out the same action in the same context many times previously, it can be termed a habit (Oulette & Wood, 1998; Verplanken & Aarts, 1999). Mindless and automatic behavior, such as the habit of watching TV, seems to be the opposite of deliberative, conscious, and volitional behavioral conduct that falls within the scope of TOPB (cf. Connor & Armitage, 1998). In this context, it is appropriate to ask whether TOPB fails to explain and predict many instances of media choice.

According to TOPB, behavior is volitional if it depends on intentions. Many researchers stress the idea that intentions are elaborate and conscious plans of action that build on a symbolic interpretation of future situations (Smith & DeCoster, 2000). Higher-order cognitive processes are involved in the symbolic anticipation of the future, enabling one to pursue a free will; i.e., to disentangle environmental or inner stimuli from behavioral responses (Kuhl & Goschke, 1994). According to this view, behavior that follows intentions and that, as such, is under volitional control, requires *higher-order cognitive elaborations* (Smith & DeCoster, 2000); these elaborations are usually costly because they demand greater cognitive resources than automatic processes. People engage in such demanding cognitive processes only if a situation does not allow a reliance on more efficient, mindless responses (Fazio & Towles-Schwen, 1999). When making a decision, people engage in elaborate cognitive processes—particularly if the decision entails a considerable risk—because important goods or considerable investments are at stake (Esser, 1996; Fazio & Towles-Schwen, 1999); however, people can only engage in higher-order cognitive processes if the situation does not require urgent action, providing the time and opportunity to think before arriving at a decision (Fazio, 1990; Payne, Bettman, & Johnson, 1993).

In contrast, if people care little about the outcomes of a decision, if they do not have time to care, or if they are simply familiar with the decision and no longer need to care, decisions are more likely to be based on mindless processes than on higher-order cognitive elaborations. From this perspective, it seems that low-involvement, impulsive, or habitual media choices rest on environmental or inner forces that only trigger mindless mental processes, not elaborate cognitive thinking (e.g., "implicit attitudes," c.f., Wilson, Lindsey, & Schooler, 2000; "reduced impulse control," Tice, Bratslavsky, & Baumeister, 2001). Accordingly, automatic media choices would not depend on an intention, and therefore would not be covered by TOPB. The scope of TOPB would then be limited to media choices that are planned, as they involve a considerable risk because they are cost-intensive (e.g., deciding to go to the movies), tap crucial values or other important personal beliefs (e.g., deciding to watch a film about the Holocaust), and/or are simply unfamiliar (e.g., deciding to use a computer for the first time).

Does TOPB indeed fail to account for many instances of media choice, then? It may also be argued that automatic processes commonly build on the same motivational dispositions as those built upon by more deliberate processes. In addition, most automatic processes may remain under volitional control to a certain extent, as people willingly let them happen but may be able to intervene if desired.

One argument in light of this perspective is that spontaneous automatic behavior may result from automatically formed attitudes, normative beliefs and control beliefs, and an intention that is quickly established on-line (Ajzen & Fishbein, 2000). The cognitive association of action-relevant beliefs (i.e., the association of possible outcomes and the estimation of their likelihood and their evaluation) is not necessarily a conscious and elaborate process: people do not need to deliberately weigh the pros and cons associated with a behavior to make a decision and perform the behavior. As suggested by Ajzen and Fishbein (2000), behavioral attitudes, as well as normative and control beliefs, may form spontaneously after the outcomes and attributes associated with the behavior have come to mind automatically and subliminally. Subsequently, these spontaneously established and implicit beliefs may guide behavior (cf. Fazio, 1990). For example, after becoming aware of their television set, people may automatically associate watching television with an enjoyable and highly desirable mood-state. Based on this association, they may quickly form a positive attitude, followed by an intention to perform the behavior. Because the opportunity already exists, they may mindlessly turn on the TV (Fazio, 1990). Zapping (Bilandzic, this volume) and avoidance behavior (Fahr & Boecking, this volume) provide other examples of such spontaneous media choices.

Spontaneous automatic behavior may rest on automatically formed or implicit attitudes, norms and control beliefs that result in a quickly established intention to perform the behavior; however, Ajzen and Fishbein

(2000) proposed that a person's spontaneous motivational disposition forms neither arbitrarily nor heuristically, but is a function of existing associations (or beliefs; for a different opinion, see Marewski et al., this volume). Related media choices would still fall within the scope of TOPB, as "at the most basic level of explanation, the [theory] postulates that behavior is a function of salient information [...] relevant to the behavior" (Ajzen, 1991, p. 189). However, researchers need to capture a person's subjective associations that in general underlie his/her media choices; i.e., a person's salient (highly accessible) belief structure (Ajzen, 1991; Connor & Armitage, 1998). However, to the extent that a person's implicit and explicit motivational disposition diverges (Wilson et al., 2000), and automatically associated aspects or salient beliefs differ between real life and in survey situations, and to the extent that people evaluate and weigh different associated aspects in a contrasting fashion, TOPB may fail to provide an accurate model of spontaneous automatic behavior.

Research on *implementation intentions* (Gollwitzer, 1993, 1999) provides another argument as to why automatic behavior may still be affected by volitional control and intentions. Implementation intentions have the format of if–then plans: "If situation X arises, then I will do Y!" (Achtziger, Gollwitzer, & Sheeran, 2008, p. 381). Accordingly, "implementation intentions create a mental link between a selected cue or situation" (e.g., the television set) and "a goal-directed response" (e.g., watching TV, Achtziger et al., 2008, p. 381). If a critical cue is present, "the respective response is executed immediately and without further conscious intent" (Gollwitzer & Brandstaetter, 1997, p. 382).

Gollwitzer (1999) suggests that people form implementation intentions based on their *general* intentions (or goal intentions), which are thought to build on the determinants suggested in TOPB. General intentions reflect more of what a person wishes to do in the long-term, whereas implementation intentions focus more on the means to achieve a chosen long-term goal. For example, a person may form the general intention to withstand the pain of loneliness. She holds a positive attitude towards this behavioral goal, and her friends strongly support her efforts to withstand loneliness. Based on her general intention, she may form the implementation intention that whenever she feels the pain of loneliness at home, she will seek to distract herself by watching television. Accordingly, the person may automatically turn on the TV at home whenever she feels painfully lonely. In the same way that she has a positive attitude about her general goal to reduce the pain of loneliness, she is likely to have a positive attitude about watching TV because the behavior has instrumental value (Vroom, 1964), helping her to reduce loneliness. For the same reasons, she may think that important others approve of her watching TV, as they also support her efforts to relieve the feeling of loneliness.

The behavior described in this example is automatic and mindless, because the person routinely triggers the TV button whenever she feels lonely. The person only relies on automatic behavior, however, because she developed an implementation intention as a means to fulfill her general intention. TOPB may predict both the person's general intention to reduce loneliness and the implementation intention to watch TV whenever she feels lonely (cf. Ajzen & Fishbein, 2005; Bamberg, Ajzen, & Schmidt, 2003, p. 185; Rise, Thompson, & Verplanken, 2003; Connor & Armitage, 1998); however, application of TOPB seems to be accurate only in the case that a person's general intention remains unchanged and thus remains in line with the derived implementation intention (Bamberg et al., 2003). If the original motivational disposition and thus the original general intention changes, however, a person's behavior may still follow an "out-dated" dragged-in implementation intention. In this case, a person may continue to mindlessly pursue behavior even if the behavior no longer has any instrumental value because the general intention has already changed and may now even be in conflict with the behavior (Ji Song & Wood, 2007).

Another category of behavior linked to implementation intentions is *habits*. Habits can be defined as "learned sequences of acts that have become automatic responses to specific cues, and are functional on obtaining certain goals or end-states" (Verplanken & Aarts, 1999, p. 104). A habit is a mental construct that relieves the brain as it passes on control over behavior to environmental stimuli (Verplanken, 2006). A habit not only includes an action routine, but also routinized decision-making (Betsch, Haberstroh, & Höhle, 2002). Some researchers argue that it is necessary for a behavior to have been conducted and successfully reinforced several times in the past (in similar situations) to establish a habit (Verplanken, 2006; Oulette & Wood, 1998). In contrast, others suggest that an implementation intention lies at the heart of every habit (Gollwitzer, 1999; Achtziger et al., 2008), implying that the basis of a habit can be established even before the behavior has ever been conducted.

It is commonly the case, however, that implementation intentions develop based on past experiences. For example, if a person learns that playing a certain video game in the evening at home causes a pleasurable rush of euphoria, she/he may form the implementation intention to play the video game again in a similar context in the future. The established implementation intention is probably stronger with increasing number of times that the behavior has been reinforced in the same context, and the more intense the repeated reinforcement (Verplanken, 2006).

If an implementation intention lies at the heart of a habit, the TOBP is also able to explain and predict habitual behavior. As argued above, however, a person's motivational disposition must remain in line with their behavioral conduct (cf. Bamberg et al., 2003). Habits are usually established by past behavior that was rewarded and thus reinforced. To the degree that a person's experienced reinforcement (e.g., a person's pleasure reactions) corresponds to his/her motivational disposition (i.e., his/her attitudes, subjective norms, and perceived control over the behavior), TOPB should provide a reliable framework in which to predict habitual behavior. Such a correspondence between reinforcement and a person's motivational disposition is not unlikely: people may fail to develop a habit if they hold a negative attitude about the behavior or if the behavior is in conflict with their present subjective norms, as this would clearly undermine the rewarding quality of the behavior. Media habits that developed based on (and that remain linked to) a person's motivational disposition may be properly predicted by TOPB. However, habits sometimes change into bad habits with a change in the original disposition that formerly promoted the behavior. Such bad media habits appear to have turned beyond volitional control, and can therefore not be explained by the TOPB.

To a certain degree, persons may still correct their bad habits and align them to their motivational disposition. Habits are difficult to control (cf. Bargh & Barndollar, 1996; Ji Song & Wood, 2007); however, an established habit can be regulated if one is able to generate sufficient willpower. Bamberg et al. (2003) demonstrated that people start to intervene and to regulate their bad habits once their motivational disposition changes and their habits come into conflict with their changed attitudes, perceived social pressure, or behavioral control (see also Wood, Tam, & Guerrero Witt, 2005). For example, a person may appreciate TV because it helps him/her to calm down; accordingly, she/he may have established a habit of watching TV before going to bed. Consider the possibility that at some point the person reads a persuasive article about the negative effects of watching TV before going to bed, and she/he experiences a change in attitude accordingly. The person may now start to revise his/her habit and to regulate the automatic drive to watch TV before going to bed. That is, the person will seek to bring the behavior back under volitional control. To the degree to which a habit can be brought back under volitional control—this may be successful if the habit is not very strong or if the person directs sufficient effort to changing the habit—it will be successfully adjusted to the changed motivational disposition. TOPB would successfully predict such re-adjusted behavior.

TOPB will fail to predict habitual behavior to the extent that people fail to change their bad habits; i.e., if habitual behavior occurs even though an intention has developed to do otherwise (cf. Heckhausen & Beckmann, 1990). For example, Ji Song and Wood (2007) revealed that very strong habits of watching TV or consuming fast food can prevail over intentions to adjust the behavior (see also Verplanken & Wood, 2006). However, the difference between single behavioral acts and repeated behavior should be noted in this regard. TOPB is often applied to the prediction of behavior on an aggregate level (e.g., amount of TV watching over the next four weeks). While it seems plausible that a single instance of overt impulsive or habitual behavior may occur that is *not* in line with a person's motivational disposition, it seems less likely that such slip-ups would happen repeatedly over a longer period, especially if the motivational disposition had changed substantially, resulting in a strong pressure to break the habit. In particular, people may succeed in regulating their behavior and adjusting it to their motivational disposition if the habit was relatively weakly developed. Accordingly, TOPB may explain particularly weak media habits or re-adjusted media exposure behavior, whereas it will fail to predict strong and bad media habits (Ajzen, 1991, 2002; Verplanken, Aarts, van Knippenberg & Moonen, 1998).

Outside the Borders of TOPB: Non-voluntary Automatic Behavior

While a habit can normally be regulated if a person invests enough effort to do so, behavior may also turn completely out of control and become *compulsive* (Loewenstein, 1996; "deficient self-regulation," LaRose, this volume). Compulsiveness can be defined as an inner urge or drive to perform a behavior that overrides a person's intention to stop it. Compulsive television use (McIlwraith, Jacobvitz, Kubey, & Alexander, 1991), Internet use (Young, 1998), and video-game use (Griffiths & Hunt, 1998) have been discussed previously in the literature. If media choice becomes compulsive, it can easily run counter to a person's motivational disposition. As stated by Berridge and Robinson (1995), a person may start to dislike the behavior, but nevertheless still feel a strong want to perform it; in this way, a person's liking and wanting may start to diverge. Therefore, compulsive media choice readily disentangles itself from attitudes, subjective norms, and considerations of behavioral control. Instead of a person's motivational disposition, environmental cues (e.g., the television set) or primes (e.g., action-related sensations or thoughts, such as a certain smell or mood) that co-occurred with the behavior in the past may trigger a want or urge to conduct the behavior. Compulsiveness commonly turns out to be problematic, as it may readily violate a person's attitudes, be in conflict with subjective norms, and come at an exceedingly high cost regarding a person's resources. Compulsive media choices are by definition outside the scope of volitional control, and are therefore beyond the scope of TOPB.

Past Applications of the Theory of Planned Behavior to Media Choice

In the past, TOPB has been used as a framework in which to explain and predict media choice in different research contexts. In particular, communication researchers involved in the Uses and Gratifications paradigm adapted the precursor of TOPB, the TRA (e.g., Babrow, 1989). Researchers studying users' appropriation of new media technology have also adapted the theoretical core of TOPB (cf. von Pape, this volume). Finally, psychologists, although not particularly interested in media choice, have on occasions examined their genuine research questions related to TOPB in the context of media use (e.g., Doll & Ajzen, 1992).

Application of TRA/TOPB in Communication Research

In the 1980s, Uses and Gratifications researchers began to study media choice by incorporating the core ideas of TRA (Fishbein & Ajzen, 1975; Babrow, 1989; Babrow & Swanson, 1988; Blood & Galloway, 1983; Galloway & Meek, 1981; LaRose & Atkin, 1988; Palmgreen & Rayburn, 1982, 1983; Rayburn & Palmgreen, 1984; Van Leuven, 1981). One such core idea is the expectancy-value rationale, which argues that people's *attitude* regarding a behavior is a function of their likelihood estimations about certain experiential (e.g., happiness) or instrumental (e.g., money) outcomes multiplied by the subjective evaluation of each outcome (Fishbein & Ajzen, 1975). In turn, the attitude is considered a determinant of the intention to perform the behavior (Fishbein & Ajzen, 1975). Van Leuven (1981) and Galloway and Meek (1981) adapted the rationale of expectancy-value beliefs by arguing that the beliefs directly determine media exposure; indeed, in a small survey study the latter authors found that expectancy-value beliefs predicted exposure to television programs.

This idea was adopted and refined by Palmgreen and Rayburn (1982, 1983). In an initial survey study, Palmgreen and Rayburn (1982) applied expectancy-value beliefs to determine both users' attitudes about television news (measured by a single item: "Overall, how satisfied are you with the job television news programs do in providing you with the things you are seeking?") and users' gratifications sought from television news (i.e., "the general tendency to seek multiple gratifications [from the medium]," p. 568; e.g., "I watch TV news to keep up with current issues and events"). The authors stressed that users' expectancy beliefs can focus on both the *attributes* of a media offering (cf. Wolling, this volume) and the *behavioral outcomes* associated with the anticipated exposure. In contrast to TRA, which links attitudes to intentions that in turn precede actual behavior, they further argued that both the attitude and gratifications are the immediate determinants of actual news exposure. It remains unclear as to why intentions were not considered in the conceptualization. In their study, Palmgreen and Rayburn found that expectancy-value beliefs regarding TV news predicted about 30 percent of the variance of both users' sought gratifications and attitude about TV news. Users' perceived importance of each anticipated aspect or outcome added little to the predictive power of the expectancy-value term (but see also van der Pligt & de Vries, 1998). Only sought gratifications (and not users' attitude to TV news) were significantly linked to actual TV news exposure; however, sought gratifications only accounted for 5 percent of the variance of exposure to TV news. The approach adopted in measuring attitude was also somewhat unusual (i.e., a single item about general satisfaction with TV news), thereby limiting the quality of the results (Babrow, 1989; Doll & Hasebrink, 1989).

A second survey study (Rayburn & Palmgreen, 1984) tested parts of the conceptualization that expectancy-value beliefs about TV news predict gratifications sought, which in turn lead to actual TV news exposure. Use of TV news, in turn, was thought to result in obtained gratifications, and the gratifications obtained by a user were thought to feed back to modify the expectancies (but not the evaluations) of attributes or behavioral outcomes associated with watching TV news. A major weakness of the survey, and despite the process character of the conceptualized model, was that it was conducted as a cross-sectional study. In addition, exposure to TV news was not assessed. The study results showed a significant correlation between expectancy-value beliefs and gratifications sought (and an even stronger correlation with gratifications obtained). In turn, gratifications obtained did indeed show a stronger correlation with users' expectancies than with their evaluations.

The link between expectancy-value beliefs and media exposure also inspired research by Babrow and colleagues (Babrow & Swanson, 1988; Babrow, 1989; Swanson & Babrow, 1989). The conceptualization of media choice suggested by Babrow and colleagues adapted TRA more carefully than the early approaches by Palmgreen and Rayburn. In an initial study, Babrow and Swanson (1988) applied a more valid measure of users' attitude and added a measurement of the intention to watch TV news. As in TRA, the intention to watch TV news was considered to rest on both users' attitudes and subjective norms about the behavior. In accordance with Palmgreen and Rayburn (1982), gratifications sought were also an object of analysis in the study; however, their role in the process of media choice remained somewhat unclear. A structural equation model was computed to test the proposed relationships. Although the overall model showed a relatively poor fit, the result of statistically significant path coefficients confirmed the validity of the TRA: expectancy-value beliefs predicted attitude about TV news, the attitude predicted intention to watch TV news, and in turn the intention predicted actual exposure to TV news. A separate analysis, however, showed that subjective norms did not predict the intention to watch TV news.

Also in line with TRA, a second study by Babrow (1989) regarding the watching of daytime soap operas replicated the finding that users' attitudes towards TV watching are a function of expectancy-value beliefs. In turn, the attitudes affected users' intention to watch, and intention significantly predicted the actual amount of watching that took place. Normative beliefs were also assessed in the study, in an even more multi-faceted manner than that suggested by TRA; however, unlike the suggestion implicit in TRA, the measurement of subjective norms only considered what respondents believed others would think about watching soap operas. The second component of subjective beliefs (i.e., respondents' motivation to comply with these expectations) remained unassessed. Still, normative beliefs exerted an influence on the intention to watch, although the effect was considerably smaller than that for attitude. In general terms, the study built upon firm theoretical grounds and led to several methodological advances. For example, the survey consisted of two waves: respondents were first asked about expectancy-value beliefs and their intention to watch soap operas over the next week; one week later they were asked about their actual viewing amount during the past week.

In summary, the above studies demonstrate that TRA provides a fruitful framework in which to study media choice, although some of the early studies were flawed (cf. Doll & Hasebrink, 1989). Surprisingly, despite these promising early steps the line of research ceased in communication research after the 1980s. Only a small number of more recent studies have sought to apply elements of TRA or TOPB to media choice. Of these, several focused almost entirely on expectancy-value theory, but did not apply the total structure of TRA or TOPB (e.g., for "news pagers," Leung & Wei, 1999; "TV prevention news stories," Cooper, Burgoon, & Roter, 2001). Other studies considered TOPB more thoroughly, but focused on users' intention to adopt a medium rather than actual media exposure (e.g., "intention to adopt the Internet," Chia, Detenber, & Lee, 2006; "intention to adopt text messaging services," Pedersen, & Nysveen, 20062; "intention to use virtual communities," Lin, 2006).

A revival of TRA/TOPB approach in communication research on media choice appears timely. Since the 1980s, TRA has been replaced by the more advanced conceptualization of TOPB, and several theoretical extensions (Conner & Armitage, 1989) and methodological improvements (Ajzen, 2006) have been suggested. Nabi and Krcmar (2004, pp. 297–299) suggested the use of TOPB in determining how attitudes are derived from media entertainment fare, and, in turn, predict future exposure to entertaining content. In a recent survey study, Hartmann and Vorderer (2006) applied TOPB in studying users' exposure to video games. Respondents' attitudes towards playing video games over the upcoming 14 days and their perceived behavioral control over playing games accounted for about 79 percent of the variance in the intention to play (subjective norms showed no effect; for similar findings, see Lin, 2006). In turn, respondents' intention predicted 23 percent of the variance of the actual amount of video game exposure measured 14 days later.

Application of TRA/TOPB to Media Choice in Other Scientific Domains

TOPB and its precursor, TRA, also inspired research on media choice in scientific domains other than communication research. The technology acceptance model (TAM; Davis, 1986; Davis, Bagozzi, & Warshaw, 1989;

Venkatesh & Davis, 2000; for overviews, see Venkatesh, Morris, Davis, & Davis, 2003; von Pape, this volume) provides one popular example. The TAM was developed as "an adaptation of TRA specifically tailored for modeling user acceptance of information systems" (Davis et al., 1989, p. 985). According to the original model, people hold a positive attitude towards using computer technology if they believe that the system is useful and easy to use. Perceived usefulness is defined as "the prospective user's subjective probability that using a specific application system will increase his or her job performance within an organizational context" (p. 985). Perceived ease of use is defined as "the degree to which the prospective user expects the target system to be free of effort" (p. 985). Departing from TRA, the original TAM further argued that the behavioral attitude (reflecting intrinsic rewards) and perceived usefulness (reflecting extrinsic rewards) predict the intention to use computer technology; subjective norms were not considered. An empirical test of the original model suggested that the conceptualization is more parsimonious if users' attitudes are neglected, and perceived usefulness and perceived ease of use are considered direct determinants of the intention to use computer technology. In a series of follow-up studies, Venkatesh and Davis (2000) further enhanced this model, demonstrating that in addition to perceived usefulness and perceived ease of use, the intention to use computer technology is affected by subjective norms.

A number of psychology-based studies that sought to either challenge or advance TOPB (e.g., Doll & Ajzen, 1992; Ouelette & Wood, 1998) or that used the model to pursue questions in applied research (e.g., Huang & Chuang, 2007; Doll, Petersen, & Rudolf, 2000) also shed light on media choice. For example, Doll and Ajzen (1992) examined the hypothesis that attitudes toward and perceived behavioral control of a behavior (e.g., using a medium) are more accessible and stable if they rest on a direct (e.g., using) rather than indirect (e.g., watching) experience with a behavioral object. The authors further examined how these behavioral beliefs, once developed, guide future behavior. To test their assumptions, they ran a laboratory experiment in which participants either watched or played six different video games, thereby forming behavioral beliefs about the playing of each game. At the end of the experiments, the participants had 45 minutes remaining to freely choose and play any game. The results showed that attitudes and behavioral control were indeed more accessible and stable if they resulted from the actual use of video games rather than merely watching the games. In turn, highly accessible behavioral beliefs affected the intention to play specific games in the 45-minute period of free time; again, intention and perceived behavioral control predicted the amount of actual exposure (see also Glasman & Albarracin, 2006).

Towards a Theory of Planned Media Choice

The reviewed studies demonstrate that TOPB, as well as its precursor TRA, provides a useful conceptualization within which to explore media choice; however, a concise and empirically corroborated theory of planned media choice has yet to be developed. Past applications of TOPB in the realm of media choice focused on a range of markedly different aspects: taken together, they do not represent a coherent line of research. Therefore, both theoretical and empirical progress is required to move ahead towards a theory of planned media choice.

Theoretical Progress

TOPB provides a powerful framework in which to predict voluntary human behavior. Despite the popularity of this theory in social psychology or health psychology, communication researchers involved in conceptualizing media choice have paid surprisingly little attention to the theory in the past. Uses and Gratification researchers took notice of TOPB's precursor, the TRA, but in general focused on expectancy-value mechanisms while neglecting any solid application of the entire framework to the realm of media choice. In addition, there exist few critical theoretical reflections of the genuine applicability of TOPB to media choice (cf. LaRose, this volume).

At its core, TOPB predicts behavior that is under complete volitional control (i.e., that builds on rather explicit and elaborate attitudes, subjective norms and control beliefs) and that results in a deliberate decision and the intention to conduct the behavior. Accordingly, TOPB should be especially capable in explaining and predicting any type of elaborate, planned or deliberate media choices. Media choices are likely to be planned if persons care about the decision because it involves a considerable risk (i.e., investment of time, money and other resources) for an uncertain outcome (Fazio, 1999; Esser, 1996; Payne et al., 1993). *Risky* media choices typically result in single behavioral acts, whereas repeated performance is more likely if the behavior is less risky (low investment costs and/or high certainty). The purchase of expensive media technology such as a computer or a television screen represents a typical example of a risky media choice; movie-going may provide another example that involves considerable risk. Media choices may also be risky, and therefore planned, if a person is highly unfamiliar with the choice and with anticipating behavioral outcomes. Next to the adoption of new media technology (cf. von Pape, this volume), other valid examples of risky media choices include choosing new software for the computer, deciding to become familiar with a new website or service on the Internet, and deciding to spent time playing a newly released video game. Seeking a certain show on television is also risky, especially if it is only broadcasted once at a specific time on a specific channel and therefore could be easily missed. All of the above choices must be based on careful, conscious anticipations if they are to result in reasonable intentions and not a waste of considerable volitional effort. TOPB should provide a valid and useful framework in which to examine such media choices.

TOPB, however, is the subject of an ongoing discussion (cf. Conner & Armitage, 1998). This discussion must not be neglected on the path towards a theory of planned media choice. It may be discussed, for example, whether the expectancy-value mechanism proposed by TOPB is a valid conceptualization of elaborate choices (e.g., Luce, Payne, & Bettman, 2000; Wolling, this volume). References to decision theory may be helpful in substantiating the discussion (cf. Marewski et al., this volume; Payne et al., 1993). In addition, the behavioral determinants laid out in TOPB may prove to be insufficient in explaining all forms of media choices. For example, next to subjective norms (e.g., "important others dis/approve of me doing..."), personal moral norms may guide planned media choices (e.g., "I personally feel that I ought to do..."; Park & Smith, 2007).

In its current version, TOPB does not fully reflect the role of emotions that underlie the development of an intention. Emotions may have a crucial impact on choices and planned media exposure (Loewenstein & Lerner, 2003), especially if the choice entails exposure to entertaining media. Furthermore, TOPB does not incorporate alternative choices (cf. Marewski et al., this volume), whereas people's media choices are commonly based on several available options (e.g., other leisure-time activities; Palmgreen & Rayburn, 1982, p. 574). For example, despite a favorable motivational disposition towards playing video games, people may still fail to form an intention to play if other more attractive alternatives exist.

Finally, TOPB primarily models the motivational stage of planned behavior (i.e., the development of an intention), but the model tells us less about the volitional stage (i.e., how selected intentions are protected against other action plans and eventually result in actual exposure; Achtziger et al., 2008; Brandstaetter, Lengfelder, & Gollwitzer, 2001; Gollwitzer, 1990). For example, despite holding an intention to play video games, people may choose not to play because they are distracted by other interfering activities or duties. On the path towards a theory of planned media choice, researchers should carefully apply the core concept of TOPB without losing track of the ongoing debate about TOPB.

Future research should also explore the question of whether TOPB, despite its name, helps to illuminate media behavior that is somewhat less voluntary; i.e., behavior that rests on largely automatic choices and that is pursued in a mindless fashion. Media habits provide typical examples of such automatic behavior. TOPB may successfully explain such media behavior if it is analyzed as repeated behavioral conduct on an aggregate level (e.g., frequency of choosing to watch a TV soap opera within a period of 14 days). I suggested in this chapter that the motivational dispositions laid out in TOPB may serve as a foundation on which to develop a media habit. Motivational dispositions that speak against a certain media choice make it less likely that the exposure will repeatedly take place; thus, the establishment of a media habit also becomes unlikely. Even if a media habit has become established, unfavorable motivational dispositions may urge a person to intervene in the behavioral conduct; however, the question of under what circumstances people may feel an urge to change a media habit, as well as under what conditions they fail or succeed to do so, remains open to discussion (cf. Ji Song & Wood, 2007). A careful consideration of socio-cognitive theory of media use (LaRose, this volume), particularly of the role of self-regulation, may be helpful in substantiating this discussion.

Empirical Progress

Past research that linked TRA or TOPB, or at least elements of both models, to the realm of media choice has led to promising results, yet few studies have appropriately adopted the full model of TOPB in predicting media choice. To develop proper assessments, researchers should consult the many recommendations made in the literature regarding how to assess the constructs of TOPB (Ajzen, 2006; Francis et al., 2004; Gagné & Godin, 2000). In general, TOPB is assessed by questionnaires, and any study should ideally include at least two waves. In the first wave, the standard constructs of TOPB are measured, including intensity or frequency of past behavior, along with the respondents' intentions to perform the same media behavior throughout a specified period in the future. After this period has elapsed, data are collected in a second wave, in which respondents are asked about how frequently or intensively they pursued the behavior. In addition, the second wave usually repeats the assessment of the constructs of TOPB (at least by applying the direct measures). Thus, test–retest reliabilities can be calculated to assess the psychometric qualities of the scales. Researchers may also test if respondents changed their motivational disposition and intention since wave 1.

Concluding Remarks

TOPB is one of the most mature and popular theories in social psychology in predicting human behavior. Sutton (1982) showed that TOPB usually predicts between 40 percent and 50 percent of the variance in intention and between 19 percent and 38 percent of the variance in behavior. In the past, application of TOPB to media choice in communication research and related disciplines did not move beyond insular efforts. It would therefore represent an innovative line of research to explain and predict media exposure based on TOPB. Such an emerging new theory on media choice may help to advance the existing body of knowledge on the topic, as it would enrich a healthy competition with other models that aim to predict people's media choices.

References

Achtziger, A., Gollwitzer, P. M., & Sheeran, P. (2008). Implementation intentions and shielding goal striving from unwanted thoughts and feelings. *Personality and Social Psychology Bulletin*, 34(3), 381–393.

Ajzen, I. (1988). *Attitudes, Personality, and Behavior*. Chicago: Dorsey Press.

Ajzen, I. (1991). The theory of planned behavior. *Organizational Behavior and Human Decision Processes*, 50, 179–211.

Ajzen, I. (2002). Residual effects of past on later behavior: Habituation and reasoned action perspectives. *Personality and Social Psychology Review*, 6, 107–122.

Ajzen, I. (2006). Constructing a TpB Questionnaire: Conceptual and Methodological Considerations. Online. Retrieved April 2007 from http://people.umass.edu/aizen/publications.html.

Ajzen, I. & Fishbein, M. (1980). *Understanding Attitudes and Predicting Social Behavior*. Englewood Cliffs, NJ: Prentice-Hall, Inc.

Ajzen, I. & Fishbein, M. (2000). Attitudes and the attitude-behavior relation: Reasoned and automatic processes. *European Review of Social Psychology*, 10, 1–33.

Ajzen, I. & Fishbein, M. (2005). The influence of attitudes on behavior. In D. Albarracín, B. T. Johnson, & M. P. Zanna (Eds.), *The Handbook of Attitudes* (pp. 173–221). Mahwah, NJ: Erlbaum.

Armitage, C. J. & Conner, M. (2001). Efficacy of the theory of planned behavior: A meta-analytic review. *British Journal of Social Psychology*, 40, 471–499.

Babrow, A. S. (1989). An expectancy-value analysis of the student soap opera audience. *Communication Research*, 16, 155–178.

Babrow, A. S. & Swanson, D. L. (1988). Disentangling the antecedents of audience exposure levels: Extending expectancy-value analyses of gratifications sought from television news. *Communication Monographs*, 55, 1–21.

Bamberg, S., Ajzen, I., & Schmidt, P. (2003). Choice of travel mode in the theory of planned behavior: The roles of past behavior, habit, and reasoned action. *Basic and Applied Social Psychology*, 25, 175–188.

Bandura, A. (1997). *Self-efficacy: The Exercise of Control*. New York: Freeman.

Bargh, J. A. & Barndollar, K. (1996). Automaticity in action: The unconscious as repository of chronic goals and motives. In P. M. Gollwitzer & J. A. Bargh (Eds.), *The Psychology of Action* (pp. 457–471). New York: Guilford.

Berridge, K. C. & Robinson, T. E. (1995). The mind of an addicted brain: Neural sensitization of wanting versus liking. *Current Directions in Psychological Science*, 4(3), 71–76.

Betsch, T., Haberstroh, S., & Höhle, C. (2002). Explaining and predicting routinized decision making: A review of theories. *Theory & Psychology*, 12, 453–488.

Blood, R. W. & Galloway, J. J. (1983). Expectancy-value measures of audience uses and gratifications for media content. Paper presented at the meeting of the International Communication Association, Dallas.

Brandstaetter, V., Lengfelder, A., & Gollwitzer, P. M. (2001). Implementation intentions and efficient action initiation. *Journal of Personality and Social Psychology*, 81(5), 946–960.

Chia, S. C., Li, H., Detenber, B. H., & Lee, W. (2006). Mining the Internet plateau: An exploration of the adoption intention of nonusers in Singapore. *New Media & Society*, 8(4), 589–609.

Conner, M. & Armitage, C. J. (1998). Extending the theory of planned behavior: A review and avenues for further research. *Journal of Applied Social Psychology*, 28, 1429–1464.

Cooper, P. C., Burgoon, M., & Roter, D. L. (2001). An expectancy-value analysis of viewer interest in television prevention news stories. Health Communication, 13, 227–240.

Davis, F. D. (1986). A technology acceptance model for empirically testing new end-user information systems: theory and results. Doctoral dissertation, Sloan School of Management, Massachusetts Institute of Technology.

Davis, F. D., Bagozzi, R. P., & Warshaw, P. R. (1989). User acceptance of computer technology: A comparison of two theoretical models. *Management Science*, 35(8), 982–1003.

Doll, J. & Ajzen, I. (1992). Accessibility and stability of predictors in the theory of planned behavior. *Journal of Personality and Social Psychology*, 63, 754–766.

Doll, J. & Hasebrink, U. (1989). Zum Einfluß von Einstellungen auf die Auswahl von Fernsehsendungen. In J. Groebel & P. Winterhoff-Spurk (Eds.), *Empirische Medienpsychologie* (pp. 45–63). München: PVU.

Doll, J., Petersen, L., & Rudolf, M. (2000). Determinanten der Internetnutzung von Gymnasiasten und Studenten: eine Anwendung der Theorie geplanten und rollengesteuerten Verhaltens [Determinants of the Internet use of grammar school students and university students: An application of the theory of planned and role-guided behavior]. *Medienpsychologie*, 12, 5–22.

Eccles, J. S. & Wigfield, A. (2002). Motivational belief, values, and goals. *Annual Review of Psychology*, 53, 109–132.

Esser, H. (1996). Die Definition der Situation. *Kölner Zeitschrift für Soziologie und Sozialpsychologie*, 48, 1–34.

Fazio, R. H. (1990). Multiple processes by which attitudes guide behavior: The mode model as an integrative framework. In M. P. Zanna (Ed.), *Advances in Experimental Social Psychology* (pp. 75–109). San Diego: Academic Press.

Fazio, R. H. & Towles-Schwen, T. (1999). The MODE model of attitude-behavior processes. In S. Chaiken & Y. Trope (Eds.), *Dual Process Theories in Social Psychology* (pp. 97–116). New York: Guilford.

Fishbein, M. & Ajzen, 1. (1975). *Belief, Attitude, Intention, and Behavior: An Introduction to Theory and Research*. Reading, MA: Addison-Wesley.

Francis, H. H., Eccles, M. P., Johnston, M., et al. (2004). Constructing questionnaires based on the Theory of Planned Behavior: A manual for health services researchers. Online. Retrieved April 2007 from www.rebeqi.org/ViewFile.aspx?itemID=212.

Frisch, D. & Clemen, R. T. (1994). Beyond expected utility: Rethinking behavioral decision research. *Psychological Bulletin*, 116, 46–54.

Gagné, C. & Godin, G. (2000). The Theory of Planned Behavior: Some measurement issues concerning belief-based variables. *Journal of Applied Social Psychology*, 30(10), 2173–2193.

Galloway, J. J. & Meek, F. L. (1981). Audience uses and gratifications: An expectancy value model. *Communication Research*, 8, 435–450.

Glasman, L. R. & Albarracin, D. (2006). Forming attitudes that predict future behavior: A meta-analysis of the attitude-behavior relation. *Psychological Review*, 132, 778–822.

Gollwitzer, P. M. (1990). Action phases and mind-sets. In E. T. Higgins & R. M.

Sorrentino (Eds.), *Handbook of Motivation and Cognition* (Vol. 2, pp. 53–92). New York: Guilford Press.

Gollwitzer, P. M. (1993). Goal achievement: The role of intentions. In W. Stroebe & M. Hewstone (Eds.), *European Review of Social Psychology* (Vol. 4, pp. 141–185). Chichester, England: Wiley.

Gollwitzer, P. M. (1999). Implementation intentions: Strong effects of simple plans. *American Psychologist*, 54, 493–503.

Gollwitzer, P. M. & Brandstaetter, V. (1997). Implementation intentions and effective goal pursuit. *Journal of Personality and Social Psychology*, 73, 186–199.

Griffiths, M. D. & Hunt, N. (1998). Dependence on computer games by adolescents. *Psychological Reports*, 82(2), 475–480.

Hagger, M. S., Chatzisarantis, N. L. D., & Biddle, S. J. H. (2002). A meta-analytic review of the theories of reasoned action and planned behavior in physical activity: Predictive validity and the contribution of additional variables. *Journal of Sport and Exercise Psychology*, 24, 3–32.

Hartmann, T. & Vorderer, P. (2006). Empirical evidence of expectancy-value structured entertainment choices. Presentation held at the 56th annual conference of the International Communication Association, ICA, Division "Mass Communication," June 19–23, Dresden.

Heckhausen, H. & Beckmann, J. (1990). Intentional action and action slips. *Psychological Review*, 97, 36–48.

Huang, E. & Chuang, M. H. (2007). Extending the theory of planned behavior as a model to explain post-merger employee behavior of IS use. *Computers in Human Behavior*, 23, 240–257.

Jaeckel, M. (1992). Mediennutzung als Niedrigkostensituation [Media use as a low-cost situation]. *Medienpsychologie*, 4, 246–266.

Ji Song, M. & Wood, W. (2007). Habitual purchase and consumption: Not always what you intend. *Journal of Consumer Psychology*, 17, 261–276.

Kuhl, J. & Goschke, T. (1994). A. theory of action control: Mental subsystems, modes of control, and volitional conflict resolution strategies. In J. Kuhl & J. Beckmann (Eds.), *Volition and Personality: Action Versus State Orientation* (pp. 93–124). Göttingen: Hogrefe.

LaRose, R. & Atkin, D. (1988). Satisfaction, demographic, and media environment predictors of cable subscription. *Journal of Broadcasting & Electronic Media*, 32(4), 403–413.

Leung, L. & Wei, R. (1999). Seeking News Via the Pager: An Expectancy-Value Study. *Journal of Broadcasting & Electronic Media*, 43, 1–17.

Lin, H. F. (2006). Understanding behavioral intention to participate in virtual communities. *CyberPsychology & Behavior*, 9, 540–547.

Loewenstein, G. (1996). Out of control: Visceral influences on behavior. *Organizational Behavior and Human Decision Processes*, 65, 272–292.

Loewenstein, G. & Lerner, J. S. (2003). The role of affect in decision making. In R. Davidson, H. Goldsmith, & K. Scherer (Eds.), *Handbook of Affective Science* (pp. 619–642). Oxford: Oxford University Press.

Luce, M. F., Payne, J. W., & Bettman, J. R. (2000). Coping with unfavorable attribute values in choice. *Organizational Behavior and Human Decision Processes*, 81, 274–299.

Madden, T. J., Ellen, P. S., & Ajzen, I. (1992). A comparison of the theory of planned behavior and the theory of reasoned action. *Personality and Social Psychology Bulletin*, 18(1), 3–9.

McIlwraith, R., Jacobvitz, R. S., Kubey, R., & Alexander, A. (1991). Television addiction theories and data behind the ubiquitous metaphor. *The American Behavioral*, 35(2), 104–121.

Nabi, R. L. & Krcmar, M. (2004). Conceptualizing media enjoyment as attitude: Implications for mass media effects research. *Communication Theory*, 4(14), 288–310.

Oulette, J. A. & Wood, W. (1998). Habit and intention in everyday life: The multiple processes by which past behavior predicts future behavior. *Psychological Bulletin*, 124, 54–74.

Palmgreen, P. & Rayburn, J. D. (1982). Gratifications sought and media exposure: An expectancy value model. *Communication Research*, 9(4), 561–580.

Palmgreen, P. & Rayburn, J. D. (1983). A response to Stanford. *Communication Research*, 10, 253–257.

Park, H. S. & Smith, S. W. (2007). Distinctiveness and influence of subjective norms, personal descriptive and injunctive norms, and societal descriptive and injunctive norms on behavioral intent: A case of two behaviors critical to organ donation. *Human Communication Research*, 33, 194–218.

Payne, J., Bettman, J., & Johnson, E. (1993). *The Adaptive Decision Maker*. Cambridge: Cambridge University Press.

Pedersen, P. E. & Nysveen, H. (2002). Using the theory of planned behavior to explain teenagers' adoption of text messaging services. Working Paper, Agder University College.

Rayburn, J. D. & Palmgreen, P. (1984). Merging uses and gratifications and expectancy-value theory. Communication Research, 11, 537–562.

Rise, J., Thompson, M., & Verplanken, B. (2003). Measuring implementation intentions in the context of the theory of planned behavior. *Scandinavian Journal of Psychology*, 44, 87–95.

Sheeran, P., Webb, T. L., & Gollwitzer, P. M. (2005). The interplay between goal intentions and implementation intentions. *Personality and Social Psychology Bulletin*, 31, 87–98.

Smith, E. R. & DeCoster, J. (2000). Dual process models in social and cognitive psychology: Conceptual integration and links to underlying memory systems. *Personality and Social Psychology Review*, 4, 108–131.

Sutton, S. (1998). Predicting and explaining intentions and behavior: How well are we doing? *Journal of Applied Social Psychology*, 28(15), 1317–1338.

Swanson, D. L. & Babrow, A. S. (1989). Uses and gratifications: The influence of gratification-seeking and expectancy-value judgments on the viewing of television news. In B. Dervin, L. Grossberg, B. J. O'Keefe, & E. Wartella (Eds.), *Rethinking Communication: Paradigm Exemplars* (pp. 361–375). Newbury Park, CA: Sage.

Tice, D. M., Bratslavsky, E., & Baumeister, R. F. (2001). Emotional distress regulation takes precedence over impulse control: If you feel bad, do it! *Journal of Personality and Social Psychology*, 80, 53–67.

Van der Pligt, J. & de Vries, N. K. (1998). Belief importance in expectancy-value models of attitudes. *Journal of Applied Social Psychology*, 28(15), 1339–1354.

Van Leuven, J. (1981). Expectancy theory in media and message selection. *Communication Research*, 8, 425–434.

Venkatesh, V. & Davis, F. D. (2000). Theoretical extension of the technology acceptance model: Four longitudinal field studies. *Management Science*, 46(2), 186–204.

Venkatesh, V., Morris, M., Davis, G., & Davis, F. (2003). User acceptance of information technology: toward a unified view. *MIS Quarterly*, (27)3, 425–478.

Verplanken, A. & Wood, W. (2006). Interventions to break and create consumer habits. *Journal of Public Policy and Marketing*, 25, 90–103.

Verplanken, B. (2006). Beyond frequency: Habit as mental construct. *British Journal of Social Psychology*, 45, 639–656.

Verplanken, B. & Aarts, H. (1999). Habit, attitude, and planned behavior: Is habit an empty construct or an interesting case of automaticity? *European Review of Social Psychology*, 10, 101–134.

Verplanken, B., Aarts, H., van Knippenberg, A., & Moonen, A. (1998). Habit versus planned behavior: A field experiment. *British Journal of Social Psychology*, 37(1), 111–128.

Vroom, V. (1964). *Work and Motivation*. New York: Wiley.

Westerik, H., Renckstorf, K., Lammers, J., & Wester, F. (2006). Transcending uses and gratifications: Media use as social action and the use of event history analysis. *Communications*, 31(2), 139–153.

Wilson, T. D., Lindsey, S., & Schooler, T. Y. (2000). A model of dual attitudes. *Psychological Review*, 107(1), 101–126.

Wood, W., Tam, L., & Guerrero Witt, M. (2005). Changing circumstances, disrupting habits. *Journal of Personality and Social Psychology*, 88, 918–933.

Young, K. S. (1998). Internet addiction: The emergence of a new clinical disorder. *CyberPsychology & Behavior*, 3, 237–244.

Chapter 4

Uses and Gratifications as Media Choice

Marina Krcmar and Yuliya Strizhakova

The uses and gratifications tradition has been used as a framework for studying audiences' motives for media use for over 60 years (Rubin, 1981). Unlike other mass communication paradigms that emphasize either media content or media effects, uses and gratifications researchers focus on media use and assume users to be active, purposeful, and selective in their media choices. Understanding why we use media or why we are motivated to choose particular types of content may offer some insight into understanding how we process media and, ultimately, how it affects us. Specifically, the now classic uses and gratifications précis seeks to understand

> the social and psychological origins of needs which generate expectations of the mass media and other sources which lead to differential patterns of media exposure (or engagement in other activities) resulting in needs gratifications and other consequences, perhaps mostly unintended ones.
> (Katz, Blumler, & Gurevitch, 1974, p. 20)

Although this early statement did not clearly lay out a program of research for uses and gratifications, various areas of investigation are imbedded in it. For example, a typical study in the uses and gratifications tradition might focus on the psychological origins of needs, linking that with a specific pattern of media exposure. Alternately, a uses and gratifications study might examine the relationship between patterns of media use and engagement in other activities. Still other research might look at motives for media use and how these moderate effects. The most traditional approach, however, utilizes a validated viewing motives questionnaire as a starting point (e.g., Rubin, 1981, 1983). By using this instrument, uses and gratifications research has documented variations in patterns of media use among different individuals (Rubin, 1983) and has demonstrated the mediating role of viewing motives in the effects of mass media (Perloff, Quarles, & Drutz, 1983).

Uses and Gratifications: A Brief History

The Media Use Scale and Typology

Some of the earliest research in the uses and gratifications tradition was related to the identification of various motives that people bring to a media use situation and assessment of the relationship between media use *motives* and media use in general, such as exposure to various content types (e.g., news), affinity for a medium, or satisfaction with it. In the context of television, one of the most widely used typologies of television viewing motives was developed by Rubin (1983) who identified nine basic motives of television use: relaxation, companionship, habit, to pass time, entertainment, social interaction, information, arousal, and escape. These earliest identified motives for television use have been applied to various media and have been both further differentiated and collapsed (e.g., Lin, 1999); however, the initial nine serve as a basis for much of the later uses and gratifications work. Specifically, these motives have been associated with 1) media exposure in general, 2) exposure to different genres, 3) television affinity, and 4) satisfaction (e.g., Abelman, 1987; Abelman & Atkin, 2000; Hawkins et al., 2001; Papacharissi & Mendelson 2007; Rubin, 1983; Nabi, Stitt, Halford, & Finnerty, 2003; Vincent & Basil, 1997). In addition, media use motives can also mediate or moderate the effect of various media on outcome behaviors.

However, there have been several inconsistencies in both the number of motives identified and their predictive power. For example, based on Rubin's (1983) nine-factor measure, Lin (1999) identified only three motives for watching television, specifically surveillance, escape/companionship, and personal identity, and Abelman and Atkin (2000) confirmed five, specifically pass time/habit, entertainment, information, companionship, and escape. Moreover, escape was a negative predictor of television exposure in Rubin's (1983) study but a positive predictor of television exposure for children in Abelman and Atkin's (2000) study. These variations led Rubin (1984) to propose that, despite the fact that television use motives could be identified as multi-dimensional, these motives could also be consolidated and collapsed into two simpler and more parsimonious dimensions: ritualistic and instrumental viewing.

Rubin (1983) initially defined ritualized media use as "a more or less habitualized use of a medium to gratify diversionary needs or motives" and instrumental media use as "a goal-directed use of media content to gratify informational needs or motives" (p. 69). Rubin (1983) concluded that a habitual viewer would typically watch more television overall, would display a definite affinity with a medium, and would watch television to fill time, for companionship, relaxation, arousal, and escape, while an instrumental viewer would seek information and would watch less television overall. Rubin (1984) further concluded that many motives for viewing television are interrelated (e.g., pass time and habit) and mainly indicate differences in audience's activity, with instrumental viewers being more active and potentially more involved than ritualized viewers.

Gratifications Sought and Obtained

A further refinement of the uses and gratifications typology emerged because researchers accurately noted that motives for use, or gratifications sought, were not always obtained. In fact, in one compelling example of this notion, Perse and Rubin (1990) found that those who sought out television for social uses sometimes ended up being more, not less, lonely after exposure to television. In other words, gratifications sought and obtained are not necessarily synonymous and must be distinguished for empirical, practical, and theoretical reasons. Gratifications sought are those that we bring to a media use situation: we want to pass time, we want to feel a sense of social companionship, we want to learn something. Gratifications obtained are those that result from a media use situation: we experienced physiological arousal, we alleviated boredom, or we exacerbated it. Gratifications sought and obtained may be similar or they may not be. In fact, as Nabi et al. (2006) pointed out, the gratifications obtained from television may be neither rewarding nor enjoyable. Therefore, in referring to media outcomes as *gratifications obtained*, the implicit assumption is that media use is, at the very least, gratifying. But this runs counter to some of the empirical findings, such as Nabi et al.'s, and to the early uses and gratifications notion that the consequences of media use may be "mostly unintended ones" (Katz et al., 1974, p. 20). Perhaps gratifications *sought* and *obtained* should be thought of as merely *needs* and *outcomes*. In fact, other conceptual and empirical criticisms have emerged over the years. Because they are reviewed thoroughly elsewhere (e.g., Rubin, 2002), we will give only a brief summary here.

Criticisms of the Uses and Gratifications Approach

The uses and gratifications approach has been criticized on several grounds over the years. Some of those criticisms have resulted in conceptual clarification and refinement and in empirical enhancement while other problems persist. For example, several critics have argued that researchers attach different meanings to the uses and gratifications constructs, depending on the issue they are investigating (Swanson, 1977, 1979). Similarly, some have criticized the lack of conceptual clarity in the concepts themselves (Blumler, 1979). This results in a lack of clarity in conceptual development and a body of findings that are scattershot and lack synthesis. For example, the notion of "gratifications obtained" may be used to assess whether or not the initial media use motive was satisfied. A researcher may examine if we set out to learn something from our media use, did this in fact occur? The initial idea of gratifications sought and obtained seems to have been framed in this way (Rubin, 2002). However, more recently, several researchers have argued that the construct of *gratification obtained* may be used to measure broader outcomes, such as satisfaction or enjoyment (Nabi et al., 2006; Strizhakova & Krcmar, 2003). Therefore, the notion of gratifications obtained still needs to be further clarified in order for integration across studies to occur.

A second problem exists in the media use typologies. Rather than investigating ways to conceptually bring together media use typologies across various media (e.g., uses of television, uses of the Internet), the number of typologies continue to proliferate (e.g. Sherry, Lucas, Greenberg, & Lachlan, 2006). It is conceivable that a new typology of media use motives could exist for every new technology that emerges. While it is certainly true that different media have different motivations for use, generating typologies with little attempt to integrate them at a broader level may do little to forward uses and gratifications as a meaningful approach.

Some of the assumptions of uses and gratifications have also come under fire, both in earlier research (e.g., Swanson, 1977) and more recently (Nabi et al., 2006). Specifically, Strizhakova and Krcmar (2003) questioned if viewers actually have access to their viewing motives. Given that some media choices are seemingly paradoxical, such as an attraction to sad media (Oliver, 1993), it is not always clear that viewers understand and are able to articulate their viewing motives. In fact, Strizhakova and Krcmar (2003) argue that a sizeable body of literature indicates that both conscious and non-conscious factors determine our behaviors, making it possible that motives for media use are not always accessible to viewers. In a related criticism, Nabi and colleagues (2006) suggested that audiences may not be as active in the media selection process as the uses and gratifications approach suggests. From the results of their study, they argue that "if we consider that those 'negative' gratifications were unintentionally obtained, we must then call into question how active, or in control, viewers are in the process of trying to fulfill various social and psychological needs if they are unable to filter out unintended effects of programming" (p. 444). In the context of the Internet, LaRose and Eastin (2004) proposed that Internet self-efficacy may moderate active consideration of uses and gratifications that predict media behavior along with habitual patterns and self-regulatory deficiencies. Therefore, both the notion of the use of self-report in uses and gratifications research and the assumption of the active audience still remain as criticisms of the approach itself.

Individual Differences in Media Use

Several studies have examined the role of personality factors in predicting selective exposure to specific types of media or specific media content (e.g.,

Hanjun, Cho, & Roberts, 2005; Lin, 1999; Tsao & Sibley, 2004). Although not all of the studies undertaken in this area have utilized uses and gratifications as the theoretical frame, these studies obliquely lend support to uses and gratifications in that they test the early notion that various psychological needs, resulting either explicitly or implicitly from personality factors, may result in different patterns of media use. In general, research into the relationship between personality characteristics and media exposure typically fall into one of three categories: studies relating personality characteristics to exposure to various types of media (e.g., Finn, 1997); studies relating personality characteristics to viewing motives (e.g., Conway & Rubin, 1991); and studies relating personality factors to exposure to specific content (e.g., Weaver, 1991).

First, in terms of preference for various *media* (e.g., television vs. newspapers), Finn (1997) attempted to link the five fundamental personality traits (extroversion, neuroticism, openness to experience, agreeableness, and conscientiousness) to exposure to various types of mass media. This large-scale study demonstrated that openness to new experiences was positively related to movie attendance and pleasure reading. To a lesser extent, extroversion negatively predicted exposure to various media. The author concluded that individuals who were more open to experience overall were also more interested in media that were novel. Similarly, Weaver (1991) found that individuals who rated high on an index of psychotocism (characterized as impulsive and nonconforming individuals) were attracted to horror films, whereas those who were more neurotic showed a preference for news and information programs. Both Finn's (1997) and Weaver's (1991) research suggest that, at the very least, personality can predict the type of media we use (e.g., newspapers vs. films). Although these studies do not clearly demonstrate a link between psychological needs and media exposure, an argument could be made that the needs deriving from extroversion, for example, cannot readily be met by media and instead may be met by other sources such as interpersonal interaction. Once again, consistent with uses and gratifications' premise that needs can be met by media or other sources, these studies lend indirect support to uses and gratifications.

Several extensions in the uses and gratifications tradition have underlined the importance of personality in predicting media *content* choices and preferences, finding that personality factors such as sensation seeking (Krcmar & Greene, 1999) and alienation (Slater, 2003) can act as predictors for media preferences such as violent television and films. In fact, sensation seeking is arguably one of the most well-documented predictors of media preferences for specific content.

Sensation seeking, both theoretically and empirically, is related to individuals' need for stimulation (Zuckerman, 1994), testing an individual's tendency to approach, rather than avoid, novel stimuli. Although the measure is strictly self-report, the theoretical basis is biological with higher sensation seekers having higher optimum levels of physiological arousal. Overall, high sensation seekers have lower arousal levels and require stronger, exciting and novel messages for attracting and holding attention, while low sensation seekers have higher arousal levels and avoid exciting stimuli (Donohew, Finn, & Christ, 1988; Donohew, Palmgreen, & Duncan, 1980). Based on these findings, Donohew and colleagues concluded messages that elicit sensory, affective, and arousal responses (i.e., have higher sensation value) are more effective for and attractive to high sensation seekers and also hold their attention more (Pugzles-Lorch et al., 1994).

Attraction to other forms of media is also related to sensation seeking. For example Arnett (1991) found high sensation seeking teens and especially high sensation seeking males, were more attracted to heavy metal music than low sensation seeking adolescents. Arnett attributes this to the fact that heavy metal is characterized by "heavily distorted electric guitars, pounding rhythms and raucous vocals all typically played at extremely loud volume" (p. 573). Due to these extremes in rhythm and vocals, high sensation seekers enjoy this high sensation-value music. Similarly, violent programs have been found to be related to arousal levels. For example, Zillmann (1971) has found that programs with violent content tend to increase arousal levels, as measured by galvanic skin response and heart rate, in viewers. Sensation seeking also predicts motives for media exposure. Conway and Rubin (1991) found that sensation seeking was positively related to the uses and gratifications constructs of passing time and escapism as motives for television viewing, but this held true only for the disinhibition dimension of the sensation seeking scale.

It is reasonable to argue, therefore, that high sensation seekers may attempt to fulfill their need for stimulation by utilizing a variety of mediated and non-mediated sources. Media sources sought out by high sensation seekers include stimuli with high sensation value like quick cuts and zooms and novel messages (Donohew et al., 1988; Donohew et al., 1980), heavy metal music (Arnett, 1991), and some forms of violent media content such as contact sports and realistic crime shows such as *COPS* (Krcmar & Greene, 1999). Consistent with uses and gratifications, therefore, the psychological need for stimulation may result in a specific pattern of media use.

Work by Nabi and colleagues (e.g., Nabi et al., 2006) applied and extended the uses and gratifications framework by using personality factors to examine the attraction and enjoyment of reality vs. fictional programming. The authors found that although voyeurism was related to interest in television programming, it was not in the predicted direction. Specifically, voyeurism was positively related to interest in fictional programming but negatively to reality programming.

Media Use Motives as Moderators and Mediators of Effects

One aspect of the uses and gratifications approach that has received attention recently is that of media use motives as moderators and mediators of effects. This approach argues that our motives for using a particular kind of media may not only dictate patterns of use but may enhance or dampen any outcomes or effects. Recently, this notion has received some support (e.g., Haridakis, 2001). For example, in a study of television news viewership, Rubin and Perse (1987) found that motives associated with instrumental use predicted a greater perceived realism of news by audiences. Those who viewed news instrumentally were also likely to have greater affinity for it and involvement with it. On the other hand, those who were ritualistic viewers of news perceived it to be less realistic and had less affinity for it. In a similar study Rubin and Step (2000) found that those with a greater sense of parasocial interaction, as well as those who had informational and pass time/habit motives felt more positively about talk radio show hosts and were more likely to follow their advice. Other motives have linked ritualized viewing of religious television with television affinity and a high level of religiosity (Abelman, 1987).

With the recent rise in reality programming, several uses and gratifications studies have also attempted to explore this genre. In general, these have found that the ritualized motives of pass time and entertainment predict affinity with reality programs (Papacharissi & Mendelson 2007), whereas voyeurism as a motive predicts enjoyment of both reality programs and some fictional programs (Nabi et al., 2003). Similarly, arousal as a motive moderates effects of violent movie previews on anticipated movie enjoyment, such that high arousal increases enjoyment; however, low arousal seems to have no effect (Xie & Lee, 2008).

Similar moderating effects of media use motives have been observed in the context of new media. In an experimental study in the U.S. and Korea, Ko, Cho, and Roberts (2005) demonstrated that those who utilized informational motives were more likely to show an engagement with commercial website content, whereas those who used motives linked to social interaction and convenience were more interested in human interactions online, such as emailing and chatting. In a review of Internet effects on social life, Bargh and McKenna (2004) concluded that the user goals of self-expression, affiliation, and competition have moderating effects on audiences' psychological well-being, relationship formation and maintenance, group memberships, and community involvement.

In addition to media use motives as moderators for effects, some researchers have proposed that media use motives may in fact mediate effects. For example, Strizhakova (2005) found that both instrumental and ritualized use either fully or partially mediated the effects of gender, alienation, aggressiveness, self-esteem, and need for cognition, on television and Internet addiction and satisfaction. Specifically, those who used media instrumentally, to learn, dream, or socialize were more likely to report television and Internet addictions. On the other hand, those who used media ritualistically, to be entertained and pass time, were more likely to report television and Internet satisfaction. In addition, Strizhakova (2005) found that ritualized users were more likely to be female and less likely to report alienation; whereas, instrumental users were more likely to have a high need for cognition, be more aggressive and report low self-esteem.

Mediating effects of specific motives have also been assessed in the context of political media. In a two-wave study of the political campaign 2000, Eveland, Shah, and Kwak (2003) found that the surveillance motivation influenced information processing, which further impacted political knowledge. These effects were reciprocal in nature and over time political knowledge increased surveillance as a motivation. In another set of studies that attempted to test the mediating role of media use motives, adolescents' motivations were also seen to act as mediators for the effects of television consumption. Specifically, Roe and Minnebo (2007) showed that family and school tensions had a positive effect on escapism motives which in turn led to increased television consumption among adolescents. Similarly, watching television to learn or to be entertained fully mediated the link between exposure to reality programs about dating and adversarial sex beliefs and negative perceptions of dating (Zurbriggen & Morgan, 2006). Taken together, these findings suggest that the reason we use media, in fact, the motivation to use it in the first place, may be the mechanism by which we are affected, whether that effect is political knowledge or sexual attitudes. Hence, across studies we find support for both moderating and mediating effects of media uses and gratifications on consumption patterns and outcomes.

Uses and Gratifications Research and New Technologies

With the introduction of various newer technologies, from cell phones to the Internet, it is important to consider the ways we use these media, our motivation for exposure and how those motives might once again, influence use patterns and outcomes. As newer technologies and media emerge, researchers have begun to consider how the uses and gratifications of older media may be similar to and different from those of newer media, such as the Internet or video games.

Internet

Recent research on the uses and gratifications of Internet use has focused on potential parallels and differences between television and Internet use (Ferguson & Perse, 2000; Lin, 1999; Papacharisse & Rubin, 2000) and on assessing motives for specific Internet activities (Althaus & Tewksbury, 2000; Diddi & LaRose, 2006; Kaye & Johnson, 2002; Leung, 2001). For example, the media substitution hypothesis proposes that audience members may substitute the use of one functionally similar medium for another (Lin, 1999). To the extent that one medium is perceived to fulfill certain needs or serve a particular function, intentional and selective media users are likely to substitute another functionally similar medium for it. At the core of this research was an identification of some basic motives, common to all media.

Specifically, Lin (1999) explored similarities between television and Internet use by applying Rubin's (1983) television motives measure to the online environment. She identified three final motives consistent across these media: surveillance, escape/companionship/identity, and entertainment, the latter being the most salient one overall. Lin (1999) concluded that even though television viewing and Internet use motives may be similar in a broad sense, they diverge when considered in specific online contexts, such as shopping, information gathering, and infotainment. In a mixed-method study, Ferguson and Perse (2000) discovered that certain television motives were not applicable to the Internet, and only four factors were consistent across the media: entertainment, pass time, relaxation, and social information, further confirming primacy of the entertainment motive for both the Internet and television use.

In addition, Flaherty, Pearce, and Rubin (1998) compared Internet to face-to-face interaction motives and concluded that people use computers to gratify a) interpersonal needs (e.g., inclusion, affection, escape, control, relaxation, and pleasure), b) mediated needs (e.g., information, entertainment, habit, pass time, and social interaction), and c) other needs (e.g., meeting people and time shifting). Papacharissi and Rubin (2000) identified that people use the Internet for interpersonal utility, convenience, pass time, information seeking, and entertainment. Korgaonkar and Wolin (1999) identified seven Internet motives, adding the dimensions of interactive and economic control; whereas, Flanagin and Metzger (2001) discussed motives of relationship maintenance, status seeking, personal insight, problem-solving and persuading others. This proliferation of scales that examine Internet use motives clearly requires conceptual clarification and could benefit from some work in synthesizing the dimensions. However, it seems clear that, at the very least, Internet use motives include information seeking and entertainment, much like the uses of television. However, the Internet offers an opportunity to satisfy a variety of interpersonal needs and the convenience of gratifying them simply and quickly.

Other researchers have examined Internet use motives in relation to specific Internet activities or emphasized specific motives of the Internet use. Althaus and Tewksbury (2000), for example, questioned whether Internet news acted as a substitute for TV and newspaper news. Indeed, heavy news readers tended to use both newspapers and the Internet, but television use was independent from that, perhaps driven simply by habit. In fact, in partial support of this contention, Diddi and LaRose (2006) found that college students were motivated by both surveillance and escapism in their use of different news outlets, but habitual use explained an overall news exposure the best. Thus, audiences appear to stress goal-directed, information seeking motives on one hand and less purposeful, entertainment motives on the other but this depends on the way the survey questions are phrased.

Similar to uses and gratifications studies in the context of television, a number of studies examined and developed scales of motives for various types of Internet use, such as e-mail (Stafford, Kline, & Dimmick, 1999), chatting (Leung, 2001), gay community sites (Yang, 2000), business websites (Eighmey & McCord, 1998; Stafford & Stafford 2001), online community sites (Grace-Farfaglia, Dekkers, Sundararajan, Peters, & Park, 2006), and political sites (Kaye & Johnson, 2002); however, they did not draw parallels between the use of the Internet in general and those specific activities. For example, Leung (2001) found that heavy users of Internet chat sites were mainly motivated by affection and sociability; whereas, light users were attracted by the novelty of the medium. Kaye and Johnson (2002) concluded that users sought guidance, information, entertainment, and social interaction in political websites. Yang (2000) identified seven motives for participating in online gay communities in Taiwan: social interaction/information, entertainment/relaxation, personal revelation, preference, escapism, pass time, and novelty. In a three-country study, Grace-Fargaglia et al. (2006) found that different cultural values, demographics and Internet connection type impacted gratifications that participants were seeking when participating in online communities.

Similar to early research on television uses, typologies for Internet use motives are diverse and lack synthesis. To address this criticism Song, LaRose, Eastin, and Lin (2004) suggests a dichotomous classification of motives, based on the degree of cognitive elaboration engaged in by Internet users and the values that users derive from either the content or the process of use. Researchers explain that, on the one hand, an active search of online information corresponds well to the active audience assumption in the uses and gratifications paradigm. On the other hand, the ability to make an active choice may be lost in the actual process of Internet use. Content-oriented motives parallel Rubin's (1984) instrumental motives, and process-oriented motives parallel ritualized motives. Stafford, Stafford, and Schkade (2004) support content- and process-oriented motives in their study of Internet users but add a third unique Internet dimension, i.e., social gratifications, associated with the interactive nature of the medium. Overall, then, regardless of the type of Internet content that researchers have studied, instrumental and ritualized motives appear to exist. In addition, however, the interactive nature of the Internet makes it likely that social uses also exist and these too can be instrumental or ritualistic.

Video Game Play

Another area of newer technology that has been examined within the uses and gratifications framework is video game play. Early attempts to measure the uses and gratifications of video game play were limited solely to arcade play because home console systems either did not exist or were not as prevalent as they are today (Selnow, 1984; Wigan, Borstelmann, & Boster, 1985). It seems very likely that patterns of uses and gratifications found in a public and social setting such as an arcade would be different from patterns of uses and gratifications for home play on the console and computer-based systems of today. Therefore, more recent research that has focused on in-home play (Sherry et al., 2006) found the most frequently reported reasons for playing video games were "challenge" and "competition." This finding underscores one of the reasons that it is difficult to apply already developed scales of media uses and gratifications to video and computer game play. Clearly "challenge" is unlikely to arise as a motive for say, television viewing. Computer and video game play is a very different experience from watching television. Unlike television viewing, video game play provides the player with a much more active experience. Although television can be watched actively (e.g., cheering on a favorite team or voting for *American Idol* contestants), it is commonly less active than video game play where a player must operate controls in order for the game to progress. In a gaming environment, instead of simply watching a television or movie character, video game players actually choose and carry out various actions. The player is able to control the action on the screen and, thus, influence the storyline to a certain extent. In fact, recent research suggests that the personality of the player affects how much violence is enacted in a given video game (Lachlan & Maloney, 2006).

In a more recent research, Farrar and Krcmar (2006) used open-ended questionnaires, and subsequently surveys, to assess the uses and gratifications of video game play. Utilizing the existing television viewing motives index (Rubin, 1981) and adapting it based on the open-ended questionnaire, they found that, overall, game play motives have a three factor structure (i.e., escapism, enjoyment, and competition/skill). Various motives are also related to satisfaction with game play. Lastly, game motives are related to physical but not verbal aggression. Furthermore, the motive of escapism moderated the relationship between game play and aggression. Those who played more computer games for more escapist motives, reported higher levels of aggression. Therefore, it appears that uses and gratifications as a framework can be applied to various media but, perhaps unsurprisingly, the motives for use as well as the gratifications obtained vary based on the type of media being used.

Uses and Gratifications: Rethinking a Framework for Future Research

The framework of uses and gratifications has spawned literally hundreds of published studies and has encouraged media researchers to consider how an active media user may choose, process, respond to and be affected by media in ways that differ precisely because choice is active and predicted by individual differences. In doing so, uses and gratifications has had a meaningful and long-lasting effect on the way media research is conceptualized and conducted. However, current research in uses and gratifications may need to be reassessed in order to continue to offer meaningful insight into media research. Why is this the case?

Consider the recent areas of research in uses and gratifications. This research has examined the uses and gratifications of various media such as the Internet or video games. Studies in uses and gratifications have continued to test the relationship between any number of personality factors and selective exposure to a similarly large array of personality variables. As such, the extant literature appears somewhat scattershot. While these various studies provide pieces of insight into the puzzle of media use and effects, a broader reconceptualization is needed. What might such a reconceptualization look like?

Although it is beyond the scope of this chapter to set forth an exhaustive model, we will outline several key points.

First, it may be useful to reintegrate the uses and gratifications approach into a broader theory of media selection and effects. While uses and gratifications has, on occasion, been referred to as a theory, more often than not, it is better thought of as a media use approach, a way of thinking about and empirically testing individuals' motives for media use. As such, media motives, and similarly, gratifications sought, may be thought of as cognitive and affective drives. Escapism, learning and social facilitation, while they are *gratifications sought*, as termed by the uses and gratifications approach, may more broadly be considered as the first stage in the process of media use. They may be brief urges, unrecognized as such, that motivate use. Separating this brief urge to watch, say, a sad movie, into a separate area of study (i.e., uses and gratifications) divorces the cognitive or affective need from the totality of the process. Reintegrating these needs into the larger model of media uses and outcomes may bring us towards a better understanding of the entire mechanism.

Second, both early research (Perse & Rubin, 1990) and recent studies (Nabi et al., 2006) have found that gratifications obtained may be far different from those sought. In fact, Nabi and colleagues argue that gratifications sought are often unintended, and, as they point out, if viewers cannot filter out negative, unintended effects, it is possible that "we must call into question how active, or in control, viewers are in the process of trying to fulfill various social and psychological needs" (p. 443). Thus, we would argue that *gratifications obtained*, as a construct, is not useful to our understanding of media use and effects. While we may be motivated to consume media for various purposes, outcomes are better thought of as *responses* to media, or sometimes *effects* of media. Enjoyment may be one such effect but others obviously exist as well. Therefore, gratifications obtained should be subsumed into the broader area of media responses and effects. Fulfillment of needs may be an effect, but it should not be separately thought of as gratifications obtained.

Third, a broader reconceptualization of media uses and gratifications may allow us to think about *media* use motives, and not motives for television use, Internet use and video game use. Once again, although it is important to consider the fact that the uses of media do in fact differ based on the type of media, it is possible that thinking about media use as a cognitive and affective process, rather than a functional one would offer two benefits in this case. First, it would allow us to integrate use motives into the larger process of media consumption and second, it would allow us to develop a typology of media use that encompasses various media. For example, while competition may be a motive for video game use, thinking of competition as an affective process (e.g., hostility) or cognitive process (e.g., strategizing) may allow researchers to integrate the very notion of media use across various media. Similarly, focusing on the cognitive and affective aspects of media use motives and media outcomes would allow us to consider these variables as common mediators and moderators across different types of media.

Overall, then, uses and gratifications has provided many insights into our understanding of media consumption; however, as we continue to consider how selective exposure may play an important role in the entire process—as a predictor of use, and as a moderator of effects—it may be important to begin to think of uses and gratifications as a one important portion in the entire process. Understanding media choices from a uses and gratifications perspective offers us insight into how and why people are motivated to make the selections that they do. Conceptually and holistically, it is crucial that we understand how and why people consume media if we are to understand the totality of the media consumption process.

References

Abelman, R. (1987). Religious television uses and gratifications. *Journal of Broadcasting and Electronic Media, 31*(3), 293–307.

Abelman, R. & Atkin, D. (2000). What children watch when they watch TV: Putting theory into practice. *Journal of Broadcasting and Electronic Media, 44*(1), 143–154.

Althaus, S. L. & Tewksbury, D. (2000). Patterns of Internet and traditional news media use in a networked community. *Political Communication, 17*, 21–65.

Arnett, J. (1991). Heavy metal music and reckless behavior among adolescents. *Journal of Youth and Adolescence, 20*, 6.

Bargh, J. D. & McKenna, K. Y. A. (2004). The Internet and social life. *Review of Psychology, 55,* 573–591.

Blumler, J. G. (1979). The role of theory in uses and gratifications studies. *Communication Research, 6,* 9–36.

Conway, J. C. & Rubin, A. M. (1991). Psychological predictors of television viewing motivation. *Communication Research, 18,* 443–463.

Diddi, A. & LaRose, R. (2006). Getting hooked on news: Uses and gratifications and the formation of news habits among college students in an Internet environment. *Journal of Broadcasting and Electronic Media, 50*(2), 193–210.

Donohew, L., Finn, S., & Christ, W. (1988). "The nature of news" revisited: The roles of affect, schemes, and cognition. In L. Donohew, H. E. Sypher, & T. Higgins (Eds.), *Communication, Social Cognition and Affect* (pp. 125–218). Hillsdale, NJ: Lawrence Erlbaum.

Donohew, L., Palmgreen, P., & Duncan, J. (1980). An activation model of information exposure. *Communication Monographs, 47,* 295–303.

Donohew, L., Palmgreen, P., & Rayburn, J. D. (1987). Social and psychological origins of media use: A lifestyle analysis. *Journal of Broadcasting and Electronic Media, 31,* 255–278.

Eighmey, J. & McCord, L. (1998). Adding value in the information age: Uses and gratifications of sites on the World Wide Web. *Journal of Business Research, 41,* 187–194.

Eveland, W. P. Jr., Shah, D., & Kwak, N. (2003). Assessing causality in the cognitive mediation model. *Communication Research, 30,* 359–386.

Farrar, K. & Krcmar, M. (November, 2006). Developing a scale to assess the uses and gratifications of video game play: Reliability and predictive validity. Paper presented at the Annual conference of the National Communication Association.

Ferguson, D. A. & Perse, E. M. (2000). The World Wide Web as a functional alternative to television. *Journal of Broadcasting and Electronic Media, 44,* 155–174.

Finn, S. (1992). Television addiction? An evaluation of four competing media-use models. *Journalism Quarterly, 69,* 422–435.

Finn, S. (1997). Origins of media exposure. *Communication Research, 24,* 507–529.

Flaherty, L. M., Pearce, K. J., & Rubin, R. B. (1998). Internet and face-to-face communication: Not functional alternatives. *Communication Quarterly, 46*(3), 250–268.

Flanagin, A. & Metzger, M. (2001). Internet use in contemporary media environment. *Human Communication Research, 27,* 153–181.

Grace-Farfaglia, P., Dekkers, A., Sundararajan, B., Peters, L., & Park, S-H. (2006). Multinational web uses and gratifications: Measuring the social impact of online community participation across national boundaries. *Electronic Commerce Research, 6,* 75–101.

Haridakis, P. M. (2001). The regulation of indecent but nonobscene computer-mediated expression and the First Amendment. In M. Seeger (Ed.), *Free Speech Yearbook* (pp. 34–56). Washington, DC: National Communication Association.

Hanjun, K., Cho, C-H., & Roberts, M. S. (2005). Internet uses and gratifications: A structural equation model of interactive advertising. *Journal of Advertising, 54,* 57–70.

Hawkins, R. P., Pingree, S., Hitchon, J., Gorham, B. W., Kannaovakun, P., Gilligan,

E., Radler, B., Kolbeins, G. H., & Schmidt, T. (2001). Predicting selection and activity in television genre viewing. *Media Psychology, 3*, 237–264.

Katz, E., Blumler, J. G., & Gurevitch, M. (1974). Utilization of mass communication by the individual. In J. G. Blumler & E. Katz (Eds.), *The Uses of Mass Communication: Current Perspectives on Gratifications Research.* Beverly Hills, CA: Sage.

Kaye, B. K. & Johnson, T. J. (2002). Online and in the know: Uses and gratifications of the web for political information. *Journal of Broadcasting and Electronic Media, 46*(1), 54–71.

Ko, H., Cho, C.-H., & Roberts, M. S. (2005). Internet uses and gratifications: A structural equation modeling of interactive advertising. *Journal of Advertising, 34*(2), 57–70.

Korgaonkar, P. & Wolin, L. (1999). A multivariate analysis of Web usage. *Journal of Advertising Research, 38*(2), 53–68.

Krcmar, M. & Greene, K. (1999). Predicting exposure to and uses of television violence. *Journal of Communication, 49*(3), 24–45.

Lachlan, K. A. & Maloney, E. K. (2006). Presence, personality, and video game violence: New conceptualizations of interactive content. Paper presented at the 91st annual meeting of the National Communication Association, San Antonio, TX.

LaRose, R. & Eastin, M. (2004). A social cognitive theory of Internet uses and gratifications: Toward a new model of media attendance. *Journal of Broadcasting and Electronic Media, 48*(1), 358–377.

Leung, L. (2001). Gratifications, chronic loneliness and Internet use. *Asian Journal of Communication, 11*(1), 96–115.

Levy, M. & Windhal, S. (1984). Audience activity and gratifications: A conceptual clarification and exploration. *Communication Research, 11*, 51–78.

Lin, C. A. (1999). Online-service adoption likelihood. *Journal of Advertising Research, 3*, 79–89.

McIlwraith, R. D., Jacobvitz, R. S., Kubey, R., & Alexander, A. (1991). Television addiction. *American Behavioral Scientist, 35*(2), 104–121.

Nabi, L. R., Biely, N. E., Morgan, J. S., & Stitt, R. C. (2003). Reality-based television programming and the psychology of its appeal. *Media Psychology, 5*, 303–330.

Nabi, R. L., Stitt, C. R., Halford, J., & Finnerty, K. L. (2006). Emotional and cognitive predictors of the enjoyment of reality-based and fictional television programming: An elaboration of the uses and gratifications perspective. *Media Psychology, 8*, 421–447.

Oliver, M. B. (1993). Exploring the paradox of the enjoyment of sad films. *Human Communication Research, 19*, 315–342.

Papacharissi, Z. & Mendelson, A. L. (2007). An exploratory study of reality appeal: Uses and gratifications of reality TV shows. *Journal of Broadcasting and Electronic Media, 51*, 355–370.

Papacharissi, Z. & Rubin, A. M. (2000). Predictors of Internet use. *Journal of Broadcasting and Electronic Media, 44*(2), 175–199.

Perloff, R. M., Quarles, R. C., & Drutz, M. (1983). Loneliness, depression, and the uses of television. *Journalism Quarterly, 60*, 352–356.

Perse, E. M. & Rubin, A. M. (1990). Chronic loneliness and television use. *Journal of Broadcasting and Electronic Media, 34*, 37–53.

Pugzles-Lorch, E., Palmgreen, P., Donohew, L., Helm, D. M., Baer, S. A., & Dsilva, M. U. (1994). Program content, sensation seeking, and attention to televised anti-drug public service announcements. *Human Communication Research, 20,* 390–412.

Reiss, S. & Wiltz, J. (2004). Why people watch reality TV. *Media Psychology, 6,* 363–378.

Roe, K. & Minnebo, J. (2007). Antecedents of adolescents' motives for television use. *Journal of Broadcasting and Electronic Media, 51,* 305–314.

Rubin, A. M. (1981). An examination of television viewing motivations. *Communication Research, 8,* 141–165.

Rubin, A. M. (1983). Television uses and gratifications: The interactions of viewing patterns and motivations. *Journal of Broadcasting, 27,* 37–51.

Rubin, A. M. (1984). Ritualized and instrumental television viewing. *Journal of Communication, 34*(3), 67–77.

Rubin, A. M. (2002). The uses and gratifications perspective of media effects. In J. Bryant & D. Zillman (Eds.), *Media Effects: Advances in Theory and Research* (pp. 409–433). Mahwah, NJ: Lawrence Erlbaum Associates, Inc.

Rubin, A. M. & Perse, E. M. (1987). Audience activity and television news gratifications. *Communication Research, 14,* 58–84.

Rubin, A. M. & Step, M. M. (2000). Impact of motivation, attraction, and parasocial interaction on talk radio listening. *Journal of Broadcasting and Electronic Media, 44,* 635–654.

Selnow, G. W. (1984). Playing videogames: The electronic friend. *Journal of Communication, 34* (2), 148–156.

Sherry, J. L., Lucas, K., Greenberg, B. S., & Lachlan, K. (2006). Video game uses and gratifications as predictors of use and game preference. In P. Vorderer & J. Bryant (Eds.), *Playing video games: Motives, responses, and consequences* (pp. 213–224). Mahwah, NJ: Lawrence Erlbaum Associates, Inc.

Slater, M. D. (2003). Alienation, aggression, and sensation-seeking as predictors of adolescent use of violent film, computer, and website content. *Journal of Communication, 53,* 105–121.

Song, I., LaRose, R., Eastin, M. S., & Lin, C. (2004). Internet gratifications and Internet addiction: On the uses and abuses of new media. *CyberPsychology & Behavior, 7*(4).

Stafford, L., Kline, S. L., & Dimmick, J. (1999). Home e-mail: Relational maintenance and gratification opportunities. *Journal of Broadcasting and Electronic Media, 43,* 659–669.

Stafford, T. F. & Stafford, M. R. (2001). Identifying motivations for the use of commercial web sites. *Information Resources Management Journal, 14,* 22–30.

Stafford, T. F., Stafford, M. R., & Schkade, L. L. (2004). Determining uses and gratifications for the Internet. *Decision Sciences, 35,* 259–289.

Strizhakova, Y. (2005). Understanding leisure consumption through modeling processes that underlie TV viewing, Internet use, and retail shopping. *Dissertation Abstracts International, 10A,* 3503.

Strizhakova, Y. & Krcmar, M. (2003, May). Do we have access to our viewing motives? Assumptions in and extensions of uses and gratifications, Paper presented at the annual conference of the International Communication Association: San Diego, CA.

Swanson, D. L. (1977). The uses and misuses of uses and gratifications. *Human Communication Research, 3,* 214–221.

Swanson, D. L. (1979). Political communication research and the uses and gratifications model: A critique. *Communication Research, 6,* 37–53.

Tsao, J. C. & Sibley, S. D. (2004). Displacement and reinforcement effects of the Internet and other media as sources of advertising information. *Journal of Advertising Research, 44,* 126–142.

Vincent, R. C. & Basil, M. D. (1997). College students' news gratifications, media use and current events knowledge. *Journal of Broadcasting and Electronic Media, 41,* 380–392.

Weaver, J. B. (1991). Exploring the links between personality and media preferences. *Personality and Individual Differences, 12,* 1293–1299.

Wigand, R. T., Borstelmann, S. E., & Boster, F. J. (1985). Electronic leisure: Video game usage and the communication climate of video arcades. *Communication Yearbook, 9,* 275–293.

Xie, G.-X. & Lee, M. J. (2008). Anticipated violence, arousal, and enjoyment of motives: viewers' reaction to violent previews based on arousal-seeking tendency. *Journal of Social Psychology, 148*(3), 277–293.

Yang, C. (2000). The use of the Internet among academic gay communities in Taiwan: An exploratory study. *Information Communication and Society, 5,* 155–172.

Zillmann, D. (1971). Excitation transfer in communication mediated aggressive behavior. *Journal of Experimental Psychology, 7,* 419–434.

Zuckerman, M. (1994). *Behavioral Expressions and Biosocial Bases of Sensation Seeking.* New York: Cambridge University Press.

Zurbriggen, E. L. & Morgan, E. M. (2006). Who wants to marry a millionaire? Reality dating television programs, attitudes toward sex, and sexual behaviors. *Sex Roles, 54*(1/2), 1–17.

Chapter 5

Money Does Matter

Helmut Scherer and Teresa K. Naab

Media Use and Costs: An Ignored Area

Costs are generally not considered a relevant factor in media use research. In most theoretical approaches to media use and media choice, the costs are ignored. This is the case for the two dominant models: the Uses and Gratifications Approach and the Mood Management Theory (Katz, Blumler, & Gurevitch, 1974; Palmgreen, Wenner, & Rosengren, 1985; Zillmann, 1988; also see Oliver in this volume and Krcmar & Strizhakova, this volume). Media use is mostly considered a low cost situation and critics assume that the level of reflection in the decision to use media is considerably overestimated (Jäckel, 1992; Neuman, 1991, P. 95f).

When taken on appearance, these thoughts seem to be justified. In this chapter we will reason why cost is seldom considered, and bring forward arguments for more carefully regarding cost situations in media use. First we will concentrate on monetary costs: We don't pay money whenever we turn on the radio or TV. The normal situation of media use is indeed generally without costs. Either the cost of media use is payable in advance or it is implicit in the purchase of other commodities. For example, commercial free TV or public free TV are a part of the culture of the industrialized nations. This means that in the actual situation of media use, the cost for television broadcasting, which is the most popular form of mass media, is non-apparent. The costs for commercial free TV are paid through advertising, which in turn is paid for by consumers buying the products advertised. Public broadcasting is generally paid for through the revenue of taxes or dues that are quite irrelevant to how often and when media is used. In countries where the daily newspaper plays a large role, such as in Germany or Switzerland, we see a similar strategy in place. A large segment of readers pay, before the actual media use, through subscriptions, which then make the costs less apparent in the actual reading situation. Only in a small number of cases are charges immediately payable for media consumption to raise the media's costs of production.

Three arguments contribute to the need for more regard to encompassing the costs of media use when conducting research. First of all, current changes in the media economy will lead to great changes in the financing of media. The ongoing media expansion could lead to a crisis in the system of advertising-based finance. More and more media compete for the advertising money. Simultaneously, advertising through media is becoming less efficient because the audience is spread over an ever increasing amount of media content. Media can counteract this phenomenon through sinking costs or finding or enlarging other sources of finance. This could also mean that in the future, users will be expected to contribute towards costs, e.g., pay TV will gain in importance. Germany has one of the largest free TV markets in the world, and the larger media players, such as RTL, intend to enlarge their percentage of pay TV (Horizont.net, 2006). Subscriptions for daily newspapers are losing their importance. It would also seem apparent that paid content Internet pages are becoming ever-more important.

Second, it could be assumed that the amount of investment required before media use indirectly influences media use. That costs are often payable in advance, and thereby not evident in the actual situation of media use, does not necessarily mean that they do not influence media use. They can influence both the choices exercised by recipients as well as the potential for gratification involved with media use.

Third, situations of media use where the costs are directly apparent, such as going to the movies or pay-per-view productions, are seldom considered in communication research.

Our aim is to ascertain which costs could play a role, and to attempt to describe these costs within an established media use model. In the following section we will differentiate types of costs in media use and also give an explanation of our concentration on monetary costs.

Types of Costs in Media Use

Costs are usually examined in the field of economics—and here with regard to goods and services provided by the producing companies. Costs are brought about through the use of resources relevant to the development, production, marketing and distribution processes of goods (compare Kiefer, 2001, p. 164; Heinrich, 1999). The definition of costs is not only applicable in the case of producers. Costs also emerge to the consumer through the acquisition, consumption or use of goods. Apart from direct costs there can also be transaction costs or opportunity costs. Transaction costs are costs that occur so that a purchase can take place (e.g. the cost of bargaining time or the cost of market research, etc.). An opportunity cost is the cost of a missed opportunity when the best alternative is not used (compare Heinrich, 1999). It is generally understood that costs are then considered to be more relevant, and the decision process more rational, when the cost of one option is both high and irreversible (compare Hartmann, 2006).

Costs concerning media use can be differentiated in a variety of ways. Schweiger (2006, p. 157) distinguishes the cost of media use in relation to the resources consumed. Schweiger sees three types of costs that could be relevant to media use: monetary costs, time and cognitive energy. He thereby assumes that time and cognitive energy can be attributed to the resource "attention." In this chapter, we wish to concentrate on the monetary costs; i.e., costs attributed to the resource "money." Energy costs are difficult to ascertain due to various individuals and situations. One individual invests more energy in the use of a particular media than another; it would seem that reading a newspaper is more demanding when one is tired than when one is well rested. Time, in relation to media use, is problematic because time is both a resource as well as a problem to be solved. That means one must find time and invest it when using media. This is however, not always considered a cost but the reason for using media, i.e. using media to fill time. To keep it manageable we will restrict this chapter to the monetary costs. Another reason is that money spans all types of costs. The importance of money is that it can be transferred into all manner of costs. Money can, quasi, buy time and energy. With money, the various types of costs are clearable, and, in turn, performances can be attributed to these costs.

Monetary costs can be further differentiated. We wish to do this in two different dimensions: a media based dimension and a communication process based dimension. The media based dimension can be distinguished between hardware and software costs. Hardware costs are costs that are attributed to the acquisition of technical equipment; software costs are all costs that go into the content. This distinction cannot, however, be applied to all media. By purchasing print media, the hardware and software costs coincide as the technical basis (printed paper) and content is purchased simultaneously. On the other hand, Internet use has hardware costs in that of the computer first, and later has software costs for content in the form of downloads.

The other distinction is along the communication process. The first type of costs are investment costs, including all costs for the acquisition of the technology necessary for the communication, but that can come about long before the communication process begins. The second type are exposure selection costs that arise immediately before the communication takes place, such as the purchase of newspapers or magazines at a newsstand. The third type are usage costs, i.e. costs that come about in the time the communication takes place. Usage costs are costs that are generated during the communication process and are thereby dependent on the duration or amount of the communication.

Investment Costs

Investment costs come about long before the situation of media use takes place, but can be highly relevant to the use situation. They determine not only which media are available for the media use situation but also the quality thereof. Investment costs are therefore monetary investments that affect potential use at a later date. They determine the options made available for use. Included in investment costs are all expenditures in technical hardware, i.e. all technical equipment necessary for media use; but also all subscription costs for pay TV, newspapers or magazines that make the media available.

Which part costs play for consumers is described in economics as price elasticity. This concept identifies a reaction of the level of demand to a change in price. High price elasticity is when a price is reduced and demand increases at a higher percentage than the reduced price would account for. When we assume that costs plays no role in media use then price elasticity should be zero (a major price change would lead to no change in media use). To prove that investment costs are relevant to media use situations it is necessary to show that price elasticity exists when investment occurs in media commodities and that the acquisition of technology or subscriptions can have an effect on the use situation. Media economics generally assumes that this is the case. Schultz (1993, p. 73), for example, states: "newspapers (...) can increase circulation by reducing subscription or newsstand prices." An indirect empirical indication for the relevance of costs on the acquisition of media technology can be seen in the role that income often plays for media equipment. Costs have to be seen in relation to the individual income. For a person with a higher income or financial resources, the price of media equipment is relatively lower than for a person with low income. It is therefore evidence for price elasticity when the willingness to buy a media technology increases with increasing income, because that means demand increases with the decrease of the relative cost. Indeed, those who can afford media technology are more likely to pay for it. We are naturally now touching on an issue of diffusion research (Rogers, 1962, also see von Pape in this volume). With regard to media innovation, Dupagne (1999) and Lin (1998) confirmed that interest in adaptation towards new media increase in relation to income. Further studies showed, in a variety of areas, that acquisition of media technology depends on income. Van den Bulte (2000) found evidence that household economic parameters, such as the income available or unemployment, have a direct consequence on the acquisition of television sets. A relation has also been clearly determined for the purchase of a computer. The US Department of Labor (Bureau of Labor Statistics, U.D.o.L., 1999) wrote: "It's almost axiomatic that the highest income groups will have the largest percentage of computer ownership" (compare also Dimmick & Wang, 2005). The German ARD Digital Project Group have shown that digital TV users belong to a higher income group and therefore assume that the investment costs necessary are an obstacle for the digital TV market (ARD-Projektgruppe Digital, 2001, p. 217). A similar situation is seen with pay TV. Schenk, Döbler, and Mühlenfeld (2001, p. 233) have confirmed that users of pay TV disproportionately belong to the higher income groups.

There is also some direct evidence for the relevance of costs when it comes to acquiring media. The so-called offliners argue that investment costs are the reason for their abstinence. In a study from Gerhards and Mende (2006) 55 percent of offliners stated that computers and accessories had to be cheaper for the Internet to be of interest to them. This is also the third most important reason for not using the Internet. Also, pay TV research shows similar results; Schenk et al. (2001, p. 233) found that for the majority of television viewers pay TV is simply too expensive.

These results show that costs play a role in that those who can more easily afford to invest in media are indeed more likely to consume, whereas those who do not invest state costs as being one of the reasons why they do not. This leads to the question of whether these decisions based on cost have an effect on media use. We would like to differentiate between three different influences: an absolute, a relative and a qualitative influence. An absolute influence takes place when consumption is only possible through the acquisition of technology. Said simply: only those who have purchased a television can view it, only those who have purchased a computer with access to the Internet can in fact use the Internet. (Sure, there are possibilities to avoid this absolute influence, like watching TV at a friend's place or surfing the net in a cyber café. But these are not the regular ways of using most media.)

In addition to this absolute influence of possessing technology on media use is relative influence. Specific investments can change the possibility of specific media use. One example of this is the purchase of a daily newspaper or magazine through subscription or at a newsstand. It can be assumed that a person who has subscribed is a more intensive user than those who purchase at a newsstand, due to the fact that the newsstand buyer may miss a day here and there. Nevertheless, anyone without a subscription is able to use the paper. Furthermore, sunk costs can urge people to (further) use a media when they have investment costs—even if there were a more gratifying media alternative. Sunk costs are costs that have been paid in the past and cannot be influenced by present decisions—as it is the case for most investment costs. The sunk cost effect refers to people who increasingly engage in an activity where they have investments that they feel have not yet paid off. Arkes summarizes that people do not want to appear to be wasteful, and "wastefulness occurs when a person does not fully utilize the item that has been purchased" (Arkes, 1996, p. 214; also Thaler, 1980). This sunk-cost effect may influence media use after raising finances for media.

Relative influences can affect the frequency of use of other media, too. Every additional purchase of media brings about changes in the use of all media because of additional alternatives. When an investment for a specific media technology has already taken place then the costs of this media use become relatively minor and this can change the relation of all media. Westermann (2004), for example, showed that the availability of a television and video recorder has a negative influence on how often one goes to the cinema because television viewing is seen as both inexpensive and it requires much less effort. Schenk et al. (2001, p. 226) argue similarly that the use of pay TV leads to fewer visits to the cinema, as well as less intensive use of rented videos.

With qualitative influence we mean that an investment in technology brings a gain in the gratification potential. A good example of this can be seen in television technology, where an investment in a bigger and better television screen also produces higher gratification in television viewing. Lombard, Reich, Grabe, Bracken, and Ditton (2000) found that a larger TV screen brings about the sensation of greater physical movement. Bracken (2005) showed that the reception of high definition TV (HDTV) lead to a greater experience of ambient and social presence. HDTV also brings a greater sense of reality, a tendency towards higher immersion levels and to greater psychological effects. This means that through technologically improved television that has to be paid for, a stronger emotional interaction to television viewing is created. The gratification potential of the media television can be improved through investment costs that take place long before the viewing experience.

Exposure Selection Costs

Exposure selection costs take place immediately prior to reception and are the basis upon which access to media is gained. They are costs such as the purchase of a newspaper, audio or videocassettes or entrance to a movie theatre, where a situational cost-use decision takes place. We assume that price elasticity exists in this case too and that demand reacts disproportionate to price. Schultz (1993) confirms this for newspapers. He assumes that a reduction in price would increase sales on newsstands. Also, Schwab (2002) shows diverse examples where at the very least a temporary increase in circulation of magazines can be observed when a radical price reduction is implemented. The magazine *PC-Welt-Manager* had an increase of circulation numbers from 490,000 to 600,000 through introducing an inexpensive pocket version in addition to the regular format. The magazine *Joy* doubled their circulation numbers through a price offensive (Schwab, 2002). Exposure selection costs play a role when purchasing music. This is clearly proven through the popularity and success of illegal music download sites. Hartmann et al. (2007) showed that music downloads were chosen because they were comparatively inexpensive, although the tone quality was seen as inferior.

One of the best examples can be seen in cinema prices. Westermann (2004) showed that cinema admissions were in a negative correlation to entrance prices (compare also Dewenter & Westermann, 2002). He therefore speaks of extraordinary high price elasticity of cinema demand (Westermann, 2004, p. 20). Also, Blanco and Pino (1997) found proof of high price elasticity in their longitudinal study of Spanish cinemas, especially when seen over a long-term view. Macmillan and Smith (2001) and Cameron (1990) found similar evidence in Great Britain. It is interesting that such a high level of research of price elasticity has been conducted with regard to cinemas, as this particular media is special: One unit of use coincides directly with one act of payment. Other media, such as newspapers, can be used a number of times, which distributes the exposure selection costs more evenly giving the impression that the purchase was more "worthwhile" (also compare sunk-costs in the previous paragraph).

Usage Costs

Usage costs are costs that come about during the communication process and are thereby dependent on the duration of the communication. They increase, for example, together with the duration and frequency of use. Usage costs are rarely seen in media reception because a media is normally purchased for later use and the repetition thereof usually is without further costs. (As stated above, the cinema is an exception to the rule. Payment is made for one viewing only. However, the costs would not be made cheaper by leaving before the end of the film.) This type of cost is important however in the telecommunication branch where prices remain competitive. In mass communication, we see usage costs in Internet use. The Internet user without a flat rate creates costs in direct relation to use. The longer one stays on the Internet the more expensive it becomes. This has a direct affect on the duration of Internet use. Gerhards and Mende (2006, p. 244) found that an argument used by offliners against Internet use were the monthly costs involved. In contrast to the direct usage costs for downloads made on the Internet, flat rates must be seen as investment costs similar to a subscription.

Usage costs are also relevant to further media. In a study on Mobile-TV's market chances Kaumanns and Siegenheim (2006) found that interest was largest among young users. Those, however, also belong to the lowest income bracket and simultaneously decided against using Mobile-TV due to expectations of high costs. The statement: "I do not use Mobile-TV because I don't want a higher phone bill" received the second highest response from this age group. Among those of the lowest income bracket, this answer received the highest response (Kaumanns & Siegenheim, 2006, p. 504).

Integrative Model

To summarize which costs can occur within the communication process: Investment costs on the one hand influence the number of alternative media available—when costs are lower, the number of alternative media available increases. On the other hand they can also influence gratification in that through purchasing a better, bigger or newer technology, a higher level of

Table 5.1 Types of Costs in the Communication Process

Cost type	Investment costs	Exposure selection costs	Usage costs
	Determine available media alternatives and their quality	Grant access to a specific alternative/content	Depend on characteristics (duration, frequency) of precise usage
Communicative phase	Long before communication	Imminent to communication	During communication
Example	Purchase of a TV set; subscription	Purchase of a newspaper at a newsstand; cinema admission price	Variable Internet costs (costs of data transfer)

performance can be attained. Exposure selection costs must be made for some media before use can take place to gain access to a media alternative. Although rare, usage costs are possible and will probably be seen more often when the mobile TV market grows. They depend on the characteristics of the precise usage.

The three costs types are arranged according to their supposed timing in the communication process. This focus on time is more a means of illustration; of course it is possible to purchase a television and immediately start using it, which would make the occurrence of the investment costs no longer well before use. The arrangement according to time within the communication process is a necessary condition. The television must be purchased before reception, but its use is possible for many years to come. Admission to a cinema, on the other hand, is payable for every viewing and usage cost for data transfer varies according to the quantity of data.

In the following we wish to integrate these assumptions into an established media use model to expand it with reflections on costs. This will be mainly based on the work of Hartmann (2006) where cost elements in the expectancy-value model of Palmgreen and Rayburn (1985) are incorporated (on expectancy-value also see Hartmann in this volume). Palmgreen and Rayburn assume that media use is explained through gratifications sought. Those are a function of both the beliefs that a particular media has the potential to meet specific needs and of the evaluation of this outcome. In this manner a recipient can have high entertainment expectations of a particular TV show; but according to Palmgreen and Rayburn, it becomes a motive for media use when the recipient, in the current situation, also places a high value on entertainment. Finally, Palmgreen and Rayburn assume that media choice is made through comparing gratifications sought, which can easily be described as the product of expectations and evaluations (GS score). In this manner, media contents are evaluated and compared to one another and the one with the highest product will be chosen. For example, when three different media alternatives a), b) and c) are evaluated, then a) will be used when it is found to have a higher level of expectation and value over b) or c).

In a traditional perspective, expectations are seen as expectations about the benefits and quality of performance of the media only. Later research incorporates cost aspects in this model. Anderson (2000) sees costs as component different from value and expectancy that influences the selection. One must not only increase the perceived task value and bolster the expectancies for success but also look at the perceived costs (Anderson, 2000, p. 5). Translated to the original expectancy-value model, this means that the gratifications sought have to be compared to the costs. Hartmann (2006, p. 148) chooses a slightly different concept. He posed the question of which components go to make up "expectation" and found them to be quality of experience, social norms and costs. Here, the GS score results from expected aspects, including cost, multiplied with their evaluation. Both approaches have in common the inclusion of costs in the final decision process; they only incorporate them at a different step (also compare LaRose in this volume, who, under a perspective of Social Cognition Theory names monetary incentives as one dimension of expected outcome).

In addition to a comparison of the quality and social standard (or of the expected gratifications, as Anderson puts it), to ascertain relevance for media use, it is necessary to also conduct a comparison of costs. It must not only be that the selected alternative a) possesses a higher level of quality of experience and properly fits social norms in comparison to the next best alternative b), but this difference in quality must also be valued higher than the difference in costs between a) and b). In other words, the surplus of quality for media a) must exceed the surplus of costs for media a).

In case it turns out that the gratification of the chosen alternative is less than expected, or one of the rejected alternatives would have been better— that is the opportunity cost being higher than expected—one might feel regret or disappointment. Zellenberg, van Dijk, Manstead, and van der Pligt state that the anticipation of these emotions "are taken into consideration when determining the expected utility of different courses of action" (2000, p. 531). According to the expectancy-value model gratifications obtained will shape future expectancies. This is why the experience of negative emotions will influence future media choices, to keep anticipated regret and disappointment low.

How can these cost considerations influence media use? Investment costs lead to a reduction in available media alternatives. This means that when investment costs are high for a particular media, it will only be available to a select group. When investment costs are reduced, then this media will be available for more and more people—an increase in media alternatives is expected. Media choice will turn out differently when the investment cost factor for the best media alternative is too high to be chosen; i.e., selection will be made of the otherwise best alternative. If investment costs for the best alternative are, however, reduced, making it more available, this one will then be used instead of the next best alternative. Investment costs can have further influence. They can change scores of gratifications sought through changing expectations of a particular media due to investments made in quality. For example, expectations of the quality of experience become higher when a better television set is purchased. That means that the product of expectation and value, i.e., the GS score, will be higher. In this manner, new comparison of media alternatives makes it possible that one alternative can receive a higher score than it previously possessed and thereby be chosen.

Investment costs and exposure selection costs are once-only costs and do not vary according to use, making them relatively cheap per unit of use. It is therefore economically sound to use a media often when it is paid for in full and for which no additional costs occur. Regarding usage costs, the comparison of costs and quality that is the comparison of gratifications sought for all alternatives has to be done every time of use, because usage costs have to be paid for every individual use. Investment cost and exposure selection costs are paid once and allow for an enduring use. This makes them risky, because if it turns out that the chosen alternative provides a lower quality than expected, the user will be disappointed and regret the decision, but must stick with it. Of course the user can also regret a decision when he paid for a single use, but in most cases this wrong decision was less expensive and is easily reversible. Here, sunk costs become relevant again: The user who paid in advance will feel the necessity to even up the sunk-cost although he is disappointed by the gratifications obtained. The person who paid for a single use has no need to compensate for the sunk costs. Therefore, usage costs are less risky because expectancies about possible regret and disappointment can more easily be changed.

Finally, it should be taken into consideration that particular needs can also be met by non-media alternatives. Generally speaking, it is safe to assume that non-media alternatives possess a higher gratification potential (compare Frey, Benesch, & Stutzer, 2007). It is more satisfying to visit a beautiful sight than to merely view a film about it. Witnessing a football game live is naturally filled with much more gratification than simply watching a game on TV. Media use can only be explained when costs are included. The media alternative is not chosen simply because it has a higher gratification potential but because it has an enormous cost advantage. The advantage in costs of media use often outweighs the gratification gained through the non-media alternative. This, however, does not necessarily remain stable. Cameron (1990) assumes that the cinema crisis can also be explained through a gain in per capita income over time. The demand for cinema falls because people have more money available to participate in expensive recreational activities. In this case, the cost advantage of media alternatives in relation to recreational activities is not valued as highly, in times of per capita income growth, as the gratification gained through non-media alternatives.

Summary

We have shown that relevant costs exist, the importance of which has been proven in many studies. From the user's perspective, there are only two methods of payment for use: The first is when costs occur irrelevant of use. These are media alternatives that have high investment costs, but when used are relatively cheap. In our opinion, the disregard of the cost factor in media use situations lies therein, that these investment costs have been completely ignored. This neglect could also apply to recipients that no longer have to think of costs, long since paid for, in the actual situation of use. The reception appears to be free. The rationally thinking user would then go on to assume that this media alternative can only be made cheaper through heavy use. In this manner, not only high investment costs, but in the case of many media, also high exposure selection costs are made more worthwhile. The other method of payment has a clear relationship between use and cost for the user because he pays exactly for how much is used—and only for this. One is designated as flat rate and the other as pay-per-use. It is interesting to note that both models, e.g., in the areas of telecommunication and Internet, use their simplicity for consumers as an advertising motto. With the one method, the costs are clear from the beginning, and with the other the recipient is assured that the costs are in relation to use.

In our opinion, the subject is by no means exhausted. Costs can influence reception in many other ways. We found in one study for example, that homeless newspapers are bought for the simple reason that the price is set so that the seller makes money on it. Other media, such as lifestyle magazines, have higher prices to signal that they belong to a higher class; i.e. the costs are used to create an image (compare Velben, 1899). Also, the costs for alternatives other than media use have to be included in the model because they influence the decision as to whether media are used or not. We hope to have at least removed any doubts as to the necessity of incorporating questions of costs within future media use research with this chapter.

References

Anderson, P. N. (2000, April 24). Cost Perception And The Expectancy-Value Model Of Achievement Motivation. A Roundtable Discussion Presented at the 2000 Annual Meeting of the American Education Research Association, New Orleans, Louisiana.

ARD-Projektgruppe Digital. (2001). Digitales Fernsehen in Deutschland—Markt, Nutzerprofile, Bewertungen [Digital TV in Germany—Market, user profiles, evaluations]. *Media Perspektiven, no Vol.*(4), 202–219.

Arkes, H. R. (1996). The psychology of waste. *Journal of Behavioral Decision Making, 9*, 213–224.

Blanco, V. F. & Pino, J. F. B. (1997). Cinema demand in Spain: A cointegration analysis. *Journal of Cultural Economics, 21*(1), 57–75.

Bracken, C. C. (2005). Presence and image quality: The case of high-definition television. *Media Psychology, 7*(2), 191–206.

Bureau of Labor Statistics, U. D. o. L. (1999). Computer ownership up sharply in the 1990s. *Issues in Labor Statistics, Summary 99*(4), 1–2.

Cameron, S. (1990). The demand for cinema in the United Kingdom. *Journal of Cultural Economics, 14*(1), 35–47.

Dewenter, R. & Westermann, M. (2002). *Cinema demand in Germany.* Issue No. 125 of the discussion articles of the Economy Department, University Duisburg-Essen.

Dimmick, J. & Wang, T. (2005). Toward an economic theory of media diffusion based on the parameters of the logistic growth equation. *Journal of Media Economics, 18*(4), 233–246.

Dupagne, M. (1999). Exploring the characteristics of potential high-definition television adopters. *Journal of Media Economics, 12*, 35–50.

Frey, B. S., Benesch, C., & Stutzer, A. (2007). Does watching TV make us happy? *Journal of Economic Psychology, 28,* 283–313.

Gerhards, M. & Mende, A. (2006). Offliner: Vorbehalte und Einstiegsbarrieren gegenüber dem Internet bleiben bestehen [Offliners: Reservations and barriers of getting started still exist]. *Media Perspektiven, no Vol.*(8), 416–430.

Hartmann, T., Scherer, H., Möhring, W., Gysbers, A., Badenhorst, B., Lyschik, C., & Piltz, V. (2007). Nutzen und Kosten von Online-Optionen der Musikbeschaffung [Use and costs of online options of obtaining music]. *Medien und Kommunikationswissenschaft, 55*(Special Issue "Music and the Media"), 105–119.

Hartmann, T. (2006). *Die Selektion unterhaltsamer Medienangebote am Beispiel von Computerspielen—Struktur und Ursachen* [The selection of entertaining media using the example of computer games—Structure and cause]. Cologne: Halem.

Heinrich, J. (1999). *Medienökonomie* [Media economy]. Wiesbaden: Westdeutscher Verlag.

Horizont.net. (29.08.2006). *RTL schnürt Pay-TV Paket* [RTL prepares Pay-TV package]. Online. Retrieved 2 May 2008 from www.horizont.net/aktuell/medien/pages/protected/show-65207.html.

Jäckel, M. (1992). Mediennutzung als Niedrigkostensituation [Media use as low cost situation]. *Medienpsychologie, 4*(4), 246–266.

Katz, E., Blumler, J. G., & Gurevitch, M. (1974). Utilization of mass communication by the individual. In J. G. Blumler (Ed.), *The Uses of Mass Communications: Current Perspectives on Gratifications Research* (pp. 19–32). Beverly Hills: Sage Publications.

Kaumanns, R. & Siegenheim, V. (2006). Handy-TV—Faktoren einer erfolgreichen Markteinführung [Mobile TV—Factors of a successful market introduction]. *Media Perspektiven, no Vol.*(10), 498–509.

Kiefer, M. (2001). *Medienökonomik* [Media economy]. Munich: R. Oldenbourg.

Lin, C. A. (1998). Exploring personal computer adoption dynamics. *Journal of Broadcasting and Electronic Media, 42*(1), 95–112.

Lombard, M., Reich, R. D., Grabe, M. E., Bracken, C. C., & Ditton, T. B. (2000). Presence and television. *Human Communication Research, 26*(1), 75–98.

Macmillan, P. & Smith, I. (2001). Explaining post-war cinema attendance in Great Britain. *Journal of Cultural Economics, 25*(1), 91–108.

Neuman, W. R. (1991). *The Future of the Mass Audience.* Cambridge: University Press.

Palmgreen, P. & Rayburn II, J. D. (1985). An expectancy-value approach to media gratifications. In K. E. Rosengren, L. A. Wenner, & P. Palmgreen (Eds.), *Media Gratifications Research: Current Perspectives* (pp. 61–72). Beverly Hills: Sage Publications.

Palmgreen, P., Wenner, L. A., & Rosengren, K. E. (1985). Uses and gratifications research. The past ten years. In K. E. Rosengren, L. A. Wenner, & P. Palmgreen (Eds.), *Media Gratification Research: Current Perspectives* (pp. 11–37). Beverly Hills: Sage Publications.

Rogers, E. M. (1962). *Diffusion of innovations.* New York: Free Press.

Schenk, M. S. B., Döbler, T., & Mühlenfeld, H. (2001). Nutzung und Akzeptanz des digitalen Pay-TV in Deutschland [Use and acceptance of digital Pay-TV in Germany]. *Media Perspektiven, no Vol.*(4), 220–234.

Schultz, D. E. (1993). Newspaper pricing and distribution. In D. E. Schultz (Ed.), *Strategic Newspaper Marketing* (pp. 71–83). Danville, Illinois: Faulstich Printing.

Schwab, I. (2002). Erkaufte Auflage [Bought circulation]. *Werben & Verkaufen, no Vol.*(14), 50–51.

Schweiger, W. (2006). Theorien der Mediennutzung in einer neuen Medienwelt [Theories of media use in a new media world]. Habilitation thesis at the Faculty of Social Sciences of the Ludwig-Maximilians University, Munich.

Thaler, R. (1980). Toward a positive theory of consumer choice. *Journal of Economic Behavior and Organization, 1*, 39–60.

Van den Bulte, C. (2000). New product diffusion acceleration: Measurements and analysis. *Marketing Science, 19*, 366–380.

Velben, T. (1899). *The Theory of the Leisure Class: An Economic Study of Institutions.* London: Macmillan Publishers.

Westermann, M. (2004). Der Kinomarkt in der Bundesrepublik Deutschland [The cinema market in the Federal Republic of Germany]. *MedienWirtschaft, 1*(1), 14–20.

Zellenberg, M., van Dijk, W. W., Manstead, A. S. R., & van der Pligt, J. (2000). On bad decisions and disconfirmed expectancies: The psychology of regret and disappointment. *Cognition and Emotion, 14*(4), 521–541.

Zillmann, D. (1988). Mood management: Using entertainment to full advantage. In L. Donohew, H. E. Sypher, & E. T. Higgins (Eds.), *Communication, Social Cognition, and Affect* (pp. 147–171). Hillsdale: Erlbaum.

Chapter 6

The Effect of Subjective Quality Assessments on Media Selection

Jens Wolling

Choice and use of media products are influenced by a number of factors. Most of the theoretical approaches in the study of media use and media product selection have sought explanations in particular human characteristics—people's motives (Rubin, 2002), moods (Zillmann, 2004), personality (Burst, 1999), attitudes (Doll & Hasebrink, 1989), etc. These approaches all assume, whether implicitly or explicitly, that the user is an active user. Other approaches focus on the conditions surrounding the use: the structure of the media market, the situation in which it is used or the personal restrictions affecting the user (Webster & Wakshlag, 1983). This second set of factors raises questions as to how active, or consciously selective, the user is and, at least, reveals the limitations under which the user operates. If in the supermarket, for example, Shoppers' Radio is broadcasting news, music and commercials, it can hardly be said that the user of the medium has made an active choice. In the case of the user taking his or her remote control and rifling through all the channels, the companion on the sofa can hardly be designated an active selector of her or his own television viewing. There are many such situations in which programs or products are used without having been actively selected.

And there are even more situations in which, indeed, there is selection, but the choice is from a very restricted range. Again, there are many examples: in the case of television, since many programs are not broadcast or are incapable of being broadcast on cable TV, the choice of program is automatically limited. In the newspaper field, the reading of news items will be predetermined by the newspaper a household has subscribed to. It is impossible, or largely so, to attribute the act of choice simply to the user's preferences (Webster & Wakshlag, 1983).

On close scrutiny, the situations where choice is exercised prove that no media selection takes place without any restrictions whatever, for it is only possible to select that which has already been produced (McQuail, 1997). It is thus necessary to keep within reason the notion of a media user with fully autonomous freedom of choice. The factors contingent to the situation on the one hand, and the social context on the other, reveal the limits set, as do the historical factors and social conditions including the structure of the media market (Wolling, Quandt, & Wimmer, 2008; Schweiger, 2007).

The Significance of Product Features in Choosing a Media Product

Although it is a banal observation that unless a thing exists it cannot be selected, the observation does remind the theoretician of something often forgotten: that conscious acts of choice always choose between pre-defined products with specific features. The features are those perceived in earlier episodes of use and therefore are expected to be present in what is offered. Especially in later stages of the selection process (Donsbach, 1991) the evaluation of these features is of importance. But even at the earliest stage of selection, the decision to turn to a particular medium and not to carry out any other activity, it can be plausibly assumed that the recipients will attribute features to the media in question, or recognize in such features an explanation for the action. This is not to say that the assessment processes are always, or even predominantly, conscious: they may well work sub-consciously and intuitively (Marewski, Galesic, & Gigerenzer, this volume). What is crucial is that the decision is based implicitly or explicitly on the ascribed or perceived features of what is offered. There is a special case, that of the choice that ensues upon a recommendation (Schweiger, 2007). However, recommendations, too, can be assumed to relate in most cases to the features of the product.

The Theory of Subjective Quality Assessment (TSQA) postulates that "decisions to use"—the selections—will be based on assessment of the features of the product by the user. Yet what are they, these "*features of the media product*"? To answer this simple question proves more difficult than one might expect, especially when one considers the epistemological problems entailed. If one looks at the question from the "uses and gratifications" approach, it is possible to take the various gratifications provided by the media as their features: their capacity to entertain the user, to inform the user, to provide the user with the stuff of conversation, to help the user escape from reality, to support the user's search for a personal identity, and so on—all these could be described as features that a media product will provide (Rosengren, Carlsson, & Tagerud, 1991). From the perspective of "mood management," features might be the product's potential to change a current mood, to raise or lower the user's level of stimulation, or to reinforce a mood.

Yet, in fact, not only the gratifications mentioned under "uses and gratifications" but also the mood modulations that have been discussed in "mood management theory" are not so much features of the media as *effects of use*: effects upon the user caused by his or her reception of the product. Either the message has provoked reactions in the recipient, as gratifications obtained or mood altered, or the recipient has adjudged it likely that the product will have such effects, i.e., gratifications sought. What Swanson in 1987 wrote about "uses and gratifications" is still one of its major problems: "The uses and gratifications approach remains essentially a conception of the audience's mass communication experience in which the role and importance of message content are not well understood" (Swanson, 1987: 245). It is thus, rather, in the effects of use that the explanation for the choice is sought and not in the desired or perceived features of the message.

Such an explanation is, however, inadequate in the eyes of the researcher who is not merely concerned with establishing that a certain effect has come of media use, but is also interested in what has caused a recipient to feel entertained or succeeded in escaping reality—or in what has improved his or her mood. These questions can only be answered by identifying the differences in content and form between the various products on offer—indeed, the differences (of form and/or of content) that are perceived by the recipients themselves as the basis of their viewing, listening, or reading choices. It is these perceived features (of form or of content) of the media product which constitute for the recipient the basis of the act of choice.

Such considerations are also implicit in well-established theories of media use. Uses and Gratifications, for example, does not assume that all motives or gratifications are of equal relevance for all media products. Rather, it is thought that certain dimensions are of greater significance for certain media (with their particular features) than for others. "Mood management" suggests, even more clearly, that if the choice of the media product is explained by "hedonic valence" or "message-behavioural affinity" (Zillmann & Bryant, 1985), such are indicators of the relevant features of the media (Hartmann, 2006: 26). Despite the abstract nature of the terms "hedonic valence" or "message-behavioural affinity," and the fact that they concentrate on only a narrow spread from within the spectrum of media product features, they are without any doubt references to the relevant aspects of content and form, i.e., the qualities.

Basic Theory

This is what TSQA takes as its starting point, rectifying the neglect of certain aspects of content and form by the established theories of media use. The theory will not be understood if too imprecise a definition of quality is in the reader's mind: "quality" in this approach is not the normative expression (recognized by grammarians as an uncountable noun) but is used as a descriptive term (and is countable): qualities are the features of any media product (to read, view, listen to and/or interact with) that are significant in the recipient's (or user's) choosing to give attention to that product.

The theory makes a basic assumption as to the part played during the process of reception by the user's desires and perceptions in respect of qualities. First, there is the assumption that recipients, or audiences, do have *desires* in respect of the qualities of the product and can indeed, specify what they are. Second, it is assumed that the *perception* of the qualities of the media products on offer is an obvious, integral element of the reception process. The third assumption is that the audience's judgement as to the qualities (its quality assessment) will be a function of the extent to which the desires in respect of the qualities are matched by the perception of the qualities. The basic thesis of the TSQA is that the recipients select and use more frequently those media products which meet their personal (subjective) desires in respect of qualities: those for which the lowest degree of discrepancy between desires and perceptions is calculated. In other words, the more positive is the quality assessment in respect of the media product, the higher is the probability that this product will be selected and regularly used.

The TSQA has in common with "uses and gratifications" that it seeks to explain patterns of media use which exhibit medium-term and long-term stability. This becomes apparent from close scrutiny of the explanation element of the theory, the quality assessment (QA). A QA is composed of desires and perceptions of qualities. It is a prerequisite for such judgements that the recipient has already gathered some experience of the media product. For the recipient, such experience is mainly obtained from serial products. Thus, the selection of a particular film or a particular book might not be seen as easy to explain under the TSQA. However, a closer look reveals that here, too, quality perceptions will play a part. At any rate, the decision in these cases will result from a transfer of quality perception from one product to another (see Figure 6.1).

This transfer is not arbitrary, but will depend on certain features exhibited by both products. In the case of a film, it might be, for example, the cast, the director or the film studio (Marewski et al., this volume). A highly important factor will, of course, be genre itself. The potential audience draws conclusions from experience and knowledge obtained from previous films—cast, directors, type of film, and so on—and applies them to the media product now in question. The qualities perceived on previous occasions with other media are then transferred if the recipient thinks there will be sufficient similarity between the products. Effectively, this sort of transfer is happening almost every time a judgment on quality is made. Even when the audience members simply judge a series on the basis of their experience of earlier episodes, and conclude from this that the quality of future episodes is likely to be similar, the conclusion is based on a transfer of perception of qualities. It is agreed that the conclusions in this case are less generalized than if the general concept of shared genre were the starting point for the said transfer.

TSQA has a foundation in theories of rational choice. The basic logic is not dissimilar to that of the Expectancy Value Theory of media gratifications sought and obtained (McQuail, 1997), though certain differences are significant. *Desires* in the TSQA is different in meaning from the expectations in the Expectancy Value Theory, where it is an expression of the probability

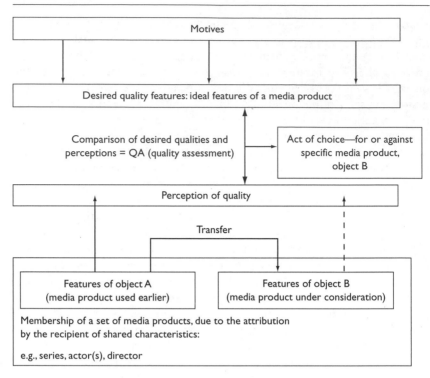

Figure 6.1 Quality perception and transfer.

that a certain media object will possess that quality. As has been stated, desire in the TSQA expresses the recipient's request that a program or other media product should possess a certain quality. The desired quality relate to features of relevance to the act of choice: they are those the audience wants the media product to have. The research in this setting must focus on *which* features the audience does actually expect of an ideal program. It is assumed that the desired qualities are influenced by the motives of the recipients.

A further significant difference from the Expectancy Value Theory is the way the second component in the TSQA is conceived. The Expectancy Value Theory takes the *evaluations* and weighs them against the expectations; the TSQA lines up the desires against the *perception* of the media features. One serious difficulty in establishing evaluations to prove the Expectancy Value Theory is that the evaluations relate to *behaviour* of the respondents, so that research involves requesting the actors to evaluate their own action. People tend to want to maintain a positive self-image and to keep up a positive public image of themselves and so there is a danger of distortion, as the method allows rationalization of one's own actions with hindsight. People can be expected to evaluate those actions (in this case media choices) more positively which they have (possibly repeatedly) adopted than those they have not. Similarly, it is to be expected that they will profile more strongly the dimensions of any evaluation which consistently and palpably justify their behaviour than they will those that (in their opinion) fail to do so. For example, it is to be expected that information and world-watching needs are mentioned as reasons for using a news program and not curiosity or recreation, even though the latter-mentioned ones might be the real reasons. This problem is especially serious in many "uses and gratifications" studies, where respondents were asked to answer questions like "I watch television because..." (Hendriks, Vettehen, & van Snippenburg, 1996). But the argument also holds true if media use and evaluations are measured independently, because in either case the evaluation is about the respondent's own behaviour and not about the evaluation of the media features. It seems to be plausible and highly probable that respondents tend to connect the questions about media use and the evaluations even if they are separated in the questionnaire by the researcher. Also in the investigation of perceptions of product features, the possibility cannot be excluded that such influences will have their effect. However, here the risk seems lower, as the people surveyed are more in the position of observers who express an opinion about an external object (the media product) than in that of people who have to judge their own activities.

The use of the expression *perception* in the theory is by no means intended to imply that reality can be recognized non-judgmentally and dispassionately. There is no doubt whatever that perception is determined not only by the actual characteristics of a product but also by characteristics of the observer him- or herself. At the same time, it is not assumed that the perception is an autonomous, purely intellectual conceptual process on the part of the recipient: theoretical consideration and empirical findings reveal that there is consonance to a greater or lesser extent between observers whenever perception takes place (Schenk & Gralla, 1993; Wolling, 2004).

The Quality Assessment

Desires and perceptions of qualities are the building blocks seen in the theory as essential to the formation of a judgment as to qualities. If recipients regard particular features as desirable for a product, and perceive them as present therein, the implication is that they have a high estimation of the quality of the product. And, in the contrary case, if recipients deplore certain features of product and then establish that they are, indeed, absent from it, this may well also imply a positive judgement as to quality (see Figures 6.2 and 6.3). What produces negative judgements on quality will, on the one hand, be the presence in a product of undesired features, and, on the other, the absence of desired features. The eight different types of arrows in Figures 6.2 and 6.3 indicate how the quality assessments are calculated for specific combinations of quality desires and perceptions.

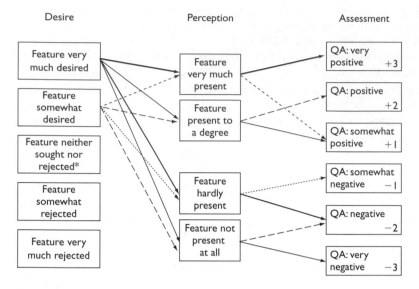

Figure 6.2 Calculating the QA for the desired features.

Note
* Not a relevant dimension: no assessment.

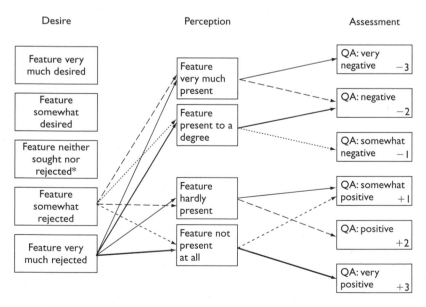

Figure 6.3 Calculating the QA for the undesired features.

Note
* Not a relevant dimension: no assessment.

If the user is disinterested, feeling neither rejection nor espousal of a particular feature, the feature is not a quality within the meaning of TSQA because it is of no significance to the user's choice of media product. In this case it does not matter how the user perceives the feature: as the dimension is irrelevant, neither the presence nor the absence will have an effect on selection.

Tackling the research in this way has advantages over the simple multiplication of the scale values which is foreseen as research method by the Expectancy Value Theory, for multiplying *evaluation* and *expectations* at times produces figures which would suggest hypotheses which are simply implausible, i.e. a larger product of multiplication is not associated in every case with higher use; neither is a lower one with lower use. This point can be easily illustrated by means of the following example: putting expectations and evaluations on a five-point scale will mean that "–2" on the evaluations axis shows a feature evaluated as very bad, and putting "1" on the expectation axis will show that it is thought very unlikely that the object of the research activity possesses the feature at all. "2," on the other hand, is the expression of very positive evaluations and "5" of high probability of presence (Figure 6.4).

It may well be plausibly argued that high estimation of a feature combined with great likelihood of its presence in a media product leads to high use of that product (Field A in Figure 6.4). Likewise, it seems logical that a positively seen feature expected to be present at least with some probability (Field B) will encourage use to a greater extent than does the same feature seen as less likely to be present (Field C). And finally, it is plausible that if the probability of presence is equal, a feature that is more highly esteemed will render use of the media product more likely (Field D) than would a feature that is not so warmly viewed (Field E). All these features can be visually represented by the multiplication method.

However, another set of associations (Field F and C) is definitely not plausible: why should the very improbable presence of a disliked feature have a negative effect on the likelihood of a product's use and the very improbable presence of a liked feature should have a positive effect? At this point the hypothesis underlying the theory—that there is a linear relationship between the multiplied result on one hand and the intensity of use (or likelihood of selection) on the other—shows a logical weakness. A means of overcoming such problems is to be found in a) replacing the central expressions by *desired qualities* and *perceptions of qualities* and b) modifying, first, the instruments of measurement (questions and scales) and, second, the way the scale values are calculated in the context of TSQA (Figures 6.2 and 6.3).

In most of the cases the simple multiplication model of the Expectancy Value Theory and the proposed calculation in Figure 2 and 3 leads to similar results but in some cases there are differences. For example: Following the TSQA model a "somewhat desired feature" being "very much present"

	Expectation				
	1	*2*	*3*	*4*	*5*
−2	−2 F	−4	−6	−8 E	−10
−1	−1	−2	−3	−4	−5
0	0	0	0	0	0
1	1	2	3	4 D	5
2	2 C	4	6 B	8	10 A

(Evaluation is labelled on the vertical axis)

Figure 6.4 Logical weaknesses in the multiplication approach of the Expectancy Value Theory.

would be an indicator of just a "somewhat positive assessment" (+1). The assessment would be higher (+2), if that "somewhat desired feature" is just "present to a degree." Applying the multiplication model of the Expectancy Value Theory the opposite would be true.

Intrinsic Tensions

Empirical results obtained from research into audience selections based on quality assessments make it clear that among the audience there are some almost irreconcilable desires in respect of quality. It is not surprising that there are such deviations among the requirements imposed by the audience, but it is interesting that very often it will be one and the same recipient who formulates contradictory expectations (Vowe & Wolling, 2004).

This phenomenon, that the varied demands as to quality may, or do, contradict one another, has also been discussed in quality research where the quality term is used in the normative way (Ruß-Mohl, 1992). In other fields of communications science, too, the thesis comes up that mutually competitive demands can be of great importance for the understanding of the processes of communication, especially of entertainment (Schönbach, 2005; Bosshart, 1994; Tannenbaum, 1980). It is also an element of the basic theory (Rational Choice) that is taken into account by the TSQA that there are divergent aims which are not easily reconciled with each other: the term used is "conflicting goals" (Eisenführ & Weber, 2003). The TSQA uses the expression "intrinsic tensions" (in German, *Spannungsbögen*) for the mutually opposed demands.

For the TSQA, identifying the conflicting requirements that are imposed by the audience on the media is of great importance, as the assumption is that recipients in making their selection prefer the media products that best meet the mutually opposed demands in combination. To predict decisions about use, taking into account the intrinsic tensions, it is thus not sufficient to view quality dimensions in isolation from one another, but necessary to work out which of the desired qualities may be such diametrically opposed pairs.

Here again, an example may clarify the issue. Taking "surprise" and "expectation fulfilment" as a pair of opposites, it seems to be essential in principle to the success of a media product that it should combine the two. There are admittedly many questions concerning how surprise and "expectation fulfilment" should be combined, in what proportion and by what means. From user group to user group, there is a variation in how much "surprise" and how much "expectation fulfilment" is found to be the ideal mixture.

The wish of recipients, having a media product distinguished both by a high degree of "surprising variety" and a high degree of "expectable continuity," cannot be fulfilled completely by media producers. They do, nonetheless, have the option of taking account of the two opposed specifications during the production process and, at least partially, attending to them both. In a television series, for instance, this may mean ensuring that certain characters and the plots associated with them are present on a long term basis, while others are only integrated into the story for a short period, and yet others appear only sporadically and unexpectedly.

The theoretical considerations would suggest that the recipient in such cases intuitively takes into account both the conflicting specifications, considering them together when forming a judgement on the product. Here the implication is that deficits in one aspect are *not* capable of compensation by particularly high performance on the opposing aspect. A media product that meets the demands as to "expectation fulfilment" but offers no "surprise" whatever should not be registered by the recipient as of moderate, but of very poor, quality. In the case of a product with at least a certain degree of "expectation fulfilment" and some "surprise," the audience approval should be significantly higher. Thus, to improve the judgment, it is necessary for *both* aspects to evince closeness between the desired qualities and the perceived qualities. Reducing the discrepancy by a modification of only one of the aspects would lead to no, or only tiny, improvements in the estimations of overall quality.

Objects of Quality-based Selection

As the TSQA operates at a fairly high degree of abstraction, it can be applied to selection and use decisions for the whole range of media. Whenever a recipient decides between varieties of media products, the choice will reflect the perceived qualities of the alternatives. The choice may be between different media, as in television and radio; or between different media products, as in the *New York Times* versus *New York Observer* or between specific programs, like *Friends* versus *King of Queens,* all these kinds of choices can be explained by the theory. The way the explanatory approach is structured permits even tinier details of recipients' decisions to be researched: why one reader selects the article XY and not column ZY in the newspaper, and why another reader took yet another option—these are questions susceptible of investigation in the light of the TSQA. Even though this broad range of applications is in principle possible, the approach may be less suitable for modelling some of the various decision situations than it is for others.

As has already been explained, decisions on selection by quality involve transfer of the quality assessment. What is crucial to the application of TSQA is that there should not be too wide an abyss between the objects to be bridged by the process of transfer. If there is a considerable *similarity* between the product previously experienced and the new products now available as the object of the choice, application of the theory is indicated and will probably be successful. The greater the dissimilarity, the less easy and certain is the transfer. To discover exactly the crucial qualities, it is, above all, necessary to know what "bridge" is carrying the transfer. Does the transfer on which the quality assessment depends derive, for instance, from a program's belonging to the same series or from a product's publication by the same provider or from whatever else there might be in common?

Another important aspect of the analysis of the quality-based selection process is the finding and setting of the appropriate evaluation level (Schweiger, 1999), since the selection which requires explanation might actually refer to other levels of the object than to the particular quality assessments. For example, if the decision to listen to a certain radio program requires analysis, finding out all desired qualities of entire radio programs may be unnecessary. It will probably make more sense to check on desired qualities and perceptions related to individual elements which make up radio: features of music, features of the news, features of presenters, features of comedy items, etc. From the quality assessments relating to these component elements, the overall assessment can be found by using aggregation rules—and this overall judgement can be used in a third step to explain the selection of that particular broadcaster (Vowe & Wolling, 2004).

It is, indeed, in just such instances of choice of a complex product (selection of a daily newspaper or regular broadcaster for instance) that there is a question concerning which parts of the product are those on which the quality assessment is made. To identify the elements and aspects to which recipients relate, it is helpful to discover which they talk about to other people when discussing the relevant media product. It seems plausible to argue that the elements they refer to in conversation are also those that are relevant to their acts of selection. For this reason, it makes sense first to identify the reference level by means of focus groups or guided interviews.

The Quality Dimensions

Exploratory procedures of this kind can, however, serve not only to determine the appropriate level of abstraction and to identify elements relevant to selection, but also to support the detection of the qualities actually relevant to the act of choice (Oehmichen, 1993; Gunter, 1997). As the success of the investigation will be crucially affected by the determination of the proper quality criteria for the quality assessment of the media product, the listing of these quality criteria requires particular care. What goes in the list should, therefore, not be merely the outcome of an inductive procedure. The quality criteria should, additionally be deduced from an overall theoretical system and their relevance for the selection justified in each case by the theory.

Nonetheless, such a process will meet with difficulties. It is actually impossible to draw up a comprehensive general catalogue of quality criteria, for the criteria found relevant by the recipients vary not only from medium to medium, but also between genre and genre, and between the evaluation levels on which the particular media products and elements are to be found. Furthermore, the criteria seen by audiences as relevant to their quality assessment appear very likely to change over time. It is this last point in particular, the variability over time of the criteria, that makes it plain that a catalogue of criteria can never be complete. It might, indeed, be possible to systematize the quality criteria, but only to a certain degree is it possible to justify their relevance by reference to overall theoretical considerations. The technical innovations being made in media production, and the development of new creative formats, may well lead to such alternatives in media products that there will be absolutely new assessment criteria to take into account. Nonetheless, there are already some catalogues of criteria, which can be used as a starting point for the evaluation of different aspects of various media products (Greenberg & Busselle, 1992; LaRose, 1992; Leggatt, 1996; Breunig, 1999; Gunter, 1994; Albers, 1994, 1996; Urban, 1999; Dahinden, Kaminski, & Niederreuther, 2004; Rössler, 2004; Bucher & Barth, 2003).

The quality criteria against which users make their assessment are, again, not only a question of the particular characteristics of the media product being selected but are the result of a social process during which the criteria are negotiated. The TSQA might lead (mistakenly) to the idea that media users make totally autonomous decisions on the significance of the criteria. But it must in fact be assumed that the qualitative criteria the recipients use are learnt in the process of media socializing—and, just as is predicted by critical theory, are susceptible of influence and manipulation by third parties. Whether this influence is deplored or welcomed is of no relevance for the TSQA. Once the user makes a decision on the relevance of the quality criteria, they have affected him or her, wherever they have come from.

Even if it is impossible to develop an exhaustive catalogue of criteria, it may, nonetheless, be possible to name certain basic dimensions and to use them systematically to group the categories by which quality may be described and assessed. What are now presented are early thoughts on the direction that might be followed.

The first distinction can be made in answer to the question of whether media quality is judged by the "how" or the "how much" (the form or the actual amount of content). That "how much" can be a dimension of quality in the TSQA sense is due to the restrictions of time and space under which both users and providers operate. The "how much"—or relative proportions of individual program elements—is a particularly significant factor for the media which are "temporally" structured, as are TV and radio. The nature of these media makes targeted selection on the part of the recipient difficult, limiting the use by the very nature of the timeline the recipients have to follow. Without doubt, the actual quantity of the various elements will then be a quality assessment criterion. Whether a radio station provides music for 50 percent or 90 percent of the time will be a major distinguishing factor in the quality assessment. It is assumed that, for the period of time they have available in which to watch and listen, users have specific desires related to the content. The disposition of the elements within the time period available to the user will actually and significantly influence the quality assessment. Where media are "spatially" organized, as with newspapers and magazines, or traditional websites, they will probably not be so much affected by the "how much" criterion. From the user's point of view it can be presumed that the only relevant aspect of the extent of the scope is whether it is extensive enough in absolute terms. The *relative* proportions of particular elements within the product will tend to be irrelevant.

A second primary distinction is the answer to the question, "Which are the points of reference for the quality criteria (Figure 6.5)?" Here there are three basic relations to be distinguished: that between the media product and reality (denoted with a "1" in the figure), that between the user and the media product ("3" in the figure), and the type marked "2," which expresses relations within and between media. Quality being a comparative concept, it requires such reference points.

Among the quality criteria that reflect the relation between the media product and reality ("1") number authenticity, fictionality, factuality, objectivity, truth, completeness, and relevance or the relative proportions of local, regional, national, or international-scale reporting. What underlies such criteria is the idea that the media should and can offer material that has a certain relation to reality. This idea exists especially in respect of the media which explicitly set out to represent reality. However, from the point of view of the TSQA the question must be asked in all cases whether the user is expecting a particular media product to depict the world realistically. Also in quality assessment of fictional media products, it may be significant whether the storyline in a film seems realistic. Even in "performing" formats, such as quizzes or talk shows, this may be relevant. For example, it may be an audience desire that a radio station offering music should reflect the whole range of current styles of music in its repertoire.

Another group of criteria, denoted as relation "2" in Figure 6.5, determines quality by comparing across and between media vis à vis both form and content. Here the dimensions might be expressed as originality, surprise versus expectation fulfilment, objectivity, professionalism, exclusivity or transparency. In the case of these criteria, quality is assessed not by whether the medium stands in a particular relationship (desired by the users) to the real world, but by the features of the medium itself: for instance, originality will be present in the fact that the product features are clearly distinct from those of any other. Creativity is another feature which can only be judged in relation to pre-existing media products, for it is measured against what is already known.

The quality criteria marked "3" in Figure 6.5 are the third group: the intrinsic tension between closeness and distance (between the media presenters and their audience), for instance,—or between comprehensibility and informativeness (Ruß-Mohl, 1992). This group reflects the relationship between the recipient and the media product. As conceived, they are close to the classic "effects of use," but because they focus on the features of the media product they have their logical home under the quality assessment roof. The development of such a structured system of quality dimensions may help the researcher to identify the relevant criteria for specific media products under investigation. It is just the first step. There is still much work to be done.

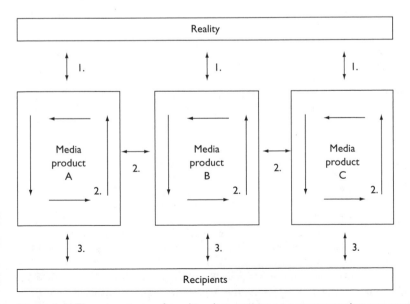

Figure 6.5 The structure of quality dimensions as a comparative concept.

Summary

The idea that qualities of media products seen subjectively will play a part in the reception process is not as new as the foregoing pages may have suggested. They do appear as "attributes" (Schenk & Rössler, 1987; Gehrau, 1997; Gunter, 1997; Greenberg & Busselle, 1996) and "stylistic features" (Himmelweit, Swift, & Jaeger, 1980) or as dimensions of "credibility" (Kiousis, 2001; Deimling, Bortz, & Gmel, 1993) and are taken into account as such in a variety of usage studies. What has been lacking so far is the conceptual framework into which to fit investigations of qualities as seen by the recipient as part of a theoretical model for the explanation of media use. That is what the TSQA offers. By differentiating desired qualities from the calculation of the quality assessment that is derived from them, the approach is able to overcome certain conceptual and methodological weaknesses in the Expectancy Value Theory and traditional direct quality evaluation. What the TSQA adds is the suggestion that quality should not be taken as a one-dimensional, linear matter, but as a balancing act between disparate desired qualities with intrinsic tensions. As such, it opens up new approaches to the art of explanation while at the same time posing new challenges to research in respect of methodology.

The TSQA has not been long on the marketplace of ideas. Time will tell if it is to find a slot in the spectrum of theories belonging to communications science and to be capable of inspiring new research. Initial empirical studies carried out on the basis of the theory do show that it has potential as an explanatory mechanism in a variety of media fields (Wolling, 2004; Vowe & Wolling, 2004). Granted, the conceptual development and theoretical hypotheses are by no means complete; neither are the means of getting empirical testing fully operational. Further developments are feasible in a number of directions. It has, for instance, been possible to demonstrate, by combining content analysis data with survey data, that there is a certain common or shared base to subjective quality perception between the recipients and the scientific observer (Wolling, 2006).

References

Albers, R. (1994). Quality in television from the perspective of the professional program maker: A Canadian view and suggested evaluation criteria. *Studies of Broadcasting*, 30, 49–86.

Albers, R. (1996). Quality in television from the perspective of the professional program maker. In S. Ishikawa (Ed.), *Quality Assessment of Television* (pp. 101–143). Luton: John Libbey Media.

Bosshart, L. (1994). Überlegungen zu einer Theorie der Unterhaltung. In L. Bosshart & W. Hoffmann-Riem (Eds.), *Medienlust und Mediennutz. Unterhaltung als öffentliche Kommunikation*. München: Ölschläger, 28–40.

Breunig, C. (1999). Programmqualität im Fernsehen. Entwicklung und Umsetzung von TV-Qualitätskriterien. *Media Perspektiven*, 3, 94–110.

Bucher, H.-J. & Barth, C. (2003). Qualität im Hörfunk—Grundlagen einer funktionalen und rezipientenorientierten Evaluierung. In H.-J. Bucher & K.-D. Altmeppen (Eds.), *Qualität im Journalismus. Grundlagen—Dimensionen—Praxismodelle* (pp. 223–245). Wiesbaden: Westdeutscher Verlag.

Burst, M. (1999). Zuschauerpersönlichkeit als Voraussetzung für Fernsehmotive und Programmpräferenzen. *Medienpsychologie*, 11(3), 157–181.

Dahinden, U., Kaminski, P., & Niederreuther, R. (2004). Gemeinsamkeiten und Unterschiede bei der Qualitätsbeurteilung aus Angebots- vs. Rezipientenperspektive. In K. Beck, W. Schweiger, & W. Wirth, (Eds.), *Gute Seiten—schlechte Seiten. Qualität in der Onlinekommunikation* (pp. 103–126). München: Reinhard Fischer.

Deimling, S., Bortz, J., & Gmel, G. (1993). Zur Glaubwürdigkeit von Fernsehanstalten. Entwicklung und Erprobung eines Erhebungsinstrumentes. *Medienpsychologie* 5(3), 203–219.

Doll, J. & Hasebrink, U. (1989). Zum Einfluss von Einstellungen auf die Auswahl von Sendungen. In J. Groebel & P. Winterhoff-Spurk (Eds.), *Empirische Medienpsychologie* (pp. 45–63). München: Psychologie Verlags Union.

Donsbach, W. (1991). *Medienwirkung trotz Selektion. Einflussfaktoren auf die Zuwendung zu Zeitungsinhalten.* Köln, Weimar, Wien: Böhlau.

Eisenführ, F. & Weber, M. (2003). *Rationales Entscheiden* (4. Auflage). Berlin: u.a. Springer.

Gehrau, V. (1997). Der Erfolg von Filmen im Fernsehen. Eine Frage der richtigen Rezeptur? In H. Scherer & H.-B. Brosius (Eds.), *Zielgruppen, Publikumssegmente, Nutzergruppen* (pp. 58–75). Beiträge aus der Rezeptionsforschung. München: Reinhard Fischer.

Greenberg, B. S. & Busselle, R. (1992). Television quality from the audience perspective. *Studies of Broadcasting*, 28, 157–194.

Greenberg, B. S. & Busselle, R. (1996). Audience dimensions of quality in situation comedies and action programmes. In S. Ishikawa (Ed.), *Quality Assessment of Television* (pp. 169–196). Luton: John Libbey Media.

Gunter, B. (1994). *Television: The Public's View 1993*. London: John Libbey.

Gunter, B. (1997). An Audience-Based Approach to Assessing Programme Quality. In P. Winterhoff-Spurk & T. H. A. van der Voort (Ed.), *New Horizons in Media Psychology: Research Cooperation and Projects in Europe* (pp. 11–54). Opladen: Westdeutscher Verlag.

Hartmann, T. (2006). *Die Selektion unterhaltsamer Medienangebote am Beispiel von Computerspielen—Struktur und Ursachen.* Köln: Halem.

Hendriks Vettehen, P. G. & van Snippenburg, L. B. (1996). Conceptualization and measurement of motivations in uses and gratifications research: A critical examination. *Communications*, 21(1), 77–92.

Himmelweit, H. T., Swift, B., & Jaeger, M. E. (1980). The audience as critic: A conceptual analysis of television entertainment. In P. H. Tannenbaum (Ed.), *The Entertainment Functions of Television* (pp. 67–106). Hillsdale, NJ: Lawrence Erlbaum.

Kiousis, S. (2001). Public trust or mistrust? Perceptions of media credibility in the information age. *Mass Communication & Society*, 4(4), 381–403.

LaRose, R. (1992). Perceived transmission quality assessment. *Studies of Broadcasting*, 28, 77–119.

Leggatt, T. (1996). Quality in television: the views of professionals. In S. Ishikawa (Eds.), *Quality Assessment Of Television* (pp. 145–167). Luton: John Libbey Media.

McQuail, D. (1997). *Audience Analysis.* London, New Delhi: Sage.

Oehmichen, E. (1993). Qualität im Fernsehen aus Zuschauerperspektive. Ansätze praxisorientierter Forschung. Media Perspektiven (1), 16–20.

Rössler, P. (2004). Qualität aus transaktionaler Perspektive. Zur gemeinsamen Modellierung von "User Quality" und "Sender Quality": Kriterien für Onlinezeitungen. In K. Beck, W. Schweiger, & W. Wirth (Eds.), *Gute Seiten—schlechte Seiten. Qualität in der Onlinekommunikation* (pp. 127–145). München: Reinhard Fischer.

Rosengren, K. E., Carlsson, M., & Tagerud, Y. (1991). Quality in programming: Views from the north. *Studies of Broadcasting*, 27, 21–80.

Rubin, A. M. (2002). The uses-and-gratifications perspective of media effects. In J. Bryant & D. Zillmann (Eds.), *Media Effects: Advances in Theory and Research* (pp. 525–548). Mahwah, New Jersey & London: Lawrence Earlbaum.

Ruß-Mohl, S. (1992). Am eigenen Schopfe ... Qualitätssicherung im Journalismus—Grundlagen, Ansätze, Näherungsversuche. *Publizistik*, 37(1), 83–96.

Schenk, M. & Gralla, S. (1993). Qualitätsfernsehen aus der Sicht des Publikums: Literaturrecherche zum Forschungsstand. *Media Perspektiven* (1), 8–15.

Schenk, M. & Rössler, P. (1987). "Dallas" und "Schwarzwaldklinik." Ein Programmvergleich von Seifenopern im deutschen Fernsehen. *Rundfunk und Fernsehen*, 35(2), 218–228.

Schönbach, K. (2005). Das Eigene im Fremden. Zuverlässige Überraschung: Eine wesentliche Medienfunktion? *Publizistik* 50(3), 345–352.

Schweiger, W. (1999). Medienglaubwürdigkeit. Nutzungserfahrungen oder Medienimage? Eine Befragung zur Glaubwürdigkeit des World Wide Web im Vergleich mit anderen Medien. In P. Rössler & W. Wirth (Eds.), *Glaubwürdigkeit im Internet. Fragestellungen, Modelle, empirische Befunde* (pp. 89–110). München: Reinhard Fischer.

Schweiger, W. (2007). *Theorien der Mediennutzung. Eine Einführung.* Wiesbaden: Verlag für Sozialwissenschaften.

Swanson, D. L. (1987). Gratification Seeking, Media Exposure, and Audience Interpretations: Some Directions for Research. *Journal of Broadcasting and Electronic Media*, 31(3), 237–254.

Tannenbaum, P. H. (1980). Entertainment as Vicarious Emotional Experience. In P. H. Tannenbaum, (Ed.), *The Entertainment Functions of Television* (pp. 107–131). Hillsday, New Jersey: University of California, Berkeley.

Urban, C. (Ed.) (1999). *Examining our Credibility: Perspectives of the Public and the Press.* Resten: ASNE.

Vowe, G. & Wolling, J. (2004). *Radioqualität. Was die Hörer wollen und was die Sender bieten.* München: Kopaed.

Webster, J. G. & Wakshlag, J. J. (1983). A Theory of Television Program Choice. *Communication Research*, 10(4), 430–446.

Wolling, J. (2004). Qualitätserwartungen, Qualitätswahrnehmungen und die Nutzung von Fernsehserien. Ein Beitrag zur Theorie und Empirie der subjektiven Qualitätsauswahl von Medienangeboten. *Publizistik*, 49(2), 171–193.

Wolling, J. (2006). Medienqualität aus Rezipientensicht. Test eines qualitätsbasierten Selektionsmodells im Rahmen eines Mehr-Methoden-Projekts. In S. Weischenberg, W. Loosen, & M. Beuthner (Eds.), *Medien-Qualitäten. Öffentliche Kommunikation zwischen ökonomischem Kalkül und Sozialverantwortung* (pp. 457–475). Konstanz: UVK.

Wolling, J., Quandt, T., & Wimmer, J. (2008). Warum Computerspieler mit dem Computer spielen. Vorschlag eines Analyserahmens für die Nutzungsforschung. In T. Quandt, J. Wimmer, & J. Wolling (Eds.), *Die Computerspieler. Studien zur Nutzung von Computergames* (pp. 13–21). Wiesbaden: Verlag für Sozialwissenschaften.

Zillmann, D. (2004). Emotionspsychologische Grundlagen. In R. Mangold, P. Vorderer, & G. Bente (Eds.), *Lehrbuch der Medienpsychologie* (pp. 101–128). Göttingen u.a.: Hogrefe.

Zillmann, D. & Bryant, J. (1985). Affect, mood, and emotion as determinants of selective exposure. In D. Zillmann & J. Bryant (Eds.), *Selective Exposure to Communication* (pp. 157–190). Hillsdale: Lawrence Erlbaum.

Chapter 7

Fast and Frugal Media Choices

Julian N. Marewski, Mirta Galesic, and Gerd Gigerenzer

Imagine you are going to the movies on a first date. Your companion asks you to choose the film you will see. How can you infer which ones will be reasonably entertaining? You quickly scan the newspaper and recognize the names of two movies, which you suggest to your date. She has only heard of one and picks that one. Possibly without even realizing it, she relied on a very simple decision strategy: the *recognition heuristic* (Goldstein & Gigerenzer, 1999, 2002). According to this simple rule of thumb, recognized *alternatives* (e.g., movies) are likely to have higher values on a criterion (e.g., being entertaining) than unrecognized ones.[1]

Media choice is based on selecting and executing different decision strategies. What cognitive processes underlie the decision making of media users? Understanding what strategies people use, how they work, and when these strategies lead to good decisions is an important step toward a full comprehension of media choice. The recognition heuristic, for example, is only one of several decision-making strategies that may guide media choice. Together with other strategies, this heuristic is investigated within the *fast and frugal heuristics approach* (e.g., Gigerenzer et al., 1999; Todd & Gigerenzer, 2000). This framework has proven to be fruitful for studying decision making in tasks that parallel those occurring in media choice (e.g., Brandstätter, Gigerenzer, & Hertwig, 2006, for risky choice; Gigerenzer & Goldstein, 1996, for inferential judgments).[2] The purpose of this chapter is to introduce the fast and frugal heuristics research program and to show how this approach can be used to study media choice.

The chapter is arranged as follows. First, we will give a brief introduction to some of this framework's historical predecessors. Second, we will provide an overview of its theoretical agenda. Third, we will describe some of the decision strategies proposed by this program. Fourth, we will compare this framework's theoretical assumptions to those made in current theories of media choice and provide a series of examples of how this framework could be used to gain insight into the way people make media choices.

Visions of Rationality

Which movies to watch, whom to court, which newspapers to read, what to eat—our days are filled with decisions, yet how do we make them? The answer to this question depends on one's view of human rationality because this view determines what kind of models of cognitive processes one believes represent people's decision strategies. There are two major approaches.

Unbounded Rationality

The study of *unbounded rationality* asks the question, if people were omniscient and omnipotent, that is, if they could compute the future from what they know, how would they behave? The maximization of subjective expected utility is one example (e.g., Edwards, 1954). When judging, for instance, which movie you should see to make it most likely that your date will kiss you, such models assume that you will collect and evaluate all information, weight each piece of it according to some criterion, and then combine the pieces to reach the mathematically optimal solution to maximize your chance of attaining the goal. Typically unbounded rationality models assume unlimited time to search for information, unlimited knowledge, and large computational power (i.e., information-processing capacity) to run complex calculations and compute mathematically optimal solutions. These models are common in economics, optimal foraging theory, and computer science.

Bounded Rationality

According to the second approach, unbounded rationality models are unrealistic descriptions of how people make decisions. Our resources—time, knowledge, and computational power—are limited. Herbert Simon (1956, 1990), the father of this *bounded rationality* view (see also Bilandzic, this volume), argued that people rely on simple strategies to deal with situations of sparse resources. One research program that is often associated with Simon's work is the *heuristics-and-biases framework* (e.g., Kahneman, Slovic, & Tversky, 1982; Tversky & Kahneman, 1974), which proposes that humans rely on rules of thumb, or heuristics, as cognitive shortcuts to make decisions.[3] Even though this program thus differs from the unbounded rationality view, it still takes unbounded rationality models—such as maximization of subjective expected utility models—as the normative yardstick against which to evaluate human decision making. According to the heuristics-and-biases tradition, decisions deviating from this normative yardstick can be explicated by assuming that people's heuristics are error prone and subject to systematic cognitive biases. Conversely, people's use of heuristics explains why decisions can be suboptimal, or irrational, when compared to the normative yardstick. In short, in this tradition the term bounded rationality mainly refers to the idea that limitations in our cognitive abilities, in our knowledge, and in other reasoning resources produce errors, biases, and judgmental fallacies (for a discussion of the "irrationality" rhetoric of the heuristics-and-biases tradition, see Lopes, 1991).

However, Simon (e.g., 1990) not only stressed the cognitive limitations of humans and proposed simple strategies we may rely on but also emphasized how the strategies are adapted to our decision-making environment: "Human rational behavior ... is shaped by a scissors whose two blades are the structure of task environments and the computational capabilities of the actor" (1990, p. 7). The fast and frugal heuristics research program (e.g., Gigerenzer et al., 1999) has taken up this emphasis. In this framework, the term bounded rationality conveys the idea that by exploiting the structure of information available in the environment, heuristics can lead to good decisions even in the face of limited knowledge, computational power, or time. This approach thus shares with the heuristics-and-biases program the idea that people rely on heuristics to make decisions, but it dispenses with the normative yardsticks that are used in the heuristics-and-biases tradition to invoke cognitive deficits and irrational errors. Instead, the fast and frugal heuristics framework has developed an ecological view of rationality through which it tries to understand *how* and *when* heuristics result in adaptive decisions (for more on the differences between the two approaches, see Gigerenzer, 2008).

Fast and Frugal Heuristics

The fast and frugal heuristics program focuses on three interrelated questions (see Gigerenzer, Hoffrage, & Goldstein, 2008). The first is descriptive and concerns the *adaptive toolbox*: What heuristics do organisms use to make decisions, and when is a particular heuristic used? The second question is prescriptive and deals with *ecological rationality*: to what environmental structures is a given heuristic adapted—that is, in what situations does it perform well? The third question focuses on practical applications: how can the study of people's repertoires of heuristics and their fit to environmental structure aid decision making? In what follows, we will focus on the first two questions and briefly touch on the third.

The Adaptive Toolbox of Ecologically Rational Heuristics

According to the fast and frugal heuristics program, boundedly rational decision makers are equipped with a repertoire of heuristics—an adaptive toolbox of the cognitive system. The toolbox contains heuristics that allow people to make inferences (e.g., about movie quality), to develop preferences (e.g., for brands), to plan interactions with others (e.g., salary negotiations

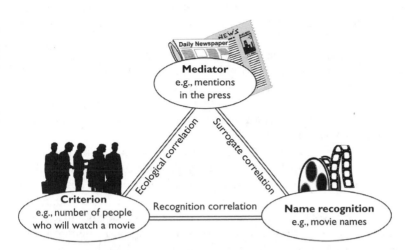

Figure 7.1 How does the recognition heuristic work? An unknown *criterion* (e.g., the number of viewers attracted by a movie) is reflected by a *mediator* (e.g., the press). The mediator makes it more likely for a person to encounter alternatives with larger criterion values than those with smaller ones (e.g., the press mentions more popular movies more frequently). As a result, the person will be more likely to recognize alternatives with larger criterion values than those with smaller ones, and, ultimately, recognition can be relied upon to infer the criterion (e.g., to infer which of two movies will be watched by more people). The relations between the criterion, the mediator, and recognition can be measured in terms of correlations.

with the boss), or to make other judgments and decisions in social and non-social contexts. By building on the way our evolved cognitive capacities work (e.g., the way recognition memory works) and by exploiting regularities in the structure of the human physical and social environment, these heuristics can yield accurate decisions in the face of limited time, knowledge, and computational power.

For instance, Figure 7.1 illustrates the ecological rationality of exploiting a sense of recognition in inferring the number of viewers attracted by a movie, say, the number of people who will watch a movie from the time of its release to the cinemas until three months later. There is an unknown criterion, namely, the number of people who watch a movie, an environmental mediator, say, the news media, and a person who infers the criterion. It is likely that the news media report more on movies that are watched by many people than on movies that attract few viewers, and as a result one is more likely to hear of the former. Correspondingly, recognizing the name of a movie alone can be informative for judging how many viewers a movie attracts, which is the principle by which the recognition heuristic works. More generally, relying on heuristics that exploit a sense of recognition is ecologically rational when there is both a substantial *ecological correlation* between the mediator and the criterion and a substantial *surrogate correlation* between the mediator and recognition. This combination yields a substantial *recognition correlation*; that is, recognized alternatives tend to have higher criterion values than unrecognized ones. If the recognition correlation is zero then it is not ecologically rational to rely on heuristics that exploit a sense of recognition.

In fact, none of the heuristics in the adaptive toolbox are all-purpose tools that can and should be applied invariantly in all kinds of situations. Rather, each heuristic is tuned to specific environmental regularities and designed for specific decision problems. Just as a screwdriver is of little use to hammer a nail into a wall but works well to attach a screw, each heuristic is a specialized tool for specific tasks. For instance, heuristics operating on recognition have little value in situations in which a person is equally likely to hear of alternatives that score high on a criterion of interest and those that score low on it. More generally, the use of a given heuristic from the adaptive toolbox is only ecologically rational when the environmental structure to which it is adapted is encountered. Humans and other organisms choose among the heuristics in their toolbox as a function of the environment.

How to Study Heuristics' Ecological Rationality

The fast and frugal heuristics framework assumes that phylogenetic evolution as well as social and individual learning processes design heuristics such that they are able to solve problems sufficiently well under the constraints of limited knowledge, computational power, and time. It is here that the heuristics' rationality needs to be understood, namely, by how well they solve given problems as they occur in the real world, and not by to what extent judgments deviate from some theoretical yardstick. Criteria for investigating the ecological rationality of heuristics include their *predictive accuracy* (e.g., in making predictions or estimations with respect to phenomena or events in the world), their *frugality* (i.e., the amount of information required in order to derive decisions), and the *speed* with which they allow for making decisions.

To study heuristics and their ecological rationality, one has to specify precise models of the heuristics. Often a high degree of precision can be achieved by describing heuristics as algorithms. Then their ecological rationality, with respect to, say, their predictive accuracy, can be assessed—for instance, by using computer simulations. And then, strong experimental tests of people's reliance on different heuristics can be designed, for instance, by comparing how well different heuristics predict people's behavior. In the fast and frugal heuristics program, heuristics are specified on an algorithmic level as *process models*; that is, they are precise enough to allow for computational modeling of *outcomes* and *processes*. For instance, in a two-alternative choice situation, say, which movie to watch, heuristics should predict both *which* of two alternatives is chosen, and *how* the corresponding decision is derived (i.e., what computational steps are involved in the decision-making process). In an experimental test of people's reliance on a heuristic, an investigator can therefore examine whether both the processes and the outcomes agree with observed behavior.[4]

Even though heuristics differ with respect to the problems they have been designed to solve, they can be understood in terms of common *building blocks* specifying the processes of how information is searched for (*search rules*), when information search is stopped (*stopping rules*), and how a decision is derived based on the information attained (*decision rules*). These building blocks are included in the mind's adaptive toolbox and can be combined into different heuristics.

The study of heuristics also requires precise concepts of environmental structure. For instance, at the time of writing this chapter, the Berlinale 2008, a famous European movie festival, is taking place. When choosing between the movies exhibited at the festival, one might consider attributes of these movies, for instance, whether the director is famous, whether the movie has won a prize, or whether the leading actor is known to be good. All of these attributes may be indicative of movie quality, which is the criterion on which one evaluates the movies. Therefore, one could use these attributes as *cues* (or clues) to infer which movie is likely to have a higher quality. More generally, in the context of inferential judgments, an environment can be described in terms of a set of alternatives from a reference class (e.g., all movies shown at the 2008 Berlinale) where each alternative is characterized by a value on an unknown quantitative criterion (e.g., movie quality) and values on a set of cues (e.g., attributes of movies). Cues are attributes of alternatives that are probabilistically related to the criterion to be inferred.

Table 7.1 illustrates the concept of an environment for a set of fictional movies that vary in the number of viewers they will attract in the next three months. Three attributes of the movies, that is, three cues for inferring the number of people who will watch each movie, are coded as 1 or 0, depending on whether an attribute is present (1) or not (0). Table 7.1 also shows how the accuracy of different heuristics in inferring the number of viewers could be studied. For instance, compare all recognized movies to all unrecognized ones by exhaustively pairing recognized with unrecognized movies: When inferring which of two movies in each pair will be watched by more people, does a heuristic that integrates the information from all three cues yield more correct inferences than the recognition heuristic? The answer is no, as a quick glance at Table 7.1 reveals: the recognition heuristic, which simply predicts more viewers for recognized movies, would yield correct

Table 7.1 Hypothetical Movie Environment

Alternatives	Criterion	Cue 1	Cue 2	Cue 3	Recognition	Retrieval fluency
(8 movies shown at a film festival)	Number of people who will watch the movie in the next 3 months	Director's name famous? (1 = yes; 0 = no)	Movie has won a prize? (1 = yes; 0 = no)	Leading actor good? (1 = yes; 0 = no)	Movie title recognized? (1 = yes; 0 = no)	How fluent is movie title's retrieval? (retrieval time in seconds)
"Rock Me"	14,000,000	1	1	0	1	0.30
"Baby Boy"	12,000,000	1	0	1	1	0.50
"Gangsters"	9,000,000	1	1	0	1	0.60
"Submarine"	7,000,000	0	0	1	1	0.80
"Hot Pot"	500,000	0	0	0	0	Not retrieved
"Red Potato"	400,000	0	0	0	0	Not retrieved
"Marry Me!"	75,000	0	0	0	0	Not retrieved
"Woman"	8,000	0	0	0	0	Not retrieved

Note
All movie names are fictional. Research in the fast and frugal heuristics framework, however, usually focuses on real-world environments, rather than on hypothetical ones.

inferences in *all* comparisons between recognized and unrecognized movies; hence a heuristic operating on cues could only equal but not outperform this heuristic.

Applications: Where are Ecologically Rational Heuristics Studied?

Ecologically rational heuristics are studied in diverse areas, including more applied ones, such as the improvement of coronary care unit allocations (Green & Mehr, 1997), first-line antibiotic prescription in children (Fischer et al., 2002), and risk communication in law and medicine (Gigerenzer, 2002; Gigerenzer & Edwards, 2003; Hoffrage, Lindsey, Hertwig, & Gigerenzer, 2000). At the same time, the fast and frugal heuristics approach is discussed in several branches of science, including philosophy (e.g., Bishop, 2006), the law (e.g., Gigerenzer & Engel, 2006), and biology (e.g., Hutchinson & Gigerenzer, 2005). In particular, in more basic research, this program has proposed a range of heuristics for different tasks—mate search (Todd & Miller, 1999), parental investment (Davis & Todd, 1999), inferential judgments (e.g., Gigerenzer & Goldstein, 1996; Goldstein & Gigerenzer, 2002), estimation (Hertwig, Hoffrage, & Martignon, 1999), categorization (Berretty, Todd, & Martignon, 1999), and choices between risky alternatives (Brandstätter et al., 2006), to name a few. Moreover, it has produced a large amount of research investigating whether and when people rely on given heuristics (Bröder & Schiffer, 2003; Mata, Schooler, & Rieskamp, 2007; Pachur, Bröder, & Marewski, 2008; Pachur & Hertwig, 2006; Pohl, 2006; Rieskamp & Hoffrage, 1999, 2008; Rieskamp & Otto, 2006), under what environmental structures the heuristics perform well (e.g., Gigerenzer & Goldstein, 1996; Hogarth & Karelaia, 2007; Katsikopoulos & Martignon, 2006; Martignon & Hoffrage, 1999), and how accurate they are for predicting events in the real world, such as the outcomes of sports events (e.g., Pachur & Biele, 2007; Scheibehenne & Bröder, 2007; Serwe & Frings, 2006) or political elections (Marewski, Gaissmaier, Schooler, Goldstein, & Gigerenzer, 2008), how much time various mammals sleep (Czerlinski, Gigerenzer, & Goldstein, 1999), or the performance of stocks (Borges, Goldstein, Ortmann, & Gigerenzer, 1999; Ortmann, Gigerenzer, Borges, & Goldstein, 2008).

Next we will illustrate this program by presenting three particularly fast and frugal heuristics in more detail: the recognition heuristic (Goldstein & Gigerenzer, 1999, 2002), the fluency heuristic (Schooler & Hertwig, 2005), and the *take-the-best heuristic* (Gigerenzer & Goldstein, 1996). All three have in common that they base decisions on just one piece of information—as opposed to weighting and adding all possible pieces, as assumed by subjective expected utility models.

Three Heuristics from the Adaptive Toolbox

The Recognition Heuristic

Which newspaper is of better quality, the *Göttinger Tageblatt* or the *Financial Times Deutschland*? Suppose you have heard of the *Financial Times* before reading this chapter, but you have never heard of the *Göttinger Tageblatt*. In this case, you could use the recognition heuristic (Goldstein & Gigerenzer, 1999, 2002) to respond: You would simply decide for the *Financial Times*, which is the alternative you have heard of before, that is, the alternative you recognize.

In its simplest form, this heuristic is designed for inferring which of two alternatives, one recognized and the other not, has a larger value on a quantitative criterion. It simply searches for recognition information and stops information search once an alternative is judged as recognized. When recognition correlates strongly with the criteria on which alternatives are evaluated, the heuristic is defined as follows.

> *Search rule*: In a comparison of two alternatives, determine which alternative is recognized and which is not.
>
> *Stopping rule*: Stop once both alternatives are classified as recognized or unrecognized.
>
> *Decision rule*: If one alternative is recognized but not the other, infer the recognized alternative to have a larger value on the criterion.

For instance, when used to infer how many people will watch the movies "Rock Me" and "Hot Pot" in the next three months (Table 7.1), the recognition heuristic would suggest that the movie "Rock Me" will be watched by more viewers than the movie "Hot Pot," because "Rock Me" is recognized while "Hot Pot" is not.

Even more so than in the case of two alternatives, recognition is particularly useful when winnowing down many alternatives. It requires almost no thinking—instead recognition is rapidly available, often before other information about an alternative can be retrieved from memory (Pachur & Hertwig, 2006). For instance, a person will more quickly know that she recognizes a movie's name than she will recall attributes of the movie, say, who the leading actors are. How does recognition help when a media user faces multiple alternatives, say, has to choose between eight movies? Many theories of choice assume a two-stage process: When evaluating multiple alternatives, first a smaller set of relevant alternatives is formed, and then a choice is made after more detailed examination of the alternatives in this *consideration set* (e.g., Alba & Chattopadhyay, 1985; Hauser & Wernerfelt 1990; Howard & Sheth, 1969). When recognition correlates strongly with the criteria on which alternatives are evaluated, the recognition heuristic generates "consideration sets" consisting of recognized alternatives (Marewski et al., 2008):

Search rule: If there are N alternatives, determine which n alternatives are recognized and which $N-n$ alternatives are not recognized.

Stopping rule: Stop once all alternatives are classified as recognized or unrecognized.

Decision rule: Rank all n recognized alternatives higher on the criterion than the $N-n$ unrecognized ones.

Consideration sets facilitate decisions by reducing the number of alternatives. To illustrate, take the movies shown in Table 7.1. A media user may want to identify the top ones, that is, those that will be watched by the most people, but she does not know the numbers yet and has to make an inference. One way to determine which of the eight movies are at the top is to rank order them. However, if the media user does not generate a smaller consideration set but instead attempts to rank *all* the movies, then she would face a total of 8! (40,320) possible rank orders. In contrast, if the recognition heuristic is used, and, say, four movies are unrecognized and four recognized, then there are only 4! (24) possible rank orders, namely, those of the recognized movies that constitute the consideration set of top ones. In a second stage, the final rank order of these movies can be determined with heuristics that use cues, such as knowledge about the movies' directors. The four unrecognized alternatives can be put aside (or ranked at random) because they are likely to score low on the criterion.

The Ecological Rationality of the Recognition Heuristic

The recognition heuristic is a specialized tool: It is only applicable when at least one alternative is recognized while others are unrecognized. If there is a positive correlation between one's recognition of alternatives and the criterion values of alternatives (e.g., number of viewers of a movie), then its application is ecologically rational, that is, it can yield accurate decisions. Recall, mediators in the environment drive such correlations: The BBC, CNN, *The Times*, and the like make it probable that we will encounter and recognize alternatives with large criterion values (c.f., Figure 7.1). In fact, the recognition heuristic has been shown to yield accurate decisions for inferring soccer teams', tennis players', and hockey teams' success in competitions (e.g., Pachur & Biele, 2007; Serwe & Frings, 2006; Snook & Cullen, 2006), the quality of universities (Hertwig & Todd, 2003), demographic and geographical variables (Goldstein & Gigerenzer, 2002; Pohl, 2006; Reimer & Katsikopoulos, 2004; Schooler & Hertwig, 2005), as well as political parties' and candidates' success in elections (Marewski et al., 2008), among others.

When do People Rely on the Recognition Heuristic?

When the correlation between one's recognition of alternatives and the criterion is substantial, people tend to make inferences in accordance with the recognition heuristic (e.g., Goldstein & Gigerenzer, 2002; Hertwig, Herzog, Schooler, & Reimer, 2008; Pachur et al., 2008; Volz et al., 2006). In contrast, when they are less pronounced, people tend not to do so. For instance, Pohl (2006) asked people to infer which of two cities is situated farther away from the Swiss city of Interlaken, and which of two cities is larger. Most people may have intuitively known that their recognition of city names is not indicative of the cities' spatial distance to Interlaken but is indicative of their size, and indeed, for the very same cities, people tended not to make inferences in accordance with the recognition heuristic when inferring spatial distance but seemed to rely on it when inferring size. There is also evidence for a range of other determinants of people's reliance on the recognition heuristic (e.g., Marewski et al., 2008; Newell & Fernandez, 2006; Pachur et al., 2008; Pachur & Hertwig, 2006).

The Fluency Heuristic

Now consider a different pair of newspapers. Which is of better quality? The *Financial Times Deutschland* or the *New York Times*? Suppose you have heard of both before reading this chapter. Thus, the recognition heuristic is of no use, because it requires that only one alternative is recognized. However, there is another heuristic you could use to make the decision.

Recognizing an alternative typically implies that a representation of this alternative is stored in one's memory. The speed of retrieving this representation from memory largely determines the time it takes to recognize the alternative. According to Schooler and Hertwig's *fluency heuristic*, a person can rely on the time it takes to retrieve alternatives, that is, their *retrieval fluency*, to infer which of two alternatives has a higher value on a given quantitative criterion.[5] When the retrieval time of an alternative correlates with a given quantitative criterion, the fluency heuristic is defined as follows:

> *Search rule:* If two alternatives are recognized, determine their retrieval time.
> *Stopping rule:* Stop once the retrieval time is determined.
> *Decision rule:* If one of the two alternatives is more quickly retrieved, then infer that this alternative has the higher value with respect to the criterion.

For instance, when used to judge how many people will watch the two recognized movies "Rock Me" and "Baby Boy" shown in Table 7.1, the fluency heuristic would suggest that the movie "Rock Me" will be watched more often than the movie "Baby Boy," because it takes more time to retrieve "Baby Boy" than "Rock Me."

The Ecological Rationality of the Fluency Heuristic

Like the recognition heuristic, the fluency heuristic is a specialized tool. First, it can only be relied on when both alternatives are recognized and when one alternative is more quickly retrieved than the other. An alternative's retrieval time largely depends on a person's history of past encounters with the alternative. Roughly speaking, the more often and the more recently an alternative, say, the name of a movie, is encountered, the more quickly it will be retrieved. Second, using the fluency heuristic is only ecologically rational when the frequency of encounters with alternatives, and consequently, their retrieval time, correlates with the alternatives' values on a given criterion (e.g., number of viewers attracted by a movie). Again, environmental mediators can create such correlations by making it more likely we will encounter alternatives that have larger values on the criterion. Thus the names of, say, popular movies tend to be more quickly retrieved than the names of less popular ones, and, ultimately, a person can rely on retrieval time to correctly infer which of two alternatives is larger on the criterion. In short, the ecological rationale of the fluency heuristic resembles very closely that of the recognition heuristic, which is illustrated in Figure 7.1. And just like the recognition heuristic, the fluency heuristic has been shown to yield accurate inferences for a range of criteria, including inferences about record sales of music artists (Hertwig et al., 2008), countries' gross domestic product (Marewski & Schooler, 2008), and the size of cities (Schooler & Hertwig, 2005), among others.

When Do People Rely on the Fluency Heuristic?

Marewski and Schooler (2008) provided evidence to suggest that the fluency heuristic is most likely to be relied on when people lack knowledge about the attributes of the alternatives they make judgments about, say, knowledge about a movie's leading actors. When knowledge about the attributes is available, people tend to rely on that knowledge rather than on the fluency heuristic. Next we will introduce a heuristic that operates on knowledge.

The Take-the-Best Heuristic

While the fluency heuristic and the recognition heuristic rely on retrieval fluency and recognition, other heuristics use knowledge about alternatives' attributes as cues to make judgments. For instance, when judging which of two newspapers is of better quality one could consider whether the newspapers are nationally distributed. Being a national newspaper might be a positive cue to quality; being a local newspaper, in turn, might be a negative cue, indicating poorer quality. Another attribute to consider might be whether the newspapers are published in a capital city. Recall, one can also think of such positive and negative cues as being coded with numbers, such as "1" (positive), and "0" (negative).

A prominent representative of such knowledge-based heuristics is Gigerenzer and Goldstein's (1996) take-the-best heuristic. It considers cues sequentially (i.e., one at a time) in the order of their *validity*. The validity of a cue is the probability that an alternative A (e.g., a newspaper) has a higher value on a criterion (e.g., quality) than another alternative B, given that alternative A has a positive value on that cue and alternative B a nonpositive value. Take-the-best bases an inference on the first cue that discriminates between alternatives, that is, on the first cue for which one alternative has a positive value and the other a negative one. Take-the-best is defined as follows:

Search rule: Look up cues in the order of validity.
Stopping rule: Stop search when the first cue is found that discriminates between alternatives.
Decision rule: Decide for the alternative that this cue favors.

The way take-the-best operates can be illustrated for the set of movies shown in Table 7.1. For inferring how many people will watch a movie, the most valid cue is whether the movie's director is famous. If one movie director is famous but not the other, then this cue discriminates and take-the-best would infer the movie with the famous director will be watched by more people. To illustrate, in a comparison of "Rock Me" and "Submarine," take-the-best would infer "Rock Me" to be more popular because the director of "Rock Me" is famous but the director of "Submarine" is not. If two movies being compared both have famous directors (or if both do not have famous directors), then the second most valid cue would be considered, that is, whether the movies have won a prize. If this piece of information discriminates between the movies, an inference would be made; otherwise the third most valid cue would be considered, until finally, a discriminating cue is found or a random guess must be made. For example, "Rock Me" and "Baby Boy" both have famous movie directors. Therefore, take-the-best would consider whether the movies have won a prize and infer a higher criterion value for "Rock Me" because this movie has won one while "Baby Boy" has not.

The Ecological Rationality of Take-the-Best

Take-the-best tends to ignore available information by looking up cues in the order of their validity and basing an inference on the first discriminating cue. Many unboundedly rational models, in turn, integrate all available information into a judgment, for instance, by weighting and adding it. Now, if a decision maker has unlimited access to information and enough computational power and time to weight and add it, should he ever rely on take-the-best instead of on strategies that integrate all information? Czerlinski et al. (1999) compared the accuracy of several models in predicting a range of diverse phenomena in 20 different real-world environments, ranging from rainfall to house prices. Take-the-best outperformed the competing models in most environments (for similar results, see also Gigerenzer & Goldstein, 1996).[6] That is, even if a decision maker could integrate all information, in these environments he would be better off not doing so but using take-the-best instead! Martignon and Hoffrage (1999) explored conditions under which different strategies work well and found that in certain environments take-the-best can actually never be outperformed by strategies that integrate all information by weighting and adding it. This happens in the environments where each cue is more valid than all less valid cues taken together. Especially in such situations, it is ecologically rational to rely on take-the-best (for more research on the ecological rationality of take-the-best and related strategies, see Baucells, Carrasco, & Hogarth, 2008; Brighton, 2006; Brighton & Gigerenzer, 2008; Gigerenzer & Brighton, 2008; Hogarth, & Karelaia, 2007; Katsikopoulos & Martignon, 2006).

On a side note, a model closely related to take-the-best has been applied to the psychologist's world of media choice, namely, to prioritizing literature searches from the PsycINFO database: Lee, Loughlin, and Lundberg (2002) examined the performance of a take-the-best variant in identifying articles that are relevant to a given topic of interest (e.g., eyewitness testimony). A researcher going by their take-the-best variant would have had to read fewer articles in order to find the relevant ones than a person behaving in accordance with an alternative model. In contrast to the take-the-best variant, the alternative model integrated all available information to rate the articles' relevance.

When do People Rely on Take-the-Best?

Numerous experiments have been conducted that investigate people's use of this simple heuristic (e.g., Bergert & Nosofsky, 2007; Bröder & Gaissmaier, 2007; Bröder & Schiffer, 2003, 2006; Rieskamp & Otto, 2006). In general, people tend to make inferences consistent with take-the-best when using it is ecologically rational. However, there are also a range of other determinants of strategy selection (see Bröder, in press, for an overview). Bröder and Schiffer (2003), for instance, showed that people are more likely to rely on take-the-best when judgments have to be made by retrieving relevant knowledge about alternatives' attributes from memory (as opposed to reading information on a computer screen).

Fast and Frugal Media Choice

Heuristics such as those introduced above can be successful because they exploit both the structure of information in the environment and the evolved capacities of the mind, such as the way memory works. In what follows, we will (i) contrast the fast and frugal heuristics approach with the assumptions theories of media choice make about decision processes and then (ii) provide a few examples of how the fast and frugal heuristics approach could be applied to studying media choice.

Assumptions About Judgmental Processes in Media Choice

The fast and frugal heuristics approach can be compared with theories of media choice on at least two dimensions, reflecting their assumptions about (i) media users' rationality (e.g., bounded or unbounded) and (ii) the role the environment plays in people's media-related behavior. First, theories of media choice differ in their view of people's resources. Some theories silently assume that people have unlimited computational power and unlimited time to process all available information about a certain problem and combine it in complex ways to come to the best solution. Others describe a case in which a solution must be found within the limits imposed by knowledge, time, and computational power.

For instance, the *uses-and-gratifications approach* (Atkin, 1985; Katz, Blumler, & Gurevitch, 1974) proposes that people actively select media content whose anticipated values exceed its anticipated costs. To illustrate, a TV program can be valuable because of the momentary gratification it provides (such as entertainment) or because it satisfies some long-term goal (such as education). It can be costly because it takes time and may cost money to watch (cf., Scherer & Naab, this volume), and because of a range of psychological and social consequences such as feelings of guilt, fear, or embarrassment stemming from exposure to certain content (e.g., pornography, a horror movie, or a mediocre soap opera). As in the broader theories of attitude formation of Fishbein and Ajzen (1975, theory of reasoned action) and Ajzen (1991, theory of planned behavior), whether to watch the program is decided by weighting the subjective evaluation of each possible positive and negative outcome by the expected likelihood that a particular media offering will lead to that outcome, and then summing the weighted evaluations. Numerous studies have used such models to predict people's media choices, though the explanatory power of such models leaves much room for further improvement (cf., LaRose, Mastro, & Eastin, 2001).

Models based on weighting and adding often assume—unrealistically—that people can predict all the consequences of their choices, are able to assign them a joint probability distribution, and can order them using a single utility function (Simon, 1983). But in real life, people rarely have the information, time, or cognitive capacity to think of all possible scenarios for the future, their likelihoods, and their subjective utilities. Moreover, life often involves so many choices and so many possible outcomes that *the* optimal solution to a problem rarely exists. Instead of trying to find the best solution, which may not be attainable, people may *satisfice* (Simon, 1997)—that is, look for solutions that are good enough for their current purposes.

This is recognized in Zillmann and Bryant's (1985) *selective exposure approach.* They proposed that people sample available media choices until they find the first alternative that is pleasing because it reduces negative or enhances positive hedonic experience. They argued that people sometimes do make elaborate evaluations of all alternatives on multiple dimensions, but that "this is the exception, even the rare exception" (p. 163). This approach, although coming from a different tradition, is closer to the fast and frugal heuristics framework—the view that people use rules to stop information search and rely on strategies that perform well even when there is little information available.

The second dimension along which the fast and frugal heuristics approach and theories of media choice differ is the emphasis they put on the interplay between the mind and the environment. While the heuristics approach highlights this interplay, some media choice theories, such as the uses-and-gratifications approach (Blumler & Katz, 1974), deal primarily with the mind and seek *internal* explanations for people's behaviors in their interests and motives. For instance, media choices are explained as serving to satisfy basic needs such as being entertained or achieving personal insight.

Other theories of media choice deal almost exclusively with the environment. For example, studies on *television inheritance effects* investigate what characteristics of TV programs make viewers more likely to watch the subsequent program on the same channel once the first program ends (Webster, 2006; see also Webster, this volume). Similarly, studies measuring *TV exposure* focus on characteristics of TV programs that make them more or less popular (cf., Webster & Wakshlag, 1985) and often treat people as merely passive receivers of media content.

Still other approaches to media choice recognize the importance of both the effects of environmental structure on people's cognitions, moods, and behaviors and the effect of people on their environments. For example, Zillmann and Bryant (1985) proposed that people try to rearrange their environments to increase the gratification they receive from them. This is reflected, for example, in their choice of TV programs—one aspect of their environment that is under their control and that they can use to modify their mood. Another example of how environment shapes people's behavior comes from a study by Dennis and Taylor (2006). They found that people stay longer on those Web pages that take longer to open, meaning that the informational structure of the Web environment affects their behavior. This parallels findings related to the foraging behavior of animals, which spend a longer time exploiting the food patches that are costlier to reach (cf., Pirolli & Card, 1999).

In sum, in line with some of the aforementioned theories, a promising approach to media choice would recognize both that people are boundedly rational and that their choices depend on the structure of the media environment. Next, we will show what corresponding models might look like.

Fast and Frugal Heuristics for Media Choice?

The best way to show that the fast and frugal heuristics program can be applied to media choice is to give concrete examples. In doing so, we will draw on the heuristics introduced above. Although these heuristics were developed primarily for inference tasks, that is, tasks where a person has to make judgments about alternatives' value on an objective criterion (e.g., number of viewers of movies), in principle they can also be applied to more subjective preferential choices—for instance, about what will make us feel good in the future. First, we describe simple strategies that could be used to pick a magazine from a large newsstand. Second, we illustrate how knowledge-based heuristics can be applied to preferential choice of TV shows. Third, we give an example of using the recognition heuristic and take-the-best to infer what is the most up-to-date health-related website. Finally, we discuss the value of using information from our social environments in making media choices. Note that all the examples should be seen as hypotheses intended to inspire research rather than summaries of empirical results.

Buying Magazines

Consider the question of how people choose a magazine at a newsstand. There are hundreds of magazines and it would take ages to read even the headlines on each one. What are possible strategies? Instead of collecting information about all alternatives and weighting and adding them, people could follow the recognition heuristic to winnow down the number of alternatives. That is, they could consider only the magazines with titles they recognize. If a person recognizes two titles, she can use the fluency heuristic to pick the one that is more quickly retrieved than the other. This can be ecologically rational in situations where recognized magazines are likely to be more interesting, appealing, or on some other criterion "good" for a person.

Choosing a TV Program

After a busy week, a person finally collapses in front of his TV and tries to find something to watch. He looks at a program guide and sees that there are five TV shows that will all start in a few minutes, of course on different stations. Being very busy lately, he has not had a chance to watch any of them before. How can he choose the one that he will be most likely to enjoy?

One option, following from the subjective expected utility approach (cf., Edwards, 1954; Savage, 1954), demands significant time and effort. First, a decision maker should collect all the available information about the shows, for instance, what genres they are, who the actors are, what the critics are saying about them, and what his friends think. Then he might weight each attribute by its correlation with his past preferences for shows. For instance, if he usually likes the shows that his friends like, he might want to put higher weight on that cue; and if he cares less about what critics say, he can discount that feature. Finally, he has to combine the scores of each program on each attribute to be able to pick the one that he is most likely to enjoy. Note that there is little evidence that this deliberate form of reasoning makes people happy (Gigerenzer, 2007; Schwartz et al., 2002).

A simpler and more efficient way is to use only a few cues that were in the past the best predictors of whether the person liked a show or not. For example, if our TV viewer almost always liked the shows his friends liked, then he could use that cue first to reduce the number of alternatives. If his friends recommended more than one show, he could use the second most predictive cue, for instance, whether any of the alternatives is in the genre he likes, say, crime investigation. If just one of them is in that genre, he can pick that show and be fairly confident that he will enjoy it (but see also Hsee & Hastie, 2006, for examples of situations in which people cannot predict what will make them happy). This strategy is a variant of the take-the-best heuristic for situations where one has to decide between multiple alternatives. It has also been called *deterministic elimination by aspects* (Hogarth & Karelaia, 2005).[7]

Choosing a Website

Let us now consider a patient who wants to find health-related information on the Web but who cannot name any medical websites off the top of her head. She types "health" into Google and gets 900 million hits. On the first Google page listing the search results, these hits include nine sponsored links, and a list of ten regular links to websites with the highest ranks as calculated by the Google search engine.[8] Let us further assume that, as many users do (cf., Brooks, 2004; Joachims, Granka, Pan, Hembrooke, & Gay, 2005), she decides to consider just these 19 hits on the initial page and to disregard the other 899,999,981. From the 19 hits, how can she choose the one link that leads to the website with the most up-to-date medical information? If people are more likely to recognize names of websites that are updated more frequently (e.g., because people talk about them more often), one hypothesis is that they could use the recognition heuristic to narrow down the initial alternatives. If our patient has not heard of any of the sponsored links nor of, say, four of the regular links, she will be left with only six possible websites to consider. Sorted in the order of their Google rank, they are the Yahoo health site, a major specialized health site, let's call it HW, and the health sections of CNN, *The New York Times*, MSNBC, and the BBC.

She could now use take-the-best to make her final pick. From her previous experience in searching for sites dedicated to specific areas (e.g., cars, sports, or movies), or from talking to her friends, she might have learned that some cues are better than others. For instance, suppose the sites dedicated to a certain topic are usually more up-to-date than more general sites. This one cue will then be enough to make the final decision: Choose HW.

The Role of Social Environments in Media Choice

Social environments are a rich source of information that people can use to solve both social and other problems. The adaptive toolbox includes heuristics that exploit properties of social environments. *Imitate-the-majority* is one example. As the literature on social comparison suggests (cf., Festinger, 1954; Suls, Martin, & Wheeler, 2002), when there are no objective standards by which to evaluate their opinions and choices, people turn to others—especially those similar to them—to make sure they are on the right track. In the world of media there is often no other standard and the popularity of a movie or a TV show may often be the cue people follow to make their media choices: Just choose the movie everybody else chooses! Whatever movie others similar to us like will most likely also be to our own taste. Imitating other people's choices has been shown to be an adaptive strategy, particularly in situations where one has little knowledge, for instance, about alternatives' attributes or other environmental characteristics (for an example from the area of food choice, see Baeyens, Vansteenwegen, De Houwer, & Crombez, 1996).

Imitating others' choices is one strategy, but people can also use their social environments to learn which cues to rely on to evaluate different media alternatives. Garcia-Retamero, Takezawa, and Gigerenzer (2006) have shown that imitation of the cues used by other successful people outperforms individual learning and other more complicated strategies of combining social information. Indeed, most of us have probably copied some of the media cues used by our friends—for instance, we would see a new movie because they praised its director. Conversations with friends about movies and TV shows can be more than a nice pastime—they can be a source of information that helps us make our media choices. This kind of social learning is also important in other areas of life where there are no clear standards for what constitutes the best decision, such as fashion or mate choice. Just like gossip can be a good way of learning about desirable qualities of prospective mates (cf., Miller & Todd, 1998), chatting about movies can help us the next time we take our date to the cinema.

Conclusion

Which of dozens of magazines, hundreds of TV programs, and thousands of websites should win our attention? Life consist of decisions, some of which are media choices. According to the fast-and-frugal heuristics framework, people rely on simple rules of thumb to make them. Most of these rules share at least one feature: They base decisions on little—but relevant—information, say a sense of recognition, while ignoring other data. Thus they differ drastically from unboundedly rational models of decision making, which assume that people integrate all the cues they can get a hold of. Everyone who has ever surfed the Internet or read a newspaper knows why: In the world of mass communication, where decision makers confront an endless stream of texts, pictures, and sounds, the art of making good choices depends on ignoring information rather than integrating all that is available.

Acknowledgments

Julian N. Marewski, Mirta Galesic, Gerd Gigerenzer, Center for Adaptive Behavior and Cognition, Max Planck Institute for Human Development, Berlin, Germany. We thank Tilo Hartmann and Rocio Garcia-Retamero for helpful comments on this chapter. We also thank Anita Todd for editing the manuscript. Correspondence concerning this article should be addressed to Julian Marewski, Center for Adaptive Behavior and Cognition, Max Planck Institute for Human Development, Königin-Luise-Straße 5, 14195 Berlin, Germany. E-mail may be sent to marewski@mpib-berlin.mpg.de.

Notes

1 In the memory literature, the term recognition is often used to refer to a person's ability to distinguish between stimuli presented in an experiment (e.g., as in a study list) and those that have not been presented in the experiment. Usually, a person has heard of both examples of stimuli before participating in the experiment (e.g., stimuli could be the names CLINTON and NIXON). Here, we adopt Goldstein and Gigerenzer's (1999, 2002; see also, e.g., Schooler & Hertwig, 2005) usage of the term to refer to a person's ability to discriminate between novel stimuli that have never been heard of before (and are hence unrecognized, e.g., the name XADALL) and those that have been heard of before (and are hence recognized; e.g., NIXON).

2 In this chapter, we use the terms "inferential judgment" and "inference" to refer to judgments about an unknown value an alternative (e.g., a movie) has with respect to a criterion (e.g., being entertaining).

3 Kahneman et al. (1982) credited Simon in the preface to the anthology although their major early papers, which appear in the anthology, do not cite Simon's work on bounded rationality. Thus this connection was possibly by hindsight (Lopes, 1992).

4 Heuristics are models of cognitive processes. This, however, does not mean that they are perfect representation of these processes. A model of mind always remains a *model* of mind. To be considered a good model, a heuristic should meet basic standards for psychological plausibility (e.g., Gigerenzer et al., 2008) and outperform alternative models by certain criteria. For instance, it should predict behavior

better than alternative models (for other model selection criteria, see Jacobs & Grainger, 1994; Marewski & Olsson, 2009; Pitt, Myung, & Zhang, 2002).

5 The term "fluency heuristic" has been used in different ways (e.g., Jacoby & Brooks, 1984; Toth & Daniels, 2002; Whittlesea, 1993). Here we use this term to refer to Schooler and Hertwig's (2005) model. Their use of the term "fluency" not only follows a long research tradition on fluency (e.g., Jacoby & Dallas, 1981), but also builds on the notion of availability (Tversky & Kahneman, 1973), which bases judgments on ease of retrieval (see Schooler & Hertwig for a discussion of the differences between their model and the notion of availability; see also Hertwig, Pachur, & Kurzenhäuser, 2005; Sedlmeier, Hertwig, & Gigerenzer, 1998, for a discussion of differences in various notions of availability).

6 A model's accuracy can be evaluated in terms of its ability to *fit* existing data and, more importantly, in terms of its ability to *predict* new data. In the first case, a model's free parameters are estimated from existing data, and the accuracy of the model in fitting the same data is measured. In the second case, the model's free parameters are estimated from existing data, and its accuracy in predicting new data with fixed parameter values is measured. Note that take-the-best outperformed, on average, competing models in the tougher test, that is, in predicting new data. (For the difference between fitting and predicting, see Pitt et al., 2002; Roberts & Pashler, 2000.)

7 Hogarth and Karelaia (2005) proposed this take-the-best variant, calling it deterministic elimination by aspects. Note that take-the-best differs from elimination by aspects (Tversky, 1972). The latter is a model of preferential choice that has no deterministic rule to order cues (i.e., attributes), and it is not specified how to compute cues' weights. Instead, it has an aspiration level for each cue and cues are quantitative. Take-the-best, in turn, is a model of inference operating on cues with binary values and a deterministic, specified order of cues.

8 Search conducted on May 15, 2007.

References

Ajzen, I. (1991). The theory of planned behavior. *Organizational Behavior and Human Decision Processes, 50,* 179–211.

Alba, J. W. & Chattopadhyay, A. (1985). Effects of context and part-category cues on recall of competing brands. *Journal of Marketing Research, 22,* 340–349.

Atkin, C. K. (1985). Information utility and selective exposure to entertainment media. In D. Zillmann & B. Jennings (Eds.), *Selective Exposure to Communication* (pp. 63–92). Hillsdale, NJ: Lawrence Erlbaum Associates.

Baeyens, F., Vansteenwegen, D., De Houwer, J., & Crombez, G. (1996). Observational conditioning of food valence in humans. *Appetite, 27,* 235–250.

Baucells, M., Carrasco, J. A., & Hogarth, R. M. (2008). Cumulative dominance and heuristic performance in binary multiattribute choice. *Operations Research, 56,* 1289–1304.

Bergert, F. B. & Nosofsky, R. M. (2007). A response-time approach to comparing generalized rational and take-the-best models of decision making. *Journal of Experimental Psychology: Learning, Memory, and Cognition, 331,* 107–129.

Berretty, P. M., Todd, P. M., & Martignon, L. (1999). Categorization by elimination: Using few cues to choose. In G. Gigerenzer, P. M. Todd, & the ABC Research Group, *Simple Heuristics That Make Us Smart* (pp. 235–254). New York: Oxford University Press.

Bishop, M. (2006). Fast and frugal heuristics. *Philosophy Compass, 1,* 201–223.

Blumler, J. G. & Katz, E. (Eds.). (1974). *The Uses Of Mass Communications: Current Perspectives on Gratifications Research.* Beverly Hills, CA: Sage Publications.

Borges, B., Goldstein, D. G., Ortmann, A., & Gigerenzer, G. (1999). Can ignorance beat the stock market? In G. Gigerenzer, P. M. Todd, & the ABC Research Group, *Simple Heuristics That Make Us Smart* (pp. 59–72). New York: Oxford University Press.

Brandstätter, E., Gigerenzer, G., & Hertwig, R. (2006). The priority heuristic: Making choices without trade-offs. *Psychological Review, 113,* 409–432.

Brighton, H. (2006). Robust inference with simple cognitive models. In C. Lebiere & B. Wray (Eds.), *Between a Rock and a Hard Place: Cognitive Science Principles Meet AI-hard Problems. Papers from the AAAI Spring Symposium* (AAAI Tech. Rep. No. SS-06-03, pp. 17–22). Menlo Park, CA: AAAI Press.

Brighton, H. & Gigerenzer, G. (2008). Bayesian brains and cognitive mechanisms: Harmony or dissonance? In N. Chater & M. Oaksford (Eds.), *The Probabilistic Mind: Prospects for Bayesian Cognitive Science.* New York: Oxford University Press.

Bröder, A. (in press). The quest for take the best—Insights and outlooks from experimental research. In P. Todd, G. Gigerenzer, & the ABC Research Group, *Ecological Rationality: Intelligence in the World.* New York: Oxford University Press.

Bröder, A. & Gaissmaier, W. (2007). Sequential processing of cues in memory-based multi-attribute decisions. *Psychonomic Bulletin and Review, 14,* 895–900.

Bröder, A. & Schiffer, S. (2003). Take the best versus simultaneous feature matching: Probabilistic inferences from memory and effects of representation format. *Journal of Experimental Psychology: General, 132,* 277–293.

Bröder, A. & Schiffer, S. (2006). Stimulus format and working memory in fast and frugal strategy selection. *Journal of Behavioral Decision Making, 19,* 361–380.

Brooks, N. (2004). *The Atlas Rank Report: How Search Engine Rank Impacts Traffic.* Seattle, WA: Atlas Institute Digital Marketing Insights. Online. Retrieved April 27, 2008 from http://app.atlasonepoint.com/pdf/AtlasRankReport.pdf.

Czerlinski, J., Gigerenzer, G., & Goldstein, D. G. (1999). How good are simple heuristics? In G. Gigerenzer, P. M. Todd, & the ABC Research Group, *Simple Heuristics That Make Us Smart* (pp. 97–118). New York: Oxford University Press.

Davis, J. N. & Todd, P. M. (1999). Parental investment by simple decision rules. In G. Gigerenzer, P. M. Todd, & the ABC Research Group, *Simple Heuristics That Make Us Smart* (pp. 309–324). New York: Oxford University Press.

Dennis, A. R. & Taylor, N. J. (2006). Information foraging on the web: The effects of "acceptable" Internet delays on multi-page information search behavior. *Decision Support Systems, 42,* 810–824.

Edwards, W. (1954). The theory of decision making. *Psychological Bulletin, 51,* 380–417.

Festinger, L. (1954). A theory of social comparison processes, *Human Relations, 7,* 117–140.

Fischer, J. E., Steiner, F., Zucol, F., Berger, C., Martignon, L., Bossart, W., Altwegg, M., & Nadal, D. (2002). Use of simple heuristics to target macrolide prescription in children with community-acquired pneumonia. *Archives of Pediatrics and Adolescent Medicine, 156,* 1005–1008.

Fishbein, M. & Ajzen, I. (1975). *Belief, Attitude, Intention, and Behavior: An Introduction to Theory and Research.* Reading, MA: Addison-Wesley.

Garcia-Retamero, R., Takezawa, M., & Gigerenzer, G. (2006). How to learn good cue orders: When social learning benefits simple heuristics. In R. Sun & N. Miyake

(Eds.), *Proceedings of the 28th Annual Conference of the Cognitive Science Society* (pp. 1352–1358). Mahwah, NJ: Lawrence Erlbaum.

Gigerenzer, G. (2002). *Calculated Risks: How to Know When Numbers Deceive You.* New York: Simon & Schuster.

Gigerenzer, G. (2007). *Gut Feelings: The Intelligence of the Unconscious.* New York: Viking.

Gigerenzer, G. (2008). *Rationality for Mortals: How People Cope with Uncertainty.* New York: Oxford University Press.

Gigerenzer, G. & Brighton, H. (2008). Can hunches be rational? *Journal of Law, Economics, and Policy, 4,* 155–175.

Gigerenzer, G. & Edwards, A. (2003). Simple tools for understanding risks: From innumeracy to insight. *British Medical Journal, 327,* 741–744.

Gigerenzer, G. & Engel, C. (Eds.). (2006). *Heuristics and the Law.* Cambridge, MA: MIT Press.

Gigerenzer, G. & Goldstein, D. G. (1996). Reasoning the fast and frugal way: Models of bounded rationality. *Psychological Review, 104,* 650–669.

Gigerenzer, G., Hoffrage, U., & Goldstein, D. G. (2008). Fast and frugal heuristics are plausible models of cognition: Reply to Dougherty, Franco-Watkins, & Thomas (2008). *Psychological Review, 115,* 230–239.

Gigerenzer, G., Todd, P. M., & the ABC Research Group. (1999). *Simple Heuristics That Make Us Smart.* New York: Oxford University Press.

Goldstein, D. G. & Gigerenzer, G. (1999). The recognition heuristic: How ignorance makes us smart. In G. Gigerenzer, P. M. Todd, & the ABC Research Group, *Simple Heuristics That Make Us Smart* (pp. 37–48). New York: Oxford University Press.

Goldstein, D. G. & Gigerenzer, G. (2002). Models of ecological rationality: The recognition heuristic. *Psychological Review, 109,* 75–90.

Green, L. & Mehr, D. R. (1997). What alters physicians' decisions to admit to the coronary care unit? *The Journal of Family Practice, 45,* 219–226.

Hauser, J. R. & Wernerfelt, B. (1990). An evaluation cost model of consideration sets. *The Journal of Consumer Research, 16,* 393–408.

Hertwig, R., Herzog, S. M., Schooler, L. J., & Reimer, T. (2008). Fluency heuristic: A model of how the mind exploits a by-product of information retrieval. *Journal of Experimental Psychology: Learning, Memory & Cognition, 34,* 1191–1206.

Hertwig, R., Hoffrage, U., & Martignon, L. (1999). Quick estimation: Letting the environment do the work. In G. Gigerenzer, P. M. Todd, & the ABC Research Group, *Simple Heuristics That Make Us Smart* (pp. 209–234). New York: Oxford University Press.

Hertwig, R., Pachur, T., & Kurzenhäuser, S. (2005). Judgments of risk frequencies: Tests of possible cognitive mechanisms. *Journal of Experimental Psychology: Learning, Memory, and Cognition, 31,* 621–642.

Hertwig, R. & Todd, P. M. (2003). More is not always better: The benefits of cognitive limits. In D. Hardman & L. Macchi (Eds.), *Thinking: Psychological Perspectives on Reasoning, Judgment and Decision Making* (pp. 213–231). Chichester, England: Wiley.

Hoffrage, U., Lindsey, S., Hertwig, R., & Gigerenzer, G. (2000, December 15). Communication of statistical information. *Science, 290,* 2261–2262.

Hogarth, R. M. & Karelaia, N. (2005). Simple models for multiattribute choice with many alternatives: When it does and does not pay to face trade-offs with binary attributes. *Management Science, 51,* 1860–1872.

Hogarth, R. M. & Karelaia, N. (2007). Heuristic and linear models of judgment: Matching rules and environments. *Psychological Review, 114*, 733–758.

Howard, J. A. & Sheth, J. N. (1969). *The Theory of Buyer Behavior.* New York: John Wiley.

Hsee, C. K. & Hastie, R. (2006). Decision and experience: Why don't we choose what makes us happy? *Trends in Cognitive Sciences, 10*, 31–37.

Hutchinson, J. M. C. & Gigerenzer, G. (2005). Simple heuristics and rules of thumb: Where psychologists and behavioural biologists might meet. *Behavioural Processes, 69*, 87–124.

Jacobs, A. M. & Grainger, J. (1994). Models of visual word recognition: Sampling the state of the art. *Journal of Experimental Psychology: Human Perception and Performance, 20*, 1311–1334.

Jacoby, L. L. & Brooks, L. R. (1984). Nonanalytic cognition: Memory, perception and concept learning. In G. H. Bower (Ed.), *Psychology of Learning and Motivation* (Vol. 18, pp. 1–47). New York: Academic Press.

Jacoby, L. L. & Dallas, M. (1981). On the relationship between autobiographical memory and perceptual learning. *Journal of Experimental Psychology: General, 110*, 306–340.

Joachims, T., Granka, L., Pan, B., Hembrooke, H., & Gay, G. (2005). Accurately interpreting clickthrough data as implicit feedback. In *Proceedings of the Conference on Research and Development in Information Retrieval* (SIGIR), 2005. Online. Retrieved April 27, 2008, from www.cs.cornell.edu/People/tj/publications/joachims_etal_05a.pdf.

Kahneman, D., Slovic, P., & Tversky, A. (Eds.). (1982). *Judgment Under Uncertainty: Heuristics and Biases.* Cambridge, UK: Cambridge University Press.

Katsikopoulos, K. & Martignon, L. (2006). On the accuracy of lexicographic strategies for pair comparison. *Journal of Mathematical Psychology, 50*, 116–122.

Katz, E., Blumler, J. G., & Gurevitch, M. (1974). Utilization of mass communication by the individual. In J. G. Blumler & E. Katz (Eds.), *The Uses of Mass Communications: Current Perspectives on Gratifications Research* (pp. 19–32). Beverly Hills, CA: Sage Publications.

LaRose, R., Mastro, D., & Eastin, M. S. (2001). Understanding Internet usage: A social-cognitive approach to uses and gratifications. *Social Science Computer Review, 19*, 395–413.

Lee, M. D., Loughlin, N., & Lundberg, I. B. (2002). Applying one reason decision-making: The prioritisation of literature searches. *Australian Journal of Psychology, 54*, 137–143.

Lopes, L. L. (1991). The rhetoric of irrationality. *Theory & Psychology, 1*, 65–82.

Lopes, L. L. (1992). Three misleading assumptions in the customary rhetoric of the bias literature. *Theory & Psychology, 2*, 231–236.

Marewski, J. N., Gaissmaier, W., Schooler, L. J., Goldstein, D. G., & Gigerenzer, G. (2008). Models of recognition-based multi-alternative inference.

Marewski, J. N. & Olsson, H. (2009). Beyond the null ritual: Formal modeling of psychological processes. *Journal of Psychology, 217*, 49–60.

Marewski, J. N. & Schooler, L. J. (2008). How memory aids strategy selection. Manuscript submitted for publication.

Martignon, L. & Hoffrage, U. (1999). Why does one-reason decision making work? A case study in ecological rationality. In G. Gigerenzer, P. M. Todd, & the ABC

Research Group, *Simple Heuristics That Make Us Smart* (pp. 119–140). New York: Oxford University Press.

Mata, R., Schooler, L. J., & Rieskamp, J. (2007). The aging decision maker: Cognitive aging and the adaptive selection of decision strategies. *Psychology and Aging*, 22, 796–810.

Miller, G. F. & Todd, P. M. (1998). Mate choice turns cognitive. *Trends in Cognitive Sciences*, 2, 190–198.

Newell, B. R. & Fernandez, D. (2006). On the binary quality of recognition and the inconsequentiality of further knowledge: Two critical test of the recognition heuristic. *Journal of Behavioral Decision Making*, 19, 333–346.

Ortmann, A., Gigerenzer, G., Borges, B., & Goldstein, D. G. (2008). The recognition heuristic: A fast and frugal way to investment choice? In C. R. Plott & V. L Smith (Eds.), *Handbook of Experimental Economics Results*: Vol. 7 (pp. 993–1003). Amsterdam: North-Holland.

Pachur, T. & Biele, G. (2007). Forecasting from ignorance: The use and usefulness of recognition in lay predictions of sports events. *Acta Psychologica*, 125, 99–116.

Pachur, T. & Hertwig, R. (2006). On the psychology of the recognition heuristic: Retrieval primacy as a key determinant of its use. *Journal of Experimental Psychology: Learning, Memory, and Cognition*, 32, 983–1002.

Pachur, T., Bröder, A., & Marewski, J. N. (2008). The recognition heuristic in memory-based inference: Is recognition a non-compensatory cue? *Journal of Behavioral Decision Making*, 21, 183–210.

Pirolli, P. L. & Card, S. K. (1999) Information foraging. *Psychological Review*, 106, 643–675.

Pitt, M. A., Myung, I. J., & Zhang, S. (2002). Toward a method for selecting among computational models for cognition. *Psychological Review*, 109, 472–491.

Pohl, R. (2006). Empirical tests or the recognition heuristic. *Journal of Behavioral Decision Making*, 19, 251–271.

Reimer, T. & Katsikopoulos, K. V. (2004). The use of recognition in group decision-making. *Cognitive Science*, 28, 1009–1029.

Rieskamp, J. & Hoffrage, U. (1999). When do people use simple heuristics and how can we tell? In G. Gigerenzer, P. M. Todd, & the ABC Research Group, *Simple Heuristics That Make Us Smart* (pp. 141–167). New York: Oxford University Press.

Rieskamp, J. & Hoffrage, U. (2008). Inferences under time pressure: How opportunity costs affect strategy selection. *Acta Psychologica*, 127, 258–276.

Rieskamp, J. & Otto, P. (2006). SSL: A theory of how people learn to select strategies. *Journal of Experimental Psychology: General*, 135, 207–236.

Roberts, S. & Pashler, H. (2000). How persuasive is a good fit? A comment on theory testing. *Psychological Review*, 107, 358–367.

Savage, L. J. (1954). *The Foundations of Statistics*. New York: Wiley.

Scheibehenne, B. & Bröder, A. (2007). Predicting Wimbledon 2005 tennis results by mere player name recognition. *International Journal of Forecasting*, 23, 415–426.

Schooler, L. J. & Hertwig, R. (2005). How forgetting aids heuristic inference. *Psychological Review*, 112, 610–628.

Schwartz, B., Ward, A. H., Monterosso, J., Lyubomirsky, S., White, K., & Lehman, D. (2002). Maximizing versus satisficing: Happiness is a matter of choice. *Journal of Personality and Social Psychology*, 83, 1178–1197.

Sedlmeier, P., Hertwig, R., & Gigerenzer, G. (1998). Are judgments of the positional frequencies of letters systematically biased due to availability? *Journal of Experimental Psychology: Learning, Memory, and Cognition, 24,* 754–770.

Serwe, S. & Frings, C. (2006). Who will win Wimbledon? The recognition heuristic in predicting sports events. *Journal of Behavioral Decision Making, 19,* 321–332.

Simon, H. A. (1956). Rational choice and the structure of the environment. *Psychological Review, 63,* 129–138.

Simon, H. A. (1983). *Reason in Human Affairs.* Stanford, CA: Stanford University Press.

Simon, H. A. (1990). Invariants of human behavior. *Annual Review of Psychology, 41,* 1–19.

Simon, H. A. (1997). *Models of Bounded Rationality, Vol. 3.* Cambridge, MA: MIT Press.

Snook, B. & Cullen, R. M. (2006). Recognizing national hockey league greatness with an ignorance-based heuristic. *Canadian Journal of Experimental Psychology, 60,* 33–43.

Suls, J., Martin, R., & Wheeler, L. (2002). Social comparison: Why, with whom, and with what effect? *Current Directions in Psychological Science, 11,* 159–163.

Todd, P. M. & Gigerenzer, G. (2000). Précis of *Simple Heuristics That Make Us Smart. Behavioral and Brain Sciences, 23,* 727–741.

Todd, P. M. & Miller, G. F. (1999). From pride and prejudice to persuasion: Realistic heuristics for mate search. In G. Gigerenzer, P. M. Todd, & the ABC Research Group, *Simple Heuristics That Make Us Smart* (pp. 287–308). New York: Oxford University Press.

Toth, J. P. & Daniels, K. A. (2002). Effects of prior experience on judgments of normative word frequency: Automatic bias and correction. *Journal of Memory and Language, 46,* 845–874.

Tversky, A. (1972). Elimination by aspects: A theory of choice. *Psychological Review, 79,* 281–299.

Tversky, A. & Kahneman, D. (1973). Availability: A heuristic for judging frequency and probability. *Cognitive Psychology, 5,* 207–232.

Tversky, A. & Kahneman, D. (1974). Judgment under uncertainty: Heuristics and biases. *Science, 185,* 1124–1130.

Volz, K. G., Schooler, L. J., Schubotz, R. I., Raab, M., Gigerenzer, G., & Cramon, D. Y. von. (2006). Why you think Milan is larger than Modena: Neural correlates of the recognition heuristic. *Journal of Cognitive Neuroscience, 18,* 1924–1936.

Webster, J. G. (2006). Audience flow past and present: Television inheritance effects reconsidered. *Journal of Broadcasting & Electronic Media, 50,* 323–337.

Webster, J. G. & Wakshlag, J. (1985). Measuring exposure to television. In D. Zillmann & B. Jennings (Eds.), *Selective Exposure to Communication* (pp. 35–62). Hillsdale, NJ: Lawrence Erlbaum Associates.

Whittlesea, B. W. A. (1993). Illusions of familiarity. *Journal of Experimental Psychology: Learning, Memory, and Cognition, 19,* 1235–1253.

Zillmann, D. & Bryant, J. (1985). Affect, mood, and emotion as determinants of selective exposure. In D. Zillmann & B. Jennings (Eds.), *Selective Exposure to Communication* (pp. 157–190). Hillsdale, NJ: Lawrence Erlbaum Associates.

Chapter 8

Cognitive Dissonance Theory— A Roller Coaster Career

How Communication Research Adapted the Theory of Cognitive Dissonance[1]

Wolfgang Donsbach

Prologue: Psychology and Communications

The field of communications today is still a relatively young discipline that is seen by some as a scientific parvenu whose right of existence is called into question. For many, Ferdinand Tönnies' statement at the annual meeting of the German Association of Sociology in 1929 still applies when he responded to the proposal to establish a press science ("Zeitungswissenschaft") alongside sociology. His answer: Why would one need it? The universities also do not have a chicken and duck science besides in biology either. Today, the field searches its identity via the social importance of the phenomena it is dealing with: social communication and particularly mediated communication (Donsbach, 2006). In its self-understanding as an "integrative science," i.e. a field that integrates methods, theories and findings from many other disciplines, it indeed shares most of its inter-disciplinary connections with psychology. The significant role of psychology for the development of communications has mainly two reasons.

First, fundamental progress in our explanatory knowledge of the communication processes could only happen because we adapted concepts, theories, and methods of psychology. For instance, psychological phenomena are found in all phases of the communication process: in the production of media content the predispositions of journalists, their subjective attitudes, group-dynamic processes, and the collective formation of opinions are playing an important role. During the reception process, psychological approaches come into play in the exposure to and the processing of information (e.g., in the concepts of attention, of selective exposure, the elaboration-likelihood model, or schema theory). Finally, psychological concepts are of utmost importance in media effects research. It starts with early persuasion research (particularly Hovland's "scientific rhetoric") and does not end with excitation theories, mood management, psychological predispositions for and effects of violence in the media, or the priming approach. However, contrary to the past, the influx of personnel from psychology has no longer the same importance as in the early days of communication research. Today, communication researchers are predominantly socialized in their own field and the majority of authors who have published in our academic journals are teaching at communication departments. However, although today there is a strong self-recruitment of the field, basic psychological knowledge still plays an important role and is often taught in the curricula of the communication field itself.

A second aid besides the supply of theory and evidence on the level of explanatory knowledge could be referred to as "epistemological mentoring of communications by psychology." Particularly in Germany, communications was traditionally influenced by historical and cultural approaches, inter alia by the continuation of pre-war traditions (e.g. Emil Dovifat). The epistemological turnaround took place in the mid-1960s. The adaptation of American research and of psychological methodology were particularly influential. Both implied the use of systematic, quantitative methods, the striving for intersubjectivity, and the awareness that one needs different methods, but not a different philosophy of science in order to analyze human beings and social issues instead of phenomena of nature.

In most parts of the discipline the awareness prevailed that the underlying social legitimization of the scientific system consists in distinguishing true from untrue statements, thus to develop and apply clear criteria for separation. Only this distinguishes science from other social systems that make assertion about reality-like literature or politics and is therefore its basis of legitimacy. For many, psychology (at least its dominant paradigm) was a beacon on which to orientate. Today communications is epistemologically more or less divided, as is the case in psychology. A survey of the members of the International Communication Association (ICA) shows some positive tendencies in that respect: the younger the members, the more they feel constrained by the quantitative-social scientific tradition. But the survey also revealed just how deep the rift is between the regions of the world in terms of their understanding of science (Donsbach, 2006).

Today, there is a reasonable division of labor between the two fields. Communications has not been primarily interested in the way people process information, but rather in the input and output to this processing, whereas input can be understood as media content and output as specific uses or effects of the media. The black box between these two remains largely unopened by communication scholars. In contrast, psychology is less interested in real settings and contents of the world of communication, and for the most part not in the mass media either, but its interests lie in the basic processes of human processing of information. However, more precise hypotheses in communications as well as more relevant examples in psychology can be generated through the cooperation of both disciplines.

When speaking about the relationship between both disciplines, one inevitably arrives at the theory of cognitive dissonance. No other theory, as will be shown, played a bigger role in the development of media effects research and no other theory is entrenched so deeply in the common knowledge of communication scientists and practitioners.

The Formation of a Research Myth

> By and large about two-thirds of the constant partisans—the people who were either Republican or Democratic from May right through to Election Day—managed to see and hear more of their own side's propaganda than the opposition's. About one-fifth of them happened to expose more frequently to the other side, and the rest were neutral in their exposure. But—and this is important—the more strongly partisan the person, the more likely he is to insulate himself from contrary points of view.
>
> (Lazarsfeld, Berelson, & Gaudet, 1944, p. 89)

With this statement the paradigm of weak media effects was born. Its basic presumption was: People selectively expose themselves to media contents according to their predispositions. The findings of the two-step-flow of communication and the role of opinion leaders stand in this context. A few years later Klapper formulated the "bolstering effect," which became standard knowledge of communications: The news media would not be able to change the opinions of people, but only bolster existing opinions This paradigm dominated the notions about media effects for three decades. However, even then these statements constituted an unreasonable simplification. As Brosius (2002) shows, the same effects size of about 8–10 percent "converted recipients" was used to indicate once strong media effects (in the "Invasion from Mars" panic) and to indicate weak media effects (in "The People's Choice").

Hardly anybody knows that Lazarsfeld and his co-authors already noted the assumptions of dissonance theory in a footnote in "The People's Choice": "The fact that people select their exposure along the line of their political predispositions is only a special case of a more general law which pervades the whole field of communication research. Exposure is always selective; in other words, a positive relationship exists between people's opinions and what they choose to listen or to read" (Lazarsfeld et al. 1944, p. 164). Thus, dissonance theory was already there in a nutshell but it was not before Festinger's publication in 1957 that it became a dominant paradigm for the perception of media exposure and effects.

Five rather non-scientific criteria can be accounted for explaining the success of this paradigm of weak media effects:

1. The paradigm of weak media effects fulfilled the normative expectations with respect to the political system. Elihu Katz (1987) writes: "Lazarsfeld and company concluded that it is a good thing for democracy that people can fend off media influence and implied that the crowd may be

less lonely and less vulnerable than mass society theorists had led us to believe … Twenty five years after the last of the decision studies was published, the model of limited effects is acclaimed as the dominant paradigm, but one that has exhausted its welcome, or worse, led the field astray" (p. 26 et sq.).

2. The paradigm also fulfilled the normative expectations with respect to the image of human beings. Raymond Bauer commented on that in "The obstinate audience": The opening sentence of Ethical Standards of Psychologist is that "the psychologist is committed to a belief in the dignity and worth of the individual human being." But what kind of dignity can we attribute to a robot (Bauer, 1964, p. 31). The more people select media contents according to their own opinions and needs, the less "robot-like" and the more free they are—completely congruent with our occidental ideal of man.

3. Furthermore, the paradigm corresponded with the image of the human being in market economy. Biocca writes: "The analogy was an attractive one because it made the media-audience transaction fit so neatly into the logic of American socio-economics. It hailed the sovereign consumer in the communications marketplace" (Biocca, 1988, p. 70). In other words: in the perception of the highly selective citizens, medium and recipient are equal partners in the market for attention.

4. The paradigm of weak media effects also made rising questions about the legitimacy of journalists' and the media's social power less prevalent. It is not surprising that of all people CBS media researcher Klapper proposed and propagated the bolstering hypothesis.

5. And finally, findings of the still young field of communications could be incorporated into those of another, more established discipline. Communications—in Germany at that time still "newspaper studies" in humanities and in a modern epistemological sense "theoryless"—suddenly had the opportunity to dock at a relatively complex construct of theory. Therefore, Festinger spoke of "borrowed theory development" 13 years later.

The result was an uncritical simplification of the theory in communications, for which a quote from the textbook by Severin and Tankard can stand as an example: "The three selective processes can be thought of as three rings of defenses, with selective exposure being the outermost ring, selective perception coming in the middle, and selective retention being the innermost ring. Undesirable information can sometimes be headed off at the outermost ring. A person can just avoid those publications or programs that might contain contrary information. If this fails, the person can exercise selective perception in decoding the message. If this fails, the person can exercise selective retention, and just not retain the contrary information" (Severin & Tankard, 1979, p. 137).

Research History

Ups and Downs

Leon Festinger proposed the following hypothesis at the beginning of his book: "The basic hypotheses I wish to state are as follows: 1. The existence of dissonance, being psychologically uncomfortable, will motivate the person to try to reduce the dissonance and achieve consonance. 2. When dissonance is present, in addition to trying to reduce it, the person will actively avoid situations and information which would likely increase the dissonance" (Festinger, 1957, p. 3). Furthermore he defined "dissonance" as "Two elements are in a dissonant relationship if, considering these two alone, the obverse of one element would follow from the other" (p. 13).

This was initially received euphorically in psychology and strengthened the already existing paradigm of consistency theories. Almost at the same time Heider's Balance Model (Heider, 1946) as well as the Consistency Model by Osgood and Tannenbaum (1955) were developed (see Zajonc, 1960 for an overview). They are all based on the "law of good gestalts." This law emanated from Gestalt Psychology and assumes a perception of environmental stimuli that strives for simplicity and order (Wertheimer, 1922).

Furthermore, these approaches were characterized by a type of pre-scientific, everyday life persuasiveness. The result were dozens of studies whose evidence, however, remained all in all unclear. Ensuing was a radical cooling-down, which was evidenced by a sharp decrease in the number of consistency theory studies. During the 1980s the theory in particular was loosing attractiveness (Bagby, Parker, & Bury, 1990). At the same time the original theoretical assumptions were increasingly revised and altered. For instance, Aronson (1968, 1969) in his "self-consistency theory" identifies in the striving of an individual for self-consistency a necessary specification of the dissonance theory. Steele and Liu (1981, 1983; Steele, 1988) in their model of "self-affirmation" consider the process of dissonance reduction independently from the reduction of existing inconsistencies with respect to self-affirmation. Cooper and Fazio (1984) in their "new look model" specify the preconditions for the emergence of dissonance and limit the validity of the theory to actions that produce aversive consequences.

These new perspectives apparently raised again awareness for the theory (Aronson, 1992) and led to the theory being intensely discussed in the 1990s. There are two indicators for this: on the one hand the increased reference to Festinger's basic assumptions such as by Beauvois and Joule (1996, 1999) with their "radical dissonance theory." Although this theory should be seen as a revision; it aims at an return to the original theory but with regard to an alternative understanding of Festinger's basic assumptions. On the other hand there has been an increased effort for integration of contradicting approaches within dissonance research, as it is done by Stone and Cooper

(2001) and Stone (2002) with the "self-standards model": This model aims at an integration of the revisions of dissonance theory with the original theory in a superordinate approach through differentiation of miscellaneous self-standards and cognitive processes deriving from them (Stone & Cooper, 2001).

Theoretical Problems

With respect to the theoretical problems of the theory of cognitive dissonance the dictum circulated: "If you want to be sure ask Leon." According to Irle and Möntman (1978) the theory had two main problems. First, it made no difference between simple cognitions (or "protocols") and hypotheses-cognitions (more general cognitions, norms, laws, etc.). But these two versions could exhibit different strengths in the system of cognitions and therefore display various effects with respect to the tendency to reduce or avoid dissonance in different situations. Both types of cognitions could also come from the individual's environment and affect the individual. The second problem derives from the role of the search for consonant and the avoidance of dissonant information: from the state of dissonance only the search can logically follow, but not the avoidance of information, because only the active search can reduce the state of tension. In a state of consonance, however, only avoidance is reasonable, because every search can create dissonance. Both, according to critics, are examined indiscriminately in Festinger's writings and studies.

Festinger struggled with the basal distinctions of human behavior in achieving/saving of pivotal goals and the quitting/avoidance of harmful or unpleasant situations for a basal law of the psychology of the human being. This concept has been prevalent in the sciences for a long time, for example in the antagonism of defense vs. working through (Freud, 1958/1914), perceptual defense vs. perceptual vigilance (Bruner & Postman, 1947), avoidance vs. vigilance (Cohen & Lazarus, 1973), repression vs. sensitization (Byrne, 1964), or selective inattention vs. selective attention (Kahnemann, 1973). However, Festinger never succeeded in establishing a general law of psychology.

Methodological Problems of Early Dissonance Research

The early dissonance research shows several methodological problems. There are three problems with respect to internal validity. (1) Concerning the *problem of direct validity* the question was raised many times whether other variables, other than dissonance, have been generated and measured that led to the same behavior. One example would be the degree of dogmatism of an individual. (2) The *problem of control* poses the question whether all variables that could have affected a given selection (e.g. the curiosity of a person) really have been controlled and measured in the experiments. (3) The *problem of reduction* alludes to the question whether the theory and the experiments that derived from it might have simplified the cognitive system of an individual in an unreasonable way. For example, a cognition can be dissonant with another, but consonant with yet a third cognition; a fact that most experiments did not consider.

Methodological problems did also arise with respect to external validity. For instance, there have always been doubts whether it is possible to generalize the results, first because most subjects in the experiments were students who, on average, are more tolerant than the rest of the population, and second because the stimuli used in the experiments were often rather irrelevant topics. With respect to measurement the problem arose how to operationalize and measure the gradation of the strength of dissonance in the experiment. Most of the time it was measured only dichotomously and not on a scale although already in his 1957 publication Festinger had pointed to the fact that the assumed effects are not linear. Today, a gradation of intensity would be easier by using the seven-scaled "dissonance-thermometer" (Elliot & Devine, 1994). Further, most of the studies had to face the aforementioned problem of distinguishing the search for from the avoidance of information (Donsbach, 1991a, p. 90).

A stab in the back of sorts was the contribution by Freedman and Sears in the well-known "TOCCAS-volume" (Abelson et al., 1968). The authors conducted a meta-analysis of 18 studies on selective exposure. In five studies the subjects preferred consonant information, in five other dissonant information, and in eight studies no significant differences occurred. The conclusion of the authors: a general psychological effect of dissonance with respect to the selection of information cannot be established.

In subsequent psychological research some methodical innovations were made. For example, the physiological confirmation of dissonance as a state of tension during the exposure to dissonant information (Donohew & Palmgreen, 1971) became possible by using a skin-galvanometer. Dissonance as a motivational condition could be measured through EEG-measurement (Harmon-Jones, 2004) or specific interviews (Elliot & Devine, 1994). As early as 1967 Brock and Balloun were able to measure the avoidance of dissonant information during an ongoing process of communication for the first time: subjects could oppress elements of a text displayed to them by pushing a button. Another methodical innovation was the possibility to measure sequential instead of simultaneous selection of information in an experiment (Jonas, Schulz-Hardt, Frey, & Thelen, 2001).

Furthermore, there were less "confounding variables" in later research. Especially curiosity, intellectual honesty, utility of information, and attractiveness of alternatives were better controlled. A couple of recent studies provide evidence for the positive relationship between the relevance of attitude and the selection of information in favor of one's own predispositions

(Holbrook, Berent, Krosnick, Visser, & Boninger, 2005; Knobloch-Westerwick, 2007).

On the theoretical side, the history of the dissonance theory can be described as an ongoing narrowing of the original hypothesis through intervening variables, whereby the scope of the basic hypotheses has become narrower over time. Figure 8.1 shows some of the most important intervening variables and allocates them to bearers and the phases of the communication process, respectively.

Frey (1984) referred to Festinger's theory as the "most influential of all cognitive dissonance theories that emanated from Gestalt-psychology" (p. 243) and at the same time as "one of the most controversial theories in social psychology" (p. 280). This ambivalence, which practically led to two camps of supporters and opponents, is surely partly responsible—as Greenwald and Ronis (1978, p. 55) ironically noticed—for its scientific history having run a course as if those who dealt with the theory wanted to prove it through their own behavior. In other words: the proponents did not take note of successful falsifications and the opponents did not notice the confirmed results.

Over 30 years after Sears and Freedman, D'Alessio and Allen conducted another meta-analysis. Their starting point was a methodical critique of the early analysis of Freedman and Sears: these 18 studies did not fulfill all necessary criteria for a statistical meta-analysis, especially since in some cases controlled experimental conditions have not been existent and some situations of decision fell short of theoretical requirements. Their new meta-analysis consisted of 16 studies (1956–1996) with 1922 subjects overall. Requirement for an inclusion in the meta-analysis was that the studies dealt with Festinger's assumptions and fulfilled the following four criteria: (1) a controlled situation (laboratory experiment); (2) the manipulation of a cognitive element (attitude, belief, opinion), which is applied in a situation of choice; (3) the demand for selection by the test persons with respect to an information offered; and (4) disclosure of statistical results. These rigorous criteria led to the exclusion of field studies, studies that conducted mood manipulation, and studies that did not offer situations in which choices, by which dissonance could be initiated or demonstrated, could be made.

The correlation between attitude and selection of consonant or dissonant information, respectively, was highly significant with a correlation coefficient of .22, however relatively low. This shows that the effect of one's own attitude on the selection of information according to Festinger's assumptions exists, but that it is relatively marginal so that feelings of dissonance have a rather low effect on selection.

Paradoxically, there was a revival of the theory of cognitive dissonance in psychology in the last years, whereas in communications, which had adapted and sustained this theory so euphorically, dissonance theory disappeared almost completely from the academic scene. Harmon-Jones and Mills did a cash check of sorts in 1999: the research today agrees with the original

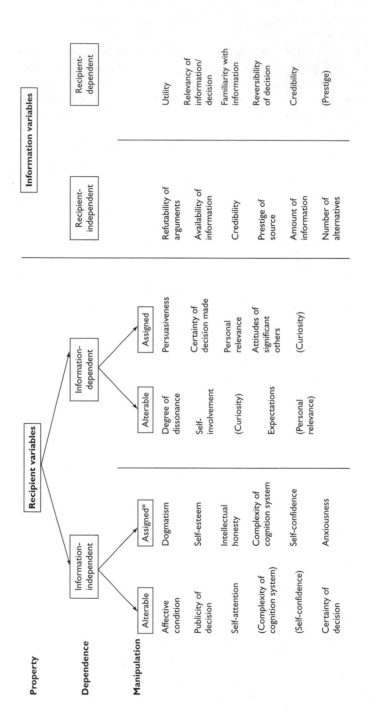

Figure 8.1 Intervening variables in the course of dissonance research.

Note

* "Assigned variables" cannot be altered, at least in the medium term, i.e., not during the experiment. In some cases the classification is not clear-cut.

assumption that dissonance was a "psychological discomfort" (Cooper & Fazio, 1984; Elliot & Devine, 1994; Harmon-Jones, 2000a, 2000b, 2004). However, there are different assessments with respect to the explanation of cause and the consequences of action. They demand to always consider cognitive, emotional, motivational, and behavioristic aspects in a situation under investigation.

Mills (1999) makes a revision of dissonance theory in three respects: (1) the differential effects of positive and negative information always has to be considered. In studies on the influence of the degree of dissonance on selective behavior Mills emphasized as early as 1965 (1965a, 1965b) that the strength of dissonance indeed results in a more intensive search for consonant information but not an increased avoidance of dissonant information. (2) Contrary to Festinger, Mills assumes—following the Choice Certainty Theory—that dissonances can appear through the anticipation of an action's consequences even before a decision is made to act a certain way. (3) Furthermore, Mills demands to factor in other cognitions that are in relationship with the two core cognitions.

Festinger's personal hope to establish the theory of cognitive dissonance as a general psychological-biological law that applies to all living creatures (as his dissonance-theoretical experiments with rats show, see Lawrence & Festinger, 1962)[2] has clearly failed. What remains is the question whether human beings generally strive for reduction or avoidance of inconsistency in their cognitions. Such Aronson already assumed in the "TOCCAS-volume" (1968, p. 26): "man cannot live by consonance alone" and Frey already listed three other theories in 1984 that are "all more or less aiming at substituting the dissonance theory completely or in part": "impression management theory" by Tedeschi (1981) among others (it traced back the findings of dissonance research to the human desire to present the social environment in a continuous, consistent character) (Tedeschi, Schlenker, & Bonoma, 1971); "self-perception theory" by Bem (1965 and others (it does not trace back cognitive changes to the existence of a state of dissonance, but explains it with the human ability to infer internal conditions from external factors); and the "curiosity and complexity theories" (see Berlyne, 1968 among others). In contrast to consistency theories they explain human behavior with the need for variety, surprise, and complexity (Berlyne, 1960; Maddi, 1961). The tendency to produce coherence among present cognitions is one, but obviously not the only driving force for the dynamic of human attitudes and perceptions of reality.

Development in Communications

Contrary to the detection of media effects, which have been found to be strong in the laboratory but low or non-existent in the field, confirmations for selectivity explained by dissonance theory frequently failed in psychological laboratory research, whereas field research in communications found many, albeit methodically deficient, indications for the purported behavior. Both phenomena could be in relationship. The majority of laboratory experiments assumedly created too unrealistic situations in order to activate the safety shield of selective exposure.

Initially, non-experimental ex-post-facto studies dominated in communications, in which selective behavior opposite to media content was correlated with present attitudes. Typical examples were and still are the relations between political preferences of readers and the editorial biases of newspapers used by them. Such studies are still being published as on the basis of attitudes towards the Iraq war (Best, Chmielewski, & Krueger, 2005; see also Chaffee, Nichols Saphir, Graf, Sandvig, & Hahn, 2001; Jonas, Graupmann, Fischer, Greitemeyer, & Frey, 2003).

However, there have also been some early quasi-experimental and experimental studies in communications. One classic is the study by Stempel (1961). He parallelized articles in a university newspaper, in which the two candidates for the chair of the student union were introduced, in terms of length and content, so that with the exception of a left right bias the same formal preconditions for selection were given on the page. Subsequently, a sample of readers was surveyed about their candidate preferences and the intensity with which they had read the two articles. However, the fact that readers had to decide beforehand whether they would read the newspaper or not created a methodological problem. Furthermore, no distinction was made between an experimental and a control group. As a result one third of the surveyed readers had read more about the candidate they preferred than about the rival candidate. For only 2 percent, it was the other way around.

A similar study was conducted by Lowin (1967) who analyzed the influence of consonance and dissonance as well as refutability of counter arguments on the exposure to campaign brochures in the election campaign between Goldwater and Johnson. In his two experiments, brochures that contained stronger and weaker arguments in favor of and against the candidates were mailed to the test persons, with the sender being clearly recognizable. The test persons could request additional information about these arguments by using a reply card. The percentage of returned cards served as the dependent variable. The response rates for these cards was 18 percent in the first experiment and 29 percent in the second experiment, respectively. As a result the general hypothesis was confirmed, but, as was suggested by dissonance theory, in case of weak dissonance or easy refutability of arguments the test persons requested the campaign information to the same degree.

Similar in its design and its results is the study by Barlett, Drew, Fahle, and Watts (1974). Letters whose sender was consonant with the candidate preference of the voters were opened twice as often as letters whose sender supported the respective rival candidate. Nevertheless: despite their methodical shortcomings, the studies by Lowin and Barlett, because of their strong field character, allow to establish connections to mass communication. As opposed to most experiments in psychological research they measured the selection of offered information without the test persons being aware of their role as subjects in an experiment, which could have resulted in atypical behavior.

Besides these studies there have been few experiments up until the 1980s, but only one study that concerned a phenomenon of news exposure: Charles Atkins (1971) analyzed the influence of available information about several standpoints as well as dissonance and consonance on the exposure to articles in newspapers. He produced eight different front pages for a university newspaper that were different only in terms of layout and headline of an article. The degree of emphasis (position and length) and the bias of the headline with respect to the Republican and Democratic Party were varied (2 × 2 design with availability high-low/supportive-non-supportive). The results showed that supporters of both the Republican and the Democratic Party picked the articles that endorsed their opinions, even when the articles were only somewhat emphasized. Emphasis was the biggest determinant for selection only when the headlines were neutral. For headlines that suggested a bias with regards to content, consonance and dissonance between offered information and the respective opinion of the reader were the decisive variables.

However, the majority of studies was merely based on correlations: Wilhoit and de Bock (1976) about exposure to the TV show "Archie Bunker"; Sweeney and Gruber (1984) about the Watergate hearings; Paletz, Koon, Whitehead, and Hagens (1972) about a critical movie on the Vietnam War; or Donsbach (1984) about the perception of published poll data during an election campaign. Also merely measuring de-facto-selectivity, but being closer to the communication process is a field study by Noelle-Neumann (1973), in which selective exposure with respect to everyday life media information was measured by means of a copy-test. The study was conducted on the basis of articles of the "Tagesanzeiger" (Zurich, Switzerland) on the Vietnam War and reforms in domestic affairs. A strong correlation was detected: from all the readers that approved of the American policy in Vietnam 44 percent had read an article that dealt with the American commitment in a positive way, whereas the same article was read by only 26 percent of opponents of the Vietnam War. Conversely, a negative article on the American Vietnam policy was read by 43 percent of the opponents of the war and by only 11 percent of the supporters.

Control in the Field: Dissonance Study Under Real Conditions

A field study by the author aimed at providing evidence for the importance of consonance and dissonance under natural conditions of selection. In the study all potential contacts between approximately 1,400 readers of four daily newspapers and around 350 articles of these newspapers were analyzed on three consecutive days of publication. In order to identify the predispositions of the recipients we conducted an opinion survey of the readers of the four newspapers on current topics and people in the news in the three newspaper issues. In order to measure the bias of the contents the three issues of the four newspapers (as well as the coverage of the previous months) was analyzed by means of a quantitative content analysis. The third component of the study was a copy-test, with which we measured the exposure of the readers to the specific articles in the three issues.

Subsequently, we generated a new unit of analysis ("contact") out of every potential contact between a reader and an article. A total of 91,389 potential contacts constituted the basis for further data analysis. This new unit of analysis consisted of attributes of both the reader and the respective article and therefore could be analyzed—among other things—with respect to consonant and dissonant combinations. Figure 8.2 illustrates the structure of the so obtained dataset. Specifically this means, for instance, that consonant or dissonant combinations were derived from the positive or negative attitudes of a reader towards, e.g., the then German chancellor Helmut Kohl, on the one hand and from the positive or negative role of Kohl in an article on the other hand. The same applied to other politicians and a total of six different topics of conflict.

The central finding for articles in which political figures appear is a differential effect of consonance or dissonance on the exposure to these articles. Across both valences a significant but only small difference is detectable between the exposure to consonant and dissonant contacts. But if one distinguishes the data between positive and negative information about the politicians, the differences become very clear in case of positive information, whereas they are leveled in case of negative information. More specifically: the positive articles were read by 42 percent of the (consonant) supporters,

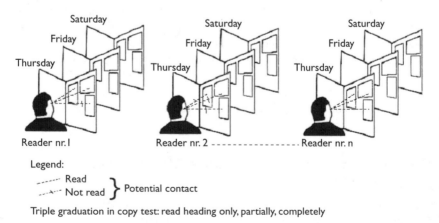

Figure 8.2 Logic of the unit of analysis.

but by only 31 percent of the (dissonant) opponents. In the case of a politician appearing in a negative role, there were virtually no differences (Figure 8.3). Thus, positive information about a politician has a considerably better chance to reach the politician's supporters than his or her opponents. This confirms previous results of surveys (see above) as well as the hypotheses of "automatic vigilance" (Pratto & John, 1991).

A number of variables, both with respect to journalistic work and the reader, are moderating the role of consonance and dissonance. The more cursory the newspaper is read every day, the bigger the selectivity in favor of the existing opinion. Furthermore, people with a high interest in politics read less selectively than do people with less or no such interest; in contrast, dogmatic persons read more selectively than tolerant ones. Selectivity in favor of one's own opinion is strongest with respect to only somewhat emphasized, i.e. disadvantageously placed and/or small, articles. The examination of photos showed a clear influence of consonant or dissonant attitudes as well. Photos on which politicians appeared favorable or likeable were viewed more often by the politicians' supporters (consonance) than by their opponents (dissonance). In contrast, opponents viewed unfavorable photos considerably more often (see Donsbach, 1991a, 1991b).

The Misunderstanding

The adaptation of cognitive dissonance in communication research probably constitutes one of the biggest misunderstandings in the history of social research. As is pointed out in chapter 3, Festinger made assertions about the

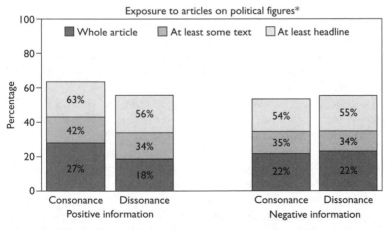

Figure 8.3 Differential effects of dissonance for positive and negative information (source: Donsbach, 1991).

Note
* Cumulated percentages including the next higher level of exposure.

state of dissonance in his hypotheses, but not about the state of consonance. Communications all but completely ignored this limitation. There is an easy explanation for this: the functional utilization of selectivity in order to reduce existing dissonance within a specific domain of the cognition system is not at the center of the interest of communication scholars. Within selection research in the field of communications media contents are not the potential instruments to reduce dissonance, but selectivity is an instrument to channel media contents according to one's own cognitive needs.

Thus, selective behavior in a non-suspense condition takes center stage in communications. We also do not regard dissonance as a normality of the recipient when he or she grabs the newspaper in the morning or watches the news at night. However, Festinger did not—as shown above—propose any hypotheses for this state of *non-existent dissonance*. Most studies in communications about the selection of information simply took the transferability of the basic hypothesis for granted with respect to this issue. It is relevant to communications whether selectivity in order to avoid dissonance can also occur in a state of consonance or is only used—as Festinger asserted—to reduce already existing dissonance. The following is a model how this problem can be solved.

Normally, one can assume a relatively consistent cognitive system for media recipients, in which no acute need for consonant information for the reduction of tension exists. In these cases one can conceive decisions of exposure as a *passive gatekeeper-situation*, in which recipients that are largely free of existing states of tension decide on the further processing of information that initially have the same chance to be considered. For example, if one keeps the degree of emphasis of articles constant, assumedly the appearance of a name or a term determines exposure in the fist phase of selection. Our results from the study mentioned above (Donsbach, 1991a, 1991b) suggest that information about politicians, on whom the reader has a positive opinion, evoke a higher interest and have a higher degree of attention than information about politicians whom the reader rather dislikes. In this first phase consonance and dissonance only play an inferior role.

In the second phase of selection the content and the tendency of the information presumably decide on further exposure first and foremost. Supporters of a politician or of a certain standpoint in an conflict issue read confirmative information intensely, but contradictory information less intensely. The opponents of a politician, who despite their low interest exposed themselves to an article, now continue reading with a higher probability if the provided information is negative, i.e. consonant for them. In other words, for supporters the dissonance that is linked to negative news puts the brakes on their initially higher interest; for the opponents the consonance linked to the same information has a rather strengthening effect on their initially lower interest. Reciprocally, positive information has a strengthening effect in the first case and a slowing-down effect in the second.

Communication scholars rarely concerned themselves explicitly with the question whether Festinger's theory of cognitive dissonance can actually be applied to the typical situation of the media user. This is in line with the aforementioned "input-output-orientation" of this discipline that is rather unconcerned about the intermediate processes in the *black box*. On the other hand, this could be seen as a reasonable division of labor between the disciplines. And finally, the rather coarse adaptation of Festinger's theory nevertheless delivered reasonable and important results about media use.

What the Theory is Still Offering Today

By now one receives the impression that the theory of cognitive dissonance experiences a revival in psychology, whereas it only sporadically appears in communications. Instead, the theory is assimilated by a variety of other disciplines. One example of this is Mood Management Theory. Festinger himself pointed out that consonance and dissonance are cognitive conditions that affect the mood: "The existence of dissonance, *being psychologically uncomfortable*, will motivate the person to try to reduce the dissonance and achieve consonance" (Festinger, 1957, p. 3). So it suggested itself that Dolf Zillmann not only referred to his Mood Management Theory as being "akin to Festinger's theory of selective exposure" (1988, p. 327), but even considered the theory of cognitive dissonance as being subordinate to his Mood Management Approach. One could view dissonance as a "bad mood that is produced by exposure to counterattitudinal persuasive messages" (Zillmann, 1988, p. 329).

Another example is the Information Utility Approach. The avoidance of dissonance is one among many considerations of utility that can motivate people to expose themselves to information from the mass media. "A message has an instrumental utility for the receiver when it provides him with a helpful input for responding to everyday environmental stimuli *or for defending personal predispositions*. He may need information to keep abreast of governmental actions, to guide his consumer decision-making, or to reinforce his political preferences" (Atkin, 1973, p. 205). Thus, a need to obtain information is generated when the individual perceives a discrepancy between his or her current and desired standard of knowledge ("criterion state") with respect to relevant issues. Atkins sees four basic types of requirements of adaptation of the individual to his or her environment, of which one is the "defensive adaptation," i.e. the motivation to erase uncertainties in one's own cognition system. Therein lies a distinct element of cognitive dissonance: "Post-cognitive uncertainty depends on the magnitude of the desire to verify cognitions currently in storage or recently learned. Similarly, the individual may not be confident that his firmly held attitudes or decisions are correct or appropriate … Each of these uncertainties resulting from self-doubt produces a need for reinforcement information" (Atkin, 1973, p. 208 et sq.).

One can expect a lot from an application of dissonance research on journalism as well. Journalists are under a considerable constraint to select and the possibility to decide in favor of one's own predispositions occurs for them in various phases, for example in the selection of issues to investigate, in the attention directed towards specific sections of speeches by politicians, in the observation of a politician's para-verbal behavior during the speech, in the spontaneous evaluation of the newsworthiness of wire reports, or in the evaluation of the relevance of a political event statement. Frey and Gaska (1993) found out that effects of dissonance on the selection of information can be expected even more strongly in groups than on the level of individuals. The strong in-group-orientation of journalists is known and confirmed (Donsbach 1982; Donsbach 2001; Crouse 1972). What this implies for the selection of media contents and the reality presented to the audience is an ever current question.

Communications has to take more cognizance of new developments in psychology including the new approaches of cognitive dissonance in that field. Today's regard for research on cognitive dissonance falls short of the current status of research in psychology. Perhaps a "normative bias"—as with the early adaptation of the rule of selection (see above)—plays a part in this: the paradigm of the active recipient within the framework of the general rational choice euphoria since the 1970s did not correspond with the actually irrational behavior the dissonance theory assumes. "Information utility" then is a euphonious and euphemistic term for the fact that one does not do exactly what is demanded by democracy theory, namely to be open to counter arguments. But the strong de-facto-selectivity, which has been repeatedly confirmed, shows that the phenomenon is still virulent and awaits further research.

Notes

1 A slightly different version of this text has been published in Trepte, S. & Witte, E. (2007). *Sozialpsychologie und Medien* [Social Psychology and the Media]. Lengerich u.a.: Pabst Science Publishers, pp. 11–34.
2 It concerns experiments in which dissonance was operationalized as the proportion/ratio between effort (running distance) and gratification (fodder). The bigger dissonance of the effort-gratification-ratio was compensated with a higher inducement of the fodder for rats that had to overcome a steeper slope.

References

Abelson, R.P., Aronson, E., McGuire, W.J., Newcomb, T.M., Rosenberg, M.J., & Tannenbaum, P.H. (Eds.). (1968). *Theories of Cognitive Consistency: A Sourcebook.* Chicago, IL: Rand-McNally.
Aronson, E. (1968). Dissonance theory: Progress and problems. In R. P. Abelson, E. Aronson, W. T. McGuire, T. M. Newcomb, M. J. Rosenberg, & P. H. Tannen-

baum (Eds.), *Theories of Cognitive Consistency: A Sourcebook* (pp. 5–27). Chicago: Rand McNally.

Aronson, E. (1969). The theory of cognitive dissonance: A current perspective. In L. Berkowitz (Ed.), *Advances in Experimental Social Psychology* (pp. 1–34). New York: Academic Press.

Aronson, E. (1992). The return of the repressed: Dissonance theory makes a comeback. *Psychological Inquiry*, 3, 303–311.

Atkin, C. K. (1971). How imbalanced campaign coverage affects audience exposure patterns. *Journalism Quarterly*, 48, 235–255.

Atkin, C. K. (1973). Instrumental utilities and information seeking. In P. Clarke (Ed.), *New Models for Communication Research* (pp. 205–242). Beverly Hills: Sage.

Bagby, R. M., Parker, J. D. A., & Bury, A. S. (1990). A comparative citation analysis of attribution theory and the theory of cognitive dissonance. *Personality and Social Psychology Bulletin*, 16(2), 274–283.

Barlett, D. L., Drew, P. B., Fahle, E. G., & Watts, W. A. (1974). Selective exposure to a presidential campaign appeal. *Public Opinion Quarterly*, 38, 264–270.

Bauer, R. A. (1964). The obstinate audience. *American Psychologist*, 19, 319–328.

Beauvois, J. L. & Joule, R. V. (1996). *A Radical Dissonance Theory*. Philadelphia, PA: Taylor and Francis.

Beauvois, J. L. & Joule, R. V. (1999). A radical point of view on dissonance theory. In E. Harmon-Jones & J. Mills (Eds.), *Cognitive Dissonance: Progress on a Pivotal Theory in Social Psychology* (pp. 43–70). Washington DC: A.P.A.

Bem, D. J. (1965). An experimental analysis of self-persuasion. *Journal of Experimental Social Psychology*, 1, 199–218.

Berlyne, D. E. (1960). *Conflict, Arousal, and Curiosity*. New York: McGraw-Hill.

Berlyne, D. E. (1968). The motivational significance of collative variables and conflict. In R. P. Abelson, E. Aronson, W. T. McGuire, T. M. Newcomb, M. J. Rosenberg, & P. H. Tannenbaum (Eds.), *Theories of Cognitive Consistency: A Sourcebook* (pp. 257–266). Chicago: Rand McNally.

Best, S. J., Chmielewski, B., & Krueger, B. S. (2005). Selective exposure to online foreign news during the conflict with Iraq. *Harvard International Journal of Press/Politics*, 10, 52–70.

Biocca, F. A. (1988). Opposing conceptions of the audience—the active and passive hemispheres of mass communication theory. In J. A. Anderson (Eds.), *Communication Yearbook*, 11, 51–80.

Brock, T. C. & Balloun, J. L. (1967). Behavioral receptivity to dissonant information. *Journal of Personality and Social Psychology*, 6, 413–428.

Brosius, H. B. (2002). Medienwirkung. In G. Bentele, H. B. Brosius, & O. Jarren (Eds.), *Öffentliche Kommunikation. Handbuch Kommunikation und Medienwissenschaft* (pp. 128–148). Wiesbaden: Westdeutscher Verlag.

Bruner, J. S. & Postman, L. (1947). Tension and tension-release as organizing factors in perception. *Journal of Personality*, 15, 300–308.

Byrne, D. (1964). Repression-sensitization on a dimension of personality. In B. A. Maher (Ed.), *Progress in Experimental Personality Research* Vol. 1 (pp. 169–220). New York: Academic Press.

Chaffee, S., Nichols Saphir, M., Graf, J., Sandvig, C., & Hahn, K. S. (2001). Attention to counter-attitudinal messages in a state election campaign. *Political Communication*, 18(3), 247–272.

Cohen, F. & Lazarus, R. S. (1973). Active coping processes, coping dispositions, and recovery from surgery. *Psychosomatic Medicine*, 35, 375–389.

Cooper, J. & Fazio, R. H. (1984). A New Look at Dissonance Theory. In L. Berkowitz (Ed.), *Advances in Experimental Social Psychology* (pp. 229–266). New York: Academic Press.

Crouse, T. (1972). *The Boys on the Bus: Riding with the Campaign Press Corps.* New York: Random House.

D'Alessio, D. & Allen, M. (2002). Selective exposure and dissonance after decisions. *Psychological Reports*, 91(2), 527–532.

Donohew, L. A. & Palmgreen, B. (1971). A reappraisal of dissonance and the selective exposure hypothesis. *Journalism Quarterly*, 48, 412–420, 437.

Donsbach, W. (1982). *Legitimationsprobleme des Journalismus. Gesellschaftliche Rolle der Massenmedien und berufliche Einstellungen von Journalisten.* Freiburg, München: Karl Alber.

Donsbach, W. (1984). Die Rolle der Demoskopie in der Wahlkampf-Kommunikation. *Zeitschrift für Politik*, 31, 388–407.

Donsbach, W. (1991a). *Medienwirkung trotz Selektion.* Köln, Wien, Weimar: Böhlau.

Donsbach, W. (1991b): Exposure to political content in newspapers: The impact of cognitive dissonance on readers' selectivity. *European Journal of Communication*, 6, 155–186.

Donsbach, W. (2001). Der kollektive Irrtum. Der Tod des kleinen Joseph: Warum Sebnitz zum Lehrstück über Journalismus wurde. *Wissenschaftliche Zeitschrift der TU Dresden*, 50(1/2), 27–28.

Donsbach, W. (2006). Presidential address: The identity of communication research. *Journal of Communication*, 56, 437–448.

Elliot, A. J. & Devine, P. G. (1994). On the motivational nature of cognitive dissonance: dissonance as psychological discomfort. *Journal of Personality and Social Psychology*, 67, 382–394.

Festinger, L. (1957). *A Theory of Cognitive Dissonance.* Stanford: Stanford University Press.

Freud, S. (1958). Remembering, repeating, and working-through. In J. Strachey (Ed.), *The Standard Edition of the Complete Psychological Works of Sigmund Freud Vol. 12* (pp. 145–150). London: Hogarth Press. (Originally published in 1914.)

Frey, D. (1984). Die Theorie der kognitiven Dissonanz. In M. Irle & D. Frey (Eds.), *Theorien der Sozialpsychologie, Volume 1: Kognitive Theorien* (pp. 243–292). Bern i.a.: Huber.

Frey, D. (1991). Informationssuche und Informationsbewertung bei Einzel- und Gruppenentscheidungen und mögliche Auswirkungen auf Politik und Wirtschaft. In D. Frey (Ed.), *Bericht über den 37. Kongreß der Deutschen Gesellschaft für Psychologie in Kiel 1990. Volume II* (pp. 45–56). Göttingen: Hogrefe.

Frey, D. & Gaska, A. (1993). Die Theorie der kognitiven Dissonanz. In D. Frey & M. Irle (Eds.), *Theorien der Sozialpsychologie. Volume I. Kognitive Theorien.* (2. Ed.) (pp. 275–324). Bern i.a.: Huber.

Greenwald, A. G. & Ronis, D. L. (1978). Twenty years of cognitive dissonance: A case study of the evolution of a theory. *Psychological Review*, 85(1), 53–57.

Harmon-Jones, E. (2000a). Cognitive dissonance and experienced negative affect: Evidence that dissonance increases experienced negative affect even in the absence of aversive consequences. *Personality and Social Psychology Bulletin* 26(12), 1490–1501.

Harmon-Jones, E. (2000b). A cognitive dissonance theory perspective on the role of emotion in the maintenance and change of beliefs and attitudes. In N. H. Frijda, A. R. S. Manstead, & S. Bem (Eds.), *Emotions and Beliefs* (pp. 185–211). Cambridge: Cambridge University Press.

Harmon-Jones, E. (2004). Contributions from research on anger and cognitive dissonance to understanding the motivational functions of asymmetrical frontal brain activity. *Biological Psychology*, 67, 51–76.

Heider, F. (1946). Attitudes and cognitive organization. *Journal of Psychology*, 21, 107–112.

Holbrook, A. L., Berent, M. K., Krosnick, J. A., Visser, P. S., & Boninger, D. S. (2005). Attitude importance and the accumulation of attitude-relevant knowledge in memory. *Journal of Personality and Social Psychology*, 88(5), 749–769.

Irle, M. & Möntmann, V. (1978). Die Theorie der kognitiven Dissonanz. Ein Resümee ihrer theoretischen Entwicklung und empirischen Ergebnisse 1957–1976. In M. Irle & V. Möntmann (Eds.), *L. Festinger: Theorie der kognitiven Dissonanz* (pp. 247–363). Bern: Huber.

Jonas, E., Graupmann, V., Fischer, P., Greitemeyer, T., & Frey, D. (2003). Schwarze Kassen, weiße Westen? Konfirmatorische Informationssuche und -bewertung im Kontext der Parteispendenaffäre der CDU. *Zeitschrift für Sozialpsychologie*, 34(1), 47–61.

Jonas, E., Schulz,-Hardt, S., Frey, D., & Thelen, N. (2001). Confirmation bias in sequential information search after preliminary decisions: An expansion of dissonance theoretical research on selective exposure to information. *Journal of Personality and Social Psychology*, 80(4), 557–571.

Kahnemann, D. (1973). *Attention and Effort*. Englewood Cliffs: Prentice Hall.

Katz, E. (1987). Communication research since Lazarsfeld. *Public Opinion Quarterly*, 51, 25–45.

Klapper, T. (1960). *The Effects of Mass Communication*. New York: Free Press.

Knobloch-Westerwick, S. (2007). Kognitive Dissonanz "Revisited." Selektive Zuwendung zu einstellungskonsistenten und -inkonsistenten politischen Informationen. *Publizistik*, 52(1), 51–62.

Lawrence, D. H. & Festinger, L. (1962). *Deterrents and Reinforcement: The Psychology of Insufficient Reward*. Stanford: Stanford University Press.

Lazarsfeld, P. F., Berelson, B., & Gaudet, H. (1944). *The People's Choice*. New York, London: Columbia University Press.

Lowin, A. (1967). Approach and avoidance: Alternative models of selective exposure to information. *Journal of Personality and Social Psychology*, 6, 1–9.

Maddi, S. R. (1961). Affective tone during environmental regularity and change. *Journal of Abnormal and Social Psychology*, 62, 338–345.

Mills, J. (1965a). Avoidance of dissonant information. *Journal of Personality and Social Psychology*, 2, 589–593.

Mills, J. (1965b). Effect of certainty about a decision upon postdecision exposure to consonant and dissonant information. *Journal of Personality and Social Psychology*, 2, 749–752.

Mills, J. (1968). Interest in supporting and discrepant information. In R. P. Abelson, E. Aronson, W. J. McGuire, T. M. Newcomb, M. J. Rosenberg, & P. H.

Tannenbaum (Eds.), *Theories of Cognitive Consistency: A Sourcebook* (pp. 771–776). Chicago: Rand McNally.

Mills, J. (1999). Improving the 1957 version of dissonance theory. In E. Harmon-Jones & J. Mills (Eds.), *Cognitive Dissonance: Progress on a Pivotal Theory in Social Psychology* (pp. 25–42). Washington: American Psychological Association.

Noelle-Neumann, E. (1973). Kumulation, Konsonanz und Öffentlichkeitseffekt. Ein neuer Ansatz zur Analyse der Wirkung von Massenmedien. *Publizistik*, 18, 26–55.

Osgood, E. E. & Tannenbaum, P. H. (1955). The principle of congruity in the prediction of attitude change. *Psychological Review*, 62, 42–55.

Paletz, D. L., Koon, J., Whitehead, E., & Hagens, R. B. (1972). Selective exposure: The potential boomerang effect. *Journal of Communication*, 22, 48–53.

Pratto, F. & John, O. P. (1991). Automatic vigilance: The attention-grabbing power of negative social information. *Journal of Personality and Social Psychology*, 61, 380–391.

Sears, D. O. & Freedman, J. L. (1967). Selective exposure to information: A critical review. *Public Opinion Quarterly*, 31, 194–213.

Severin, W. J. & Tankard, J. W. (1979). *Communication Theories: Origins, Methods, Uses.* New York: Hastings House.

Steele, C. M. (1988). The psychology of self-affirmation: Sustaining the integrity of the self. In R. F. Baumeister (Ed.), *The Self in Social Psychology: Key Readings in Social Psychology* (pp. 372–390). Philadelphia: Psychology Press.

Steele, C. M. & Liu, T. J. (1981). Making the dissonant act unreflective of self: Dissonance, avoidance, and the expectancy of a value-affirming response. *Journal of Personality and Social Psychology Bulletin*, 7(3), 393–397.

Steele, C. M. & Liu, T. J. (1983). Attitude and social cognition: Dissonance processes as self-affirmation. *Journal of Personality and Social Psychology*, 45(1), 5–19.

Stempel, G. H. (1961). Selectivity in readership of political news. *Public Opinion Quarterly*, 25, 400–404.

Stone, J. (2001). Behavioral discrepancies and the role of construal processes in cognitive dissonance. In G. B. Moskowitz (Eds.), *Cognitive Social Psychology: The Princeton Symposium on the Legacy and Future of Social Cognition* (pp. 41–58). Mahwah, NJ: Erlbaum.

Stone, J. & Cooper, J. (2001). A self-standards model of cognitive dissonance. *Journal of Experimental Social Psychology*, 37(2), 228–243.

Sweeney, P. D. & Gruber, K. L. (1984). Selective exposure: Voter information preferences and the Watergate affair. *Journal of Personality and Social Psychology*, 46, 1208–1221.

Tedeschi, J. T. (Ed.) (1981). *Impression Management Theory and Social Psychological Research.* New York: Academic Press.

Tedeschi, J. T., Schlenker, B. R., & Bonoma, T. V. (1971). Cognitive dissonance: Private ratiocination or public spectacle? *American Psychologist*, 26, 680–695.

Wertheimer, M. (1922). Untersuchung zur Lehre von der Gestalt. *Psychologische Forschung*, 1, 47–58.

Wilhoit, G. C. & de Bock, H. (1976). "All in the family" in Holland. *Journal of Communication*, 26(4), 75–84.

Zajonc, R. B. (1960). The concept of balance, congruity and dissonance. *Public Opinion Quarterly*, 24(2), 280–296.

Zillmann, D. (1988). Mood Management Through Communication Choices. *American Behavioral Scientist*, 31, 327–340.

Chapter 9

Informational Utility as Determinant of Media Choices

Matthias R. Hastall

Everyday questions like "has anything important happened in the world?," "what's on TV tonight?," or "what's the weather going to be tomorrow?" can initiate a distinct and frequently observable kind of media use: informational and educational message selections, performed with the intention to monitor the environment, to learn and to understand, to form opinions, or to find guidance regarding upcoming events and decisions. Informational utility approaches are among the few theoretical frameworks that were specifically developed to explain such informational-educational media choices. The basic idea was formulated decades ago: "It seems likely that the greater the perceived utility of the information the greater will be the subject's desire to be exposed to it" (Freedman & Sears, 1965, p. 81).

Two informational utility models have been proposed and will be portrayed later in this chapter: the classic informational utility framework by Atkin (1973) and the recent model by Knobloch-Westerwick and colleagues (e.g., 2005a and b, 2002). Their specific assumptions, limitations, and empirical outcomes will be discussed with the hope that this chapter will have a preferably high informational utility for the reader, herewith defined as *anticipated or experienced potential of media offerings to provide comprehension and guidance with respect to relevant past, current, and future events or developments.*

Informational Utility and Media Choices: A Theoretical Clarification

Although we may have reached the entertainment age after all (e.g., Vorderer, 2001), the quantity of available informational-educational media offerings on virtually all media types casts doubt that we have ever left the information age. Instead, it appears that people enjoy more informative and educational media content than ever before (e.g., U.S. Census Bureau, 2006; Ridder & Engel, 2005), and informational utility considerations belong to the central self-reported media use motives for almost all media types (Ridder & Engel, 2005; Atkin, 1985). For example, Ridder and Engel (2005) present the results of a German media use survey with 4,500 respondents (representative for Germans, age 14 and up) which included standardized questions about reasons for media consumption. As the most important motive for newspaper, Internet, and television use emerged "to be informed" (accumulated percentages for "applies completely" and "applies to a large extent": 98 percent, 91 percent, and 90 percent); for radio use, this motive emerged as second important factor (84 percent). These and essentially comparable findings in other questionnaire-based investigations (e.g., Atkin, 1985; Lichtenstein & Rosenfeld, 1983) suggest two conclusions: First, the perceived utility of media offerings plays an important role in individuals' explanations of media choices. Second, media types differ regarding their perceived utility to satisfy informational-educational needs.

Informational utility models assume, similar to other functional approaches, that media offerings differ in their ability to fulfill certain wishes and desires of the audience. With putting the audience and their needs in the centre of a theoretical framework, this view implies that humans are a) at least to some extent aware of their informational needs, b) capable to estimate the potential of media offerings to satisfy these needs, and c) motivated to select those offerings that best satisfy them. Such a perspective seems plausible at first glance, mainly because the opposite assumption—according to which media users would generally prefer media content that rather sharpens their desires—appears far less likely (but see also Hsee & Hastie, 2006).

Merits and Pitfalls of Functional Logic: Consequences Versus Causes, and Causes Versus Reasons

The functional logic of utilitarian media choice models, however, received severe criticism, particularly regarding their application in the uses and gratifications approach (e.g., Vorderer & Groeben, 1992; McQuail, 1984; Carey & Kreiling, 1974; see also Bredemeier, 1955). In short, it was pointed out that functional *consequences* of media behavior must be conceptually distinguished from the *causes* of such behavior. Given an observation in which people choose highly entertaining media content, claims that this behavior was simply caused by a need for entertainment are properly diagnosed as "pure tautology" (McQuail, 1984, p. 182) or as revealing a "striking theoretical weakness" (Vorderer & Groeben, 1992, p. 363).

Also, most functional analyses relied exclusively on self-report data. Although newer findings in neuroscience challenge the idea of a free will in the sense of human autonomy (e.g., Roskies, 2006), there is little doubt that the conscious experience of agency still constitutes a central part of most people's self-images. As a result, humans can be presumed to always see—at least some—sense in whatever they are doing or not doing, and furthermore are capable of giving verbal explanations for their behavior in almost any particular situation. It is unclear, however, to what extent such *reasons* are connected with the actual *causes* of behavior (cf. Locke & Pennington, 1982; Davidson, 1963), as people obviously appear to have very limited access to higher-order processes that govern their behavior (e.g., Nisbett & Wilson, 1977). In any case, the universal tendency of humans to experience almost any own behavior as functional may complicate research on the true determinants of media choices.

Despite such substantial criticism on theoretical and empirical grounds, the functional perspective still enjoys great popularity inside and outside the scientific community. The reasons for that might be manifold: The underlying view of humans as active media users who purposefully select media offerings to attain desired goals simply must appear positive and favorably to humans (see also Biocca, 1988; Levy & Windahl, 1984). Second, this view may save researchers from dealing with conflicting findings about human nature in other disciplines, and from perhaps rather emotional discussions on this topic. Finally, such a view may reassure us of the adequacy of our favored self-report-based research designs.

Given this listing of possible pitfalls of functional logic, however, one may doubt the scientific value of such concepts, including informational utility approaches: After all, what could be left to outweigh these downsides? As long as informational utility approaches are concerned, three arguments can be brought up in favor of them: First, as described above, informational utility considerations appear constantly among the most important self-reported motives for the use of certain media content and thus should not be ignored. Many scientific and every-day observations confirm the notion that informational media content is sought (and paid) to find helpful information regarding various kinds of uncertainties and challenges.

Second, informational utility assumptions are restricted to informational-educational media offerings. While it seems rather unlikely that individuals are completely aware of neurological processes and states that guide entertainment choices (e.g., Shrum, 2006), there is little doubt that most informational-educational message choices are initiated by top-down processes rather than bottom-up processes (i.e., cognition-activated rather than stimulus-triggered). Hence, informational media choices are activated and controlled by the same *rational, cognitive system* in humans (e.g., Epstein, 2003) that also primarily processes such messages and that eventually produces verbal responses in questionnaires about media use motives. As a result of this systemic proximity, self-reported reasons for informational-educational message selections should be stronger related to their actual causes than can be true for arousing entertainment content, when selection and processing is largely determined by a distinct *non-verbal, affect-driven system* in humans (c.f., Chaiken & Trope, 1999) to which we have very limited if any cognitive access (Nisbett & Wilson, 1977; but see also Marewski & Galesic in this volume).

Third, experimental investigations by Knobloch-Westerwick and colleagues described later in this chapter investigated the impact of high versus low informational utility news messages on the measured—instead of self-reported—amount of exposure time, thus allowing causal inferences about the relationships between utility and message choices.

The Meaning of Utility

But what exactly is utility? Precise definitions are required to determine which media behavior is utilitarian—and perhaps more important, which is *not*. The term utility has been employed with a great variety of meanings and connotations, but hardly ever precisely defined. One of the few, if not the only explicit definition in media choice research has been formulated by Levy and Windahl (1985) who understood it in a rather broad sense as anticipated or actual use of "mass communication for manifold social and psychological purposes" (p. 112). Their ambitious utility conceptualization nonetheless appears somewhat incompatible with the common understanding of this concept as it can be found elsewhere in the media choice literature.

Despite a lack of precise utility definitions, some central aspects of utility seem to have broad consent among many media choice researchers (e.g., Knobloch, Patzig, & Hastall, 2002; Zillmann, 2000; Atkin, 1985; Atkin, 1973; Sears & Freedman, 1967). According to this view, media use determined by informational utility is perceived as *cognitive* controlled rather than as affective, and furthermore as primarily motivated by a *desire for orientation and uncertainty reduction*. In contrast to media behavior driven by hedonistic impulses towards immediate emotional pleasure maximization (cf. Knobloch-Westerwick, 2006; Zillmann, 1988), utilitarian media use motivation can even lead to counter-hedonistic media and message choices. For example, a person experiencing high levels of uncertainty regarding a particular health threat might prefer rather emotionally unpleasant but presumably helpful medical information, instead of selecting an unrelated but highly entertaining television show. As media offerings have the potential to satisfy different needs simultaneously, the same individual could also turn to a health-unrelated media offering with the intention to escape frightening or disturbing thoughts (e.g., Krohne, 1993; Katz & Foulkes, 1962). Likewise, a high informational utility message could be avoided if individuals perceive their opinions and believes as threatened by the message content (e.g., Cooper, 1999; Festinger, 1957; see also Donsbach in this volume).

In sum, utility considerations are perceived as one among other rivaling motives for media choices and as principally independent of hedonistic desires. This counter-hedonistic notion of utility, which also seems to be implied by the distinction between *uses* and *gratifications* in the so-named approach (e.g., Atkin, 1985; Blumler & Katz, 1974), is an essential agreement among researchers and at the same time a first step to determine what utility is *not*. This chapter follows this non-hedonistic understanding of informational utility as anticipated or experienced potential of media offerings to improve comprehension and to provide guidance with respect to relevant past, current, and future events.

It must be noted, however, that this view is incompatible with the utility definition by Levy and Windahl (1985) that, referring to psychological purposes, encompasses the exclusive satisfaction of affective needs. This understanding of utility also differs from psychological conceptualizations that comprise hedonistic components (e.g., Eccles & Wigfield, 2002; Kahneman, Wakker, & Sarin, 1997).

Towards a Theoretical Model of Informational Utility

The notion of informational utility emerged in different contexts and with different labels in the media choice literature. It was mostly brought up to explain unexpected findings, for example in cognitive dissonance research (Cotton, 1985; Donohew & Tipton, 1973; Sears & Freedman, 1967; Freedman & Sears, 1965; Canon, 1964), knowledge gap research (e.g., Wanta & Elliott, 1995, McLeod & Perse, 1994), and mood management studies (Zillmann, 2000). Typically for such occurrences was the belief that the perceived utility of media content was powerful enough to interfere with whatever was in the focus of the investigation—and thus responsible for counter-hypothesized or nil findings. With the exception of Zillmann (2000), not much theoretical elaboration has been given to informational utility in these instances.

Informational utility models portray humans as active problem solvers who purposefully approach messages that appear as helpful to solve informational needs. Such a top-down perspective on media choices naturally does not emphasize physiological attention levels to formal media attributes. Instead, this perspective starts at the content level of media offerings and moves from there towards their relationship to the media users' informational desires and uncertainties. With hedonistic considerations understood as largely independent of utilitarian motives, a somewhat narrowed but consistent picture of media choices is drawn that combines audience-oriented and media-oriented components, and which has been classified in the area of "cognitive growth" theories (instead of cognitive preservation, affective growth, or affective preservation theories; see Wenner, 1985; McGuire, 1974). Two specific informational utility models have been proposed, the classic model by Atkin (1973) and the model by Knobloch-Westerwick and colleagues (e.g., 2005a and b, 2002). Both will be outlined and discussed in the following two sections.

The Informational Utility Model by Atkin (1973)

Atkin's (1973) informational utility model combines functionalistic ideas of message choices with expectancy-value assumptions, information seeking concepts, and cognitive dissonance postulations. A message's *informational* or *instrumental utility*—both terms were used interchangeably by Atkin (1985)—is conceptualized as a function of an individual's *needs for information* and *message attributes*. Only the core postulations of this complex model can be outlined here.

Extrinsic Motivations for Media Choices

Somewhat resembling the dichotomy of immediate versus delayed rewarding news categories by Schramm (1949), Atkin distinguishes between intrinsic and extrinsic motivations for media choices: Intrinsic motivations refer to affective and mental states which demand immediate satisfaction, for instance, media selections on the basis of the entertainment appeal or due to a high personal topical interest. Extrinsic media use motivations, on the other hand, are understood as goal-oriented pursued with the intention to solve daily life problems, to cope with environmental demands, or to guide decision-making. Dominant exposure motivation is the anticipated post-exposure application of the information gained from media consumption, in contrast to any instant satisfaction during media exposure: "A message has instrumental utility for the receiver when it provides him with a helpful input for responding to everyday environmental stimuli or for defending personal predispositions. He may need information to keep abreast of governmental actions, to guide his consumer decision-making, or to reinforce his political preferences" (Atkin, 1973, p. 205).

Atkin (1973) furthermore distinguishes between two general processes called (a) *orientation formation*, the desire to form a cognitive, affective, or behavioral orientation towards a potential relevant extrinsic stimuli, and (b) *orientation confirmation*, the desire to reinforce previously formed orientations. Both occur if individuals perceive a discrepancy between the current and the aspired criterion state of certainty. Extrinsic uncertainty, also a key concept in Atkin's model, causes specific needs for information (see Figure 9.1).

Within orientation formation, three distinct types of adaptation processes towards extrinsic uncertainty are proposed by Atkin: (1) *Cognitive adaptation*, initiated by awareness uncertainty and understanding uncertainty towards a potential meaningful object, creates a need for surveillance information. (2) *Affective adaptation* occurs when individuals feel the need to form an opinion about an object (evaluative uncertainty) or when uncertainty about the proper choice in a decisional situation is experienced (decisional uncertainty). These uncertainties produce a desire for guidance information. (3) *Behavioral adaptation* is characterized through uncertainties regarding prospective actions (communicatory uncertainty, enactment uncertainty, task uncertainty) and results in a need for performance information. The fourth and last adaptation type is proposed only for the process of orientation confirmation: (4) *Defensive adaptation*, an individual's desire to confirm previous cognitive, affective, or behavioral orientations (evoked by post-cognitive,

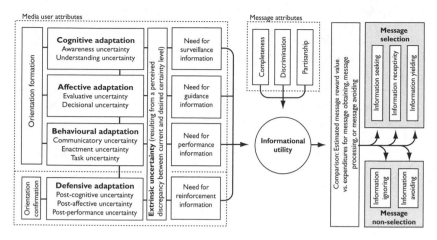

Figure 9.1 Basic assumptions of the informational utility model by Atkin (1973).

post-affective, or post-performance uncertainty) that generates a need for reinforcement information.

Although informational utility is conceptualized as a combination of both an individual's needs for information and message attributes, only three message characteristics are exemplary mentioned by Atkin (1973): completeness, multi-object discriminability, and partisanship. Much more consideration is given to the connection between utility and subsequent media behavior: Instead of proposing a simple and direct link between both, informational utility is predicted to constitute the main component of the perceived reward value of messages. In line with other expectancy-value assumptions (e.g., Palmgreen & Rayburn, 1985), it is assumed that messages will be selected when their estimated reward value exceeds the projected costs for message obtaining, processing, or avoiding. Thus, the media users' resources (money, time, energy, mental attributes; see also Scherer & Naab in this volume) are considered in this model as well. As non-exposure may be utilitarian in some situations, for example to avoid obtrusive advertising messages, the resources that are required for message avoidance are also taken into account.

Beyond Exposure Versus Avoidance

In an attempt to overcome the simple dichotomy of message selection versus avoidance, Atkin (1973) introduces a more differentiated view: *Message selection* actions are distinguished as being either (a) *information seeking*, in which a positive cost-expenditure relationship is given, or (b) *information yielding*, in which a message exposure occurs because of otherwise to high costs to avoid exposure. Information seeking is sub-classified as either (a1) *informa-tion search* or (a2) *information receptivity.* Information search refers to pur-poseful initiated search behavior, while information receptivity denotes a state of sheer openness to message topics without the explicit ex ante intention to look for something specific.

Two types of *message non-selections* are distinguished: (c) *Information ignorance* occurs when individuals feel that a message is not worth spending the expenditures that would be necessary to obtain or decode it. (d) *Infor-mation avoidance,* in contrast, describes the purposeful intention to not come into contact with a particular message, what also involves some expenditure. Atkin (1973) concludes that "the individual will respond to various states of uncertainty by seeking out some messages, avoiding others, and ignoring the vast majority. Occasionally, the prominence of a message will lead to yielding when benefits are not present" (p. 238).

Empirical Support

Atkin (1973) presents a total of 14 empirical investigations, nine of them conducted by him and colleagues, which bolster the importance of the pro-posed four adaptation types and the role of expenditures for message selec-tions. It is important to note, however, that none of these studies was conducted as an explicit test of the proposed informational utility model, and that all investigations were non-experimental and exclusively based on self-reports. For example, findings of a study by McLeod, Ward, and Tancill (1965–1966), in which 180 adults were interviewed about their motivation for newspaper use, were cited in support for cognitive adaptation. Asked about the most important reasons for newspaper consumption, 88 percent replied with "to help me keep up with things" and 67 percent answered "for interpretation of important events." Compared to other factors like escapist considerations or reading pleasure, these aspects emerged as much more important. In a later paper, Atkin (1985) reviews and organizes a large number of studies that throughout support his argument, and presents results of an own investigation designed to explore the importance of four informational utility motives (providing conversational material, providing advice, learning about life, learning new behaviors) across different media types and genres. Altogether, the findings indicate that most media exposure is—at least partially—determined by utilitarian considerations, which are stronger related to the use of classic information sources (general newspaper, magazines, nonfiction books) than to typical entertainment sources like tele-vision, theater films, fiction books, and music.

The Informational Utility Model by Knobloch-Westerwick and Colleagues

About 30 years after Atkin first published his informational utility model, an alternative framework was developed by Knobloch-Westerwick and colleagues (e.g., 2005a and b, 2002). This model is more specific in a number of aspects that were left rather vague in Atkin's approach, and at the same time considerably less complex with respect to the number of proposed processes. Similar to Atkin, this model understands informational utility as a function of both media user and media message attributes, and as basically independent of hedonistic drives. In contrast, origins of informational utility considerations are neither limited to external demands in this model, nor have dissonance reduction motives found a place in it. The authors explicitly apply their model to positive events that suggest chances and opportunities, as well as to negative events like potential threats and other unfavorable developments.

Four Dimensions of Utility

The initial model (e.g., Knobloch, Carpentier, & Zillmann, 2003; Knobloch, Patzig, & Hastall, 2002) comprised three independent dimensions of informational utility: "Specifically, this model predicts that information relating to individuals' immediate and prospective encounter of threats and opportunities will have utility, which will vary with (a) the perceived *magnitude of challenges or gratifications*, (b) the perceived *likelihood* of their materialization, and (c) their perceived *immediacy* (i.e., the proximity in time of their materialization)" (Knobloch, Carpentier, & Zillmann, 2003, p. 95; italics in original). A fourth dimension, (d) the perceived *efficacy* to influence the consequences of described events, was added later (Knobloch-Westerwick, Hastall, Grimmer, & Brück, 2005; Knobloch, Grimmer, Hastall, & Brück, 2004). These dimensions are assumed to contribute separately—and thus in an additive manner—to the overall informational utility of media offerings (see Figure 9.2).

As an example for this view on utilitarian media choices, let's consider media coverage about new tax regulations that just passed the congress. According to this model, it is assumed that the informational utility of related media messages will be higher to the extent that generally intense—positive as well as negative—financial consequences of this regulation are expected, compared to little or no changes (magnitude). Likewise, high informational utility is presumed if the media user belongs to the target group of this regulation and thus will be presumably affected by it, and lower utility in situations in which this would not be the case (likelihood). A high utility is furthermore predicted if this regulation would come into effect very soon, while lower levels are expected if it still takes years or decades until it

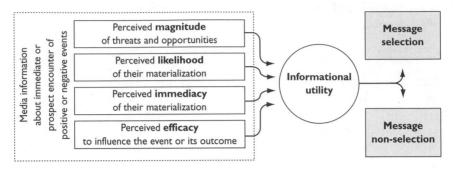

Figure 9.2 Assumptions of the informational utility model by Knobloch-Westerwick, Hastall, Grimmer, and Brück (2005).

becomes official law (immediacy). Finally, messages that suggest that people have a certain chance to increase or limit the positive and negative consequences of this regulation are expected to have a higher utility than messages that do not indicate such a personal influence on the outcome (efficacy).

While the combination of these four utility dimensions in a media choice model can be seen as innovative, the factors are not novel in media research. Most can be traced back to persuasion models in which they have been proposed and tested, although in different combinations and sometimes with different names (for an overview, see Knobloch-Westerwick, Hastall, Grimmer, & Brück, 2005). The relevance of magnitude, likelihood and immediacy for the perception of risks and resulting persuasive effects was described decades ago (e.g., Hovland, Janis, & Kelley, 1953). The notion of self-efficacy (e.g., Bandura, 1997) is incorporated in persuasion models like protection motivation theory (Maddux & Rogers, 1983; Rogers, 1975) or the extended parallel process model (Witte, 1992). The dimensions magnitude, likelihood and immediacy may also on first sight resemble some factors that can be found with different names in some news value classifications (e.g., Galtung & Ruge, 1965; Östgaard, 1965). But, as will be outlined later, both approaches differ fundamentally in their understanding of such factors. Moreover, this approach conceptualizes magnitude and likelihood as distinct factors, in contrast to, for example, Rogers' (1975) work. In sum, this informational utility model comprises factors that emerged as highly influential in existing media effect models, arranged them in a coherent media choice model and clarified the theoretical relationships between them.

Empirical Support

A series of experimental investigations was conducted by Knobloch-Westerwick and colleagues to test the hypotheses derived from this model. Most of these studies employed a very similar research design: Online news outlets, largely analogous in form and function to those available in the World Wide Web, were created and served as means to present manipulated and unmanipulated articles at the same time. Each magazine advertised six to eight articles on an overview page with a headline, sometimes with an additional sub-headline, and with the first few words of the first paragraph. Respondents were instructed to browse through the magazine and read whatever they find interesting, just as they normally would. The specific instructions, which were presented both verbally and written, were formulated to encourage a most "natural" media use situation. Selectivity was furthermore facilitated through the presentation of more reading material than could be consumed in the given time span that ranged between three and six minutes per online magazine. Most of the investigations were conducted in university computer labs with Internet access, which were also normally frequented by students to read online news.

From the magazines overview page, the whole articles could be assessed through hyperlinks. Unbeknownst to the respondents, browsing behavior was automatically recorded to the split second by server-sided scripts. Exposure time to all manipulated articles was accumulated later and served as main dependent variable for data analysis. An online questionnaire that collected additional respondent information was automatically uploaded when the end of the scheduled browsing time was reached. Informational utility was experimentally varied (as high vs. low, and as single informational utility dimension or in combination with others) in half of the articles, while the remaining articles were provided as competing reading material. Stimulus material was pre-tested to ensure valid informational utility manipulations, and article placement on the overview page was controlled through rotation.

Seven investigations with a total of 677 US and 503 German participants have employed this method of data collection to test the impact of informational utility on the selective exposure to a variety of positive and negative online news topics (Knobloch-Westerwick, Hastall, Grimmer, & Brück, 2005; Knobloch & Hastall, 2005; Knobloch-Westerwick, Carpentier, Blumhoff, & Nickel, 2005; Knobloch, Carpentier, & Zillmann, 2003; Knobloch, Patzig, & Hastall, 2002). Significant differences in reading times, without exception in the predicted direction, were found for magnitude in six out of seven investigations, for likelihood and immediacy in five out of six, and for efficacy in two out of two tests. In six out of seven studies, the utility dimensions under investigation influenced selective exposure in the predicted additive manner. Overall, these studies corroborate the impact of the four utility dimensions as independent determinants of selective exposure to online news for positive as well as negative news, for different news topics and across two cultures.

The most exhaustive test of this model was conducted by Knobloch-Westerwick, Hastall, Grimmer, & Brück (2005) who manipulated two magazines regarding all four informational utility dimensions. The first magazine

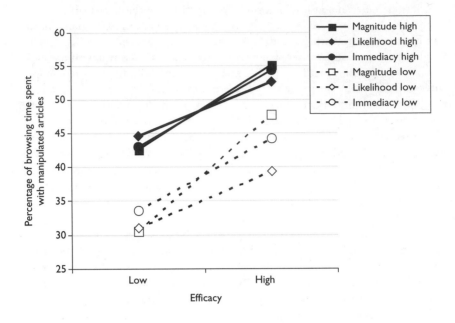

Figure 9.3 Selective exposure to positive and negative news combined as function of informational utility (data from Knobloch-Westerwick, Hastall, Grimmer, & Brück, 2005).

contained negative news reports and the second news reports that described positive events. 309 German students browsed through both magazines. Half of the six articles in each magazine were manipulated regarding a combination of efficacy and one of the remaining three utility dimensions (e.g., efficacy high and magnitude low). The findings are displayed in Figure 9.3.

Efficacy emerged as powerful predictor of news reading times, with high levels of efficacy resulting in 24 percent longer exposure times, compared to the low-efficacy version. The remaining three informational utility dimensions affected browsing time and the number of selected articles almost as strong as efficacy did.

Relationship to Other Media Choice Approaches

What alternative theoretical approaches are at hand to explain informational-educational media use? Without doubt, the uses and gratifications approach (e.g., Rosengren, Wenner, & Palmgreen, 1985; Blumler & Katz, 1974) must be named here, which claims to explain all media choices. This framework, however, received severe criticism regarding basically all underlying assumptions (e.g., McQuail, 2004; Vorderer & Groeben, 1992).

Although uses and gratifications and informational utility models share a few functional postulations, the latter approach appears to a greater extent unchained of rather problematic or even ideological assumptions and, above all, does not claim or imply that the mechanism for selecting informational-educational media content is the same as for entertainment offerings. The theoretical predictions of informational utility models are thus more focused, and the available experimental investigations allow causal inferences about the accuracy of all important model assumptions.

Several information seeking models have been developed in different fields and with great variability in their theoretical predictions (e.g., Afifi & Weiner, 2004; Järvelin & Wilson, 2003; Brashers, Goldsmith, & Hsieh, 2002; Wilson & Walsh, 1996; Johnson & Meischke, 1993; Donohew & Tipton, 1973). As a detailed characterization lies beyond the scope of this chapter (see, for example, Afifi & Weiner, 2004; Wilson & Walsh, 1996), only some main differences to informational utility models can be pointed out here which cannot apply to all models to the same extent: First, the core concept to explain informational behavior varies greatly. For example, many information seeking approaches refer to uncertainty and related constructs which are perhaps not as universal in nature as utility considerations, but instead more influenced by personality traits like uncertainty tolerance (e.g., Grenier, Barrette, & Ladouceur, 2005; Dalbert, Kulla, & Samer, 2002). Second, these models differ remarkably regarding their main dependent variable, as many information seeking models have been originally proposed to explain particular actions like interpersonal communication, exposure to specific health information, or the realization of specific search tasks; not all of them appear hassle-free applicable to everyday mass media use. In sum, both traditions emphasize the importance of non-hedonistic factors for people's exposure to informational-educational messages. But apart from that, the approaches differ in many aspects and are far from being simply substitutable.

News value classifications differ greatly regarding the number and kind of factors contained to explain media choices. Originally developed to explain journalistic news selections (e.g., Galtung & Ruge, 1965; Östgaard, 1965), this approach was recently extended to audiences selections (Eilders, 2006; Eilders & Wirth, 1999). Factors like "relevance" (Schulz, 1976; Galtung & Ruge, 1965), "actual utility/success" or "possible utility/success" (Staab, 1990) can be found in some of these models and may appear related to utility dimensions on first glance. These factors are, however, basically conceptualized as inherent message characteristics and not as audience-attributed features of messages. An example shall illustrate further theoretical differences: For a newscast about a celebrity and his/her repeated failure to develop a successful romantic relationship, news value approaches would predict a generally intensified exposure to such news due to the assumed presence of factors like "sensationalism" (Östgaard, 1965), "reference to persons," "reference to elite people," or "negativism" (e.g., Galtung &

Ruge, 1965). Informational utility approaches, on the other hand, would draw a more differentiated picture: According to them, some people would attend such newscast due to a perceived high informational utility (e.g., to acquire conversational material, to feel informed about this celebrity, etc.), while others would be predicted to ignore or avoid it based on a perceived low informational utility for them. Combining attributes of media users and media messages, informational utility models thus offer a more differentiated view on media choices.

Informational Utility and Media Use: A Conclusion

This chapter reviewed the theoretical and empirical developments regarding one of the most prominent determinants of media use, the perceived informational utility of media offerings. The underlying assumptions of such approaches were discussed and the two available frameworks, the model by Atkin (1973) and by Knobloch-Westerwick and colleagues (2005b), were reviewed.

Atkin's model is fairly complex and subsumes a variety of processes including cognitive dissonance reduction motives, but restricts utility considerations to external demands and thus ignores intrinsic motivations for information seeking. The large number of postulated cognitive processes makes comprehensive model tests complicated, if not impossible. While the general idea of informational utility was welcomed by scholars and frequently cited, the empirical output is limited: Less than a handful studies explicitly tested at least a few of the numerous model assumptions (e.g., Wang, 1977). Despite its intuitive charm, this framework was unable to generate sufficient empirical support to back its assumptions. In contrast, the four dimensions of informational   utility   proposed   in   the   alternative   model   by Knobloch-Westerwick and colleagues emerged as theoretically as well as empirically powerful predictors of actual media behavior. It certainly remains a matter of opinion whether this list of dimensions is exhaustive or not, although it may be not easy to identify factors as basic and independent as the four currently proposed.

We are still amazingly far from a comprehensive understanding of causes for everyday phenomenon like daily morning newspaper reading, and many other frequently observable types of informational-educational media choices. Informational utility approaches, however, might be a promising step in that direction.

References

Afifi, W. A. & Weiner, J. L. (2004). Toward a theory of motivated information management. *Communication Theory, 14*(2), 167–190.

Atkin, C. K. (1973). Instrumental utilities and information seeking. In P. Clarke (Ed.), *New Models for Mass Communication Research* (pp. 205–242). Beverly Hills, CA: Sage.

Atkin, C. K. (1985). Informational utility and selective exposure to entertainment media. In D. Zillmann & J. Bryant (Eds.), *Selective Exposure in Communication* (pp. 63–91). Hillsdale, NJ: Lawrence Erlbaum.

Bandura, A. (1997). *Self-Efficacy: The Exercise of Control.* New York, NY: Freeman.

Biocca, F. A. (1988). Opposing conceptions of the audience: The active and passive hemispheres of mass communication. In J. A. Anderson (Ed.), *Communication Yearbook 11* (pp. 51–80). Beverly Hills, CA: Sage.

Blumler, J. G. & Katz, E. (Eds.). (1974). *The Uses of Mass Communications: Current Perspectives on Gratifications Research.* Beverly Hills, CA: Sage.

Brashers, D. E., Goldsmith, D. J., & Hsieh, E. (2002). Information seeking and avoiding in health contexts. *Human Communication Research, 28*(2), 258–271.

Bredemeier, H. C. (1955). The methodology of functionalism. *American Sociological Review, 20*(2), 173–180.

Canon, L. K. (1964). Self-confidence and selective exposure to information. In L. Festinger (Ed.), *Conflict, Decision, and Dissonance* (pp. 83–95). Stanford, CA: Stanford University Press.

Carey, J. W. & Kreiling, A. L. (1974). Popular culture and uses and gratifications: Notes toward an accommodation. In J. G. Blumler & E. Katz (Eds.), *The Uses of Mass Communications: Current Perspectives on Gratifications Research* (pp. 225–248). Beverly Hills, CA: Sage.

Chaiken, S. & Trope, Y. (Eds.). (1999). *Dual-process Theories in Social Psychology.* New York: Guilford Press.

Cooper, J. (1999). Unwanted consequences and the self: In search of the motivation for dissonance reduction. In E. Harmon-Jones & J. Mills (Eds.), *Cognitive Dissonance: Progress on a Pivotal Theory in Social Psychology* (pp. 149–173). Washington, D.C.: American Psychological Association.

Cotton, J. L. (1985). Cognitive dissonance in selective exposure. In D. Zillmann & J. Bryant (Eds.), *Selective Exposure in Communication* (pp. 11–33). Hillsdale, NJ: Lawrence Erlbaum.

Dalbert, C., Kulla, C., & Samer, E. (2002). Individuelle Unterschiede im Aufsuchen gesundheitsrelevanter Informationen. Der Einfluss der Ungewissheitstoleranz. (Individual differences in selective exposure to health-related information: The impact of uncertainty-tolerance.) *Report Psychologie, 27*(4), 246–251.

Davidson, D. (1963). Actions, reasons, and causes. *Journal of Philosophy, 60*(23), 685–700.

Donohew, L. & Tipton, L. (1973). A conceptual model of information seeking, avoiding, and processing. In P. Clarke (Ed.), *New Models for Mass Communication Research* (pp. 245–268). Beverly Hills, CA: Sage.

Eccles, J. S. & Wigfield, A. (2002). Motivational beliefs, values, and goals. *Annual Review of Psychology, 53*, 109–132.

Eilders, C. (2006). News factors and news decisions: Theoretical and methodological advances in Germany. *Communications, 31*(1), 5–24.

Eilders, C. & Wirth, W. (1999). Die Nachrichtenwertforschung auf dem Weg zum Publikum: Eine experimentelle Überprüfung des Einflusses von Nachrichtenfaktoren bei der Rezeption. (News value research on the way to the audience: An experimental investigation of the impact of news values on media reception.) *Publizistik, 44*(1), 35–57.

Epstein, S. (2003). Cognitive-experiential self-theory of personality. In T. Millon & M. J. Lerner (Eds.), *Handbook of Psychology* (Vol. 5: Personality and social psychology). New York: John Wiley & Sons.

Festinger, L. (1957). *A Theory of Cognitive Dissonance.* Stanford, CA: Stanford University Press.

Freedman, J. L. & Sears, D. O. (1965). Selective exposure. In L. Berkowitz (Ed.), *Advances in Experimental Social Psychology* (Vol. 2, pp. 58–98). New York: Academic Press.

Galtung, J. & Ruge, M. H. (1965). The structure of foreign news: The presentation of the Congo, Cuba and Cyprus crisis in four Norwegian newspapers. *Journal of Peace Research, 2*(1), 64–91.

Grenier, S., Barrette, A.-M., & Ladouceur, R. (2005). Intolerance of uncertainty and intolerance of ambiguity: Similarities and differences. *Personality and Individual Differences, 39*(3), 593–600.

Hovland, C. I., Janis, I. L., & Kelley, H. H. (1953). *Communication and Persuasion: Psychological Studies of Opinion Change.* New Haven, CT: Yale University Press.

Hsee, C. K. & Hastie, R. (2006). Decision and experience: Why don't we choose what makes us happy? *Trends in Cognitive Sciences, 10*(1), 31–37.

Järvelin, K. & Wilson, T. D. (2003). On conceptual models for information seeking and retrieval research. *Information Research, 9*(1), paper 163. Online. Retrieved on July 20, 2007 from http://informationr.net/ir/9–1/paper163.html.

Johnson, J. D. & Meischke, H. (1993). A comprehensive model of cancer-related information seeking applied to magazines. *Human Communication Research, 19*(3), 343–367.

Kahneman, D., Wakker, P. P., & Sarin, R. (1997). Back to Bentham? Exploration of perceived utility. *The Quarterly Journal of Economics, 112*(2), 375–405.

Katz, E. & Foulkes, D. (1962). On the use of the mass media as "escape": Clarification of a concept. *Public Opinion Quarterly, 26*(3), 377–388.

Knobloch, S. & Hastall, M. R. (2005). *Effects of informational utility and exemplification on selective exposure to health news.* Paper presented at the annual meeting of the International Communication Association (ICA), New York.

Knobloch, S., Carpentier, F. D., & Zillmann, D. (2003). Effects of salience dimensions of informational utility on selective exposure to online news. *Journalism & Mass Communication Quarterly, 80*(1), 91–108.

Knobloch, S., Grimmer, D., Hastall, M., & Brück, J. (2004). *Predicting selective exposure to media information: The efficacy dimension in the informational utility model.* Paper presented at the annual meeting of the International Communication Association (ICA), New Orleans.

Knobloch, S., Patzig, G., & Hastall, M. (2002). "Informational Utility." Einfluss von Nützlichkeit auf selektive Zuwendung zu negativen und positiven Online-Nachrichten. ("Informational Utility." The impact of utility on selective exposure to negative and positive online news.) *Medien- und Kommunikationswissenschaft, 50*(3), 359–375.

Knobloch-Westerwick, S. (2006). Mood management: Theory, evidence, and advancements. In J. Bryant & P. Vorderer (Eds.), *Psychology of Entertainment* (pp. 239–254). Mahwah, NJ: Lawrence Erlbaum.

Knobloch-Westerwick, S., Carpentier, F. D., Blumhoff, A., & Nickel, N. (2005a). Selective exposure effects for positive and negative news: Testing the robustness of the informational utility model. *Journalism and Mass Communication Quarterly, 82*(1), 181–195.

Knobloch-Westerwick, S., Hastall, M., Grimmer, D., & Brück, J. (2005b). "Informational Utility." Der Einfluss der Selbstwirksamkeit auf die selektive Zuwendung zu Nachrichten. ("Informational Utility." The impact of efficacy on selective exposure to news.) *Publizistik, 50*(4), 462–474.

Krohne, H. W. (Ed.). (1993). *Attention and Avoidance: Strategies in Coping with Aversiveness.* Seattle: Hogrefe & Huber.

Levy, M. R. (1977). Experiencing television news. *Journal of Communication, 27*(4), 112–117.

Levy, M. R. & Windahl, S. (1984). Audience activity and gratifications: A conceptual clarification and exploration. *Communication Research, 11*(1), 51–78.

Levy, M. R. & Windahl, S. (1985). The concept of audience activity. In K. E. Rosengren, L. A. Wenner, & P. Palmgreen (Eds.), *Media Gratifications Research: Current Perspectives* (pp. 109–122). Beverly Hills, CA: Sage.

Lichtenstein, A. & Rosenfeld, L. B. (1983). Uses and misuses of gratifications research: An explication of media functions. *Communication Research, 10*(1), 97–109.

Locke, D. & Pennington, D. (1982). Reasons and other causes: Their role in attribution processes. *Journal of Personality and Social Psychology, 42*(2), 212–223.

Maddux, J. E. & Rogers, R. W. (1983). Protection motivation and self-efficacy: A revised theory of fear appeals and attitude change. *Journal of Experimental Social Psychology, 19*(5), 469–479.

McGuire, W. J. (1974). Psychological Motives and Communication Gratification. In J. G. Blumler & E. Katz (Eds.), *The Uses of Mass Communications: Current Perspectives on Gratifications Research* (pp. 167–196). Beverly Hills, CA: Sage.

McLeod, D. M. & Perse, E. M. (1994). Direct and indirect effects of socioeconomic status on public affairs knowledge. *Journalism Quarterly, 71*(2), 433–442.

McLeod, J. M., Ward, S., & Tancill, K. (1965–1966). Alienation and uses of the mass media. *Public Opinion Quarterly, 29*(4), 583–594.

McQuail, D. (1984). With the benefit of hindsight: Reflections on uses and gratifications research. *Critical Studies in Mass Communication, 1*(2), 177–193.

McQuail, D. (2004). With more hindsight: Conceptual problems and some ways forward for media use research. In K. Renckstorf, D. McQuail, J. E. Rosenbaum, & G. Schaap (Eds.), *Action Theory and Communication Research: Recent Developments in Europe* (pp. 35–50). Berlin: Walter De Gruyter.

Nisbett, R. E. & Wilson, T. D. (1977). Telling more than we can know: Verbal reports on mental processes. *Psychological Review, 84*(3), 231–259.

Östgaard, E. (1965). Factors influencing the flow of news. *Journal of Peace Research, 2*(1), 39–63.

Palmgreen, P. & Rayburn, J. D. (1985). An expectancy-value approach to media gratifications. In K. E. Rosengren, L. A. Wenner, & P. Palmgreen (Eds.), *Media Gratifications Research: Current Perspectives* (pp. 61–72). Beverly Hills, CA: Sage.

Ridder, C.-M. & Engel, B. (2005). Massenkommunikation 2005: Images und Funktionen der Massenmedien im Vergleich. (Mass communication 2005: Images and functions of mass media in comparison.) *Media Perspektiven, 9,* 422–448.

Rogers, R. W. (1975). A protection motivation theory of fear appeals and attitude change. *Journal of Psychology, 91*(1), 93–114.

Rosengren, K. E., Wenner, L. A., & Palmgreen, P. (Eds.). (1985). *Media Gratifications Research: Current Perspectives.* Beverly Hills, CA: Sage.

Roskies, A. (2006). Neuroscientific challenges to free will and responsibility. *Trends in Cognitive Sciences, 10*(9), 419–423.

Schramm, W. (1949). The nature of news. *Journalism Quarterly, 26*(3), 259–269.

Schulz, W. (1976). *Die Konstruktion von Realität in den Nachrichtenmedien. Analyse der aktuellen Berichterstattung.* (The construction of reality in news media. An analysis of the current news coverage.) Freiburg/München: Alber.

Sears, D. O. & Freedman, J. L. (1967). Selective exposure to information: A critical review. *Public Opinion Quarterly, 31*(2), 194–213.

Shrum, L. J. (2006). Perception. In J. Bryant & P. Vorderer (Eds.), *Psychology of Entertainment* (pp. 55–70). Mahwah, NJ: Lawrence Erlbaum.

Staab, J. F. (1990). Nachrichtenwerttheorie. Formale Struktur und empirischer Gehalt. (News value theory. Formal structure and empirical capacity.) Freiburg/München: Alber.

U.S. Census Bureau (2006). *Statistical Abstract of the United States: 2007.* Washington, D.C.

Vorderer, P. (2001). It's all entertainment—sure. But what exactly is entertainment? Communication research, media psychology, and the explanation of entertainment experiences. *Poetics, 29*(4–5), 247–261.

Vorderer, P. & Groeben, N. (1992). Audience research: What the humanistic and the social science approaches could learn from each other. *Poetics, 21*(4), 361–376.

Wang, G. (1977). Information utility as a predictor of newspaper readership. *Journalism Quarterly, 54*(4), 791–793.

Wanta, W. & Elliott, W. R. (1995). Did the "magic" work? Knowledge of HIV/AIDS and the knowledge gap hypothesis. *Journalism & Mass Communication Quarterly, 72*(2), 312–321.

Wenner, L. A. (1985). The nature of news gratifications. In K. E. Rosengren, L. A. Wenner, & P. Palmgreen (Eds.), *Media Gratifications Research: Current Perspectives* (pp. 171–193). Beverly Hills, CA: Sage.

Wilson, T. & Walsh, C. (1996). *Information Behaviour: An Inter-disciplinary Perspective* (British Library Research and Innovation Report 10). London: British Library Research and Innovation Centre. Online. Retrieved July 20, 2007 from http://informationr.net/tdw/publ/infbehav/.

Witte, K. (1992). Putting the fear back into fear appeals: The extended parallel process model. *Communication Monographs, 59*(4), 329–349.

Zillmann, D. (1988). Mood management: Using entertainment to full advantage. In L. Donohew, H. E. Sypher, & E. T. Higgins (Eds.), *Communication, Social Cognition, and Affect* (pp. 147–171). Hillsdale, NJ: Lawrence Erlbaum.

Zillmann, D. (2000). Mood management in the context of selective exposure theory. In M. E. Roloff (Ed.), *Communication Yearbook 23* (pp. 103–123). Thousand Oaks, CA: Sage.

Chapter 10

Affect as a Predictor of Entertainment Choice

The Utility of Looking Beyond Pleasure

Mary Beth Oliver

Individuals are faced with a dizzying array of possibilities in deciding on an evening's choice of entertainment. Not only are there countless genres and titles that are available, recent technological changes have brought about additional control over selections, with individuals now able to choose entertainment "on demand" via their cable providers or download entire motion pictures from the Internet. Given this increasing breadth of selection opportunity, it is arguably more difficult than ever to predict viewers' choices. Critical acclaim, recommendations from friends, popularity of titles, movie promotions, and enduring personal tastes undoubtedly all play important roles. But with all of these variables exerting influence, it is important to keep in mind that many media preferences vary from one moment to the next. At one point in time, a given individual with a given set of preferences may opt for a comedy that is anticipated to deliver mirth and humor, and at another point in time this same individual may prefer a suspenseful film that is anticipated to engender anxiety if not terror. It is at these state-level variations that the importance of affect as a predictor of media choice becomes most critical, for it as this level where individuals' *feelings* or *affective states* likely exert the most influence over what is selected and what is avoided. This chapter first overviews existing research and theorizing on affect as a predictor of media choice, noting the common methodological approaches and theoretical assumptions that have been utilized. Subsequent sections then consider different types of media content that seem puzzling in light of existing research, overviewing how various theoretical perspectives may account for these seemingly paradoxical media selections. Finally, I provide a template for broader conceptualizations of affect and media gratifications that may more fully capture the breadth of individuals' media choices and that may help to address some of the limitations of current models.

Theoretical Approaches to Exploring Affective Predictors of Media Choice

The importance of affect in predicting media choice has arguably received the greatest attention from two theoretical perspectives: uses and gratifications

(U&G) and mood management (and its variants). These two perspectives share many similarities, though they differ on a number of important dimensions, including their focus on affect, the extent to which viewers are assumed to be cognizant of their media choices, and the methodological approaches that are most commonly employed.

Uses and Gratifications

Conceptualizations of audiences as active in their media selection and use is readily understood to be as assumption adopted by U&G perspectives (Katz, Blumler, & Gurevitch, 1974; Rubin, 2002). In general, this approach identifies media use as an activity that is performed on the basis of individuals' felt needs and the expected gratifications that are thought to be enjoyed when these needs are met. Because "needs" are typically conceptualized very broadly, the types of uses and gratifications that are examined from this perspective include more than affect-related variables, but also social, cognitive, and temporal variables as well (e.g., passing the time, habit, learning). Nevertheless, an examination of the variety of reported needs associated with the selection of a diversity of media content reveals that individuals often report motivations and expected gratifications that contain affective components.

McGuire's (1974) categorization of human motives that may be related to media-selection behaviors included both cognitive motives (information processing tendencies) and affective motives (characterized by feeling states). Within the affect-motives category, McGuire argued that four of the eight motives were associated with the desire to maintain equilibrium (tension reduction, expression, ego-defense, and reinforcement), and four were associated with the desire to enhance or improve one's state (assertion, affiliation, identification with attractive characters, and observation of successful role models). Many of these needs have also been noted in other U&G studies, as researchers have commonly identified using media for purposes of excitation and relaxation as common motives (Conway & Rubin, 1991; Rubin, 1979). The breadth of gratifications identified by McGuire is also similar to the array of basic desires that Reiss and Wiltz (2004) argued may be consequential in individuals' media-selection patterns, including needs for romance, tranquility, vengeance, and power, among others.

Given prior research on individuals' uses of media content for purposes related to arousal and affect regulation, it seems reasonable to assume that the experience of different affective states would make these motivations more salient at some times than at others. For example, the experience of boredom should make motivations to use media for purposes of arousal more pronounced than at other times when an individual may be experiencing pleasant feelings of calmness or, in contrast, experiencing feelings of stress or anxiety. However, U&G has arguably tended to treat affective media-use motivations as more enduring or stable preferences. Consequently, one potentially fruitful avenue of research within the U&G domain would be to expand upon how motivations (and their associated affect) can vary within individuals at different time periods.

Mood Management

Whereas U&G research examines affect-related needs as one among many different types of motivations for media use, the focus of mood management, as the name implies, is almost exclusively on the role of affect in predicting individuals' media selections. Specifically, mood management theory proposes that one primary motivation for media-choice behaviors is the regulation of moods, with individuals' choices reflecting hedonistic motivations—the maintenance or intensification of positive affect, and the termination or reduction of negative affect (Knobloch-Westerwick, 2006; Oliver, 2003; Zillmann, 1985, 1988a, 2000; Zillmann & Bryant, 1986). Further, unlike research from a U&G perspective, mood management does not assume that individuals are necessarily cognizant of the role of affect in influencing their media choices (Zillmann & Bryant, 1985). Consequently, research from a mood-management perspective typically (though not exclusively) employs experimental procedures in which positive or negative affective states are induced, and selective exposure to media messages are assessed.

In describing the types of media portrayals that may assist in mood regulation, Zillmann and his colleagues have identified four different characteristics of media content that may serve these ends (Zillmann, 1985, 1988a, 1988b, 2000; Zillmann & Bryant, 1986). The excitatory potential of media content refers to the extent to which the media portrayals may serve to regulate arousal, with individuals who are under-aroused (bored) predicted to choose exciting fare, and individuals who are over-aroused (stressed) predicted to choose calming fare. The behavioral affinity of media content refers to the similarity between the media portrayals and the context of the viewer's current mood state, with individuals in negative moods predicted to avoid content high on behavioral affinity. The absorbing potential of media content refers to the extent to which the portrayals are involving or absorbing to the viewer, with individuals in negative states predicted to choose content high on absorbing potential because such content presumably disrupts rumination about the negative mood, thereby decreasing its intensity. Finally, the hedonic valence of the media content refers to the extent to which the depictions are positive or negative in tone, with all viewers (but particularly viewers in negative affective states) predicted to avoid negatively valenced content.

Support for these general propositions has been obtained in a variety of contexts and for a diversity of media content. For example, Bryant and Zillmann (1984) found that overly aroused (stressed) participants spent significantly longer than did under-aroused (bored) participants viewing calming programming such nature programs or soothing musical performances over exciting programming such as game-show playoffs or sporting events. Likewise, Knobloch and Zillmann (2002) reported that participants in negative mood states induced via bogus feedback on a recognition task spent significantly more time than did participants in positive mood states listening to upbeat, lively, and energetic music over more somber musical selections. In addition to demonstrating evidence for mood management under laboratory conditions, research has also provided support for this theory's basic propositions in more naturalistic contexts. For example, Meadowcroft and Zillmann (1987) reported that women in the premenstrual phase of their menstrual cycle were more likely than women in other phases to indicate a preference for viewing situation comedies as the evening's entertainment lineup. Finally, although the propositions of mood management have been studied most extensively in the context of entertainment programming, some evidence suggests that it may also be applicable to the selection of news content (Biswas, Riffe, & Zillmann, 1994).

Paradoxes and Potential Explanations

Although U&G and mood management differ on a number of noteworthy dimensions, both perspectives point to the idea that individuals' media use is generally gratifying at some level or, more specifically in the case of mood management, is successful in repairing negative affective states or in prolonging positive ones. Consistent with this idea, many entertainment offerings appear to readily conform to this characterization of media use, as genres such as comedies presumably result in feelings of mirth, many dramas result in feelings of inspiration, and many sporting events result in feelings of elation.

With these "understandable" forms of media in mind, however, it is evident that many popular forms of media entertainment stray considerably from unambiguously positive hedonic tones. Tragedies, tear-jerkers, and mournful love songs are but a few of the numerous examples of popular media content that elicit negative affective responses, including sorrow, upset, and distress, among other responses (Oliver, 1993). Perhaps even more puzzling than the simple popularity of these genres, however, is the appeal that they appear to hold for individuals in negative affective states (Gibson, Aust, & Zillmann, 2000; Strizhakova & Krcmar, 2007). Because such appeal appears to be inconsistent with hedonic considerations, alternative frameworks for understanding the role of affect in predicting media choices may be useful (and necessary) to help more fully account for the variety of means by which affect can predict and guide individuals' selection patterns.

Affect as a Predictor of Processing Style

Identifying sad films, tragedies, and mournful love songs as "paradoxical" genres (and particularly when selected by viewers in sad or negative moods) implies that the most important function of affect in media selection is in terms of hedonically driven affect regulation. Although this assumption has arguably garnered the greatest attention among scholars and is therefore treated more fully in the sections that follow, it may be useful to first consider alternative frameworks for interpreting the relationship between affect and media selection. Namely, research on "affect as information" suggests that affective states and media choice may be related, but not necessarily as a reflection of motivations related to mood regulation, but rather as a reflection of different processing strategies associated with different types of affect (Schwarz, 2002; Schwarz & Clore, 2007). As such, the relationship between affect and media selection may not be directly related, but may rather be mediated by different processing styles.

In general, "affect as information" suggests that affective states have informational value for individuals, with negative states signifying that the individual should attend carefully to the situation so as to alleviate or address the presumed problem giving rise to the state, and positive states signifying that "all is well," and that one can continue with one's normal functioning (Schwarz, 2002). In their overview of research in this area, Schwarz and Clore (2007) explained that this informational function of feeling states leads to different processing strategies, with negative states leading to more systematic or "bottom up" processing (that would presumably aid in identifying and rectifying problems that gave rise to the state), and positive states allowing for default heuristic or "top down" processing.

What might these differential processing styles imply about seemingly counter-hedonistic choices? First, approaching media selection from an "affect as information" perspective may suggest that the most proximate predictor of attraction to sad films or tragedies may not actually be negative affect in and of itself, but rather the more narrow, focused, careful, and systematic processing that more frequently accompanies negative over positive feelings. In many ways, it makes sense that more dramatic and contemplative entertainment (including dramas, sad films, and tragedies) would be more attractive to individuals processing in systematic as opposed to heuristic ways. Not only might the enjoyment of this type of entertainment fare require a substantial amount of cognitive effort to appreciate the subtleties and nuances of human drama, entertainment that features only predictable (if not silly) portrayals (such as comedies or action flicks) may be seen as too superficial or shallow to be meaningful or enjoyable.

This interpretation is also consistent with Reber, Schwarz, and Winkielman's (2004) argument that the ease with one can process information associated with an object or task can further serve as a source of information that heightens perceptions of beauty or truth: "We suggest that aesthetic experience is a function of the perceiver's processing dynamics: The more fluently the perceiver can process an object, the more positive is his or her aesthetic response" (p. 365). Applied to the enjoyment of tragedy, then, this reasoning would imply that people in negative affective states may more readily (and easily) process more contemplative entertainment over more light-hearted fare, thereby leading to heightened perceptions of aesthetic quality (and hence, enjoyment).

Of course, the application of "affect as information" to enjoyment of sad films is purely speculative at this point, though some existing evidence suggests that it may be a fruitful avenue for future research. For example, although experimental studies have yet to examine the idea that higher levels of systematic processing lead to greater attraction to dramatic entertainment, other existing research does suggest that individual differences in processing styles predict more stable or enduring entertainment preferences. Namely, Oliver (2007) reported data showing that higher levels of need for cognition (Cacioppo & Petty, 1982) were positively associated with preferences for and enjoyment of dramatic entertainment, but were unrelated to preferences for hedonically-positive entertainment (e.g., comedies). If *trait*-like measures indicating a propensity to engage in systematic processing usefully predict attraction to seemingly counter-hedonic media choices, it seems reasonable to assume that *state*-like differences in processing styles arising from positive and negative feeling states could operate in comparable ways.

Affective Forecasting

In contrast to "affect as information" approaches, the bulk of research in media psychology has tended to examine affective predictors in terms of their motivational functions. In this regard, in considering why people may make media choices that appear counter-hedonistic, it may be useful to first recognize that individuals' behaviors and preferences may be misplaced or mistaken. In other words, although individuals may ultimately be motivated to behave in ways that serve hedonic ends, they may be unable to accurately identify the most effective means that serve this goal. Such an interpretation is consistent with a growing body of research suggesting that individuals are often not particularly adept at identifying their moods and the causes of their moods, nor are they particularly effective at managing their moods in ways that are desired (Watson, 2000). As Wilson and Gilbert (2005) describe, "Research on affective forecasting has shown that people routinely mispredict how much pleasure or displeasure future events will bring and, as a result, sometimes work to bring about events that do not maximize their happiness" (p. 131). Situated in the context of media-choice patterns, research on individuals' problems in affective forecasting might suggest that the choice of sad (or seemingly counter-hedonistic) media selections among individuals in sad or bad moods reflects mistaken judgment. Such an explanation is somewhat dissatisfying, however, given that it fails to fully explain *why* this mistaken judgment would arise in the first place and/or why it would persist. In other words, if we assume that individuals are motivated by hedonic concerns, why might there be a tendency for individuals to routinely, mistakenly believe that sad films or tragedies could serve those ends?

On the one hand, the answer to this question may well be that sad films or tragedies ultimately *do* result in mood repair and therefore do not reflect counter-hedonic selections or problems in affective forecasting—a position that I will consider below. On the other hand, if sad films are not successful in diminishing negative feelings, Loewenstein and Schkade's (1999) discussion of intuitive theories of well-being may help address this puzzle. Namely, these authors point out that many problems in affective forecasting may reflect individuals' reliance on lay theories of what will or will not function in bringing about happiness or positive affect, and that these intuitive theories often fail to account for more proximate or accurate actual causes and outcomes.

The idea that individuals have lay theories or intuitions regarding media influence has yet to garner a great deal of research attention in general, much less in regards to specific questions concerning affect regulation. However, the "lay theory" suggesting that sad films or tear-jerkers can have "cathartic" effects does appear to enjoy wide-scale popularity. References to "having a good cry" or "getting it all out" are commonplace, with popular books such as *Cinematherapy: The Girl's Guide to Movies for Every Mood* (Peske & West, 1999) encouraging readers to select "weepies" and "tear jerkers" when feeling blue, low, or melancholy as a means of purging and venting. Indeed, Cornelius' (1997) review of popular advice columns concerning weeping and catharsis revealed that almost all of the columns (94 percent) advised readers that crying and weeping was healthy and beneficial.

Consistent with the idea that intuitive theories of affect are often based on faulty reasoning, research on the popularly endorsed notion of catharsis has concluded that this function of media has very limited empirical support (Zillmann, 1998). What, then, may encourage individuals' continued reliance on this seemingly misplaced "intuitive" belief? Although the answer to this question is unclear at this point, Loewenstein and Schkade's (1999) discussion of the importance of salience may be relevant. Namely, these authors point out that in remembering or forecasting affect, people place a disproportionate emphasis on situations or stimuli that are salient or that are the focus of attention, even if the salient or attended to stimuli are not the actual or most proximate causes. As such, in the context of viewing sad films or tragedies, it may be useful to note that crying and expressions of grief often result in comforting, soothing, or supportive behaviors by others, and particularly for some individuals (e.g., females) more so than others (Vingerhoets, Cornelius, Van Heck, & Becht, 2000). Consequently, negative affect as a predictor of consuming sad films may reflect an expectation of actual comfort (as in the case of co-viewing) or imagined comfort (as experienced previously), with these positive affective experiences mistakenly attributed to the films themselves or the experience of viewing—arguably the most salient component of the media-consumption experience. Of course, such an interpretation awaits empirical validation, though it does point to the importance of researchers considering that "paradoxical" media selections may more aptly be called "mistaken" media selections or "misplaced" media selections that reflect problems associated both with individuals' identification of their affective states and their ability to effectively manage their states in ways that are intended.

Prolonging Negative States

In contrast to the idea that individuals may be motivated to rid themselves of negative affect, some researchers have explored the idea that under some circumstances, individuals may be motivated to prolong negative states if the situation or circumstances suggest that negative affect may be particularly appropriate or beneficial. For example, Zillmann (2000) pointed out a distinction between spontaneous and telic hedonism, with spontaneous hedonism referring to immediate gratification seeking, and telic hedonism referring to putting off immediate gratification for some future (and presumably larger) benefit. Applied to media consumption, Zillmann argued that whereas the majority of entertainment choices are likely governed by immediate, hedonic considerations, there might be circumstances where people opt to prolong their negative states for some future, positive outcome.

Similar to this line of reasoning, Knobloch's (2003) research on mood adjustment suggests that although individuals may generally be motivated to terminate negative moods in hedonically driven ways, they may sometimes opt to expose themselves to media portrayals that prolong negative affect when they have expectations of future interactions or tasks for which positive affective states may be inappropriate or ineffective. Such reasoning obtained empirical support in Knobloch's research on selective exposure to music, with participants tending to avoid joyful and energetic music when they anticipated having to perform in a cognitively engaging task (see also Knobloch-Westerwick & Alter, 2006).

Although this line of research provides a compelling rationale for why at some points in time individuals may opt for media selections that prolong (or at least do not disrupt) negative affective states, this perspective does not fully account for why negative affect appears to predict attraction to sad or mournful genres across a variety of circumstances. Namely, the use of this theory to explain why sad individuals appear to be attracted to sad films, for example, would necessitate the assumption that sad individuals routinely anticipate future interactions or tasks for which positive affective states would be undesirable—an assumption that seems somewhat unrealistic or improbable.

In contrast to Knobloch's (2003) mood-adjustment approach, Erber and Erber's (2000) social constraints model makes no assumption that individuals may be normally motivated by mood-repair considerations. Rather, Erber and Erber provide evidence that the default behavioral tendency for most individuals is to act in ways that maintain their moods (including sad moods) *unless* social constraints call for adjustments to a more neutral state. As a result, and counter to hedonistic assumptions, sad individuals should have a tendency to act in ways that maintain their sadness—a tendency that Erber and Erber imply may provide individuals with a greater opportunity for contemplation or reflection. As such, whereas both mood adjustment and social constraints models account for why negative affect may predict consumption of sad or tragic entertainment fare, it would appear that the social constraints model may be better able to account for more consistent patterns of sadness as a predictor of sad-media selection, as the maintenance of moods (including sad or negative moods) is conceptualized as the default behavioral tendency.

Therapeutic Purposes

Related to Erber and Erber's (2000) idea that sad mood may allow for greater reflection, a final consideration for why negative affect may be a predictor of sad or negative media choices is that consumption of such fare ultimately has therapeutic functions in helping the viewer "work through" his or her negative affective state. In this regard, conceptualizations of sad films as "cinematherapy" are consistent with the previously discussed idea of "delayed gratification," and are further consistent with the characterization of media selection as hedonically driven.

One of the most readily understood and intuitively appealing explanations for the enjoyment of tragedies is that they may help viewers put their own problems into perspective. For example, Mares and Cantor (1992) reasoned that for some viewers, self comparisons with tragic or pitiable media characters may lead to more positive affective states via the process of downward social comparison (Festinger, 1954). As such, individuals experiencing negative affect may be the ones most in need of downward comparison opportunities and may therefore be most likely to choose entertainment that serves these ends, and particularly when the entertainment features characters for whom comparisons are applicable or appropriate (i.e., similar to the viewer on a variety of characteristics). In support of this reasoning, Mares and Cantor found that higher levels of loneliness among their sample of older participants was associated with greater preference for viewing negative over positive media portrayals, and particularly so for negative portrayals featuring older characters. Further, among lonely participants, actual viewing of a media segment featuring a portrayal of a sad, downtrodden, older man resulted in higher levels of positive affect, whereas the opposite was true among non-lonely participants in the sample.

Although feeling better as a result of others' suffering may constitute some form of "therapy" in the broadest sense of the term, such therapy may be unlikely to help individuals with long-term coping or resolution of the circumstances giving rise to negative affective states. Rather, greater insight about or information concerning the issues giving rise to negative affective states would likely be a more stable and effective means of addressing concerns. Similar to this line of reasoning, Zillmann (2000) suggested that some negatively-valenced entertainment may ultimately prove comforting to listeners by making them feel understood by others who share similar fates. As such, learning of others' misfortunes should be particularly comforting in helping the viewer feel that he or she is "not alone" when the sufferer shares similar characteristics with the viewer that could encourage identification (see Knobloch & Zillmann, 2003). In addition to arguing that media may be comforting to viewers, Zillmann (2000) also suggested that the selection of negatively valenced entertainment may reflect information-seeking. That is, the experience of negative affect may motivate individuals to consume media content featuring characters experiencing similar circumstances, as such portrayals may provide viewers with information that would assist in addressing problems or rectifying troublesome situations.

Summary

Extant research has provided a variety of possible explanations for affective predictors of seemingly paradoxical media selections. These explanations identify a number of different variables that undoubtedly have important functions, including social constraints, cognitive processing, and immediate versus delayed gratifications. However, they all seem to share a focus on the idea that the valance (positive versus negative) of the affective experience both as a predictor and an outcome of media choice is a crucial component of the process. In this last section of the chapter, I raise the idea that a more complete picture of the role of affect in media selection and enjoyment may be obtained by broadening our conceptualization of both affective predictors of entertainment and our conceptualization of audience gratifications.

A Broader Conceptualization of Media Gratifications and Their Affective Predictors

Many of the seeming paradoxes that negatively valenced entertainment presents to theorizing in media psychology may be due to the tendency for researchers to focus on the notion of *enjoyment* (emphasizing positive affect) over other gratifications and motivations that people may have for media consumption. As a consequence of the focus on enjoyment (and its accompanying affect), it stands to reason that researchers have tended to examine affective predictors and reactions that are either consistent with this focus or salient in their inconsistencies in terms of affective valence. In other words, extant research may have reported "puzzling" results suggesting conclusions such as "sad people like sad films" because sadness specifically was measured (and therefore salient) rather than alternative types of affective predictors, responses, or gratifications that may be more descriptive but that were not considered or assessed. Consequently, broadening the scope of our focus to include gratifications and motivations other than only enjoyment may not only provide a fuller and more apt description of entertainment experiences, but may also help to address some of the seeming paradoxes in extant research concerning affective predictors of entertainment.

Gratifications of Human Meaningfulness

Although enjoyment and hedonic concerns undoubtedly capture a large portion of viewers' media-selection motivations, it is important to note that many forms of entertainment provide additional gratifications that go beyond mere amusement. Zillmann (1998), too, considered the idea that the experience of *enjoyment* may not be the most appropriate means of describing the gratifications that viewers experience from drama, tragedy, or other somber forms of entertainment:

> It may be considered ill-advised, in fact, to focus on enjoyment as a redeeming value of tragedy. Perhaps we should return to Aristotle's (*Poetica*) declaration of tragedy's object, namely the evocation of pity, and grant redeeming value to tragic drama's capacity for honing our empathic sensitivities and for making us cognizant of our vulnerabilities, compassions, and needs for emotional wellness—a capacity that tragedy seems to posses to a greater degree than alternative dramatic forms.
>
> (p. 12)

Indeed, the experience of "enjoyment" does not seem apply to many types of entertainment, including tragic plays, poignant dramas, or heart-wrenching sad films. To say that one "enjoyed" films such as *Schindler's List*, *One Flew Over the Cuckoo's Nest*, or *Saving Private Ryan* seems misplaced if not odd. However, it is clear that viewers *do* derive some gratification from consuming such fare, though it seems unlikely that the maximization of pleasure or the minimization of pain are the primary forces at work. Rather, it seems evident that positive affect may be inconsequential, orthogonal, or secondary to viewers' experience of gratification for some types of fare. Instead, greater insight, meaningfulness, understanding, and reflection appear to be more important components of entertainment gratification, and particularly as they relate to contemplations of human poignancies and human connection. This distinction between hedonic gratifications and gratifications associated with meaningfulness is analogous to researchers' distinctions between psychological and subjective well-being. For example, Keyes, Shmotkin, and Ryff (2002) noted that subjective well-being is associated with high levels of positive affect and low levels of negative affect, whereas psychological well-being is associated with feelings of personal growth, self-acceptance, and purpose in life. Likewise, Waterman (1993) the employed the Aristotelian terms *eudaimonia* to refer to happiness that is conceptualized in terms of personal expressiveness, and *hedonic happiness* that is conceptualized in terms of pleasure.

Perhaps because of the emphasis on *enjoyment* over other types of viewer responses in extant entertainment research, gratification associated with greater insight, meaningfulness, or understanding has yet to garner much empirical attention, and particularly within experimental contexts. However, some research from a U&G approach does suggest that individuals are motivated to view some entertainment for more than laughs or fun. For example, Katz, Gurevitc, and Haas's (1973) early research on the use of media to fulfill "important needs" identified self-gratification as a need reported by the majority of respondents. Consistent with assumptions of hedonic considerations, this gratification was associated with using media for purposes of entertainment and release of tension. At the same time, however, this gratification was also associated with using media for purposes of raising morale and experiencing beauty. Similarly, Tesser, Millar, and Wu (1988) identified three primary motivations that individuals reported for their movie-going behaviors, including a motivation that they called "self-development." Important to the present discussion, self-development motivations appear to be akin to *eudaimonic* motivations (introspection and expressiveness), as they included wanting to view movies to see how others think and feel, and selecting films that were successful in producing strong emotions. Further, this motivation was associated with preferences for films such as *Kramer vs. Kramer* and *Ordinary People*, and a dislike of more superficial fare such as *Porky's*.

Affective Predictors of Appreciation

Assuming that individuals may derive gratification from entertainment that focuses on human meaningfulness (eudaimonic motivations) over human comedy or pleasure (hedonic motivations), what might this distinction imply for the seeming paradoxes in extant research? In other words, how might such a distinction aid in our understanding of why, under some circumstances, people who are sad or blue appear to be drawn toward sad films, melancholy songs, or tragic plays? In recent research I have tried to suggest that by not fully recognizing gratifications associated with human insight and meaningfuless (i.e., eudaimonic gratifications), research in media psychology may have focused too narrowly on *sadness* or negative affect as both the most salient feature of genres such as "sad films" *and* as the most salient affective predictor (Oliver, 2007, 2008).

First, research that has examined "sad films" or tragic movies has tended to characterize these films in terms of viewers' presumed affective response. This characterization is understandable, as sad films and related fare go by a host of affect-identified names, including "tear-jerkers," "weepies," or "three-hankie movies." Despite the salience of sadness or grief that may be associated with this type of fare, though, it's not evident that sadness per se is the most important, defining element of entertainment in this genre. Rather, sad films arguably do much more than elicit sadness, but also present poignant, dramatic, moving contemplations of *human relationships* and *human connection*. Consequently, sad films may be considered to be but one example of a broader class of entertainment that may be best characterized in terms of human drama and contemplations concerning the human condition. Consequently, the first step in untangling the "paradox" of sad films may be in a broader conceptualization that characterizes this type of entertainment in terms of its focus on human conditions (both its joys and its sorrows) rather than in terms of the affective responses it elicits.

In addition to having a narrow focus on *sad* entertainment, research on affective predictors of entertainment has also tended to measure, manipulate, or assume feeling states by focusing on sad or bad moods versus happy or good moods specifically. Measures of affect have been employed to assessed naturally occurring feelings (Mares & Cantor, 1992; Strizhakova & Krcmar, 2007), bogus feedback on tasks has been provided to induce moods (Knobloch & Zillmann, 2002; Zillmann, Hezel, & Medoff, 1980), and affect has been assumed by asking participants to imagine hypothetical scenarios (Gibson et al., 2000; Knobloch, Weisbach, & Zillmann, 2004). Across all of these studies, however, it is interesting to note that the most consistent evidence for hedonic media selections is for studies in which bad moods were induced via instrumental tasks (i.e., bogus feedback on a task). In contrast, studies that have explored loneliness or heartbreak have often reported contrary evidence for mood management considerations, suggesting that sad moods or bad moods appear to heighten preferences for sad or mournful entertainment. Such an interpretation is understandable, as sad affect as a predictor is salient in these situations and is therefore often the focus of measurement. However, sadness per se may be only one component of the affective (and cognitive) states that accompany heartbreak, relational loss, or human poignancies, with other affective components also present (but not frequently assessed). If this interpretation is correct, then broadening the conceptualization of feeling states to include affective (and cognitive) blends could include additional descriptors such as *wistful, bittersweet, nostalgic, introspective*, or even *brooding* that may be more fruitful in signifying an interest in and desire to contemplate profound human conditions and to seek meaningfulness. Such a blend is analogous to Sedikides, Wildschut, and Baden's (2004, pp. 202–203) discussion of the existential function of nostalgia:

> Nostalgia is an existential exercise in search for identity and meaning, a weapon in internal confrontations with existential dilemmas, and a mechanism for reconnecting with important others. Nostalgia keeps "the wolf of insignificance" from the door.
>
> (Bellow, 1970, p. 190)

The idea that certain affective states may signify an interest in or readiness to consume entertainment that focuses on profound human conditions has yet to receive much research attention within media psychology. However, several studies point to the potential viability of this argument in explaining what appears to be counter-hedonistic media selection among individuals in serious if not negative affective states. For example, research on the phenomenon of terror management suggests that the contemplation of one's own mortality (thoughts that are arguably devoid of joy for most people) causes people to become more reflective and to search for meaningfulness in human life beyond their individual lives (Greenberg, Solomon, & Pyszczynski, 1997). One implication is that mortality salience increases the importance placed on culture, as culture represents a larger, more enduring representation of human life than an individual's own fleeting existence. Furthermore, various aspects of culture, including entertainment, are thought to provide individuals with coping mechanisms that help them to process thoughts of their own inevitable deaths. Based on this reasoning, Goldenberg, Pyszczynski, Johnson, Greenberg, and Solomon (1999) suggested that tragedy should be particularly attractive and emotionally involving when mortality salience is high, as tragic entertainment provides individuals with the opportunity to confront their fears in a safe and nonthreatening environment. Although these authors provided evidence for this reasoning by showing that mortality salience was associated with greater emotional responses to and enjoyment of tragedy, these authors did not assess the specific feelings that were elicited when participants were instructed to think of their own deaths. Consequently, it is unclear if participants' responses to tragedy were the result of feelings of fear or terror, or of some other feelings associated with mortality salience that may serve to make tragedy particularly appealing or moving.

In an attempt to examine specific affective states that may predict interest in viewing tragic or moving entertainment, I recently argued that the affective state of "tenderness" was an important precursor to individuals' interest in viewing media entertainment focused on human relationships (Oliver, 2008). Tenderness was conceptualized and operationalized as an affective blend of social emotions, including such feelings as "warmth," "tenderness," "sympathy," and "kindness." Consistent with predictions, higher levels of actual and imaged feelings of tenderness were associated with greater interest in viewing "touching" entertainment featuring portrayals of human conditions, including tragic portrayals, dramatic portrayals, and romantic portrayals. Unfortunately, this research assessed tenderness as experienced or imagined states rather than manipulating actual affect. Consequently, this line of research would benefit from future research that could induce tender affective states and that could provide greater insight into the types of experiences and cognitions that give rise to these feelings that appear to heighten interest in more contemplative entertainment.

Summary and Conclusions

The importance of affective states in predicting media selection is well established in social scientific studies. Further, individuals appear to have an intuitive notion that media content may serve as an effective means of regulating moods, as it is common to hear phrases such as "I feel like a comedy," or "I'm in the mood for a good mystery." With this background in mind, however, extant research has tended to focus its attention on mood repair, on the role of affect over cognition, and on entertainment that is assumed to result in positively-valenced affective states. This focus has resulted in considerable theorizing in attempts to resolve seemingly paradoxical media selections. By broadening our conceptualization of affect to allow for mixed affective and cognitive states, we may be in a stronger position to examine how media entertainment can not only serve our needs for enjoyment, but also our needs for greater insight, feelings of meaningfulness, and contemplation of human poignancies.

References

Biswas, R., Riffe, D., & Zillmann, D. (1994). Mood influence on the appeal of bad news. *Journalism Quarterly, 71*, 689–696.

Bryant, J. & Zillmann, D. (1984). Using television to alleviate boredom and stress: Selective exposure as a function of induced excitational states. *Journal of Broadcasting, 28*, 1–20.

Cacioppo, J. T. & Petty, R. E. (1982). The need for cognition. *Journal of Personality and Social Psychology, 42*, 116–131.

Conway, J. C. & Rubin, A. M. (1991). Psychological predictors of television viewing motivation. *Communication Research, 18*, 443–463.

Cornelius, R. R. (1997). Toward a new understanding of weeping and catharsis? In A. J. J. M. Vingerhoets, F. J. Van Bussell, & A. J. W. Boelhouwer (Eds.), *The (Non) Expression of Emotions in Health and Disease* (pp. 303–321). Tilburg: University Press.

Erber, R. & Erber, M. W. (2000). The self-regulation of moods: Second thoughts on the importance of happiness in everyday life. *Psychological Inquiry, 11*, 142–148.

Festinger, L. (1954). A theory of social comparison processes. *Human Relations, 7*, 117–140.

Gibson, R., Aust, C. F., & Zillmann, D. (2000). Loneliness of adolescents and their choice and enjoyment of love-celebrating versus love-lamenting popular music. *Empirical Studies of the Arts, 18*, 43–48.

Goldenberg, J. L., Pyszczynski, T., Johnson, K. D., Greenberg, J., & Solomon, S. (1999). The appeal of tragedy: A terror management perspective. *Media Psychology, 1*, 313–329.

Greenberg, J., Solomon, S., & Pyszczynski, T. (1997). Terror management theory of self-esteem and cultural worldviews: Empirical assessments and conceptual refinements. In M. P. Zanna (Ed.), *Advances in Experimental Social Psychology* (Vol. 29, pp. 61–139). Sand Diego: Academic Press.

Katz, E., Blumler, J., & Gurevitch, M. (1974). Utilization of mass communication by the individual. In J. Blumler & E. Katz (Eds.), *The Uses of Mass Communications: Current Perspectives on Gratifications Research* (pp. 19–32). Beverly Hills: Sage.

Katz, E., Gurevitc, M., & Haas, H. (1973). Use of mass media for important things. *American Sociological Review, 38*, 164–181.

Keyes, C. L. M., Shmotkin, D., & Ryff, C. D. (2002). Optimizing well-being: The empirical encounter of two traditions. *Journal of Personality and Social Psychology, 82*, 1007–1022.

Knobloch, S. (2003). Mood adjustment via mass communication. *Journal of Communication, 53*, 233–250.

Knobloch, S. & Zillmann, D. (2002). Mood management via the digital jukebox. *Journal of Communication, 52*, 351–366.

Knobloch, S. & Zillmann, D. (2003). Appeal of love themes in popular music. *Psychological Reports, 93*, 653–658.

Knobloch, S., Weisbach, K., & Zillmann, D. (2004). Love lamentation in pop songs: Music for unhappy lovers? *Zeitschrift für Medienpsychologie, 16*, 116–124.

Knobloch-Westerwick, S. (2006). Mood management: Theory, evidence, and advancements. In J. Bryant & P. Vorderer (Eds.), *Psychology of Entertainment* (pp. 239–254). Mahwah, NJ: Lawrence Erlbaum Associates.

Knobloch-Westerwick, S. & Alter, S. (2006). Mood adjustment to social situations through mass media use: How men ruminate and women dissipate angry moods. *Human Communication Research, 32*, 58–73.

Loewenstein, G. & Schkade, D. (1999). Wouldn't it be nice? Predicting future feelings. In D. Kahneman, E. Diener, & N. Schwarz (Eds.), *Well-being: Foundations of Hedonic Psychology* (pp. 85–105). New York: Russell Sage Foundation.

Mares, M. L. & Cantor, J. (1992). Elderly viewers' responses to televised portrayals of old age: Empathy and mood management versus social comparison. *Communication Research, 19*, 459–478.

McGuire, W. J. (1974). Psychological motives and communication gratification. In J. G. Blumler & E. Katz (Eds.), *The Uses of Mass Communications: Current Perspectives on Gratification Research* (pp. 167–196). Beverly Hills, CA: Sage.

Meadowcroft, J. M. & Zillmann, D. (1987). Women's comedy preferences during the menstrual cycle. *Communication Research, 14*, 204–218.

Oliver, M. B. (1993). Exploring the paradox of the enjoyment of sad films. *Human Communication Research, 19*, 315–342.

Oliver, M. B. (2003). Mood management and selective exposure. In J. Bryant, D. Roskos-Ewoldsen, & J. Cantor (Eds.), *Communication and Emotion: Essays in Honor of Dolf Zillmann* (pp. 85–106). Mahwah, NJ: Lawrence Erlbaum Associates.

Oliver, M. B. (2007, May). An exploration of eudaimonic motivations for viewing entertainment. Paper presented at the Colloquium Series of the Department of Communication Arts, University of Wisconsin-Madison.

Oliver, M. B. (2008). Tender affective states as predictors of entertainment preference. *Journal of Communication, 58,* 40–61.

Peske, N. K. & West, B. (1999). *Cinematherapy: The Girl's Guide to Movies for Every Mood:* London: Dell Trade Paperback.

Reber, R., Schwarz, N., & Winkielman, P. (2004). Processing fluency and aesthetic pleasure: Is beauty in the perceiver's processing experience? *Personality and Social Psychology Review, 4,* 364–382.

Reiss, S. & Wiltz, J. (2004). Why people watch reality TV. *Media Psychology, 6,* 363–378.

Rubin, A. M. (1979). Television use by children and adolescents. *Human Communication Research, 5,* 109–120.

Rubin, A. M. (2002). The uses-and-gratifications perspective of media effects. In J. Bryant & D. Zillmann (Eds.), *Media Effects: Advances in Theory and Research* (2nd ed., pp. 525–548). Mahwah, NJ: Lawrence Erlbaum Associates.

Schwarz, N. (2002). Situated cognition and the wisdom of feelings: Cognitive tuning. In L. F. Barrett & P. Salovey (Eds.), *The Wisdom in Feeling* (pp. 144–166). New York: Guilford Press.

Schwarz, N. & Clore, G. L. (2007). Feelings and phenomenal experiences. In A. W. Kruglanski & E. T. Higgins (Eds.), *Social Psychology: Handbook of Basic Principles* (2nd ed., pp. 385–407). New York: Guilford Press.

Sedikides, C., Wildschut, T., & Baden, D. (2004). Nostalgia: Conceptual issues and existential functions. In J. Greenberg, S. Koole, & T. Pyszczynski (Eds.), *Handbook of Experimental Existential Psychology* (pp. 200–213). New York: Guilford Press.

Strizhakova, Y. & Krcmar, M. (2007). Mood management and video rental choices. *Media Psychology, 10,* 91–112.

Tesser, A., Millar, K., & Wu, C. H. (1988). On the perceived functions of movies. *Journal of Psychology, 122,* 441–449.

Vingerhoets, A., Cornelius, R. R., Van Heck, G. L., & Becht, M. C. (2000). Adult crying: A model and review of the literature. *Review of General Psychology, 4,* 354–377.

Waterman, A. S. (1993). Two conceptions of happiness: Contrasts of personal expressiveness (eudaimonia) and hedonic enjoyment. *Journal of Personality and Social Psychology, 64,* 678–691.

Watson, D. (2000). Basic problems in positive mood regulation. *Psychological Inquiry, 11,* 205–209.

Wilson, T. D. & Gilbert, D. T. (2005). Affective forecasting. *Current Directions in Psychological Science, 14,* 131–134.

Zillmann, D. (1985). The experimental exploration of gratifications from media entertainment. In K. E. Rosengren, L. A. Wenner, & P. Palmgreen (Eds.), *Media Gratifications Research: Current Perspectives* (pp. 225–239). Beverly Hills, CA: Sage.

Zillmann, D. (1988a). Mood management through communication choices. *American Behavioral Scientist, 31,* 327–340.

Zillmann, D. (1988b). Mood management: Using entertainment to full advantage. In L. Donohew, H. E. Sypher, & E. T. Higgins (Eds.), *Communication, social cognition, and affect* (pp. 147–171). Hillsdale, NJ: Lawrence Erlbaum Associates.

Zillmann, D. (1998). Does tragic drama have redeeming value? *Siegener Periodikum für Internationale Literaturwissenschaft, 16,* 1–11.

Zillmann, D. (2000). Mood management in the context of selective exposure theory.

In M. E. Roloff (Ed.), *Communication Yearbook* (Vol. 23, pp. 103–123). Thousand Oaks, CA: Sage.

Zillmann, D. & Bryant, J. (1985). Selective exposure phenomena. In D. Zillmann & J. Bryant (Eds.), *Selective Exposure to Communication* (pp. 1–10). Hillsdale, NJ: Lawrence Erlbaum Associates.

Zillmann, D. & Bryant, J. (1986). Exploring the entertainment experience. In J. Bryant & D. Zillmann (Eds.), *Perspectives on Media Effects* (pp. 303–324). Hillsdale, NJ: Lawrence Erlbaum Associates.

Zillmann, D., Hezel, R. T., & Medoff, N. J. (1980). The effect of affective states on selective exposure to televised entertainment fare. *Journal of Applied Social Psychology, 10*, 323–339.

Chapter 11

Media Choice as Avoidance Behavior

Avoidance Motivations During Television Use

Andreas Fahr and Tabea Böcking

Many studies of audience research invoke what is probably the most popular approach in communication research when describing reasons for media exposure: the Uses-and-Gratifications Approach (UGA) (Katz, Blumler, & Gurevitch, 1974; for a summary, see Rubin, 2002). The paradigm conceives TV exposure primarily as a proactive approach process in which individuals preferably use media content that promises to satisfy their needs; however, in addition to substantial doubts that have been raised concerning the extent of viewers' proactivity (for an overview, cp. Vorderer, 1992; for differentiations, cp. for example Bilandzic, 2004), this perspective is often criticized because of its exclusive conceptualization of TV exposure as an *approach* process driven by *explicit motivations* that individuals are *aware* of. Recent research has shown that the process involved in switching channels can also be understood in terms of evasion: viewers change channels to avoid certain media contents; not solely because of unfulfilled needs, but to escape from unpleasant content (Perse, 1998).

The goal of this chapter is to further illuminate the question of TV exposure as an avoidance process. First, theoretical insights from classical gratification research are discussed, as well as those from cognitive and emotional psychology research. Based on these considerations, empirical data are presented that conceptualize TV exposure as avoidance behavior; reasons are introduced as to why we avoid certain content within a selected program. Finally, in discussing the implications of these findings an escape perspective is added to the UGA-perspective, conceptualizing emotions or affects as moderators of program choice.

From the Gratification Discrepancy Model to the Escape Model

The UGA serves as the basis for the gratification discrepancy model, which postulates that viewers are generally aware of their needs and therefore purposefully and intentionally choose certain types of media, shows or programs to satisfy their needs (Rubin, 2002). For example, many of us have a "need for information" (see also Hastall, this volume), which is why we turn on the daily news. Likewise, if we wish to relax, we turn to an "entertainment program." If our expectations are not met, we change the program until the media content satisfies the sought-after gratification. In other words, media exposure is accompanied by a constant comparison between "gratifications sought" (GS) and "gratifications obtained" (GO) (Palmgreen & Rayburn, 1982; Palmgreen, Wenner, & Rosengren, 1985; Rayburn & Palmgreen, 1984). As long as GO equals or exceeds GS, the gratification discrepancy model predicts that a viewer will stay with a program. If GO falls below GS for a period of time, a program change can be expected.

For the model to work, it incorporates certain assumptions that can be summarized in the following postulates. First, conscious and elaborate cognitions drive program or content choices. Media choice is somehow "concept-driven;" the process follows a *"top-down"* mode whereby wishes or needs function as explicit motivators. Second, and following on from the first point, a mainly *approach-related motivation* (Updegraff, Gable, and Taylor, 2004) guides media use. Third, individuals seek to *maximize* their benefit to attain an optimum state (Blumler, 1979; Rubin, 2002).

If we consider past studies that bring together individual needs and viewing behavior, we find that explicit motives such as general gratification expectations are often inadequate predictors of program selection in a given situation. Indeed, existing selection options, the success and popularity of shows and the situative conditions surrounding media exposure are commonly better predictors of content choice than general needs (e.g., Klövekorn, 2002; see also Webster, this volume). That is because TV viewing is mainly a habitual behavior, learned via long-term media socialization. During media exposure, general individual needs are blurred, unconscious and volatile. At best, media choice is driven by implicit motives (cp., McClelland, 1999) of which we are usually unaware. Moreover, television viewing amounts to a "low-cost situation" in which unmet gratifications do not entail serious consequences; therefore, no great effort is exerted when choosing or changing a program.[1]

Strategies of media choice are often guided by the satisficing principle (Newell & Simon, 1972; Simon, 1955), meaning that humans are satisfied with a less-than-optimal outcome provided that it suffices for their current purposes. Klein takes this view to its extreme in stating that, "Viewers watched programs not because they liked them, but because they didn't dislike them: People will not tune in for the best show, but they will tune in for the least objectionable program that is on" (Klein, quoted in MacFarland, 1997; see also Hirsch, 1980; Jeffres, 1978).

Avoidance as a Predictor of Media Choice

While definable needs become less important during media exposure, we are vulnerable to peripheral cues that intervene in the GS/GO process. In such a situation it is possible that program selection is not solely guided by the need to optimize the benefits: it may also be guided by the desire to minimize potential damage. For example, we may watch the news in accordance with our need for information (GS), but we may suddenly change the channel because graphic footage from a war-torn country becomes unbearable. The information need (GS) remains with us, but is now superceded by an affective process. In this case, a proactive-approach-related motivation turned into a reactive avoidance process that is, at least for a short period, detached from the GS/GO screening, potentially leading to a change in channel.

For example, within advertising research, Woltman Elpers, Wedel, and Pieters (2003) show that avoidance behavior is an integral part of media use: during exposure, individuals may decide to avoid advertising due to specific cognitive or affective reactions invoked by the running program (cp. Forgas, 2001). The authors identify a high information value and low entertainment value, in addition to a combination of high information value and high entertainment value, as the cause of the decision to end exposure. The findings of Walker and Bellamy (1991) and Walker, Bellamy, and Traudt, 1993 also point to the existence of an avoidance process in the context of TV exposure. Their work identifies the avoidance of media content as the main reason for remote-control usage, rather than a search for gratification. Other authors also emphasize the importance of avoidance behavior during media exposure (cp. Heeter, 1988; Heeter & Greenberg, 1985; McLeod & Becker, 1974; Perse, 1998; Van den Bulck, 2001). This perspective emphasizes the way in which viewers select programs via a negative selection process, thereby choosing the program considered the least unpleasant.

Two Processes

Of course, at this point some researchers might object to the proposal that avoidance-related motivations are not based on an autonomous process, but merely represent inverse gratification expectations. For example, one might argue that when we switch channels because we dislike a particular talk-show host, it is actually our need for parasocial interaction and relaxation that is not being satisfied. The result is a discrepancy in gratification that makes us search for a different talk show with a more likeable host. In such a case, the avoidance perspective would not have any additional explanatory value in terms of media choice; however, selectivity research strongly suggests that avoidance and approach behaviors are two different processes.

McLeod and Becker (1974) pointed to avoidance behavior as a complementary rather than inverse process. Support for this reasoning has come from research conducted by Kahneman, Knetsch, and Thaler (1991), who found that damage-avoidance commonly dominates the optimization of benefits. In particular, their research showed that damage and missed benefit are not proportional to each other. Individuals possess an anthropologically based fear of losses and damages, and this aversion commonly exceeds the maximization of benefits. This argument parallels a longstanding discussion among researchers of emotions as to whether negative and positive affects are best conceptualized as opposite poles in a single dimension or as independent processes—as it turns out, the latter appears to be true (Russell and Carroll, 1999). The hypothesis of two independent processes received further support from a study by Cacioppo and Berntson (1994), as their results indicated that negative and positive affects are based on different neurological processes. The argument is also corroborated by research that demonstrates the existence of two differing control mechanisms in the human brain (Staats & Eifert, 1990): one that controls approach-positive emotions and another that controls avoidance-negative emotions. Staats and Eifert (1990) interpret these findings as indicating the existence of "reward" and "punishment" loci in the human brain.

In summarizing our reasoning to this point, the following characteristics can be applied to avoidance processes that supplement the gratification discrepancy model. First, unconscious and unreasoned processes drive program or content selection. Media choice is commonly somewhat "content-driven" rather than volitional, and the process follows a "bottom-up" mode in which implicit motivations play a crucial role. Because this mode is barely under active control, it is susceptible to situational factors and sudden turns in content. Second, avoidance-related motivations invoked by psychologically (potentially) aversive contents guide media use under certain circumstances. Third, TV viewers seek to protect themselves and minimize damage or psychological costs rather than optimize gratifications.

Theoretical Approaches to Explaining Avoidance Behavior

Up to this point, we have proposed reasonings that suggest avoidance processes can, as moderators of the GS/GO process, explain TV viewing behavior. We now turn to a discussion of theoretical reasons for avoidance behaviors during media exposure, with a focus on cognitive and affective factors (for TV avoidance in general, see Sicking, 2000).

One way to explain avoidance behavior is to refer to consistency theories, which predict a change in behavior as a possible reaction to the perceived dissonance. When viewers absorb information that conflicts with their knowledge, opinion, attitudes and behavior, they experience a psychological state of tension that can be avoided by changing the channel. As such, in explaining behavioral changes, consistency theories assign priority to the cognitions that develop during exposure situations. For example, dissonances can result from cognitive overtaxing, leading to an end to TV exposure (Anderson, Lorch, Field, Collins, & Nathan, 1986; see also Zillmann, Hezel, & Medoff, 1980). Next to dissonance, but still from a cognitive perspective, a lack of interest may be another reason why users avoid a program (cf. Moriarty, 1991). This is consistent with Berlyne's theory of curiosity and motivation (Berlyne, 1950, 1960), which identifies unfamiliar stimuli as an important factor in the decision to continue exposure. In addition, studies concerned with reasons for zapping demonstrate that viewers defend themselves against perceived attempts to influence them ("reactance" of Brehm & Brehm, 1981; see also Niemeyer & Czycholl, 1994; Woltman Elpers et al., 2003).

A further theoretical approach that can be employed in explaining avoidance behavior deals with decision processes. These approaches assume that viewers are rational in balancing the costs of media usage against its benefits (cp. Jungermann, Pfister, & Fischer, 1998; Payne, Bettman, & Johnson, 1993). For example, the "information utility approach" (Atkin, 1985) posits that exposure is terminated at the point where the costs of watching a program exceed the benefits. Beneficial factors are the support of one's own predispositions and the informative value of the media content, while cost factors are money, time, physical and mental effort, and possible feelings of guilt, fear, irritation and dissonance. In addition, Kahneman et al. (1991) proposed that fear of possible damage or loss is much more influential in determining decision behavior than any potential benefit or gain. These costs are not inevitably the opposite of sought-after gratifications, and they are rarely discussed in uses-and-gratifications studies.

While cognitive factors can be plausibly invoked in explaining users' avoidance behavior, aversion is ultimately closely linked to feelings and emotions. Therefore, a closer examination of the psychology of emotions would further illuminate the reasons why users may turn away from media content. Research has shown that exposure to media stimuli is characterized by involvement and emotional participation.[2] Important factors in the genesis of emotions are valence and activation: valence describes the experienced pleasantness of a stimulus, while activation describes the actual arousal, which is in part induced and commonly moderated by this stimulus (Larsen & Diener, 1992; Russell & Carroll, 1999). Focusing on the arousal component, it seems plausible that viewers switch channels when their activation level becomes too high or too low. For example, Rice et al. (1982) demonstrated that stimuli that are too weak (e.g., familiar, simple, redundant, repeated) lead to boredom, while those that are too intense and complex (e.g., brand new, incompatible with former experiences, inconsistent, unpredictable, surprising) lead to overstimulation and are overly taxing (cp. Berlyne, 1960).

The theory of affect-dependent stimulus arrangement and mood management theory both postulate a medium excitation level as being optimal: a state that viewers wish to reach and maintain (Bryant & Zillmann, 1984; Zillmann, 1988; Zillmann & Bryant, 1985; Zillmann & Rohloff, 2000). To this effect, mood management theory suggests that viewers turn away from media content if it threatens the sought-after arousal-regulation.

In an analogy to the psycho-biological concept of approach/avoidance behavior, program avoidance could be seen as a protection mechanism that is supposed to prevent excessive (psychological) damage (Updegraff et al., 2004). This behavior may also be connected to the overriding process of mood management that commonly takes place during exposure. Wirth and Schramm (2005) describe several ways in which such mood regulation occurs, which in many cases is clearly affected by the wish to avoid damage and/or optimize benefits.

In general, emotion researchers generally interpret escape and avoidance behavior as one possible response to negative emotions (Schmidt-Atzert, 1995). Taking the valence component of emotions into account, viewers are also posited to avoid contents that induce a negative mood or affect (Meadowcroft and Zillmann, 1987; Oliver, 1993; Perse, 1998; Walker & Bellamy, 1991; Zillmann & Bryant, 1985; Zillmann & Rohloff, 2000; see also Oliver, this volume) or those that remind them too much of their own life and consequently prevent an escapist media use (Tamborini, Zillmann, & Bryant, 1984). Therefore, it seems likely that strongly negative emotions can be responsible for overriding the GS/GO process (cp. Bartsch, Mangold, Viehoff, & Vorderer, 2006; Miron, 2006; Schreier, 2006), thereby leading to content avoidance.

In summary, against the background of the actual TV landscape, usage patterns and cognitive as well as emotional psychology, avoidance behavior seems to be an important part of TV exposure, intervening into GS/GO adjustments. In particular, the emotional experience during TV exposure appears to be a crucial predictor of media exposure, especially in terms of avoiding negative affects rather than obtaining pleasant feelings. From this perspective, cost factors and program avoidance as a whole have yet to be analyzed, and, most notably, situational avoidance has escaped attention; however, this is especially important because in reaction to the specific program content, affective and cognitive reactions perpetually change during exposure, resulting in specific behaviors.

Program Avoidance According to the Audience

Against the background described above, we would like to present in greater detail a number of reasons why viewers switch away from a running TV program (cp. Fahr & Böcking, 2005), addressing the questions of, Which dimensions of program avoidance underlie these reasons? and, To what extend do these dimensions correspond with the postulates of the UGA?

To arrive at a broad, yet manageable, list of potential reasons for switching channels, we pursued a combination of theory-guided and empirically based courses of action. Based on our literature review, we derived (theory-led) general (i.e., not genre-specific) reasons for switching channels. For the empirical approach, we observed the switching behaviors of a small sample of viewers watching TV at home. These qualitative observations were complemented by follow-up or parallel interviews asking the viewers to explain their switching behavior. Based on these findings, 55 items indicating avoidance behavior were used in a main investigation (264 interviews). We inquired about exposure situations in which interviewees had watched TV by themselves, as the presence of other people (friends, family members, etc.) has been proven to influence program choices (i.e., Heeter, 1988; Heeter & Greenberg, 1985; Webster & Wakshlag, 1983). We also chose not to investigate the question of why viewers switch channels during commercial breaks, as extensive research already exists on this topic (e.g., Hofsümmer & Müller, 1999; Ottler, 1998; Woltman Elpers et al., 2003).

Using exploratory factor analysis, we derived six factors from the 55 items explaining program avoidance (see Table 11.1). One comprehensive explanation seems plausible and, at least ex post, theoretically tenable: it seems that viewers change channels when they experience negative emotions, dissonance or boredom, even though these emotions are not always represented in their prototypical forms.

Factor 1 is best described as indicating artificiality or lack of *authenticity*: viewers switch channels when they perceive the content to be superficial, biased, unprofessional and implausible. The viewers complain about a lack of authenticity and quality (cp. Heuvelman, Peeters, & van Dijk, 2005; Shaver, Schwartz, Kirson, & O'Connor, 1987), and that they feel intellectually insulted and/or overtaxed. The characteristics incorporated in the items also appear to counteract the view of television as a "window to reality." Suspension and relaxation appear to be impossible in such cases.

Factor 2 is connected to the strong negative emotions of *disgust* and *repugnance* (Ulich & Mayring, 1992). Viewers may switch channels "in disgust" when they judge media content to be repulsive, shocking, offensive or too violent (cp. Heuvelman et al., 2005). Feelings of disgust and repugnance are aroused by an extreme disapproval of a subject or behavior (Ulich & Mayring, 1992). Together with contempt and anger (see below), disgust and repugnance form the so-called "hostility triad" (Izard, 1981) in the emotion literature, and are also (together with hate) classified as aggression-related emotions.

Along these lines, the factor also comprises items that describe conditions of strain, irritation, instability and loss of control (Davitz, 1969). For this reason, the factor also includes the items—which at first glance appear mismatched—"loud and shrill" and "everything happens too fast." From the perspective of the psychology of emotion, high activation in tandem with a negative valence appears to play a decisive role here (Larsen & Diener, 1992). Some items also point to the experience of embarrassment and shame (Roos, 1988). These feelings arise from discrepancies between the real and ideal self, meaning that they are related to subjective moral concepts that become activated or even disturbed with exposure to the media content: the

Table 11.1 Factor Analysis: Reasons for Program Avoidance

Reasons: I switch programs, when...	M	1	2	3	4	5	6	Factor names
it is trivial/undemanding	3.8	0.68						authenticity
the people are superficial	3.4	0.68						
it is not plausible	3.7	0.65						
it is stereotyped/full of clichés	3.6	0.63						
it has nothing to do with real life	3.2	0.58						
the description of men and women is biased	3.0	0.57						
it is unprofessional/poor	4.0	0.55						
the pictures seem too artificial	3.7	0.55						
the program does not provide me with topics to discuss	3.1	0.49						
the program is superficial	3.7	0.46						
I can foresee what's happening	3.0	0.45						
the people do not interest me	3.6	0.45						
I feel treated like a child	3.4	0.43						
they show violence	3.6		0.78					disgust
it is offensive and vulgar	3.6		0.69					repugnance
it shocks me	3.4		0.65					
they show sex	2.9		0.63					
I find it disgusting	4.1		0.61					
people are mistreated	3.4		0.59					
animals are mistreated	3.6		0.55					
I think it is immoral	3.4		0.55					
it is very loud and shrill	3.9		0.51					
minorities are portrayed negative	3.1		0.45					
I feel embarrassed	3.1		0.42					
it reminds me of my own life	2.2			0.66				dejection
the program makes me brood about something	2.1			0.66				loss of distance
the people remind me of my peer	2.3			0.61				
it concerns me personally	2.5			0.57				
it gets too realistic/too genuine	2.2			0.56				
it makes me feel sad	2.7			0.56				
the program emotionally exhausts me	2.6			0.53				
they show people suffering	3.1			0.43				
I do not appreciate the expressed opinions	3.5				0.68			dissonance
I do not like the people	3.8				0.57			reactance
I feel treated as an idiot	4.0				0.56			anger
the people apparently do not have any idea	3.8				0.51			
I think they try to give me feelings of guilt	3.3				0.48			
the people talk in an unpleasant manner	3.4				0.43			
I cannot really forget my everyday life	2.8					0.68		sophistication
I cannot unwind watching	2.8					0.65		boredom
I do not get to know anything new	3.2					0.50		
I see pictures repeatedly	3.7					0.45		
it is boring	4.5					0.40		
I cannot plunge into the story	3.3						0.59	anxiety
it makes me nervous	3.6						0.56	nervousness
I am scared	3.0		0.51				0.52	
I am not interested in the topics	4.2						0.41	
Explained variance in % (total: 45.8)		10.9	10.8	7.8	6.5	5.3	4.5	
Eigenvalues		12.2	3.7	2.4	2.0	1.8	1.7	

Notes

Base: N = 264 participants; factor analysis; KMO sample adequacy: >.88; Extraction method: PCA; criterion for extraction: parallel analysis (Horn, 1965; see also Lautenschlager, Lance, & Flaherty, 1989); rotation method: Varimax; Factor values<.40 not displayed. The following items showed factor loadings <.40 on all factors and are therefore omitted: "it is not realistic" "it is too private" "everything happens too fast" "the content gets too complicated" "nothing really happens." The item "it is very thrilling" was eliminated because of a low arithmetic mean. M = arithmetic mean; Scale 1 = "I never switch;" 5 = "I switch every time."

user unexpectedly feels a state of increased self-awareness, feels unmasked, helpless and rejected (Izard, 1981). Compassion is also incorporated in this dimension: the users are affected, experiencing someone else's negative emotions (pain, misery) as their own. Compassion requires sympathy and the ability to adopt another's point of view; this appears to evoke empathy, stress, leading to avoidance behavior.

Factor 3 shows explicit emotion-related characteristics such as *dejection*, *loss of distance*, sadness and grief. In contrast to factor 2, we assume average activation and negative valence to be at work here (Larsen & Diener, 1992). Drawing from the literature on emotions, we consider that viewers switch channels because the media content reminds them of their own state or situation, which is characterized by feeling miserable, hopeless, unsatisfied, sad, depressed, empty, tired, lonely and weak (Diener, Smith, & Fujita, 1995; Ulich & Mayring, 1992). The trigger in this case would be media content that reminds viewers of their own (object or role) losses, diseases, or misfortunes (Scherer, 1988). Such stimuli raise viewers' cognitive awareness to the point that the threat of losing control or the lack of coping resources becomes highly evident.

In summary, the third factor can be interpreted as dejection and loss of distance triggered by media content that, to use an idiom, "hits too close to home." As such, the factor shows parallels with the UGA escapism factor: certain media contents apparently have the potential to block one's escape from reality. Consequently, viewers switch channels when they feel unpleasantly reminded of their own defeats (cp. Tamborini et al., 1984).

Factor 4 points to the emotions of *anger* and wrath (Ulich & Mayring, 1992), but also to cognitive responses such as *dissonance* and *reactance*. Similar to factor 2, we assume that an activated unpleasant affect is of major influence here (Larsen & Diener, 1992). Such emotions arise when people encounter pointless, unjustified obstacles during goal attainment. For example, anger results when viewers gain the impression that they are impeded, annoyed or pestered without just cause, in turn making them feel tense, overtaxed and irritable (Izard, 1981). Previous research has commonly related anger, rage and wrath to the frustration–aggression hypothesis. In the case of rage, the affective excitation overweighs; in the case of wrath it is the moral indignation. These facets are reflected in the items that ask the viewers whether they are annoyed by an expressed opinion or feel they are being treated like an idiot.

We also find contempt to be represented in the fourth factor. As with disgust and repugnance, contempt expresses an aversion, but this feeling is based more on cognitive assessments (appraisals) than on arousal-triggered feelings. Contempt results from notions of one's own superiority and low opinions of the behavior of others or the TV actors. The focus of the items in this factor reminds of the understanding of dissonance adopted by communication science, which can also lead to the devaluing of a person or an object, including their subsequent rejection. Interestingly, persons or objects perceived to impede one's goal attainment are frequently considered to be malicious and to possess a hostile intent.

Factor 5 indicates *boredom* on the one hand and *sophistication* and excessive demands on the other. Both aspects correspond with UGA and emotion psychology. People are likely to avoid a level of complexity and aspiration that is subjectively too high or too low. Being bored, viewers experience negatively toned apathy, tiredness, disinterest, indifference, and the feeling of being insufficiently challenged; this is accompanied by a distorted sense of time, inner restlessness, unease and imbalance (Plattner, 1990). A primary feature of boredom is the fact that the viewer has lost his/her subjective goal(s) (Ulich & Mayring, 1992).

Anxiety and *nervousness* appear to play a role when talking about program escape (factor 6). These feelings are particularly commonly mentioned by people when asked for escape reasons. Anxiety is experienced as a strong, non-specific concern that makes one feel confined, nervous, insecure, lonely and inferior (Diener et al., 1995; Ulich & Mayring, 1992). Similar to anger, this is more likely to be experienced as an activating and unpleasant affect (Larsen & Diener, 1992). From a cognitive perspective, viewers evaluate situations as being alarming and ominous in conjunction with uncertainty about one's coping potential for such situations.

To further evaluate the significance of the six factors, we calculated the mean values for all factor indices. Rank ordering shows that viewers switch channels most often when annoyed ($M = 3.65$), followed by fear ($M = 3.53$), authenticity ($M = 3.47$), disgust and repugnance ($M = 3.41$), sophistication and boredom ($M = 3.10$) and finally dejection and loss of distance ($M = 2.45$). Unfortunately, a lack of space prohibits any discussion of subgroup differences at this point; however, the principal goal of the current investigation was to identify those dimensions hidden behind the statement: "I switch channels when I don't like the program."

Discussion

Taken together, our findings demonstrate that it is worthwhile to view media exposure not only from the perspective of sought-after and obtained gratifications, but also to consider the role of the instantaneous costs of viewing and the following avoidance processes. In terms of watching TV, avoidance processes seem to explain and predict program choice equally as well as approach processes, especially with TV increasingly becoming a background noise or piped medium. At the very least, affects are important intervening factors that moderate the quest for gratification, thereby explaining media use and media exposure. For the sake of brevity, we discuss the main findings of our study in the following points.

1. Viewers switch channels, thereby interrupting their exposure to a program that they started watching, not solely because they did not obtain a

priori expected gratifications. Complementing the notions inherent in the UGA, our findings indicate the existence of a separate, predominantly affectively controlled avoidance process. Building on this agreement, we extend this rationale by suggesting that there exist four archetypical reactions to exposure situations, depending on the nature of discrepancy in gratification and emotional experience/positive or negative affects (see Figure 11.1). Specifically, as depicted in the upper-right quadrant of Figure 11.1, the consonance of gratification and pleasantness represents the well-known view of the UGA as an approach process (gratifications obtained meet gratifications sought). Moreover, as shown in the upper-left quadrant, a discrepancy in gratification sought and obtained can be dominated by positive affect leading to a further exploration of program offerings (e.g., when we "actually" wanted to see something else but the current program attracted our interest and an implicit set of motivations, appealing to us in a positive way). As a third possibility, gratification consonance can also be accompanied by unpleasant emotions or negative affect as in the news example described above, without leading to an interruption to TV exposure (labeled "toleration;" see the lower-right quadrant of Figure 11.1). The viewer endures a negative affect and does not attain the sought-after gratification because a long-term objective dominates short-term attempts to escape (cp. Heck-

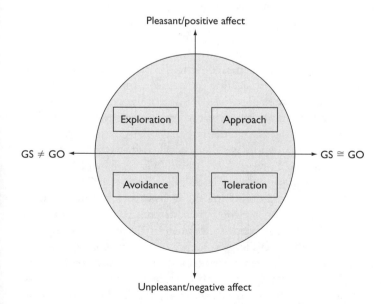

Figure 11.1 Affect as moderating factor in the gratification discrepancy model.

Note
GS = gratifications sought; Go = gratifications obtained.

hausen & Heckhausen, 2006). For example, one tolerates negative news because it is important to be able to talk about such issues with friends and colleagues. Moreover, negative-affect experiences endured while watching thrillers lead to positive evaluations subsequent to exposure, because we overcame the situation and therefore experience feelings of control (cp., Oliver, 1993; see also Oliver, this volume).

Finally, avoidance behavior may be invoked when perceived gratification discrepancies are accompanied or dominated by unpleasant emotions or negative affects (lower-left quadrant in Figure 11.1). This experience leads to avoidance and program escape.

We suggest that the four "ideal types" are likely to be separated by gradational borders. It also remains to be seen whether the four dimensions are orthogonal to each other or whether a configuration that situates positive experience and the gratification consonance closer to one another is more appropriate.

2. Our data indicate that the avoidance process is foremost triggered by "viewing costs" such as negative emotions (e.g., disgust, repugnance, fear, anxiety, anger, rage, compassion, boredom, and shame). Although these emotions emerge rather clearly in our factor–analytic investigation, it should be noted that some of the factors are tainted by items that poorly reflect their respective factors. Readers are therefore advised to regard our interpretations with caution until our claims have been substantiated by follow-up studies. The testing and confirmation of our items with other samples and in other countries represent challenges for future research.

3. Negative emotions or affects should not be regarded as the sole reason for switching channels to avoid media content. In our survey, we did not inquire about failure to meet gratification as a reason for avoidance behaviors. An investigation of this possibility was not one of the goals of this study, and none of the interviewed individuals in the preliminary examination provided such an explanation for their avoidance behavior. In other words, these findings do not disprove the hypothesis that people switch channels because of unfulfilled gratifications; however, we argue that both avoidance *and* approach processes occur in parallel (cp. McLeod & Becker, 1974), with the costs of the actual exposure situation being the decisive factor in determining which process is responsible for switching away from a particular show. We also assume that the avoidance process dominates gratifications sought in most cases because of the prevailing influence of affect components on behavior, especially in low-involvement situations. In reference to developmental psychology, we point to the fact that humans learn to recognize dangers early in life and thus are able to react rapidly in the case of peril; reactions are therefore improved even before elaborate cognitive control processes can evaluate whether present media content serves expected gratifications that are latently conscious.

4. We would also like to note that switching away from programs is only

one coping strategy for dealing with unpleasantly experienced inter- and intra-transactions. Distance, confrontational coping, self-control, search for social support, making oneself responsible, planned problem-solving and developing new, positive attitudes (Weber & Laux, 1990) are other possible outcomes that would not necessarily trigger escape behaviors (see, e.g. Wirth & Schramm, 2005 on media-bound mood-regulation; see also Oliver & Sanders, 2004). As noted above, it is possible to conceive of situations in which viewers "endure" or tolerate a show when gratification consonance and negative affects arise simultaneously (Heckhausen & Heckhausen, 2006). This holds especially true when the gratifications are regarded as being of personal importance.

5. A challenge for future research will be to identify the extent to which the discrepancy between gratification sought and obtained is accompanied by unpleasant affects or, to put it the other way, identify to what extent positive emotions correlate with consonance in gratifications sought and obtained. Our findings indicate that a sudden increase in negative affects can dominate the basic GS/GO process, possibly leading to "programmed escape."

In conclusion, we argue that viewing costs, such as the experience of negative emotions during exposure, are currently poorly integrated (or at least not sufficiently explicitly integrated) into existing models of program choice. We also consider, as advocated by previous authors, that it is time to revise the notion that negative emotions merely represent the reciprocal of sought gratifications. Risk- and loss-aversion play an important role in approaching our goals in everyday life. Based on our findings, we can provide a better explanation of program choice if we integrate approach and avoidance processes into our models of media choice.

Notes

1 See Barwise, Ehrenberg, and Goodhart, 1982; Bless and Schwarz, 2002; Doll and Hasebrink, 1989; Gensch and Shaman, 1980; Heeter and Greenberg, 1988; Hirsch, 1980; Jäckel, 1992; Jeffres, 1978; Jungermann, Pfister, and Fischer, 1998; Levy and Windahl, 1984; Perse, 1990, 1998; Rubin, 1984; Rubin and Perse, 1987; Salomon, 1984; Vorderer, 1992; Webster and Wakshlag, 1983; Weidenmann, 1989. See also Bilandzic, this volume; Marewski, Galesic and Gigerenzer, this volume.

2 See Charlton and Borcsa, 1997; Maio and Esses, 2001; Mangold, 1998; Oatley, Smelser, and Baltes, 2001; Perse, 1998; Suckfüll, 2004; Suckfüll, Matthes, and Markert, 2002; Vorderer, 1992; Woltman Elpers et al. 2003; Zillmann and Rohloff, 2000.

References

Anderson, D. R., Lorch, E. P., Field, D. E., Collins, P. A., & Nathan, J. G. (1986). Television viewing at home: Age trends in visual attention and time with television. *Child Development, 57,* 1024–1033.

Atkin, C. (1985). Informational utility and selective exposure to entertainment media. In D. Zillmann & J. Bryant (Eds.), *Selective Exposure to Communication* (pp. 63–91). Hillsdale, NJ: Erlbaum.

Bartsch, A., Mangold, R., Viehoff, R., & Vorderer, P. (2006). Emotional gratifications during media use—An integrative approach. *Communications: The European Journal of Communication Research, 31*, 261–278.

Barwise, T. P., Ehrenberg, A. S., & Goodhart, G. J. (1982). Glued to the box? Patterns of TV repeat-viewing. *Journal of Communication, 32*, 22–29.

Berlyne, D. E. (1950). Novelty and curiosity as determinants of exploratory behavior. *British Journal of Psychology, 41*, 68–80.

Berlyne, D. E. (1960). *Conflict, Arousal and Curiosity.* New York: McGraw Hill.

Bilandzic, H. (2004). *Synchrone Programmauswahl. Der Einfluß formaler und inhaltlicher Merkmale der Fernsehbotschaft auf die Fernsehnutzung.* München: R. Fischer.

Bless, H. & Schwarz, N. (2002). Konzeptgesteuerte Informationsverarbeitung. In D. Frey & M. Irle (Eds.), *Motivations-, Selbst- und Informationsverarbeitungstheorien* (pp. 257–278). Bern: Huber.

Blumler, J. G. (1979). The role of theory in uses and gratifications studies. *Communication Research, 6*, 9–36.

Brehm, S. S. & Brehm, J. W. (1981). *Psychological Reactance: A Theory of Freedom and Control.* New York: Academic Press.

Bryant, J. & Zillmann, D. (1984). Using television to alleviate boredom and stress: Selective exposure as a function of induced excitational states. *Journal of Broadcasting, 28*, 1–20.

Cacioppo, J. T. & Berntson, G. G. (1994). Relationship between attitudes and evaluative space: A critical review, with emphasis on the separability of positive and negative substrates. *Psychological Bulletin, 115*, 401–423.

Charlton, M. & Borcsa, M. (1997). Thematische Voreingenommenheit, Involvement und Formen der Identifikation: Diskussion eines Modells für das aktive Zuschauerhandeln anhand eines empirischen Beispiels. In M. Charlton & S. Schneider (Eds.), *Rezeptionsforschung: Theorien und Untersuchungen zum Umgang mit Massenmedien* (pp. 254–267). Opladen: Westdeutscher Verlag.

Davitz, J. R. (1969). *The Language of Emotion.* New York: Academic Press.

Diener, E., Smith, H., & Fujita, F. (1995). The personality structure of affect. *Journal of Personality and Social Psychology, 69*(1), 130–141.

Doll, J. & Hasebrink, U. (1989). Zum Einfluß von Einstellungen auf die Auswahl von Fernsehsendungen. In J. Groebel & P. Winterhoff-Spurk (Eds.), *Empirische Medienpsychologie* (pp. 45–63). München: PVU.

Fahr, A. & Böcking, T. (2005). Nichts wie weg? Ursachen der Programmflucht. *Medien & Kommunikationswissenschaft, 53*(1), 5–25.

Forgas, J. P. (2001). The affect infusion model (AIM): An integrative theory of mood effects on cognition and judgments. In L. L. Martin & G. L. Clore (Eds.), *Theories of Mood and Cognition: A User's Guidebook* (pp. 99–134). Mahwah, NJ: Erlbaum.

Gensch, D. & Shaman, P. (1980). Models of competitive television ratings. *Journal of Marketing Research, 17*, 307–315.

Heckhausen, J. & Heckhausen, H. (Eds.). (2006). *Motivation und Handeln* (3rd ed.). Heidelberg: Springer.

Heeter, C. (1988). The choice process model. In C. Heeter & B. S. Greenberg (Eds.), *Cableviewing* (pp. 11–32). Norwood, NJ: Ablex.

Heeter, C. & Greenberg, B. S. (1985). Cable and program choice. In D. Zillmann & J. Bryant (Eds.), *Selective Exposure to Communication* (pp. 203–224). Hillsdale, NJ: Erlbaum.

Heeter, C. & Greenberg, B. S. (1988). A theoretical overview of the program choice process. In C. Heeter & B. S. Greenberg (Eds.), *Cableviewing* (pp. 33–50). Norwood, NJ: Ablex.

Heuvelman, A., Peeters, A., & van Dijk, J. (2005). Irritating, shocking, and intolerable TV programs: Norms, values, and concerns of viewers in the Netherlands. *Communications: The European Journal of Communication Research, 30*, 325–342.

Hirsch, P. M. (1980). An organizational perspective on television (Aided and abetted by models from economics, marketing, and the humanities). In S. B. Withey & R. P. Abeles (Eds.), *Television and Social Behavior: Beyond Violence and Children* (pp. 83–102). Hillsdale, NJ: Erlbaum.

Hofsümmer, K.-H. & Müller, D. K. (1999). Zapping bei Werbung—ein überschätztes Phänomen. *Media Perspektiven* (6), 296–300.

Horn, J. L. (1965). A rationale and test for the number of factors in factor analysis. *Psychometrika, 30*, 179–185.

Izard, C. E. (1981). *Die Emotionen des Menschen*. Weinheim: Beltz.

Jäckel, M. (1992). Mediennutzung als Niedrigkostensituation: Anmerkungen zum Nutzen- und Belohnungsansatz. *Medienpsychologie, 4*, 246–266.

Jeffres, W. (1978). Cable TV and viewer selectivity. *Journal of Broadcasting, 22*, 167–177.

Jungermann, H., Pfister, H.-R., & Fischer, K. (1998). *Die Psychologie der Entscheidung*. Heidelberg: Springer.

Kahneman, D., Knetsch, J. L., & Thaler, R. H. (1991). Anomalies: The endowment effect, loss aversion, and status quo bias. *Journal of Economic Perspectives, 5* (1), 193–206.

Katz, E., Blumler, J. G., & Gurevitch, M. (1974). Utilization of mass communication by the individual. In J. G. Blumler & E. Katz (Eds.), *The Uses of Mass Communications. Current Perspectives on Gratifications Research* (pp. 19–32). Beverly Hills, CA: Sage.

Klövekorn, N. (2002). *Sehen wir, was wir wollen? Die Fernsehprogrammauswahl unter Berücksichtigung langfristiger Zuschauerpräferenzen und Programmierungsstrategien der Fernsehsender*. München: R. Fischer.

Larsen, R. J. & Diener, E. (1992). Promises and problems with the circumplex model of emotion. In M. S. Clark (Ed.), *Review of Personality and Social Psychology* (pp. 25–59). Newbury Park, CA: Sage.

Lautenschlager, G. J., Lance, C. E., & Flaherty, V. L. (1989). Parallel analysis criteria: Revised equations for estimating the latent roots of random data correlation matrices. *Educational and Psychological Measurement, 49*, 339–345.

Levy, M. R. & Windahl, S. (1984). Audience activity and gratifications: A conceptual clarification and exploration. *Communication Research, 11*, 51–78.

MacFarland, D. T. (1997). *Future Programming Strategies. Cultivating Listenership in the Digital Age*. Mahwah, NJ: Erlbaum.

Maio, G. R. & Esses, V. M. (2001). The need for affect: Individual differences in the motivation to approach or avoid emotions. *Journal of Personality, 69* (4), 583–615.

Mangold, R. (1998). Emotionale Wirkungsaspekte während der Fernsehrezeption. In W. Klingler, G. Roters, & O. Zöllner (Eds.), *Fernsehforschung in Deutschland. Theorien—Methoden—Akteure* (pp. 641–660). Baden-Baden: Nomos.

McClelland, D. C. (1999). *Human Motivation* (6 ed.). Cambridge: Cambridge University Press.

McLeod, J. M. & Becker, L. B. (1974). Testing the validity of gratification measures through political effects analysis. In J. G. Blumler & E. Katz (Eds.), *The Uses of mass communications. Current Perspectives on Gratification Research* (pp. 137–164). Beverly Hills, CA: Sage.

Meadowcroft, J. M. & Zillmann, D. (1987). Women's comedy preferences during the menstrual cycle. *Communication Research, 14*, 204–218.

Miron, D. (2006). Emotion and cognition in entertainment. In J. Bryant & P. Vorderer (Eds.), *Psychology of Entertainment* (pp. 343–364). Mahwah, NJ: Erlbaum.

Moriarty, S. E. (1991). Explorations into the commercial encounter. In R. Homann (Ed.), *Proceedings of the 1991 Conference of the American Academy of Advertising*. New York.

Newell, A. & Simon, H. A. (1972). *Human Problem Solving*. Englewood Cliffs, NJ: Prentice-Hall.

Niemeyer, H. G. & Czycholl, J. (1994). *Zapper, Sticker und andere Medientypen: eine marktpsychologische Studie zum selektiven TV-Verhalten*. Stuttgart: Schaeffer-Poeschel.

Oatley, K., Smelser, N. J., & Baltes, P. B. (2001). Emotion in Cognition. In N. J. Smelser & P. B. Baltes (Eds.), *International Encyclopaedia of the Social and Behavioral Sciences* (pp. 4440–4444). Amsterdam: Elsevier.

Oliver, M. B. (1993). Exploring the Paradox of the Enjoyment of Sad Films. *Human Communication Research, 19*, 315–342.

Oliver, M. B. & Sanders, M. (2004). The appeal of horror and suspense. In S. Prince (Ed.), *The Horror Film* (pp. 242–260). New Brunswick, NJ: Rutgers University Press.

Ottler, S. (1998). *Zapping—Zum selektiven Umgang mit Fernsehwerbung und dessen Bedeutung für die Vermarktung von Werbezeit*. München: R. Fischer.

Palmgreen, P. & Rayburn, J. D. (1982). Gratifications sought and media exposure: An expectancy value model. *Communication Research, 9*, 561–580.

Palmgreen, P., Wenner, L. A., & Rosengren, K. E. (1985). Uses and gratifications research: The past ten years. In K. E. Rosengren, L. A. Wenner & P. Palmgreen (Eds.), *Media Gratifications Research: Current Perspectives* (pp. 11–37). Beverly Hills, CA: Sage.

Payne, J. W., Bettman, J. R., & Johnson, E. J. (1993). *The Adaptive Decision Maker*. Cambridge: Cambridge University Press.

Perse, E. M. (1990). Audience selectivity and involvement in the newer media environment. *Communication Research, 17*, 675–697.

Perse, E. M. (1998). Implications of cognitive and affective involvement for channel changing. *Journal of Communication, 48* (3), 49–68.

Plattner, I. (1990). *Zeitbewußtsein und Lebensgeschichte*. Heidelberg: Asanger.

Rayburn, J. D. & Palmgreen, P. (1984). Merging uses and gratifications and expectancy-value theory. *Communication Research, 11*(4), 537–562.

Rice, M. L., Huston, A. C., Wright, J. C., Pearl, D., Bouthilet, L., & Lazar, J. B. (1982). The forms of television: Effects on children's attention, comprehension, and social behavior. In National Institute of Mental Health (Ed.), *Television and Behavior: Vol. 2. Ten Years of Scientific Progress and Implications for the 80's* (pp. 24–38). Washington D.C.: Government Printing Office.

Roos, J. (1988). *Die Entwicklung der Zuschreibung komplexer Emotionen am Beispiel der Emotion 'Peinlichkeit'*. Frankfurt: Lang.

Rubin, A. M. (1984). Ritualized and instrumental television viewing. *Journal of Communication, 2*, 67–77.

Rubin, A. M. (2002). The uses-and-gratifications perspective of media effects. In J. Bryant & D. Zillmann (Eds.), *Media Effects: Advances in Theory and Research* (pp. 525–548). Mahwah, NJ: Erlbaum.

Rubin, A. M. & Perse, E. M. (1987). Audience activity and television news gratifications. *Communication Research, 14* (1), 58–84.

Russell, J. A. & Carroll, J. M. (1999). On the Bipolarity of Positive and Negative Affect. *Psychological Bulletin, 125*, 3–30.

Salomon, G. (1984). Television is "easy" and print is "tough": The differential investment of mental effort in learning as a function of perceptions and attributions. *Journal of Educational Psychology, 76*, 647–658.

Scherer, K. R. (Ed.). (1988). *Faces of Emotion*. Hillsdale, NJ: Erlbaum.

Schmidt-Atzert, L. (1995). *Lehrbuch der Emotionspsychologie*. Stuttgart: Kohlhammer.

Schreier, M. (2006). (Subjective) well-being. In J. Bryant & P. Vorderer (Eds.), *Psychology of Entertainment* (pp. 389–404). Mahwah, NJ: Erlbaum.

Shaver, P., Schwartz, J., Kirson, D., & O'Connor, C. (1987). Emotion knowledge: Further exploration of a prototype approach. *Journal of Personality and Social Psychology, 52*, 1061–1086.

Sicking, P. (2000). *Leben ohne Fernsehen: Eine qualitative Nichtfernseherstudie*. Wiesbaden: DUV.

Simon, H. A. (1955). A behavioral model of rational choice. *Quarterly Journal of Economics, 69*, 99–118.

Staats, A. W. & Eifert, G. H. (1990). The paradigmatic behaviorism theory of emotions. *Clinical Psychology Review, 10*, 539–566.

Suckfüll, M. (2004). *Rezeptionsmodalitäten. Ein integratives Konstrukt für die Medienwirkungsforschung*. München: R. Fischer.

Suckfüll, M., Matthes, J., & Markert, D. (2002). Rezeptionsmodalitäten: Definition und Operationalisierung individueller Strategien bei der Rezeption von Filmen. In P. Rössler, S. Kubisch, & V. Gehrau (Eds.), *Empirische Perspektiven der Rezeptionsforschung* (pp. 193–211). München: R. Fischer.

Tamborini, R., Zillmann, D., & Bryant, J. (1984). Fear and victimization: Exposure to television and perceptions of crime and fear. In R. N. Bostrom (Ed.), *Communication Yearbook* (Vol. 8, pp. 492–513). Beverly Hills, CA: Sage.

Ulich, D. & Mayring, P. (1992). *Psychologie der Emotionen*. Stuttgart: Kohlhammer.

Updegraff, J., Gable, S. L., & Taylor, S. E. (2004). What Makes Experiences Satisfying? The Interaction of Approach-Avoidance Motivations and Emotions in Well-Being. *Journal of Personality and Social Psychology, 86* (3), 496–504.

Van den Bulck, J. (2001). News avoidance: The paradox of viewer selectivity. In K. Renckstorf, D. McQuail, & N. Jankowski (Eds.), *Television News Research: Recent European Approaches and Findings* (pp. 173–184). Berlin: Quintessenz.

Vorderer, P. (1992). *Fernsehen als Handlung*. Berlin: Sigma.

Walker, J. R. & Bellamy, R. V. (1991). The gratifications of grazing: An exploratory study of remote control use. *Journalism Quarterly, 68*, 422–431.

Walker, J. R., Bellamy, R. V., Jr., & Traudt, P. J. (1993). Gratifications derived from remote control devices: A survey of adult RCD use. In J. R. Walker & R. V.

Bellamy, Jr. (Eds.), *The Remote Control in the New Age of Television* (pp. 103–112). Westport, CT: Praeger.

Weber, H. & Laux, L. (1990). Bringing the person back into stress and coping measurement. *Psychological Inquiry, 1*, 37–40.

Webster, J. G. & Wakshlag, J. J. (1983). A theory of television program choice. *Communication Research, 10*, 430–446.

Weidenmann, B. (1989). Der mentale Aufwand beim Fernsehen. In J. Groebel & P. Winterhoff-Spurk (Eds.), *Empirische Medienpsychologie* (pp. 134–149). München: PVU.

Wirth, W. & Schramm, H. (2005). Media and Emotions. *Communication Research Trends, 24*, 3–39.

Woltman Elpers, J. L. C. M., Wedel, M., & Pieters, R. G. M. (2003). Why Do Consumers Stop Viewing Television Commercials? Two Experiments on the Influence of Moment-to-Moment Entertainment and Information Value. *Journal of Marketing Research, 40* (4), 437–453.

Zillmann, D. (1988). Mood management: Using entertainment to full advantage. In L. Donohue, H. E. Sypher, & E. T. Higgins (Eds.), *Communication, Social Cognition and Affect* (pp. 147–172). Hillsdale, NJ: Erlbaum.

Zillmann, D. & Bryant, J. (1985). Affect, mood, and emotion as determinants of selective exposure. In D. Zillmann & J. Bryant (Eds.), *Selective Exposure to Communication* (pp. 157–190). Hillsdale, NJ: Erlbaum.

Zillmann, D., Hezel, R. T., & Medoff, N. J. (1980). The effect of affective states on selective exposure to televised entertainment fare. *Journal of Applied Social Psychology, 10*, 323–339.

Zillmann, D. & Rohloff, M. E. (2000). Mood management in the context of selective exposure theory. In *Communication Yearbook* (Vol. 23, pp. 103–123). Thousand Oaks, CA: Sage.

Chapter 12

Media Choice on a Micro Level

On-line Selective Strategies in Watching Television

Helena Bilandzic

In expanding television environments, viewers are confronted with an abundance of channels to compose their television fare. It is up to the viewers to decide with which programs they spend their time in front of the set, and which programs they choose to ignore. While planned choices aided by program guides exist, and habitual use is still important, many viewers use the remote control to inform themselves about the current options and to eventually choose one (Heeter & Greenberg, 1988a). Other motivations for channel changes may be to avoid less liked content, e.g., advertising, and to watch multiple shows at a time (Heeter, 1988; Walker & Bellamy, 1991; see also Fahr & Böcking in this volume). Such behaviors can be summarized as *on-line selective strategies*—selections that are made by changing channels with the remote control.

On-line selective strategies are investigated on a micro level if the main interest of research lies in explaining individual variations in television selections. However, the same data basis—individual-level data on channel changes—may inform macro level investigations if the goal of the analysis is to trace aggregate fluctuations in the size and composition of television audiences. For example, aggregate level research has been done regarding the overlap between audiences of different shows and time slots (e.g., Barwise & Ehrenberg, 1988; Cooper, 1993; Webster, 1985). This line of research is particularly useful in applied audience research to build smooth transitions between shows or from shows to commercials and back in order to keep as many viewers as possible and manage the "audience flow" (Adams, 1993; Eastman, Newton, Riggs, & Neal-Lunsford, 1997; Eastman & Newton, 1995). These aggregate (or macro) level approaches use television units as a basis of analysis—a show, a time slot, a genre, etc., and observe audiences movements. An individual (or micro) level perspective, which is the main concern of this chapter, seeks to explain television selections with individual factors (ones that vary across individuals), often by making use of the viewers' subjective interpretations of their actions, intentions, motivations and mental processes. However, to complete the picture of individual on-line selections, the influence of external factors (e.g., television content) will be briefly summarized as well even if it usually belongs to aggregate level research. After all, on-line selections are the result of an interaction between television content and the viewer, and factors from both sides need to be considered for complete explanations.

This chapter summarizes research about on-line television selections. First, measurement issues of investigating channel changes will be discussed and some descriptive results will be presented. Then, internal and external factors for channel changes will be delineated and research on each of these will be presented. Finally, process-oriented explanations for channel changes will be synthesized and discussed.

Measurement Issues in Studying Channel Changes

Three methods are generally used to capture channel changing: self report, observation, and meter data (Webster & Lichty, 1991; Webster & Wakshlag, 1985). These methods generate different results on the rate of channel changes. While all media behaviors are sensitive to the methods that are used to investigate them, channel changing stands out from other media behavior in several respects that make it even more sensitive. First, changing channels is a mundane behavior that is given little attention by the viewer (Ferguson, 1994). Second, it occurs repeatedly during television viewing, which means that viewers cannot remember every single instance. Third, it varies within viewers from context to context, depending on factors such as the current program options, available time budget, motives, or the viewing group.

All of these characteristics of channel changing make the use of self reports difficult. Self reports of behavior are generally intricate because they do not measure actual behavior but a *subjective estimate* of the behavior. Viewers cannot remember the frequency of channel changes very well, and they usually underestimate their actual rate (Ferguson, 1994; Kaye & Sapolsky, 1997). Typical reasons for using the switch (e.g., to avoid commercials) might be better remembered than atypical reasons. Generalizing across many situations may also result in superficial explanations, e.g., the motive was to avoid boring or annoying content. Self report is strong in assessing stable behavior and behavior that is accessible to a respondent's consciousness (Anderson & Field, 1985)—both of which are not the case here. Apart from memory problems, integrating many experiences into a judgment of how often one switches through channels requires some sort of cognitive algebra across situations that may represent merely (forced) guesses or at best be biased by factors such as recent experiences. Finally, spending time flipping from channel to channel is not an activity that is socially desirable. Thus, respondents might try to embellish their actual behavior. However, despite these disadvantages, self-reports are widely used (e.g., Ferguson, 1992; Hawkins, Pingree, Fitzpatrick, Thompson, & Bauman, 1991; Heeter &

Greenberg, 1988a), because they have a decisive advantage compared to more "objective" methods like observation or meter data: in a self report, respondents are able to indicate the *sense* of their channel changes, e.g. the motivations for and the importance of channel changing relative to other aspects of television use.

Observing channel changes unburdens the viewer from making those difficult judgments about their own behavior. There are different possibilities how to do an observation: First, a human observer may be present to note ongoing channel changes (Eastman & Newton, 1995). Second, a video cassette recorder (or digital recorder) may register all channel changes that are visible on the television set (Bilandzic, 1999; Traudt, 1993). Third, a video camera may record both the television image and the viewer at the same time (Copeland & Schweitzer, 1993). Although these methods are more precise and less demanding for the viewers, both the human observer and the video camera are obtrusive and may disturb the viewer's privacy. Both video based observational methods have the downside of providing uncoded material that needs processing before it can be analyzed; training and sending human observers to households is just as costly.

Another method that provides data on channel changes uses electronic meters to track instances in which the television set is turned on and off, and which channels are selected at what precise moment in time. Such methods are costly; technical equipment distributed in representative samples is mostly used in commercial audience research for broadcasting companies that provide ratings of programs and advertisement, e.g., Nielsen ratings in the U.S. or the German ratings organized by the Gesellschaft für Konsumforschung (GfK). These data mostly serve the function to provide program ratings as a basis for advertisement pricing, not primarily for tracking channel changes. Obviously, the advantage of meter data lies in the high precision and reliability of the data (provided that the meter devices are properly used by the respondents). Respondents do not have to observe themselves, or make inferences or summaries of their own behavior. However, meter data do not provide any interpretation of behavior—that is, what viewers intended to do when they switched the channel. Deciding on a method is a trade-off between precision and objectivity on one hand, and getting to know the subjective sense of channel changes on the other.

Descriptive Data on Channel Changing

The Rate

Depending on the meter technology, different rates for channel changes are found. Heeter, d'Alessio, Greenberg, and McVoy (1988) used a meter that measured television use once every minute—channel changes that occurred between two measurements were not recorded by the system. They found

4.4 channel changes per hour that were mostly positioned at the full and the half hour, indicating orienting behavior (Heeter et al., 1988; for similar results see Kaplan, 1985). For Germany, Jäckel (1993) found 10 to 11 channel changes per hour, depending on the week day—also using a meter that only recorded changes every 21 seconds. Bilandzic (1998), using a meter that recorded all channel changes at any point in time, found 16 channel changes per hour. A detailed analysis showed that the average gives a false impression of the actual behaviors: half of the viewers switched 6 times or less, while 10 percent of the viewers switched more than 40 times per hour.

There is some indication that viewers have increased their switching rate in the course of the past decade. Ettenhuber (2007) found an increase in channel changes from 1995 to 2005 using representative meter data from Germany. While viewers changed channels every 6.4 minutes in 1995, they accelerated their rate to channel changes every four minutes in 2001; the rate has remained more or less constant since then.

Demographics of Channel Changers

While precise measurement of actual channel changing is sensitive to different methods, the demographic characteristics of those who switch and those who do not is consistent across different methods, samples and countries (Bellamy & Walker, 1996). In a survey, Heeter (1988) found that switching through the channels for orientation about what is on and re-evaluation is more frequent in men and younger persons. Heeter and Greenberg (1988a), also using survey data, found that men and younger persons generally use the remote control more often compared to women and older persons. Meter data in the US (e.g., Greenberg, Heeter, & Sipes, 1988) and Germany (Bilandzic, 1998; Ettenhuber, 2007) confirmed this finding.

Internal Factors for Channel Changing: Intentions, Motives, and Traits

From the individual's perspective, channel changes may have different functions. In the past, researchers have developed taxonomies of what channel changes mean and how they can be explained. There are some frequently used terms that characterize the viewers' intentions of channel changes, but that are used somewhat differently across different studies. The clearest terms are zapping and hopping. *Zapping*, in a narrow sense, is avoiding television commercials by changing the channel, sometimes also in the sense of physical zapping—leaving the room when the commercial break begins (Heeter, 1988; Heeter & Greenberg, 1988b). In a wide sense (and in everyday language), zapping is used as a synonym for channel changes regardless of their reason. *Zipping* is a variant of commercial avoidance, where the viewer fast-forwards a videotaped show to skip commercials. In digital recorders, zipping is enabled by various fast-forwarding speeds, functions that skip through the program in 30 second slots or automated functions that get rid of commercials during recording (Woltman Elpers, 2003). *Hopping* is a term for watching several shows at the same time by switching back and forth between two or more channels (e.g., Heeter, 1988; Heeter & Greenberg, 1988b). *Flipping* or *switching* through the program are usually used synonymously to express channel changes with the goal of orientation and searching a program to watch. *Scanning* denotes the same thing, albeit with a connotation of a quick succession through the channels. *Grazing* is also used to express consecutive channel changes (e.g., Eastman & Newton, 1995; Walker & Bellamy, 1991), but this time with the negative connotation of aimlessness.

One of the first categorizations of channel changing motives was provided by Heeter and Greenberg (1988a): Viewers switch channels to see what else is on, to avoid commercials, out of boredom, for variety, and to watch multiple shows. To obtain a more coherent and precise categorization of channel changing motives, Walker and Bellamy (1991) developed a 47-item questionnaire from an exploratory study using open-ended questions about the gratifications of channel changing. In a survey of 455 college students, seven dimensions emerged in a factor analysis. They found that viewers use the remote control to (1) selectively avoid political ads, news, politicians, journalists and other persons they do not like, (2) control what is being watched, to annoy or tease co-viewers, (3) inform themselves about the current program without getting up or consulting a television guide, (4) get more from television, to make it more interesting, (5) avoid commercials, (6) watch music videos and (7) watch news. It becomes apparent that content drives many of the channel changes—in either avoidance or search. But channel changes can also increase enjoyment of television by giving the viewers the freedom to initiate or end their attention to given options. The remote control as a means of power within the family or another viewing group is also independent of content. At the same time, these dimensions are analytical, but not mutually exclusive. When a viewer switches from a program, she may avoid certain content, but at the same time look for a different option and establish her position of power in her viewing group. Music and news were mentioned as the only formats that viewers seek. While quite different, they are similar in a formal sense: Both are available on specialized channels all day and both are composed of small, self-contained segments that are ideal for on-line selection. Of course, viewers do look for other content as well—but that may be so diverse that it is hidden in the dimension "getting more from television." The study by Walker and Bellamy (1991) confirmed some of the reasons for using the remote control found earlier by Ainslie (1989; cited in Walker, Bellamy, & Traudt, 1993). Specifically, when forced to indicate only one reason for remote control use, almost a third of the respondents indicated that they use the remote control when they get bored with the program and another third indicated to look for better programs. More than a fifth chose zapping and a tenth hopping (Ainslie, 1989; cited in Walker et al., 1993).

Walker et al. (1993) replicated the study with a representative sample of adults using a reduced set of 24 gratification items and found a similar factor structure as in the student sample. In another study with students, Wenner and Dennehy (1993) extracted a similar factor structure, again with selective avoidance, aggressive play (annoy co-viewers), commercial avoidance, music scanning, news scanning and, differently from previous studies, environmental convenience (not getting up, adjust sound).

To avoid typical problems of situation-independent self report, several studies investigated channel changes in the actual viewing situation so respondents did not have to reproduce and reflect their own actions. Traudt (1993) explored the use and the meaning of the remote control in a mix of observation, interviews and additional self report supported by the observation. He videotaped television viewing behavior including all channel changes of five voluntary participants for at least one and a half hours. During the interviews, these recordings were used to ask specific questions about channel changes and their function for the individual viewer. Traudt (1993) found three recurring patterns of RCD use. First, in the "surveillance phase," viewers switch channels in a fast pace to learn what programs are on at a given time, either when they first turn on the set, or between viewing longer segments. Usually, the viewers' goals are unspecific; they try to find something to watch, or at least to narrow down their choice to a set of channels. Second, in the "cluster viewing" phase, viewers have chosen a smaller set of channels to view a program or to review the given options again. Third, "within cluster viewing" means that individuals view a longer portion of a program. This can be either initiated after a phase of surveillance or as the result of planned viewing. Traudt (1993) sees television viewing as the result of external conditions, such as the technology of the remote control and the available program options, and internal states such as program preferences and habits. Both of these determine how viewers use the remote control.

Two studies by Bilandzic (1999; 2002) also involved a combination of observation and self report. Again, channel changing behavior was recorded and used as a basis for self-report; more specifically, respondents were instructed to retrospectively think aloud while they watched the tape of their own television viewing. They were not prompted to deliver reasons for their channel changing, they just had to verbalize any thoughts they had while watching in order to avoid rationalizations. In the two studies involving a sample of 12 students and a sample of 20 adolescents, invariant elements of selective television viewing could be reconstructed from the selective behavior and the content of the shows or fragments watched, on one hand, and the verbal protocols on the other. Similar patterns of subjective interpretations of behavior emerged in both studies. First and foremost, viewers were busy recognizing what is on, in varying degrees of thoroughness. Recognition was oriented towards different aspects of the television content, most of it concerned with classifications of the television message, such as topic, genre, show, and to a lesser extent stimulus characteristics such as images or tones. What was recognized may initiate five types of cognitive activities. First, viewers express positive or negative evaluations of what they recognized. Second, they refer to habits connected to television content they see. Third, they generate expectations towards content, channel or show. Fourth, viewers associate personal experiences with television content by referring to biographical information and events, or by telling about other media experiences and elaborating what is said on television by knowledge otherwise acquired. Fifth, viewers spend a substantial portion of their viewing time to explore the television options, to get an overview of all options or by watching options a little longer to get information on the type of show or the topic and then to decide whether to stay with it or switch on. Verbal reports were more detailed when viewers remained with an option for a longer period, while rapid fire switching was not commented in much detail. This is partly due to lack of time to verbalize thoughts (even though respondents had the opportunity to stop the tape during their verbal report to elaborate). Also, it is possible that the thoughts are considerably reduced in these rapid fire phases of selective television use and that people employ routinized, stereotypic, low-effort decision strategies that more or less match the available situation with memorized situations and typical actions, rather than use rational and conscious strategies (see also Marewski, Galesic, & Gigerenzer in this volume). These findings mirror the results in a study by Perse (1998) who found out that viewers were more likely to change channels when they are not mentally engaged, their attention as well as their cognitive involvement into the program is low or when they experience negative affect with a program.

Instead of exploring subjective interpretations of channel changing another approach is to categorize mere behavior and to distinguish different actions on the remote control from each other. Cornwell et al. (1993), in order to avoid biases in self-reports, recorded the television set in ten households during six days from five p.m. to one a.m. These recordings were coded for four different behaviors involving the remote control. Grazing was defined as switching at least through three channels while not remaining more than five seconds with each of them. Hopping was defined as watching multiple shows, and operationalized as switching back and forth between two channels at least three times within five minutes. Zapping was leaving a channel at least three seconds before a commercial ends. Zipping was fast-forwarding a video tape during the commercial break. Zapping and grazing were the most common behaviors, while zipping and hopping were less popular. The strength of this study in terms of methods is that exact operational definitions of the different remote control behaviors were developed, which enables an unbiased assessment of the purpose of channel changes.

Eastman and Newton (1995) also employed an observational method to investigate different uses of the RCD. Instead of video cameras, trained students observed 253 adults and children during three hours of prime time viewing, recording every remote control operation. They coded punching (choosing a channel with the numbers pad of the remote control), arrowing (pressing the up and down button very quickly to get to a predetermined channel), scanning (pressing the up and down button more slowly to get an impression of the program), jumping (use of the previous channel button), muting (changing or eliminating the volume) and inserting (placing additional programs on the screen). The authors interpret punching, arrowing, jumping and inserting as purposeful activities. They found out that such purposeful activities taken together are much more prevalent than scanning— which is seen as a less purposeful activity indicating browsing around aimlessly in the television landscape. Men used the remote control more often to punch in a specific channel, to jump and to scan, which corresponds to self report studies. Channels changes were equally distributed across program types, with higher rates during sports programming and lower rates during pay-cable movies. Especially at the start and end of programs, channel changes increased. Also, individual viewers switched more than viewers in groups, but used the remote control for the same operations.

Wenner and Dennehy (1993) looked for predictors of channels changes, focusing on the psychological origins of remote control gratifications and the frequency of its use (which adds a trait component to the repertoire of explanations and thus a less intentional momentum on the nature of these television decisions). The use of the remote control to see what is on after viewers switch on the television was predicted by white (compared to non-white) race, U.S. citizenship, novelty seeking, low television affinity, low cognitive television gratifications, few available channel options and, as the strongest predictor, being motivated to use the remote control to avoid commercials. Actual levels of commercial avoidance were first and foremost predicted by the motivation to avoid commercials, followed by the respondent's high technological affinity and a low use of program guides. Watching multiple programs at the same time was predicted by the amount of television exposure, cable viewing, the tendency to view alone, news scanning, and, again most strongly, by the motivation to use the remote control for commercial avoidance. Similarly, grazing was best predicted by the amount of television exposure, cable viewing, the tendency to view alone, and being motivated to avoid commercials. Overall, the motivation for commercial avoidance in many cases was the strongest predictor for remote control use. Desirability of control was only related to muting the sound and overall remote control use. This means that most of the specific reasons for remote control use were not connected to the desire to shape one's environment according to one's ideas. Rather than just serving as a tool for purposefully controlling the television environment, the remote control may be more appropriately seen as a toy that helps to get pleasure from television and from exploring it without a particular goal in mind (Wenner & Dennehy, 1993).

External Factors for Channel Changing

The studies discussed so far were mainly concerned with internal factors for channel changing such as intentions, motivations, and personality traits. However, there is also some research on the influence of external factors on channel changes which may be present in some characteristics of the content and in characteristics of the viewing situation.

Characteristics of the Content

While no program is really safe from the viewers' loose thumb on the remote control, content does matter for the frequency of switching. Reinold (1994, cited in Ettenhuber, 2007) investigated channel changing frequency in meter data according to genres and found 2.2 channel changes per hour in information programs, 2.8 in sport, 1.7 in entertainment shows, 1.5 in fiction and 5 in commercials. This corresponds well to the finding from self reports that commercial avoidance is one of the most important reasons for channel changing (Heeter & Greenberg, 1988a; Walker & Bellamy, 1991). But not all commercials are equally subject to zapping. The zapping rate is influenced by a number of characteristics of the commercial itself. For example, commercials with a brand-differentiating message—one that makes an explicit claim how to distinguish a brand from others and emphasizes the uniqueness of the product—are less likely to be zapped (Siddarth & Chattopadhyay, 1998). However, there may be a ceiling effect for the benefits of information: Woltman Elpers, Wedel, and Pieters (2003) found that the amount of information in a commercial is related to the tendency of viewers to stop watching it. This discrepancy might be due to different methods to measure information in commercials—ratings for the brand-differentiating message were based on how much the information contained in a commercial makes the product unique (Siddarth & Chattopadhyay, 1998), while information value is the sum of all facts, arguments and benefits of the product (Woltman Elpers et al., 2003). Another study corroborates this interpretation: When an ad was rated to be high in fact-related attributes (e.g., rational or factual appeals), viewers saw less of it, while attributes that stressed feelings like aesthetic, artistic or beauty appeals, extended viewing time (Olney, Holbrook, & Batra, 1991).

Further, a commercial that is placed within a program is less likely to lose viewers (Siddarth & Chattopadhyay, 1998; van Meurs, 1998). The loss of viewers at breaks between programs is even more extreme when programming before and after changes in terms of program type and target group (van Meurs, 1998). Also, there seems to be an effect of ad repetition: While first exposures to an ad decrease the likelihood of zapping, after about 14 exposures, the likelihood increases (Siddarth & Chattopadhyay, 1998).

Characteristics of the Viewing Situation

Some characteristics of the viewing situation may enhance the frequency of switching. First and foremost, the presence of an remote control is crucial for switching: The switching rate is higher for viewers who have an remote control at their disposal than for those who do not (Bryant & Rockwell, 1993; Danaher, 1995; Kaplan, 1985). Of course, remote controls have an excellent household penetration as they automatically come with new sets (Klopfenstein, 1993). Another technical-structural factor in the use of the remote control is channel availability. There is a tendency for viewers to use the remote control more often if they have more programs available through a cable subscription (Ferguson, 1992; Weimann, 1995).

The viewing group is an important factor for channel changing. There are two aspects of this issue. First, flipping channels in the presence of other people also means exerting a form of control over the co-viewers. Several studies associated using the remote control with male dominance (Copeland & Schweitzer, 1993; Morley, 1986) or with the motive to annoy other people (Walker & Bellamy, 1991, 1993; Wenner & Dennehy, 1993). However, the remote control is more often used to switch channels when viewers watch alone than when they watch in a group (Eastman & Newton, 1995; Wenner & Dennehy, 1993). This is also true for commercial zapping (van Meurs, 1998). Bellamy and Walker (1996) interpret this discrepancy as an indicator that the annoying or controlling behaviors are "short-lived, if memorable because of the emotions they provoke" (p. 137).

Types of Selective Strategies

Channel changing sometimes means that viewers are not straightforward and rational in their intentions and their choices (Wenner & Dennehy, 1993). They scan television options, stop once in a while, go on, take in some bits and pieces of the television world, drift away again. Television viewing consists of many of these episodes and single actions, many different strategies for coping with the multitude of options. While motive catalogues are typically focused on outcomes (like not watching commercials, watching favourable shows), the scanning strategy itself remains rather vague. Heeter (1988) proposes a choice process model that delineates scanning strategies, first analyzing the type of decision situation a viewer has to handle when choosing a program to watch. The main interest lies in the situation in which cable subscribers do not yet know what program to watch; they have an indefinite goal, one that can be achieved by several alternatives (for example, being entertained may be achieved by a crime movie or a situation comedy). The "task" is complex, because there are many options to chose from and many criteria to base the decision on; and it is uncertain, because the viewer has to find a set of alternatives from an almost unmanageable amount of options. The basic process is that viewers inform themselves about the possibilities, match their needs with those options and eventually select a program. A dominant feature of the television decision is that it occurs regularly, making it a "routinely structured decision-making task" (Heeter, 1988, p. 13). In Heeter's model, viewers can inform themselves with the TV guide, or they can scan the programs and sample what is on. This on-line "orienting search" has three dimensions. The first is processing mode, which can be either automatic, when channels are checked in the order that they are programmed into the television set, or controlled, when channels are checked in a different, purposive order created by the viewer. The second dimension is the search repertoire which can be elaborate when a viewer searches all or most available channels, or restricted when only a subset of channels is searched. The third dimension is evaluation, which is exhaustive when viewers first consider all options before choosing one, or terminating when viewers stop the search at the first acceptable option. An orienting search may result in an option that is viewed; the decision, however, may be subject to revision in the course of viewing. Heeter (1988) calls this phenomenon "reevaluation." For reevaluation, viewers may leave a show or a commercial to start searching again, or they may simultaneously watch several shows.

In a study of 232 cable households the relationships of orienting search and reevaluation with household and individual characteristics were investigated. Heeter (1988) found out that guide use was stronger in households with a pay cable subscription and with children as well as in individuals with higher cognitive novelty-seeking and younger females. Elaborated and exhaustive on-line searches as well as reevaluation were more prevalent among men, while exhaustive and terminating search were not related to sex. All types of searches and reevaluation were more common among young viewers compared to old ones. Sensate novelty seeking was related to all orienting searches and reevaluation, while cognitive novelty seeking only correlated with exhaustive search and reevaluation.

Heeter's (1988) model shows that the television choice is embedded in a complex process and consists of several actions directed at a constantly changing television environment. Dynamics in the content (which may have been suspenseful at first and become slower), but also in viewer attributes (a viewer may become tired after an hour of watching, too stressed or understimulated by a program) complicate the decision process and promote playful television behavior—as opposed to rational choices that weigh options according to their uses. A typical multi-channel television environment with a remote control encourages the viewer to transcend traditional boundaries of individual shows and view only bits and pieces of shows. This counteracts the intended structure of televised segments and creates a new flow of sense specific to an individual viewer. Choices become idiosyncratic, depending on spontaneous evaluations of what is currently shown on television. This represents a challenge to both theory and method: Both need to be anchored in the viewing situation and to account for dynamic relations between content, perception of the content and actual choices throughout a viewing sequence.

Process-oriented Explanations of Channel Changing

Following that idea, Vorderer (1993) investigated how channel changing is related to the way viewers experience a film. He distinguishes between two modes of viewing experience: First, involvement which is defined as the viewer's experience of living within the fictional world of a film and second, the analytic mode which is defined as reflecting and thinking about the film in a more distanced way. Involvement and analysis were measured in two groups with a device that prompted respondents once per minute to give estimates of the level of involvement or analysis they perceived at that very moment. These data were correlated with meter data from a representative sample that indicated how many viewers switched into the film when it was aired, and how many people left the film. Thus, it was possible to trace relationships between the levels of involvement or analysis (from the experiment) and channel changing behavior of the audience (from the meter data). The results indicated that involvement was lower in the four minutes prior to major channel changes in the meter data. This suggests that viewers leave a film when their involvement is low. Analysis did not have this effect. These results confirm Perse's (1998) findings that channel changing increases when viewers are not mentally engaged and pay less attention to the program they watch.

To test the relationship between attention and channel changes more directly, Lang et al. (2005) measured heart rate as an indicator for cognitive effort and skin conductance as an indicator for arousal and investigated the relationship of these variables with channel changes. Results showed that channel changes were related to declining physiological arousal—cognitive effort as well as arousal decreased up to the point when the channel was changed and then increased again. Also, stimuli were varied to offer the respondents choices differing in production pacing (number of cuts and edits) and story length. The goal was to find out whether short stories and fast pacing prevented viewers from changing channels. An effect of these two factors could only be traced for younger viewers—but only for consistent combinations: younger viewers prefer to watch either slow-paced, long stories, or fast-paced short stories, but not inconsistent combinations.

Woltman Elpers et al. (2003) employed a process-oriented design to commercials. In a moment-to-moment analysis, the situational reactions of viewers to the entertainment and information value of commercials were investigated. Entertainment value indicates how much commercial content is amusing, warm or playful, while information value refers to arguments, facts and benefits of the product mentioned in the commercial. Both were rated by trained student judges who in a continuous measurement assessed commercials from "very unentertaining" to "very entertaining" and "very uninformative" to "very informative," respectively. The researchers found out that a high entertainment value increases the likelihood that viewers continue watching a commercial, while a high information value increases the likelihood that viewers switch away from a commercial. Also, a high information value overrides the benefits of a high entertainment value: Viewers tend to stop watching commercials that are high on both entertainment and information.

Vorderer (1993), Lang et al. (2005) and Woltman Elpers et al. (2003) use a process-oriented design instead of situation-independent self report. While Vorderer (1993) relies on subjective viewing experiences to explain switching, the other two studies assess qualities of the content to explain selective processes (story length and pacing in Lang et al., 2005, and entertainment and information value in Woltman Elpers et al., 2003). The nature of the explanation is different from the studies following a uses and gratifications paradigm. Channel changes are not seen as purely intentional, motivated actions, but as reactions to content; the viewer may not be conscious of the reasons for the channel changes. What appears on the phenomenological surface (that is, in self reports) as "boredom with a show" may be specified as inconsistent in content and form (in pacing and length), or as displeasing quality (high information value).

Conclusions

There is constant change in a viewing situation: Television content, alternative options as well as the viewers' motives, moods and energy level vary with time, just as the evaluation of current television content. On-line selections arise from an interaction of these constantly changing states and circumstances. The studies presented here focus on different aspects of this process. In a uses and gratifications paradigm, the process is condensed into overall judgments about switching motivations in a retrospective self-report. This provides a good impression of what people intentionally seek to achieve by changing channels. But the study of channel changes is complicated by the mundane and situational nature of these selections. Spontaneous switching is difficult to reproduce for the viewer outside the viewing situation. Moreover, research on the gratifications of channel changing often creates the impression that switching is sufficiently explained by intentional reasons and obfuscates the possibility that switching might also be reaction, and not only action. Viewers might not be aware of the more spontaneous, reactive part of switching; the reasons for such behavior might be difficult to verbalize or altogether not accessible to the viewer. If switching is a mix of (intentional) action and (non-intentional) behavior, considering both on the theoretical level and using methods that capture both seems appropriate. While there is some accordance between the reasons that viewers indicate and that were found out without reliance on self report—for example, the decrease in attention before a channel change in the Lang et al. (2005) study corresponds to viewers indicating boredom as a reason to switch away—there is also some divergence when viewers do not interpret an aspect of the viewing situation as relevant for their actions. For example, pacing and story length (Lang et al., 2005) are not mentioned in free self-reports (e.g., Bilandzic, 2002; Traudt, 1993). Considering both intentional and non-intentional reasons make the explanation of channel changing complete, and there is still much research needed to understand the interaction between the two. For example, on-line selections might be composed of varying levels of intentionality and non-intentionality; just as viewers choose from different channels, genres, shows, stories or single bits of information, they also choose a rule according to which to decide (Jungermann, Pfister, & Fischer, 1998; Marewski, Galesic, & Gigerenzer in this volume)—in certain situations, viewers may go for what they always watch out of convenience, sometimes they may weigh expected consequences of the different options to watch (and engage in a rational choice). This means that there is not a single decision rule for television selections, but a multitude, depending on situation, current content, current state and goals of the viewer. This is closely related to the way viewers inform themselves about available options. Choosing from a television guide endorses thorough processing of information about the options and a rational choice (that is, matching expectations, evaluations and options). Scanning channels with the remote control leaves little time to consider the program closely and does not allow for thorough processing of content, story, or arguments. Rather, when viewers have little time to view an option, they tend to process in a more superficial way. In this case, viewers pick up cues that are easy to decode even in a time-constrained situation and use them as a rule of thumb, or working hypothesis that allows the viewer to make quick judgments about the options (Bilandzic, 2004). If this first step in the decision is positive (that is, the option seems promising at the first superficial sight), the option may be viewed a little longer and the decision either reinforced or revoked. In a study combining content analysis and meter data, Bilandzic (2004) could show that viewers flipping through channels often stop and remain with a program when it is currently transitioning from one segment to the next (e.g., when a new story begins in a newscast). Also, scanning viewers tend to choose programs for closer evaluation whose genre they habitually watch; however, habits could not predict watching the whole show, but only stopping the scanning search and initiating an extended evaluation.

Although research on channel changing has somewhat declined in the past decade, new challenges call for further research. One of the fields that still needs to be addressed is conceptualizing on-line selections as a mix of intentional and non-intentional aspects and finding appropriate ways to operationalize it. Also, new technological developments might alter the phenomenon that needs explaining: Digital media multiply channels available for viewing; at the same time, electronic program guides may be even more convenient than switching the remote control manually to narrow choices down to a few channels. However, channel changing is not merely an unliked yet necessary means to find the best program; switching through the channels has become an integral part of enjoying television as much as actually watching a show—the "toy" function of the remote control and with it the enjoyment of browsing through channels of the television world might be too valuable to be given up easily by the audience because of new technology that just facilitates selection. Exploring the situation and reactive, spontaneous channel changes might further help to overcome the focus on instrumental interpretations of on-line selections.

References

Adams, W. J. (1993). TV program scheduling strategies and their relationship to new program renewal rates and rating changes. *Journal of Broadcasting and Electronic Media, 37*, 465–474.

Ainslie, P. (1989). The new TV viewer. In *How Americans Watch TV: A Nation of Grazers* (pp. 9–20). New York: C.C. Publishing.

Anderson, D. R. & Field, D. E. (1985). Online and offline assessment of the television audience. In J. Bryant & D. Zillman (Eds.), *Responding to the Screen* (pp. 199–216). Hillsdale: Lawrence Erlbaum.

Barwise, T. & Ehrenberg, A. (1988). *Television and its Audience*. London: Sage.

Bellamy, R. V. & Walker, J. R. (1996). *Television and the Remote Control*. New York, London: The Guilford Press.

Bilandzic, H. (1998). Formale Merkmale individueller Fernsehnutzung [Formal features of individual television use]. In W. Klingler, G. Roters, & O. Zöllner (Eds.), *Fernsehforschung in Deutschland [Television research in Germany]* (pp. 743–763). Baden-Baden: Nomos.

Bilandzic, H. (1999). Psychische Prozesse bei der selektiven Fernsehnutzung [Mental processes in selective television use]. In U. Hasebrink & P. Rössler (Eds.), *Publikumsbindungen. Medienrezeption zwischen Individualisierung und Integration [Audience ties. Media use between individualization and integration]* (pp. 89–110). München: R. Fischer.

Bilandzic, H. (2002). Situative Frames in der Dynamik der Fernsehrezeption. Eine Inhaltsanalyse von Gedankenprotokollen zur selektiven Fernsehnutzung [Situational frames in the dynamics of television use: A content analysis of think aloud protocols on selective television use]. In P. Rössler, S. Kubisch, & V. Gehrau (Eds.),

Empirische Perspektiven der Rezeptionsforschung [Empirical perspectives of audience research] (pp. 75–95). München: R. Fischer.

Bilandzic, H. (2004). *Synchrone Programmauswahl. Der Einfluss formaler und inhaltlicher Merkmale der Fernsehbotschaft auf die Fernsehnutzung [Synchronous television program choice: The influence of formal and content-related features of the television message]*. München: R. Fischer.

Bryant, J. & Rockwell, S. C. (1993). Remote control devices in television program selection: Experimental evidence. In J. R. Walker & R. V. Bellamy (Eds.), *The Remote Control in the New Age of Television* (pp. 73–85). Westport: Praeger.

Cooper, R. (1993). An expanded integrated model for determining audience exposure to television. *Journal of Broadcasting and Electronic Media, 37*(4), 401–418.

Copeland, G. A. & Schweitzer, K. (1993). Domination of the remote control during family viewing. In J. R. Walker & R. V. Bellamy (Eds.), *The Remote Control in the New Age of Television* (pp. 155–167). Westport: Praeger.

Cornwell, N. C., Everett, S.-L., Everett, S., Moriarty, S., Russomanno, J. A., & Tracey, M. (1993). Measuring RCD use: Method matters. In J. R. Walker & R. V. Bellamy (Eds.), *The Remote Control in the New Age of Television* (pp. 43–56). Westport: Praeger.

Danaher, P. (1995). What happens to television ratings during commercial breaks? *Journal of Advertising Research, 35*, 37–47.

Eastman, S. T. & Newton, G. D. (1995). Delineating grazing: Observations of remote control use. *Journal of Communication, 45*, 77–95.

Eastman, S. T., Newton, G., Riggs, K., & Neal-Lunsford, J. (1997). Accelerating the flow: A transition effect in programming theory? *Journal of Broadcasting and Electronic Media, 41*, 265–283.

Ettenhuber, A. (2007). *Die Beschleunigung des Fernsehverhaltens [Acceleration of television behavior]*. München: R. Fischer Verlag.

Ferguson, D. A. (1992). Channel repertoire in the presence of remote control devices, VCRs and cable television. *Journal of Broadcasting and Electronic Media, 36*(1), 83–91.

Ferguson, D. A. (1994). Measurement of mundane TV behaviors—remote-control device flipping frequency. *Journal of Broadcasting & Electronic Media, 38*(1), 35–47.

Greenberg, B. S., Heeter, C., & Sipes, S. (1988). Viewing context and style with electronic assessment of viewing behavior. In C. Heeter & B. S. Greenberg (Eds.), *Cableviewing* (pp. 123–139). Norwood: Ablex.

Hawkins, R., Pingree, S., Fitzpatrick, M. A., Thompson, M., & Bauman, I. (1991). Implications of concurrent measures of viewer behavior. *Human Communication Research, 17*, 485–504.

Heeter, C. (1988). The choice process model. In C. Heeter & B. S. Greenberg (Eds.), *Cableviewing* (pp. 11–32). Norwood: Ablex.

Heeter, C. & Greenberg, B. S. (1988a). Profiling the zappers. In C. Heeter & B. S. Greenberg (Eds.), *Cableviewing* (pp. 67–73). Norwood: Ablex.

Heeter, C. & Greenberg, B. S. (1988b). A theoretical overview of the program choice process. In C. Heeter & B. S. Greenberg (Eds.), *Cableviewing* (pp. 33–50). Norwood: Ablex.

Heeter, C., d'Alessio, D., Greenberg, B. S., & McVoy, D. S. (1988). Cableviewing behaviors: an electronic assessment. In C. Heeter & B. S. Greenberg (Eds.), *Cableviewing* (pp. 51–66). Norwood: Ablex.

Jäckel, M. (1993). *Fernsehwanderungen. Eine empirische Untersuchung zum Zapping [Television fluctuations: An empirical study on zapping].* München: R. Fischer Verlag.

Jungermann, H., Pfister, H.-R., & Fischer, K. (1998). *Die Psychologie der Entscheidung [Decision psychology].* Heidelberg, Berlin: Spektrum Akademischer Verlag.

Kaplan, B. M. (1985). Zapping—the real issue is communication. *Journal of Advertising Research, 25,* 9–12.

Kaye, B. K. & Sapolsky, B. S. (1997). Electronic monitoring of in-home television RCD usage. *Journal of Broadcasting & Electronic Media, 41,* 214–228.

Klopfenstein, B. C. (1993). From gadget to necessity: the diffusion of remote control technology. In J. R. Walker & R. V. Bellamy (Eds.), *The Remote Control in the New Age of Television* (pp. 23–39). Westport: Praeger.

Lang, A., Shin, M., Bradley, S. D., Wang, Z., Lee, S., & Potter, D. (2005). Wait! Don't turn the dial! More excitement to come! The effects of story length and production pacing in local television news on channel changing behavior and information processing in a free choice environment. *Journal of Broadcasting and Electronic Media, 49*(1), 3–22.

Morley, D. (1986). *Family Television: Cultural Power and Domestic Leisure.* London: Comedia.

Olney, T. J., Holbrook, M. B., & Batra, R. (1991). Consumer responses to advertising: The effects of ad content, emotions, and attitude toward the ad on viewing time. *Journal of Consumer Research, 17,* 440–453.

Perse, E. M. (1998). Implications of cognitive and affective involvement for channel changing. *Journal of Communication, 48*(3), 49–68.

Reinold, A. (1994). Patterns of individual TV usage. In *ARF (Advertising Research Foundation)/ESOMAR (European Society for Opinion and Marketing Research) Worldwide Electronic and Broadcasting Audience Research Symposium (Paris)—vol. 2* (pp. 67–78). Amsterdam, New York.

Siddarth, S. & Chattopadhyay, A. (1998). To zap or not to zap: A study of the determinants of channel switching during commercials. *Marketing Science, 17*(2), 124–138.

Traudt, P. J. (1993). Surveillance and cluster viewing: Foraging through the RCD experience. In J. R. Walker & R. V. Bellamy (Eds.), *The Remote Control in the New Age of Television* (pp. 57–72). Westport: Praeger.

van Meurs, L. (1998). Zapp! A study on switching behavior during commercial breaks. *Journal of Advertising Research, 38,* 43–53.

Vorderer, P. (1993). Audience involvement and program loyalty. *Poetics, 22,* 89–98.

Walker, J. R. & Bellamy, R. V. (1991). Gratifications of grazing: an exploratory study of remote control use. *Journalism Quarterly, 68*(3), 422–431.

Walker, J. R. & Bellamy, R. V. (1993). *The Remote Control in the New Age of Television.* Westport: Praeger.

Walker, J. R., Bellamy, R. V., & Traudt, P. J. (1993). Gratifications derived from remote control devices. In J. R. Walker & R. V. Bellamy (Eds.), *The Remote Control in the New Age of Television* (pp. 103–112). Westport: Praeger.

Webster, J. G. (1985). Program audience duplication: a study of television inheritance effects. *Journal of Broadcasting and Electronic Media, 29*(2), 121–133.

Webster, J. G. & Lichty, L. (1991). *Ratings Analysis: Theory and Practice.* Hillsdale, NJ: Lawrence Erlbaum.

Webster, J. G. & Wakshlag, J. (1985). Measuring exposure to television. In D. Zillman & J. Bryant (Eds.), *Selective Exposure to Communication* (pp. 35–62). Hillsdale, NJ: Lawrence Erlbaum.

Weimann, G. (1995). Zapping in the Holy Land: Coping with multi-channel TV in Israel. *Journal of Communication, 45*(1), 96–102.

Wenner, L. A. & Dennehy, M. O. (1993). Is the remote control a device or a toy? Exploring the need for activation, desire for control and technological affinity in the dynamic of RCD use. In J. R. Walker & R. V. Bellamy (Eds.), *The Remote Control in the New Age of Television* (pp. 113–134). Westport: Praeger.

Woltman Elpers, J. L. C. M. (2003). *Consumers' Moment-to-moment Processing of Television Commercials*, from http://irs.ub.rug.nl/ppn/256275823.

Woltman Elpers, J. L. C. M., Wedel, M., & Pieters, R. (2003). Why do consumers stop viewing television commercials? Two experiments on the influence of moment-to-moment entertainment and information value. *Journal of Marketing Research, XL*, 437–453.

Chapter 13

The Role of Structure in Media Choice

James G. Webster

Most theories of media choice rely heavily on the psychological predispositions of individuals to explain their patterns of consumption. This chapter argues that the structural features of the media environment play an important, if less appreciated, role in determining choice. I begin by outlining a comprehensive theory of media choice that views agency and structure as mutually constituted, what Giddens (1984) termed the "duality of structure." I describe how people use the resources offered by the media environment to enact their preferences and, in doing so, shape the very structures within which they operate. This happens with both "linear" media systems and newer "non-linear" modes of delivery. However, because the duality of media structure depends largely upon aggregating agents into audiences, it is best understood at a higher level of analysis than is typical of psychologically grounded theories of choice.

Towards a Comprehensive Theory of Media Choice

Some years ago, Jack Wakshlag and I published an article arguing for a comprehensive theory of television program choice (Webster & Wakshlag, 1983). We observed that existing bodies of theory, specifically uses and gratifications and economic models of choice, didn't do a very good job of explaining observed patterns of audience behavior, and suggested that theorists needed to be more cognizant of factors that mediated individual preference as a determinant of choice. We proposed a model that integrated viewer needs and program type preferences with a number of other factors including the structure of program options, viewer awareness, and viewer availability. These factors continue to be important determinants of media choice, though the characteristics of new media are altering their relative importance and the ways in which they operate.

Although I didn't know it at the time, the approach we were advocating was broadly compatible with the "theory of structuration" proposed by Giddens (1984). He argued for a "duality of structure" in which human agency and social structure were mutually constituted. That is, while people were free to act, they did so within structures that, through their very actions, they helped reproduce. In the theoretical vocabulary of Giddens, Jack and I were arguing that most students of media choice had focused on agents while turning a blind eye to the role of structure.

The theoretical balance is still heavily tilted in favor of the individual agent. The literature on media choice typically posits various affective and/or cognitive states as determinative of behavior. Uses and gratifications research maintains its characteristic commitment to need gratification as the genesis of media use (e.g., Finn, 1997; Rubin, 2002; Ruggiero, 2000). Newer work on selective exposure, mood management, flow states, sensitivity theory, or simply "enjoyment" (e.g., Reiss & Wiltz, 2004; Sherry, 2004; Vorderer, Klimmt, & Ritterfeld, 2004; Zillmann, 2000) is similarly committed to psychologically grounded theories of media choice. In fact, many of the contributors to this volume employ such a framework. By arguing for a fuller consideration of structure, I don't mean to minimize the importance of a psychological approach to media choice. It helps us appreciate what motivates individuals to use media and explains the pleasures and utilities of those encounters. But more is required to understand how choices are made in dynamic media environments.

Structuration theory can offer an alternative framework that reconciles the motivations of individual agents with the media structures they employ. It has been adapted to study how information technology is used within organizations (e.g. DeSanctis & Poole, 1994; Orlikowski, 1992; Poole & DeSanctis, 2004), but is not widely used to understand the more general phenomenon of media consumption. I'd like to encourage the latter by applying Giddens' vocabulary to the particulars of media choice. Before I do, let me be clear about the theoretical assumptions I make, most of which will sound familiar to students of Giddens.

Agents

In this context, agents are the people who choose media. Their choices are purposeful and can, in principle, occur whenever they wish. However, media consumption is typically embedded in the routines of day-to-day life, and so has a predictable, recursive quality. People know a good deal about the media environments within which they operate, reflect upon how they use those environments, and can, if asked, provide a rational account of their actions. It does not follow, however, that they know everything there is to know about the causes or consequences of their choices. Indeed, they are complicit in many unintended consequences of which they are largely unaware. Conceptualizing agents in this way is consistent with most economic and psychological theories of choice, a topic that I develop below.

Structures

People choose media within highly structured social and technological environments. For the most part, governments and/or industries provide the infrastructures people need to enact their media preferences. Those resources include a vast array of media services and materials, and the hardware needed to deliver them. The institutions that provide media have their own motives for doing so and attempt to manage consumption toward those ends. They do so by catering to what they perceive to be audience preferences, and exploiting the unintended consequences of media use. In the short term, media structures are relatively "hard" constraints on individual action. Over time, those structures are considerably more malleable.

Duality of Structure

Media choices result from the interaction of agents and structures. It is an iterative process that implicates both in perpetuating and/or reshaping the structural features of the environment. This duality of media is heavily dependent upon aggregating individual actions. Institutions, for their part, can only respond to what they "see." Agents are most visible when they are constituted as markets, publics and/or audiences—a concept that Ettema and Whitney have referred to as "institutionally effective audiences" (1994, p. 5). Aggregation is the lens through which institutions both understand and attempt to manage consumption. Agents, too, are increasingly dependent on various forms of aggregation, as these often constitute the structures that guide choice-making in non-linear environments.

Structures of the Media Environment

The media environment provides the resources necessary for people to act. It has two basic modes of delivery, each with its own structural features. The first, a linear system, has been characteristic of electronic media since the beginning of broadcasting. Radio, and later television, programs were strung together in a temporal sequence determined by the broadcaster. Though this system itself is changing, for reasons I develop below, I believe it will persist well into the future. The second, a non-linear system, makes discrete items of content available to individuals as they request them. Non-linear delivery systems, such as video "on-demand," DVRs, websites, or media downloaded over the Internet, are much newer phenomena—at least for electronic media.

The Webster and Wakshlag (1983) model of choice identified three factors that bear on a consideration of structure: the structure of available program options, viewer availability, and curiously enough, viewer awareness. I'll touch on each of these as I discuss modes of delivery.

Linear Media

At last count, linear media were responsible for roughly 70 percent of all the time Americans spent consuming media. That included the use of broadcast, cable, and satellite television, as well as broadcast and satellite radio services (Veronis Shuler Stevenson, 2006). The building blocks of this environment are channels. Over the years, the sheer number of channels in the U.S., Europe, and most of the world has increased dramatically. I've argued that as this happened: 1) the media environment offered people more diverse content; 2) content became correlated with channels; and 3) channels became differentially available (Webster, 1986; Webster & Phalen, 1997). The structural features of this environment have a powerful effect on program choice.

The most obvious constraint on choice is simple channel availability. Despite the growing abundance of linear media, a surprising number of channels are beyond the reach of most households. A recent analysis of television audience behavior in the U.S. indicated that while there are over 300 national networks, only a handful of the major broadcast networks came close to being universally available (Webster, 2005). Nor was there any relationship between the number of households that could receive a channel and the intensity with which the channel was used. HBO, for example, was available in only a third of homes, yet its viewers spent as much time watching it as a major broadcast network. Failing to subscribe to HBO might indicate a lack of interest, or a lack of money, or some technical impediment. But surely, among the two thirds of the audience who couldn't choose HBO at any point in time, many would occasionally prefer to watch its programming. The same might be said of any cable channel. Excluding broadcast networks, the top 50 cable networks were, on average, unavailable in a third of television households.

Prior (2007) has recently demonstrated that changes in channel availability over time have had a dramatic affect on news consumption. Specifically, as the proliferation of cable channels have made it possible for some viewers to opt out of watching television newscasts, the overall consumption of news has become increasingly polarized. These shifts have occurred without any change in the underlying distribution of audience program type preferences. Media choice, then, can only be understood within the context of what is available to each individual at each moment in time—a factor not well explained by viewer psychology alone.

Beyond simple channel availability, linear media by their very nature runs many streams of content opposite one another. This has the effect of offering people an endless succession of forced-choice situations. The phenomenon of "multi-tasking" notwithstanding, a person can only consume one item of content at a time. Hence, people may have to choose between two, equally preferred options at one time and be forced to settle for some "least objectionable" program at another time. While it once seemed that VCRs would free people from this dilemma, they proved too cumbersome to have much effect. DVRs will undoubtedly make time-shifting easier, but they introduce other structural biases I'll discuss in the section on non-linear media.

Not only can linear streams of content force choices among equally preferred alternatives, they have the effect of privileging some programs over others. "Audience flow" is a routinely observed feature of audience behavior in which the audience for a program stays tuned to the succeeding program in disproportionate numbers (Webster, 2006). In effect, this structural device "stacks the deck" in favor of the succeeding item of content, by increasing the odds that individuals using the channel will consume the next program the network has scheduled, or the next song the radio station plays.

Audience flow also demonstrates the duality of structure in action. It is doubtful that individuals set out to create this phenomenon, or that they are aware of it when they do. It is a feature of audience behavior that is visible only through aggregation. Television programmers, who constantly monitor audience ratings, are well aware that the "lead-in" program offers an opportunity to entice viewers with material they might not otherwise choose. Of course, it makes sense to offer them something that they will find appealing. So individual preferences, insofar as the media can respond to them, are instantiated in the structured arrangement of programming. People are always free to do something other than follow along, but many do not. For a variety of reasons, they choose what is laid before them. If this juxtaposition of content works in the channel's favor, it will recur. If it does not, the schedule will change. Hence, individuals express their preferences within the structures available to them and, in doing so, both reproduce and alter that very system. In the short term, the structure of program options constrains and directs, in the long term, its very design depends on the actions of agents.

Indeed, the uncoordinated activity of individuals is responsible for many unintended consequences that institutions see and, in turn, use to structure the environment. The most salient of these, from media's point of view, are patterns of audience availability. Since media use is intertwined with the rhythms of day-to-day life, it tends to produce habitual, and therefore predictable, patterns of consumption (Rosenstein & Grant, 1997; Webster & Phalen, 1997). When people commute to work, many listen to radio. When they return home, many turn on the television. Of course, media industries know in a general sort of way what kinds of people are likely to be available at certain times, and do their best to factor that into their programming. In fact, "drive time" and "prime time" are occasions for particularly intense, well-financed competitions since the prizes are especially large.

With rare exceptions, though, people's patterns of availability are determined by things other than the scheduling practices of the media. Not all those who might be interested in a particular show, or song, or news broadcast, are available when it airs. Rather, choice proceeds in two stages. People first decide to use a medium, which typically reflects the structure of daily routines. Second, they consider specific content options and, within those bounds, exercise their preferences. In a linear media environment, behavior is infused with factors that are essentially random with respect to the psychological determinants of choice—most notably audience availability. In a non-linear environment, things change.

Non-linear Media

The strictures of linear media are giving way to non-linear delivery systems. Increasingly, specific items of content can be retrieved directly from "libraries" in accordance with a person's preferences. Although it's tempting to think of this as a world devoid of structure, it is not. The influence of its architecture may be less apparent to users, but it is still driven by institutional self-interests. Even the producers of "consumer-generated media" often have an interest in managing consumption.

The sheer volume of media materials from which to choose is growing at an extraordinary rate. Precise estimates are hard to come by, but Lyman and Varian (2003) have reported that the total amount of new information produced each year grew by 30 percent from 1999 to 2002. In 2002 alone, over 100 million hours of new broadcast programming was produced worldwide. At this writing, Technorati tracks some 70 million blogs worldwide. More and more, media of all types are digitally created and stored on hard drives. More and more, it accumulates in a form that is accessible over broadband distribution systems.

In such a world, media are not in short supply. Rather, what constrains media consumption are money and time. Subscribing to cable, satellite, DVR or Internet service providers, renting or buying DVDs and videogames, and downloading music or movies all cost money. The average American will spend close to $800 a year on media content, not to mention expenditures on consumer electronics (Veronis Shuler Stevenson, 2006). Obviously, each individual's willingness and/or ability to bear these expenses varies widely across the population. Everyone, though, has only 24 hours in a day.

The Nobel laureate Herbert Simon famously observed, "a wealth of information creates a poverty of attention, and a need to allocate that attention efficiently among the overabundance of information sources that might consume it" (1971, p. 40). Some 35 years later, the problem is considerably more acute. An inescapable requirement of non-linear media consumption is navigating that ever-expanding universe in order to find what you want when you want it. There are two basic mechanisms for doing so: search and recommendation.

Search is an exercise in finding what you're looking for. It's certainly not unique to non-linear media. People have used printed guides to find television programs for a long time. More recently, digital cable and satellite systems have begun offering electronic guides that allow viewers to scroll through hundreds of channel options. These, however, can be unwieldy and are typically occasions for people to limit their searches to idiosyncratic "channel repertoires" (Neuendorf, Atkin, & Jeffres, 2001; Yuan & Webster, 2006). Search engines are a more powerful way to sort though large inventories of content. They report a list in response to a search term. Although search algorithms vary, results are usually sorted as a function of an item's popularity. Google, for example, sorts websites possessing the requisite search terms by the number and importance of their inbound links (Battelle, 2005). The user, of course, must wade through the list to determine the relevance of each item. For search terms that generate several pages of results, it's doubtful most are even considered.

Recommendation systems alert you to things you weren't necessarily looking for. There are many types of recommendation systems beyond simple word-of-mouth. Advertising and promotional announcements are familiar, if transparently self-serving, forms of recommendation. The outbound links on websites constitute recommendations and form the architecture of the "blogosphere" (Benkler, 2006). Social networking software, with which people indicate their preferences by rating, bookmarking, or tagging media content, is becoming commonplace. The most powerful systems use "collaborative filtering" software to sort through databases of media rentals or product purchases to "guess" what you might like. In effect, they match each individual's profile to other consumers who've made similar purchases. It's plausible, for example, that you'd like other books that were purchased by readers with comparable profiles. Amazon.com is well known for using this technique, and those of us who visit its website to buy books are often tempted by new titles brought to our attention.

Search and recommendation systems share some important similarities. Both are essentially exercises in becoming aware of media content. To learn of a thing's existence does not guarantee it will be chosen, but it establishes the boundaries within which choices will be made. It is unlikely that a person would choose something of which they were unaware. The most elaborate, and seemingly "objective," systems are built by aggregating people's preferences as demonstrated in their behaviors and/or declarations. Hence, recommendations may carry an additional dose of social influence (e.g., Salganik, Dodds, & Watts, 2006). Media institutions can manipulate these increasingly important dimensions of awareness by manufacturing a structured set of options that guide media choice. Agents are always free to choose what they like, but they often enact their preferences by using such content-finding systems. And, in another demonstration of duality of structure, their actions reproduce and reconstitute the very structures that shape subsequent consumption.

In a world where time is limited, search and recommendation systems have another consequence. Initiating searches, weighing the results, following links, or considering recommendations all involve time and effort. In the parlance of economists, they impose "search costs." It's certainly possible for a person to specifically search for and queue every song she wants to hear as she commutes to and from work, but it's quicker and often just as satisfactory to listen to a radio station or satellite network. Further, many people value the judgments of human editors and programmers to bring timely or unexpected items to their attention. I suspect these attributes will sustain linear media into the future. How people will allocate their time across linear and non-linear modes of delivery is an open question. There is likely to be considerable variation across the population, was well as variation within individuals over time. But no matter the nature of media environments, all will structure choice.

Expanding the Playing Field

It seems to me that if we hope to understand media choices, we need to expand the theoretical playing field. To date, our efforts have been too "user-centric." Making individuals the center of attention is hardly surprising. Giddens himself noted that, for much of the academy, "The human agent is treated as the prime focus of social analysis. That is to say, the main concern of the social sciences is held to be the purposeful, reasoning actor" (1987, p. 59). Unfortunately, too much escapes our notice if we try to understand media choice exclusively in terms of the psychological predispositions of agents. In my view, there are two related problems with this approach.

First, focusing on individuals can blind us to the role of structure. At best, this theoretical formulation provides only half the explanatory power we need. Indeed, if one takes Giddens seriously, agency itself cannot be fully understood in isolation because structure is the "very medium ... of human agency" (1987; p. 220). Second, since institutions typically respond to media consumers in the aggregate, using individuals as the unit of analysis fails to adequately illuminate their impact on the duality of structure. Let me briefly revisit the concept of agency, then make a case for understanding media choice at a higher level of analysis.

The economic models of choice that Wakshlag and I (Webster & Wakshlag, 1983) used as a point of departure made a number of simplifying assumptions about the nature of program choice that, in effect, constructed an archetypal agent. Among them was the explicit assertion that individuals had distinct, pre-existing program type preferences, and the implicit assumption that viewers were perfectly aware of their viewing options all times. Those assumptions, coupled with the "free good" nature of advertiser-supported television, lead to a direct, cause and effect relationship between viewer affect and media choice (see for example, Owen, Beebe, & Manning, 1974). Such reasoning, which is not unique to rational-choice economics, is problematic for a number of reasons. I've noted how patterns of availability and imperfect awareness complicate this relationship in modern media environments. The assumption that people's preferences exist *a priori*, fully formed and ready to drive choices, is also troublesome (e.g., Gandy, 1992). It seems more likely that a person's preferences, or expectations of need gratification, are continuously conditioned by the media environment. A person is unlikely to prefer media forms with which they have no experience. And media institutions are unlikely to offer programming for which there is no demonstrated market. In the current environment, both are capable of adapting rather quickly. But it is a dynamic process with influence flowing in both directions. I doubt that even the most self-reflexive people are fully aware of how their preferences and subsequent actions are cultivated by and determinative of the structures that surround them.

A revealing site of inquiry, then, might focus on how agents use and shape media structures over time. The duality of structure certainly depends on this mechanism. To understand the machinery, though, we need to conceptualize choices at a higher level of analysis. That's because the institutions that are integral to the process typically see and respond to media consumers as audiences or markets. And agents themselves are evermore dependent upon intelligence about what others are doing to guide their own choice-making. Audience dynamics, revealed through aggregation, fuel the process.

Audiences, however, are different analytical entities than individual actors. While they are necessarily built upon collections of the latter, different patterns of behavior and alternate explanatory frameworks become apparent at this level of analysis (e.g., Salganik, et al. 2006; Watts, 2003). We've seen how broadcasters exploit audience flow to manage consumption (Webster, 2006). Audience fragmentation and polarization are other forms of institutionally salient behavior that only come into view in the aggregate (Webster, 2005; Webster & Phalen, 1997). More recently, analysts have noted the "long tails" that characterize all manner of cultural consumption. These ubiquitous patterns describe everything from the rates at which people download songs from iTunes, to theatrical attendance, to the linking architecture of the Web (Anderson, 2006; Benkler, 2006; DeVany, 2004). All are important manifestations of choice that are amenable to explanation with reference to structural variables, but not particularly tractable when forced into the theoretical framework of psychological predispositions.

Focusing on a macro-level duality of structure has additional benefits. First, aggregated behaviors are often stable and susceptible to modeling. Some have been formulated as rules of thumb or even "laws," such as the 80/20 rule, the duplication of viewing law, and the law of double jeopardy (e.g., Anderson, 2006; Goodhardt, Ehrenberg, & Collins, 1987; McPhee, 1963). In fact, Web usage is so law-like that physicists routinely model its architecture (e.g., Barabasi, 2001; Huberman, 2001; Watts, 2003). Second, knowing the behavior of audiences, which are readily conceptualized as publics, speaks not only to business interests but to larger social issues. Many commentators, for instance, have worried about the polarizing potential of new media (e.g. Katz, 1996; Sunstein, 2001; Turow, 1997). These social concerns can be cast in much sharper relief by understanding large-scale trends in consumption (e.g., Couldry, Livingston, & Markham, 2007; Prior, 2007; Webster, 2005).

Noting that we live in an "entertainment age," Bryant (2004; p. 392) argued that legitimizing and advancing entertainment theory was one of the most important challenges facing communication research. To do that, he recommended using "hedonistic psychology." If understanding the patterns of media choice that I've just described is on the agenda of entertainment theory, we will need to know more than people's hedonistic impulses. The media structures that enable and/or constrain choice must be reflected in any fully formed theory. While such calls are hardly new (e.g. Elliot, 1974; Weibull, 1985), structure remains conspicuously absent from the literature on media choice. As the media environment grows in size and complexity, this will be an increasingly serious omission. I'd like to conclude with a few thoughts about why we seem to have such difficulty expanding the playing field.

First, for some, granting structural factors a role in program choice has seemed tantamount to a declaration of audience passivity (e.g., Adams, 1997; Rugerio, 2000). This view conceives of structures as acting upon hapless media consumers, thus denying them any meaningful notion of agency. Our discipline, on the contrary, has been more inclined to celebrate the active media user. Unfortunately, if we see structures as separate and unbending, activity can only play out in the arena of individual action. This is a needlessly limiting conceptualization of agency. People, both as consumers and creators of media, are undoubtedly more active today than they have ever been. But the media structures they use are not neutral or fixed. They both shape and are shaped by the choices agents make. If we want to foreground activity, we should recognize it in its most potent form. It is the agency of audiences, not individuals, that brings institutions to heel.

This leads to a second problem: scaling down structural factors to the level of an agent. Balancing micro/macro tensions is nothing new to social scientists (e.g., Alexander et al., 1987; Salganik et al., 2006). In fact, reconciling those tensions is an important purpose of structuration theory. But acknowledging that doesn't make it any easier to design studies that accommodate both perspectives. In most micro-level research designs I've seen, the complications of structure are assumed away. Pivotal factors like awareness and availability are ignored or taken as given. Likewise, the structured arrangement of media offerings, if it is considered at all, is simplified and static. The grander scale of structural determination across time and space is difficult to capture in short-term laboratory experiments or cross-sectional surveys that depend entirely upon self-reports from purposeful, reasoning agents. I'm not willing to concede that the micro-level orientation of agency and macro-level influence of structure are incommensurable, but moving between levels is a challenge. It's only by meeting that challenge, that we will fully understand the nature of media choice.

References

Adams, W. J. (1997). Scheduling practices based on audience flow: What are the effects on new program success? *Journalism and Mass Communication Quarterly, 74*, 839–858.

Alexander, J. C., Giesen, B., Munch, R., & Smelser, N. J. (Eds.). (1987). *The Micromacro Link*. Berkeley, CA: University of California Press.

Anderson, C. (2006). *The Long Tail: Why the Future of Business is Selling Less or More*. New York: Hyperion.

Barabasi, A. L. (2001, July). The physics of the Web. *Physics World*. Online. Retrieved June 10, 2006 from http://physicsweb.org/articles/world/14/7/9.

Battelle, J. (2005). *The Search: How Google and its Rivals Rewrote the Rules of Business and Transformed our Culture*. New York: Portfolio.

Benkler, Y. (2006). *The Wealth of Networks: How Social Production Transforms Markets and Freedom*. New Haven, CN: Yale University Press.

Bryant, J. (2004). Critical communication challenges for the new century. *Journal of Communication, 54*(3), 389–401.

Couldry, N., Livingston, S., & Markham, T. (2007). *Media Consumption and Public Engagement: Beyond the Presumption of Attention*. New York: Palgrave Macmillan.

DeSanctis, G. & Poole, M. S. (1994). Capturing the complexity in advanced technology use: Adaptive structuration theory. *Organization Science, 5*(2), 121–147.

DeVany, A. (2004). *Hollywood Economics: How Extreme Uncertainty Shapes the Film Industry*. London: Routledge.

Elliot, P. (1974). Uses and gratifications research: A critique and a sociological alternative. In J. G. Blumer & E. Katz (Eds.), *The Uses of Mass Communications: Current Perspectives on Gratifications Research*. Beverly Hills, CA: Sage, 249–268.

Ettema, J. S. & Whitney, D. C. (1994). The money arrow: An introduction to audiencemaking. In J. Ettema & D. Whitney (Eds.). *Audiencemaking: How the Media Create the Audience*. Thousand Oaks: Sage, 1–18.

Finn, S. (1997). Origins of media exposure: linking personality traits to TV, radio, print, and film use. *Communication Research, 24*(5) 507–529.

Gandy, O. H. (1992). The political economy approach: A critical challenge. *Journal of Media Economics, 5*, 23–42.

Giddens, A. (1984). *The Constitution of Society: Outline of the Theory of Structuration*. Berkeley, CA: University of California Press.

Giddens, A. (1987). *Social Theory and Modern Sociology*. Stanford, CA: Stanford University Press.

Goodhardt, G. J., Ehrenberg, A. S. C., & Collins, M. A. (1987). *The Television Audience: Patterns of Viewing*. (2nd ed.). Westmead, UK: Gower.

Huberman, B. A. (2001). *The Laws of the Web: Patterns in the Ecology of Information*. Cambridge, MA: MIT Press.

Lyman, P. & Varian, H. R. (2003). *How Much Information?* Retrieved from www.sims.berkeley.edu/how-much-info-2003, on September 14, 2006.

Katz, E. (1996). And deliver us from segmentation. *Annals of the American Academy of Political and Social Sciences, 546,* 22–33.

McPhee, W. N. (1963). *Formal Theories of Mass Behavior.* New York: The Free Press.

Neuendorf, K., Atkin, D., & Jeffres, L. (2001). Reconceptualizing channel repertoire in the urban cable environment. *Journal of Broadcasting & Electronic Media, 45* (3), 464–482.

Orlikowski, W. J. (1992). The duality of technology: Rethinking the concept of technology in organizations. *Organization Science, 3,* 398–427.

Owen, B. M., Beebe, J. H., & Manning, W. G. (1974). *Television Economics.* Lexington, MA: Lexington Books.

Poole, M. S. & DeSanctis, G. (2004). Structuration theory in information systems research: Methods and controversies. In M. E. Whitman & A. B. Woszczynski (Eds.), *Handbook of Information Systems Research.* Hershey, PA: Idea Group, 206–249.

Prior, M. (2007). *Post-broadcast Democracy: How Media Choice Increases Inequality in Political Involvement and Polarizes Elections.* Cambridge, UK: Cambridge University Press.

Reiss, S. & Wiltz, J. (2004). Why people watch reality TV. *Media Psychology, 6,* 363–378.

Rosenstein, A. W. & Grant, A. E. (1997). Reconceptualizing the role of habit: A new model of television audience activity. *Journal of Broadcasting & Electronic Media, 41,* 324–344.

Rubin, A. M. (2002). The uses-and-gratifications perspective of media effects. In J. Bryant & D. Zillmann (Eds.), *Media Effects: Advances in Theory and Research.* Mahwah, NJ: Erlbaum, 525–548.

Ruggiero, T. E. (2000). Uses and gratifications theory in the 21st century. *Mass Communication & Society, 3* (1), 3–37.

Salganik, M. J., Dodds, P. S., & Watts, D. J. (2006, February 10). Experimental study of inequality and unpredictability in an artificial cultural market. *Science, 311,* 854–856.

Sherry, J. L. (2004). Flow and media enjoyment. *Communication Theory, 14*(4), 328–347.

Simon, H. (1971). Designing organizations for an information-rich world. In M. Greenberger (Ed.), *Computers, Communications and the Public Interest.* Baltimore: The Johns Hopkins Press, 40–41.

Sunstein, C. (2001). *Republic.com.* Princeton, NJ: Princeton University Press.

Turow, J. (1997). *Breaking up America: Advertisers and the new media world.* Chicago: University of Chicago Press.

Veronis Shuler Stevenson. (2006). *Communications Industry Forecast: 2006–2010.* New York: Author.

Vorderer, P., Klimmt, C., & Ritterfeld, U. (2004). Enjoyment: At the heart of media entertainment. *Communication Theory, 14*(4), 388–408.

Watts, D. J. (2003). *Six Degrees: The Science of a Connected Age.* New York: Norton.

Webster, J. G. (1986). Audience behavior in the new media environment. *Journal of Communication, 36*(3), 77–91.

Webster, J. G. (2005). Beneath the veneer of fragmentation: Television audience polarization in a multichannel world. *Journal of Communication, 55*(2), 366–382.

Webster, J. G. (2006). Audience flow past and present: Television inheritance effects reconsidered. *Journal of Broadcasting & Electronic Media, 50*(2), 323–337.

Webster, J. G. & Phalen, P. F. (1997). *The Mass Audience: Rediscovering the Dominant Model.* Mahwah, NJ: Erlbaum.

Webster, J. G. & Wakshlag, J. J. (1983). A theory of television program choice. *Communication Research, 10*(4), 430–446.

Weibull, L. (1985). Structural factors in gratifications research. In K. E. Rosengren, L. A. Wenner, & P. Palmgreen (Eds.), *Media Gratifications Research: Current Perspectives.* Beverly Hills, CA: Sage, 123–147.

Yuan, E. & Webster, J. G. (2006). Channel repertoires: Using peoplemeter data in Beijing. *Journal of Broadcasting & Electronic Media, 50*(3), 524–536.

Zillmann, D. (2000). Mood management in the context of selective exposure theory. *Communication Yearbook, 23*, 103–122.

Chapter 14

Media Choice Despite Multitasking?

*Cees M. Koolstra, Ute Ritterfeld, and
Peter Vorderer*

Most chapters in this book presume that media users usually have particular *reasons* or an identifiable *motivation* to select (or not to select) specific media and certain forms of content at any given point in time. If we look at patterns of media use today, however, one of the most striking characteristics seems to be that many (more than anything else: younger) users do *not* always select one medium and one form of content over another anymore. Instead, some, and increasingly more individuals use different media and different content simultaneously. They play a computer game while listening to music, they watch a TV program while talking to a friend over the phone, etc. and thereby engage themselves in what has been called multitasking.

One reason for this particular form of media behavior certainly results from the increased availability of various media. From a psychological point of view, however, we need to explore the users' underlying reasons, motivations, or goals to understand the phenomenon.

Research in media psychology and communication has a long tradition in attempting to identify the one and only reason or—in the context of uses-and-gratifications research—the specific motivation for each particular exposure situation to media content (Sherry & Boyan, 2008; Vorderer, 2008). Those attempts have usually started with a definition of what needs to be explained (the explanandum), and this, in almost all cases, was the use of *one* particular medium or of some *specific* content. From there, it was often tried to identify the drives, motives, or goals (as explanans) that explain the observed selection and responses to the particular media usage. Although about one fourth of all the media-related choices of U.S. children and adolescents appeared in the context of multitasking even a few years ago (cf., Foehr, 2006) and although this phenomenon is widely discussed in public (e.g., Wallis, 2006) it has hardly been recognized in media exposure theory. Multitasking challenges the very idea of media users making a more or less deliberate decision about what kind of media they are going to use and what specific content they are willing to expose themselves to.

Instead of asking why one person watches TV or selects a specific show the question now rather seems to be: Why does somebody combine the use of various media at the same time? Is this to simultaneously gratify several needs or does multitasking indicate a person's difficulties in selecting one media (content) over the other?

In order to shed some light on this relevant question for media exposure theory and research, we will start with an overview of how multitasking has been conceptualized so far within communication studies, summarize the most important empirical studies on the prevalence of the phenomenon, turn to the motivational question of why media users involve themselves in this specific kind of activity and then refer to the most important findings about the effects of multitasking currently known. On the basis of this summary, we will end the chapter with some conclusions for future research.

What is Media Multitasking?

Multitasking refers to doing two or more things at the same time. The term originates from computer science as a description of a central processor performing two or more tasks simultaneously. Like computers, people frequently do more than one task at the same time, e.g., singing while taking a shower, and listening to the radio while driving a car. In the context of the social sciences, however, the term multitasking most commonly refers to a situation in which people are engaged in two or more information-processing tasks at the same time. More specifically, media multitasking or "simultaneous use of (multiple) media" pertains to using two or more media simultaneously (Foehr, 2006; Koolstra, 2008). Doing two or more different information-processing tasks using one and the same medium may also be considered as media multitasking. An example for this is reading an email message while listening to music by means of the same medium, such as a computer, a PDA, or a mobile phone. However, when using one medium that involves two or more sensory channels, e.g., using a TV to watch a movie and listen to the sound of the same movie, we speak of "multi-modal (or in this example bi-sensory) processing" (e.g., Stephens, 2007) and not of media multitasking. More difficult to define is the use of media content that consists of different unrelated elements in *multi-message formats* presented simultaneously (cf., Bergen, Grimes, & Potter, 2005) such as *CNN's Headline News* combined with lexical news *crawls* at the bottom of the TV screen. In these cases, it matters what the mind of the user is occupied with and what is set as *primary* and *secondary* media use. An example is when reading a newspaper as a primary task is combined with listening to the radio as a secondary task (or background medium); or doing homework while keeping the television on in the background. The terminology about "primary" and "secondary" media use refers to the idea that people choose to focus most of their attention on one (the primary task) and little attention on an additional (the secondary) task. During multitasking, a person may choose to switch focus from one to the other: The primary task becomes secondary and the secondary task becomes primary; for example, when somebody briefly interrupts reading the newspaper because most of his or her attention is focused on an interesting discussion broadcast on television.

Related but different to media multitasking is the *sequential* or *serial* use of media. Whereas media multitasking assumes that people use different media simultaneously, sequential media use assumes that users switch between media. An example of this would be when a person has two or more media (such as a TV and a computer) available and "on" while at a certain point in time all of the available attention is focused on one of the two only (e.g., TV), after which all of the attention is switched (back) to the other medium (e.g., the computer). The distinction between media multitasking and media switching seems to be hypothetical in a situation in which different media are on/available and switching is done very rapidly. In fact, the assumption may be that when two or more media are on and readily available, it would be difficult to engage in "total" task switching, because at least some attention may always be related to the secondary medium. At the same time, it should be noted that there is increasing evidence from psychological dual-task studies that indicate that on a micro-level "doing things at the same time" may consist of doing tasks in a serial rather than in a parallel mode (e.g., Ruthruff, Pashler, & Hazeltine, 2003). This means that attentional capacity is switched from one task to the other, and that the idea of central tasks sharing attentional capacity may not be valid.

Prevalence of Media Multitasking

There have been remarkably few studies investigating how frequently people engage in media multitasking. A recent one with a sample of 8- to 18-years-old US Americans (Foehr, 2006) shows that among people in that age group multitasking is actually very common. This conclusion was based on two types of data: Survey data collected among a representative U.S. sample (N = 2,032) and diary data collected from a subgroup of this sample (N = 685). When asked how often additional media were dealt with when using each of four different media, print, TV, music, and computer, a majority of the children/adolescents (53 percent or more) reported that they engaged in media multitasking "most of the time" or "some of the time." Dependent on the type of medium, only 12 percent to 19 percent said they "never" do so. The diary data in which "time spent with multiple media" was measured regardless of whether they were primary or secondary showed that for 17 percent of the time television viewing was combined with another medium. Much higher percentages were found for media combinations while using email (83 percent), visiting websites (74 percent), instant messaging (74 percent), playing computer games (67 percent), and doing homework on the computer (60 percent). Additional data in which the distinction between primary and secondary media use was made showed that television (to which young people still devote the most amount of their media time) and video games are the least likely and the computer is the most likely primary medium to be combined with other media. For example, of the total time devoted to computer use as a primary activity, 27 percent was spent on doing secondary tasks with the same computer (i.e., computer-based multi-tasking), 13 percent on listening to music, 8 percent on reading, and 7 percent on doing homework (not on the computer).

There also is evidence that media multitasking is increasingly *popular* among young people: Whereas in 1999, children at the age of 8 to 18 years spent 16 percent of their media time on multiple media use, in 2004 the percentage had risen to 26 percent (Roberts, Foehr, & Rideout, 2005). The popular and seemingly effortless use of media multitasking among young people has even inspired some researchers to coin names for this age group, such as the *M Generation* (Roberts et al., 2005), *digital natives* (Prensky, 2001), *Net Generation* (Oblinger & Oblinger, 2005), and *teen-media-juggling act* to describe their specific media behavior (cf., www.kff.org).

Although the above-mentioned studies suggest that young people who grew up with the latest media technologies are more frequently engaged in media multitasking than adults, a Dutch study on the prevalence of media multitasking, in which adolescents as well as adults were included (SPOT, 2007) tells a somewhat different story. When the distinction was made between children/adolescents (13 through 19 years old, *n* = 399) and adults (20 through 65 years old, *n* = 3,002), percentages of time engaged in media multitasking were similar between the two age groups. For example, listening to music was combined with using another medium for 89 percent of the time among the younger age group, whereas it was combined for 85 percent of the time among the group of adults. Other highly comparable multitasking proportions among the young and adult group were found for reading a newspaper (69 percent and 69 percent), using a mobile phone (67 percent and 67 percent), and watching television (37 percent and 36 percent), respectively. There were, however, also differences between the two groups: Young people were multitasking more frequently when surfing the Internet (76 percent of the time) and using email (82 percent of the time) than adults (56 percent and 65 percent, respectively). In contrast, adults were multitasking more than the youngsters while playing computer games (49 percent among the adults versus 38 percent among the young) and while chatting through the Internet (64 percent of the time among the adults versus 55 percent among the young). These findings indicate that the younger generation is not always engaged more in media multitasking than the older generation but that the choice to engage in multitasking may depend on age as well as on the type of medium. Frequently used combinations among the younger were chatting as the primary activity with secondary use of the Internet (35 percent of the time) or television (12 percent of the time), surfing the Internet with chatting (35 percent) or watching TV (19 percent), and playing computer games with watching TV (25 percent) or chatting (6 percent). Among the adult group reading the newspaper was often combined with watching TV (23 percent) or listening to the radio (18 percent), and reading a magazine also with watching TV (27 percent) or listening to the radio (12 percent).

Another U.S. study also shows that adults are frequently engaged in multitasking: The so-called *Middletown Media Studies* estimated that almost 24 percent of adults' media time is spent with using more than one medium simultaneously (Papper, Holmes, & Popovich, 2004). This study used three different types of data about media use: telephone surveys, diaries, and observations. A striking finding was that when the question was simply whether a particular medium was used increasing uses were reported from survey to diary to observation. Media multitasking time proportions were also higher when being observed than self-reported in diaries: The diaries indicated that 12.4 percent of the total media time was spent on media multitasking whereas observations show that media multitasking was prevalent in 23.7 percent of the media time. According to those observations television as a primary medium was rarely combined with other media, whereas television was by far the most popular secondary medium while media multitasking. This outcome seems to be consistent with another U.S. study on media multitasking among more than 5,000 online respondents (Luth Research, 2007). Although conducted by a non-academic research institution that did not document which specific questions were asked, this study concluded that people nowadays spend about 20 hours per week on media multitasking and that television is "a key companion medium of other media" (p. 3): Nearly half of the respondents reported to use TV as a secondary medium while they were engaged in surfing the Internet or in doing email. In addition, 20 percent of the respondents reported to use TV as a background medium to reading newspapers, magazines, or books.

Finally, there were a series of bi-annual online surveys among very large U.S. samples (N's > 7,000) conducted by BIGresearch (Pilotta & Schultz, 2005; Pilotta, Schultz, Drenik, & Rist, 2004). These so-called SIMM studies (Simultaneous Media Consumption) have also shown that media multitasking is a very common way of using the media. Again, television was the most popular secondary medium when surfing the Internet, using email, reading the newspaper or reading magazines. The second most popular secondary medium was radio as a background to surfing the Internet, using email, and reading magazines. Based on the findings that people regularly seem to *listen* to television as a secondary medium (rather than watch it as a primary medium) and shift their attention from and to multiple media, Pilotta and Schultz (2005) concluded that: "The simultaneous media experience is a non-narrative form with no beginning, middle, or end, with one media flowing through the other—synesthesia" (p. 24).

Why Do People Engage in Media Multitasking?

To our knowledge, there have not been any systematic studies that explored the question *why* users would be media multitasking. Based on general knowledge about people's media use there may, however, be several reasons. First, there is an increase in the availability of media. In particular, within the highly industrialized countries households are media saturated not only in respect to different types of media (TV, radio, computer, telephone, books, video games, magazines, etc.) but also in respect to converging media (e.g., reading books, watching movies, and listening to music by means of the same media such as a computer or PDA). In addition to media saturation in homes more and more of such media can now also be used *outside* of homes (e.g., mobile phones, mp3-players, car navigation systems, or PDA's). Second, from a uses-and-gratifications point of view, the surveillance function of the media may be fulfilled best by attending to surveillance-type media such as TV or radio news channels (or both) in the background of other media. Third, because many people have become used to doing several things simultaneously, this general behavior pattern may also apply to the use of media. It even might support the feeling or at least the illusion that several things are actually done at the same time. Fourth, different media can complement each other in specific aspects. For example, when students are doing homework, the Internet (by using a computer) may be used for its recency of information in addition to a book, which may provide the more established, basic information about the same topic. Another example would be a situation that is filled with executing dull tasks, e.g., paying several bills by using a computer, which can be turned into something more interesting by using another medium in the background. Also, as media can be used for mood-management (e.g., Knobloch-Westerwick, 2007; Knobloch-Westerwick & Scott, 2006), the use of secondary media may enhance one's mood while performing a task using a primary medium. Fifth, somewhat related to the complementary-functions argument, using background media may stimulate the effectiveness of tasks performed with a primary medium. For example, putting on music may help the performance of another media task in situations in which the background music "overrides" disturbing background noises such as outside traffic or neighbors shouting at each other.

With these assumptions we imply that multitasking is a deliberate choice. Some authors, however, point to the necessity to multitask, for example in working spheres (González & Mark, 2004). Information workers are found to spend an average of two minutes on any computer task before switching to the next. The resulting high discontinuity encompasses computer work (text, programming), hand held planners and calculators, and media based communication (phone, email). About half of the discontinuity was prompted by external factors such as incoming emails or ringing phones whereas the other half was initiated by the worker him/herself. Most interestingly, the majority of subjects in this study criticized the unpredictability of external disruptions and reported a preference for less fragmented work. A follow up study conducted by Mark, González, and Harris (2005) confirmed the high fragmentation of information work. In addition, the authors identify private activities as the main cause for internal interruptions whereas external interruptions are often a result of prioritizing. However, high priority activities were interrupted more often (60.3 percent) than peripheral work (41.7 percent). A similar conclusion was derived from a Microsoft research team, which used log files to analyze computer activities of information workers (Horvitz, Kadie, Paek, & Hovel, 2003). Moreover, this study reveals the high affordance of incoming emails: 40 percent of all incoming mails elicit an immediate response from their addressees. In turn, each of these responses resulted in an averaged 15 minute interruption in the work flow.

Possible Effects of Media Multitasking

To date, only a few studies on the effects of media multitasking are available. However, it may be argued that research in the context of dual-task performance can inform us—at least to some extent—about the effects of multitasking. These studies indicate that doing two tasks simultaneously (or switching between tasks) costs more time and results in a lower task performance than doing the same tasks in succession (see for a review, Pashler, 1994), suggesting that there is support for a *central bottleneck model* of dual-tasking (e.g., Ruthruff et al., 2003). In addition, dual-tasking seems to be more difficult if tasks are more complex and more unfamiliar (e.g., Rubinstein, Meyer, & Evans, 2001). However, there is also evidence that younger people have less problems with dual-tasking than older people (e.g., Göthe, Oberauer, & Reinhold, 2007) and that practice may help to decrease dual-task costs (e.g., Kramer, Larish, & Strayer, 1995; Schumacher et al., 2001).

Two other types of psychological studies inform why media multitasking may result in compromised information-processing. First, there is research on distraction effects of background noise, speech or music (e.g., Broadbent, 1979). In general, these studies indicate that background sound hinders cognitive performance in experimental (e.g., Salamé & Baddeley, 1987) as well as in ecological settings such as offices (e.g., Evans & Johnson, 2000). Second, another set of studies are based on the assumption that the ability to process information is limited (e.g., Basil, 1994; Kahneman, 1973; Lang, 2000). The so called limited capacity information-processing model states that information gets lost because a person chooses to allocate too few resources to a task, or because a task requires more resources than the person has available. In media multitasking, the simultaneous tasks compete for limited information-processing resources, which may result in an overload of information exceeding the processing capacity, so that only part of the information can be processed and the remaining information is lost. Some neurophysiological data seem to support the limited capacity model, especially for single-modal activities (Lavie, 2005; Marois & Ivanoff, 2005).

Limited-capacity theorists hold two alternative views to explain capacity overload when people are multitasking (Bourke, Duncan, & Nimmo-Smith, 1996). One position states that there is a general processing capacity that can be exceeded: Information processing might suffer when two or more tasks require more capacity than available in one's general resources. The alternative view states that overload might occur when two tasks compete for the same specific information-processing resource and the capacity of the specific resource is exceeded, a phenomenon referred to as "structural interference" (Bourke et al., 1996). According to this latter view, tasks might interfere with each other even if the total processing capacity is not exceeded. Structural interference may arise, for example, when reading is combined with watching a talk show, because both activities require the processing of linguistic information. A supplementary explanation as to why media multitasking might lead to loss of information is that some messages elicit "orienting responses" (Lang, 2000). Orienting responses involve automatic allocation of resources to a medium as a reaction to novel or interesting stimuli such as sound effects, visual complexity, movements, cuts, and zooms, presented in a television program (Lang, 2000). If a secondary medium also elicits such orienting responses, most or all of the processing resources are allocated to the newly presented stimulus with the result that fewer or no resources are left to process the former, primary information-processing task(s).

It should be noted that the above mentioned psychological studies and theoretical models pertain to multitasking on a micro-level in the sense that tasks are almost always very short and time measurements are very precise (into milliseconds). In addition, studies are almost always conducted in an experimental setting that does not resemble the situation in which media users at home may be engaged in media multitasking. Also, many studies are concerned with a "meaningless" background such as noise, whereas in media multitasking backgrounds of secondary media content are almost always meaningful. The few studies that investigated effects of media multitasking with meaningful backgrounds and longer tasks in a more daily-life setting pertain to the effects of using background media on homework performance among students. A series of studies conducted by Armstrong and colleagues indicated that background television might cause reduced performance in reading comprehension (Armstrong, Boiarsky, & Mares, 1991) and spatial problem solving (Armstrong & Greenberg, 1990), and that deleterious effects of background television on reading arise during the encoding process (Armstrong & Chung, 2000). A series of experiments conducted by Pool and colleagues investigated not only effects of background TV but also of background radio (music or speech). It was found that background radio, whether it was music or talk radio, and music video clips such as shown on MTV, did not lead to performance decreases in homework (Pool, van der Voort, Beentjes, & Koolstra, 2000; Pool, Koolstra, & van der Voort, 2003a). Background TV soaps operas, however, caused a decreased performance on difficult tasks as well as some extension of the time needed to complete the tasks (Pool, Koolstra, & van der Voort, 2003b). This last experiment also included observations to investigate how students divide their attention, measured by *eyes-on-screen*, between the homework task and the television screen. It was established that the extension of homework time in the soap television conditions, which amounted to 28 percent as compared with the control condition, was due to the fact that students looked at the TV at moments when the soap opera was becoming more interesting (for example because of romantic or aggressive scenes). On average, students shifted their attention 2.5 times per minute from their homework task to the TV.

Conclusion

In light of the fact that in highly industrialized countries people spend about one quarter of the time they use the media with multitasking, there are strikingly few scientific studies on this phenomenon. The few studies on the prevalence of media multitasking that are available today were either conducted by commercial research institutes and/or they are not published in academic communication journals. This suggests that this phenomenon, which is becoming increasingly important not only for individuals but also for society at large, has not been acknowledged yet among mainstream media researchers.

The overall conclusion of the available studies on the prevalence of media multitasking is that not only young people but also adults are frequently engaged in such activities. Media that are often used as a secondary source or background medium are TV and radio (or listening to music), whereas the most popular primary media during media multitasking are the computer (used for email, the Internet, chatting and instant messaging) and print media (newspapers, magazines, and books). When engaged in media multitasking, TV is rarely chosen as the primary medium. New studies on the question of *why* people are engaged in media multitasking may show that primary media often pertain to using only one sensory channel, whereas secondary media are chosen to pertain to another sensory channel. In addition, it may be suggested that secondary media fulfill the roles of mood management, companionship, and/or surveillance.

An interesting new question arises about how we should look at the present knowledge about the effects of media use. On the one hand it may be expected that media effects established in past experimental studies may no longer be valid, because they cannot be generalized to real-life settings in which people use more media at the same time. At the same time, effects of multiple media use in real life may be expected to be smaller than those established in controlled single media settings, because the limited attentional capacity has to be divided among several media resources. On the other hand, effects pertaining to variables such as uncertainty and confusion may be much larger in media multitasking, because of the same limitation of attention to be divided over more than one media source. Examples are that people who have limited attention focused on background television may have problems making a distinction between trustworthy and untrustworthy sources of information as well as deciding about whether the content of the information was fictional or realistic. In these situations sleeper effects of media multitasking could occur: Because specific characteristics of media content are processed subconsciously or heuristically, decisions about information made after exposure may be incorrect with the possible result that information from a low-credible source could increase in effectiveness (for a review on sleeper effects, see Pratkanis, Greenwald, Leippe, & Baumgardner, 1988).

Many questions about media multitasking are still unanswered. Does media multitasking really involve doing more than one task simultaneously or does it involve switching between media tasks? Observational data indicate that when concurrent media tasks ask for much attention, people switch between tasks (e.g., Pool et al., 2003b; Schmitt, Woolf, & Anderson, 2003), although some attention may be focused on the secondary medium to be able to *monitor* it while doing the primary task. In contrast, psychological studies on dual-tasking suggest that at least central processing pertains to doing one type of task at the same time.

Another question relates to how media multitasking can be measured reliably. When people use visual media such as television and computers, observation seems to be a good choice, for example by recording eyes-on-screen, but when media (also) include auditory channels, observation does not work. Measuring exposure through self-reported recognition of visual and/or auditory content might work, but it would not guarantee that stimuli that are processed automatically will be reported.

In this chapter, we have tried to give some preliminary answers to the question of how media multitasking is related to media choice. The high prevalence of media multitasking and its many unknown aspects and consequences ask for more studies on the phenomenon. As compared with media behavior 50 years ago, the explosion of new forms of communication today seems to have reshaped our media behavior with many more media concurrently competing for our attention. In line with this phenomenon we also need to reshape our research on media use.

References

Armstrong, G. B. & Chung, L. (2000). Background television and reading memory in context: Assessing TV interference and facilitative context effects on encoding versus retrieval processes. *Communication Research, 27*, 327–352.

Armstrong, G. B. & Greenberg, B. S. (1990). Background television as an inhibitor of cognitive processing. *Human Communication Research, 16,* 355–386.

Armstrong, G. B., Boiarsky, G. A., & Mares, M. (1991). Background television and reading performance. *Communication Monographs, 58,* 235–253.

Band, G. P. H., Jolicoeur, P., Akyürek, E. G., & Memelink, J. (2006). Integrative views on dual-task costs. *European Journal of Cognitive Psychology, 18*(4), 481–492.

Basil, M. D. (1994). Multiple resource theory I: Application to television viewing. *Communication Research, 21,* 177–207.

Bergen, L., Grimes, T., & Potter, D. (2005). How attention partitions itself during simultaneous message presentations. *Human Communication Research, 31*(3), 311–336.

Bourke, P. A., Duncan, J., & Nimmo-Smith, I. (1996). A general factor involved in dual-task performance increment. *The Quarterly Journal of Experimental Psychology, 49,* 525–545.

Broadbent, D. E. (1979). Human performance and noise. In C. S. Harris (Ed.), *Handbook of Noise Control* (2nd ed., pp. 17.1–17.20). New York: McGraw-Hill.

Evans, G. W. & Johnson, D. (2000). Stress and open-office noise. *Journal of Applied Psychology, 85,* 779–783.

Foehr, U. G. (2006). *Media Multitasking Among American Youth: Prevalence, Predictors and Pairings.* Kaiser Family Foundation. Online. Retrieved March 5, 2007 from www.kff.org/entmedia/7592.cfm.

González, V. M. & Mark, G. (2004). "Constant, constant, multi-tasking craziness": managing multiple working spheres. *Proceedings of the SIGCHI Conference on Human Factors in Computing Systems, 6*(1), 113–120.

Göthe, K., Oberauer, K., & Kliegl, R. (2007). Age differences in dual-task performance after practice. *Psychology and Aging, 22*(3), 596–606.

Horvitz, E., Kadie, C. Paek, T., & Hovel, D. (2003). Models of attention in computing and communication: From principles to applications. *Communication of the ACM, 46*(3), 52–59.

Kahneman, D. (1973). *Attention and Effort.* Englewood Cliffs, NJ: Prentice Hall.

Knobloch-Westerwick, S. (2007). Gender differences in selective media use for mood management and mood adjustment. *Journal of Broadcasting & Electronic Media, 51*(1), 73–92.

Knobloch-Westerwick, S. & Scott, A. (2006). Mood adjustment to social situations through mass media use: How men ruminate and women dissipate angry moods. *Human Communication Research, 32*(1), 58–73.

Koolstra, C. M. (2008). Multitasking. In W. Donsbach (Ed.), *The International Encyclopedia of Communication* (pp. 3165–3168). Oxford: Blackwell Publishing.

Kramer, A. F., Larish, J. F., & Strayer, D. L. (1995). Training for attentional control in dual task settings: A comparison of young and old adults. *Journal of Experimental Psychology: Applied, 1*(1), 50–76.

Lang, A. (2000). The limited capacity model of mediated message processing. *Journal of Communication, 50*(1), 46–70.

Lavie, L. (2005). Distracted and confused? Selective attention under load. *Trends in Cognitive Science, 9*(2), 75–82.

Levine, L. E., Waite, B. M., & Bowman, L. L. (2007). Electronic media use, reading, and academic distractibility in college youth. *Cyberpsychology & Behavior, 10*(4), 560–566.

Luth Research (2007). *Indicator EDG Research: Media Multitasking.* Online. Retrieved October 22, 2007 from at www.luthresearch.com.

Mark, G., González, V. M., & Harris, J. (2005). No task left behind? Examining the nature of fragmented work. *Proceedings of the SIGCHI Conference on Human Factors in Computing Systems,* 321–330.

Marois, R. & Ivanoff, J. (2005). Capacity limits of information processing in the brain. *Trends in Cognitive Sciences, 9,* 296–305.

Oblinger, D. G. & Oblinger, J. L. (2005). *Educating the Net Generation.* Boulder, CO: Educause.

Papper, R. A., Holmes, M. E., & Popovich, M. N. (2004). Middletown media studies: Media multitasking ... and how much people really use the media. *The International Digital Media and Arts Association Journal, 1*(1), 5–50.

Pashler, H. (1994). Dual-task interference in simple tasks: Data and theory. *Psychological Bulletin, 116*(2), 220–244.

Pilotta, J. J. & Schultz, D. E. (2005). Simultaneous media experience and synesthesia. *Journal of Advertising Research, 45*(1), 19–26.

Pilotta, J. J., Schultz, D. E., Drenik, G., & Rist, P. (2004). Simultaneous media usage: A critical consumer orientation to media planning. *Journal of Consumer Behaviour, 3*(3), 285–292.

Pool, M. M., Koolstra, C. M., & van der Voort, T. H. A. (2003a). The impact of background radio or television on high school students' homework performance. *Journal of Communication, 53,* 74–87.

Pool, M. M., Koolstra, C. M., & van der Voort, T. H. A. (2003b). Distraction effects of background soap operas on homework performance: An experimental study enriched with observational data. *Educational Psychology, 23,* 361–380.

Pool, M. M., van der Voort, T. H. A., Beentjes, J. W. J., & Koolstra, C. M. (2000). Background television as an inhibitor of performance on easy and difficult homework assignments. *Communication Research, 27,* 293–326.

Pratkanis, A. R., Greenwald, A. G., Leippe, M. R., & Baumgardner, M. H. (1988) In search of reliable persuasion effects: III. The sleeper effect is dead. Long live the sleeper effect. *Journal of Personality and Social Psychology,* 54(2), 203–218.

Prensky, M. (2001). Digital natives, digital immigrants. *On the Horizon NCB University Press, 9*(5), 1–6.

Roberts, D. F., Foehr, U. G., & Rideout, V. (2005). *Generation M: Media in the Lives of 8–18 Year-olds.* Kaiser Family Foundation. Online. Retrieved March 22, 2007 from www.kff.org/entmedia/7251.cfm.

Rubinstein, J., Meyer, D., & Evans, J. (2001). Executive control of cognitive processes in task switching. *Journal of Experimental Psychology, 27*(4), 763–797.

Ruthruff, E., Pashler, H. E., & Hazeltine, E. (2003). Dual-task interference with equal task emphasis: Graded capacity sharing or central postponement? *Perception & Psychophysics, 65*(5), 801–816.

Salamé, P. & Baddeley, A. D. (1989). Effects of background music on phonological short-term memory. *Quarterly Journal of Experimental Psychology, 41,* 107–122.

Schmitt, K. L., Woolf, K. D., & Anderson, D. R. (2003). Viewing the viewers: Viewing behaviors by children and adults during television programs and commercials. *Journal of Communication, 53,* 265–281.

Schumacher, E. H., Seymour, T. L., Glass, J. M., Fencsik, D. E., Lauber, E., J., Kieras, D. E., & Meyer, D. E. (2001). Virtually perfect time sharing in dual-task performance: Uncorking the central cognitive bottleneck. *Psychological Science* *12*(2), 101–108.

Sherry, J. L. & Boyan, A. (2008). Uses and gratifications. In W. Donsbach (Ed.). *The International Communication Encyclopedia* (pp. 5239–5244). Oxford: Blackwell Publishing.

SPOT (2007). *Aandacht voor multitasking: Conclusies uit het SPOT tijdbesteding- sonderzoek 2006* [Attention for multitasking: Conclusions from the SPOT time use study of 2006]. Amstelveen, The Netherlands: SPOT.

Stephens, K. K. (2007). The successive use of information and communication tech- nologies at work. *Communication Theory, 17*, 486–505.

Vorderer, P. (2008). Exposure to communication content. In W. Donsbach (Ed.), *International Encyclopedia of Communication* (pp. 1658–1668). London: Black- well.

Wallis, C. (2006). The multitasking generation. Online. Retrieved March 22, 2006 from www.time.com/time/magazine/article/0,9171,1174696,00.html.

Chapter 15

Media Synchronicity and Media Choice

Choosing Media for Performance[1]

Alan R. Dennis, Robert M. Fuller, and Joseph S. Valacich

One of the most widely used media theories is Media Richness Theory (MRT), which argues that task performance will be improved when task information needs are matched to a medium's information richness (later called just "media richness"). Media capable of sending "rich" information (e.g., face-to-face meetings) are better suited to equivocal tasks (where there are multiple interpretations for information) and less "rich" media (e.g., computer-mediated communication) are best suited to tasks with a lack of information.

MRT was developed to theorize which media should prove *most effective*, not to theorize how managers *choose* media (Daft & Lengel, 1986; Dennis & Kinney, 1998). Nonetheless, the expected effectiveness of using a media, is one important factor influencing the choice to use it (Daft, Lengel, & Trevino, 1987). Empirical tests of MRT for "new media" such as computer-mediated communication have not been convincing, (Burke & Chidambaram, 1999; Carnevale et al., 1981; Dennis & Kinney, 1998; El-Shinnawy & Markus, 1992; Kinney & Watson, 1992; Lee, 1994; Markus, 1994; Mennecke, Valacich, & Wheeler, 2000; Ngwenyama & Lee, 1997; Rice & Shook, 1990; Trevino, Lengel, Bodensteiner, Gerloff, & Muir, 1990; Valacich, Paranka, George, & Nunamaker, 1993; Vickery et al. 2004). In this paper, following from the Fit-Appropriation Model (Dennis, Wixom, & Vandenberg, 2001), we argue that the fit of media capabilities to the *communication* needs of a task influence the appropriation and choice to use a medium.

Prior Media Theories

Theories about communication and media are abundant (Fulk & Boyd, 1991; Putnam, Phillips, & Chapman, 1996). Perhaps the most influential theory, at least for the "new media" (Rice, 1992), is Media Richness Theory (Daft & Lengel, 1986). MRT initially did not consider new media, but they have been retroactively fit into it (Dennis & Kinney, 1998). MRT is similar to other media theories of its era (e.g., social presence theory: Short, Williams, &

Christie, 1976), in arguing that media differ in their ability to transmit certain information or cues (cf. cues-filtered out theory, Sproull & Kiesler, 1991). MRT argues that media differ in "richness" ("the ability of information to change understanding within a time interval," Daft & Lengel, 1986, p. 560). Face-to-face communication is the richest, while media capable of sending fewer cues (e.g., no vocal inflections) or providing slower feedback (e.g., written communication) are "leaner." Communication and task performance will improve when managers use richer media for equivocal tasks (where there are multiple and conflicting interpretations of information) and leaner media for non-equivocal tasks (Daft & Lengel, 1986; Daft, Lengel, & Trevino, 1987).

Most studies of MRT have used it for media choice, not performance (Dennis & Kinney, 1998). Because MRT did not accurately reflect managers' choices, Trevino, Daft, and Lengel (1987) proposed a symbolic interaction extension to it by arguing that some media carry symbolic meaning above and beyond the content of the message (e.g., written media are more formal). This symbolic meaning "deflect[s] media choice behavior away from the rational matching of task ambiguity and media richness" (Fulk & Boyd, 1991, p. 410) so that media choice is based on the users' perceptions about symbolic meaning as well as actual characteristics.

Social information processing theory (later called social influence theory) argues that media richness is not an objective, physical, property of a medium (Fulk, Schmitz, & Steinfield, 1990; Fulk, Steinfield, Schmitz, & Power, 1987). Instead, media richness is in part socially constructed and different individuals may hold different perceptions of richness (cf. Lee, 1994). This theory focuses on media choice, not communication performance, but researchers have concluded that factors beyond media richness also affect other outcomes (see Fulk & Boyd, 1991; Rice 1992).

Walther (1992) argues that rather than looking at media characteristics, we need to also consider the people using the media. He argues that over the long run, communication transcends media (i.e., the medium is *not* the message). Communicators are motivated by the same drivers regardless of media used, so deep personal relationships can be developed through very "lean" media, although it may take much longer. He concludes that "over time, computer mediation should have very limited effects on relational communication" (Walther, 1992, p. 80), other than to slow it.

In a different perspective on media and communication performance, DeSanctis and Poole's (1994) adaptive structuration theory argues that it is not the objective physical characteristics of the medium that matter, but rather how those characteristics are appropriated and used. Communication participants may appropriate and use media characteristics as intended by the designers, or they may appropriate and use them in ways not intended or even expected. The physical characteristics that are used are influenced by the participants' existing social structures and how the media's physical structures are understood. The physical structures that are appropriated in turn influence the social structures that participants use, that in turn may influence future appropriation and use.

Channel expansion theory builds on MRT (Carlson & Zmud, 1999), arguing that the perceived richness of a medium depends not only on its characteristics, but also on the users' experience using it, and with each other, and perhaps also on the task and the organizational context in which the use occurs. Thus, while the physical characteristics of a medium may be fixed, users' perceptions depend upon their experiences, which may change over time.

Yoo and Alavi (2001) argue—and provide empirical evidence—that social presence, the extent to which the media enables the perception of others' presence (Short et al. 1976), is affected not only by objective characteristics of the medium (e.g., cues), but also by the nature of the individuals using it. They found that in established groups, whose members had worked together for several weeks, the level of group cohesion (i.e., members' attraction to the group) was directly related to the perception of the social presence provided by a medium. Members of highly cohesive groups reported higher social presence for both audio-only conferencing and desktop videoconferencing with application sharing, but social presence had no impact on task performance.

More recently, Kock's (2004) psychobiological model argues that humans have evolved to favor face-to-face communication, and the lower the "naturalness" of a medium (i.e., co-location, synchronous communication, facial cues, body language, and especially spoken words), the greater the cognitive effort required to use it. As individuals appropriate and use a medium, they can adapt to it, so cognitive effort decreases with use (e.g., DeLuca, Gasson, & Kock, 2006). Because such adaptation is learned, the cognitive effort required to use a non-natural medium depends upon the extent to which the communicating individuals hold similar views about the medium and how to use it. Improved communication performance and the choice to use a medium could come about through the learned reduction of cognitive effort required to use the medium.

A major consideration for any media theory is the facilitation of interactions necessary for the sharing of information and the development of meaning(s) ascribed to that information. Miranda and Saunders (2003) argue that one key outcome of communication is the development of intersubjective meaning of the information held by the participants: *"meaning derives from interactive interpretation by multiple persons, not simply from the cognition of a single individual"* (p. 88, original emphasis). In other words, meaning is co-constructed by the communication participants (Eisenberg, 1991; Weick, 1979). Understanding is not just transmitted from one participant to another, but evolves from the interactions among participants. Understanding of meaning is not possible without this interaction. For media theories, this means that the impact of media on communication performance (and ultimately the choice to use it) will derive from its ability to facilitate the interactions necessary to support meaning development.

Our Fundamental Assumptions

Our approach follows the "conduit metaphor" (Putnam et al., 1996), and treats the medium as a conduit among participants. We move beyond the transmission of information through this conduit to understand how the information is processed by the receiver. The conduit may be best thought of as a "reagent" (Lee, 1994, p. 154), in that information received can trigger extensive information processing as a receiver elaborates (Petty & Cacioppo, 1986) on a message to understand it, integrate it into his or her cognitive schema, and possibly draw implications far beyond the message itself (Lee, 1994; Petty & Cacioppo, 1986). The medium enables the transfer and processing of information which creates meaning (Sitkin, Sutcliffe, & Barrios-Choplin, 1992; Miranda & Saunders, 2003).

We begin with five fundamental assumptions, which represent boundary conditions to our theory. First, we start with the premise that the purpose of communication is to develop shared understanding (Miranda & Saunders, 2003; Rogers, 1986; Te'eni, 2001). We explicitly do not address situations in which the intent of some participants is to deceive other participants, although some parts of our theory may be useful in this research area (e.g., Carlson & George, 2004).

Second, we believe that such shared understanding *can* be co-constructed by the communication participants (Eisenberg, 1991; Miranda & Sanders, 2003; Weick, 1979), but that co-construction does not *always* occur (Sitkin et al., 1992). With co-construction, communication participants jointly create meaning and shared understanding so that the communication changes everyone's understanding of the information and its meaning. We believe that it is possible but not necessary for communication to involve co-construction; sometimes communication changes everyone's understanding, other times no one's understanding changes.

Third, the spirit by which shared understanding is developed is what Habermas terms *ideal speech*: "to ensure that (a) all voices in any way relevant can get a hearing, and that (b) the best arguments we have in our present state of knowledge are brought to bear, and that (c) disagreement or agreement on the part of the participants follows only from the force of the better argument and no other force" (Habermas & Nielsen, 1990, p. 104). We do not specifically address situations where some participants desire to manipulate or control how other participants interact so that the shared understanding that is developed does not reflect the information and opinions of all participants; however, parts of this theory may be useful in this research area as well.

Fourth, a medium has objective physical characteristics (e.g., it can or cannot transmit voice, it can or cannot store a copy of a message) that we prefer to call *media capabilities*. These capabilities may or may not be well understood by communication participants, and thus may or may not be appropriated and used as expected (DeSanctis & Poole, 1994). The media capabilities that are used can induce the creation of subjective, socially developed characteristics that may be perceived differently by different users, or perceived differently by the same user over time (Carlson & Zmud, 1999; Fulk et al., 1990; Walther, 1992). Our theory begins with a set of physical media capabilities that can induce the creation of a socially developed characteristic that we term media synchronicity, which may differ from person to person and over time.

Finally, most prior media theories have focused on media choice. Our theory is a theory of *communication performance*, which we argue is a fundamental factor influencing *media choice*. We do not address the myriad of factors beyond expected performance that influence media choice.

Rethinking task

"Task" has been a key element in the development and testing of media theories (Daft & Lengel, 1986; Dennis & Kinney, 1998; Mennecke et al., 2000; Rice, 1992; Suh, 1999; Zigurs & Buckland, 1998). However, studies comparing task performance between individuals working on different tasks with different media have not convincingly shown that a better match of media to the task will yield better task performance (Dennis & Kinney 1998; Hollingshead, McGrath, & O'Connor, 1993; Mennecke et al., 2000; Rice, 1992; Straus & McGrath, 1994; Straus, 1997; Suh, 1999).

Our primary thesis is that communication performance comes from the matching of media capabilities to the communication processes required to accomplish a task, not to the overall task itself. We contend that regardless of the type of task (e.g., equivocal or uncertain: Daft & Lengel, 1986; negotiation or decision-making: McGrath, 1984), individuals working together perform a similar set of more fundamental micro-level communication processes. This is not to say that task is unimportant, but that it is at the wrong level of analysis; it is too broad.

We believe that "task" is best thought of in terms of the fundamental communication processes that must be performed. This is analogous to the concept of *steps* which are the underlying acts required to accomplish a task (McGrath, 1991). To better understand task outcomes, we must understand how individuals perform these underlying steps in terms of which steps they choose to perform, in what order, and when. Every task involving more than one person requires a mix of different communication processes to perform these steps.

Communication Processes: Conveyance and Convergence

Communication has been defined as "a process in which participants create and share information with one another in order to reach a mutual understanding" (Rogers, 1986, p. 199). Sharing information is inherently an exchange process, in which developing meaning requires a dissemination of information (*information transmission*) and individual processing of that information (*information processing*). Developing shared meaning requires that individuals not only understand the information they have, but also understand how others interpret it.

Based on the need to both transmit and process information, we identify two fundamental communication processes relevant to all tasks: conveyance and convergence. *Conveyance processes* are the transmission of a diversity of new information—as much new, relevant, information as needed—to enable the receiver to *create* and *revise* a mental model of the situation. Individuals using conveyance engage in substantial information transmission so that a potentially large, diverse, set of information can be exchanged in a variety of information formats. Individuals participating in conveyance processes will often require time to perform information processing—the cognitive processes necessary to analyze the information, make sense of it, and build their mental models.

Convergence processes are the discussion of pre-processed information about each individual's *interpretation* of a situation, not the raw information itself. The objective is to agree on the meaning of the information, which requires individuals to reach a common understanding *and* to mutually agree that they have achieved this understanding (or to agree that it is not possible) (Lind & Zmud, 1991). Convergence typically needs rapid, back and forth transmission of small quantities of pre-processed information. Convergence can require less information processing than conveyance when it focuses on the verification of and/or modest adjustments to existing mental models. If individuals agree on the interpretation of some or many elements of the situation, then those elements do not need much information processing; the scope of the information space is reduced and thus individuals need to devote less information processing to those elements than they did during the initial consideration of the situation when the information was first conveyed. Information processing is reduced, as it focuses on a smaller set of information than the entire information space. However, when individuals have large differences in their understandings, convergence may require as much or more cognitive processing than conveyance.

Most tasks (e.g., decision-making, negotiation) will require *both* conveyance and convergence processes, regardless of the task's type or level of equivocality or uncertainty, although the proportion and duration of these fundamental communication processes will vary from task to task and from individual to individual. Yet, these two processes have fundamentally different implications for media choice.

Media Synchronicity Theory

We argue that the fit between the information transmission and information processing needs of the communication processes and the information transmission and information processing capabilities of media will influence communication performance and selection of media (see Figure 15.1). In many cases, media choice is based on expectations of performance, thus if we understand performance, we can make predictions about media choice. We contend that convergence processes have a greater need for rapid information transmission and lesser needs for information processing while the reverse is true for conveyance processes. Convergence processes benefit from "synchronicity" (defined below) while conveyance processes do not. We contend that certain media capabilities influence the way individuals can transmit and process information and the degree they can work together— their level of synchronicity. Thus there is a fit between communication processes and media capabilities that facilitates media choice, leading to a better outcome.[2]

Media Synchronicity

Synchronicity is a state in which actions move at the same rate and exactly together (Random House, 1987). Synchronicity exists among individuals when they exhibit a shared pattern of coordinated synchronous behavior with

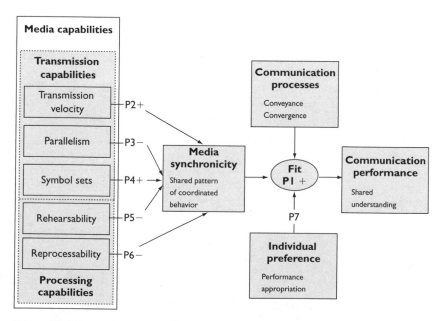

Figure 15.1 Media Synchronicity Theory implications for media choice.

a common focus (Harrison, Mohammed, McGrath, Floret, & Vanderstoep, 2003; McGrath & Kelly, 1986). Research shows that when individuals use electronic media synchronously, they often attend to information asynchronously (Miranda & Saunders, 2003). Thus synchronous use of media does not always imply true *synchronicity*. Synchronous communication is necessary but not sufficient for synchronicity; although individuals may work synchronously, they may not achieve synchronicity. We define *media synchronicity* as the extent to which the capabilities of a communication medium enable individuals to work together at the same time with a shared pattern of coordinated behavior.

Media Synchronicity and Communication Processes

Conveyance and convergence processes have different requirements for information transmission, information processing, and consequently, synchronicity. Conveyance focuses on the transmission of large amounts of raw information and subsequent retrospection, suggesting that individuals will have less need to transmit and process information at the same time (Robert & Dennis, 2005). Alternatively, convergence focuses on the transmission of abstractions of information and negotiations of these abstractions to existing mental models, suggesting that individuals will have greater need to quickly transmit and process smaller volumes of information to develop a shared understanding. See Table 15.1.

When people work together at the same time with a shared pattern of coordinated behavior (i.e., high synchronicity) there is a greater level of interaction and shared focus between message senders and the recipients than when they do not (Ballard & Seibold, 2004). High synchronicity is associated with reduced cognitive effort to encode and decode messages, yielding faster message transmissions, so a message can be assessed and modified quickly, even during transmission itself (Clark, 1992; Kock, 2004; Zmud, Lind, & Young, 1990). High synchronicity can also provide individuals with

Table 15.1 Communication Process Characteristics

Communication process	Information transmission characteristics	Information processing characteristics	Media synchronicity required
Conveyance	Higher quantity Various formats Multiple sources	Retrospective Slower	Lower
Convergence	Lower quality Specific format Specific sources Faster	Verification Adjustment Negotiation Faster	Higher

the ability to receive immediate feedback, enabling the message sender to use communication patterns such as "installments" which enable the sender to break up a message and seek the recipient's feedback after each installment is sent (Clark & Wilkes-Gibbs, 1986), or offer trial references to test the recipient's agreement and understanding (Clark & Brennan, 1991).

Lower synchronicity implies that individuals can take more time between messages, allowing them more time for information processing to analyze the content of a message or to develop meaning across messages (Robert & Dennis, 2005). Likewise, lower synchronicity implies that individuals will have the opportunity to craft messages, taking into consideration other issues such as the context in which the receiver will receive the message (Kock, 1998). Lower synchronicity is derived from a decreased level of interaction between sender and the recipient.

We propose that for communication performance on convergence processes, higher levels of media synchronicity will be beneficial to support the interactive give-and-take required for sensemaking strategies, leading to more efficient convergence. Convergence requires less deliberation on new information, so in situations where individuals have shared mental models, encoding and decoding familiar information should be faster (Minsky, 1986). Since convergence involves a simpler contextualization of information, media capable of supporting higher levels of synchronicity can better provide the ability to coordinate and verify understanding (Graetz, Boyle, Kimble, Thompson, & Garloch, 1998; Rogers 1986). Because the goal is to understand others' *interpretations* of information, *not* the information itself, the ability of the medium to provide synchronicity is important for convergence. Alternatively, using media low in synchronicity can negatively impact convergence processes by increasing delays that impede the rapid development of shared understanding.

For conveyance processes, media lower in synchronicity will lead to better communication performance. To transmit information and enable the analysis typical of conveyance, individuals do not need to work together or at the same time. If the message is complex, with large amounts of diverse information (Campbell 1988), individuals will require more time to assess and deliberate. Media can influence the way in which individuals use them (Dennis & Reinicke 2004). Media supporting higher levels of synchronicity can generate expectations of rapid interaction that can interfere with deliberation processes. Using media with higher synchronicity for conveyance processes (which require deliberation) may impair development of understanding as individuals may not have time to fully process the information (Robert & Dennis, 2005). This may induce greater cognitive load (Te'eni, 2001) and premature action (Weick & Meader, 1993). Therefore:

> P1: Communication performance will depend on the fit between a medium's synchronicity and the fundamental communication processes being performed.

a) For communication processes in which convergence on meaning is the goal, use of higher synchronicity media will lead to better communication performance.

b) For communication processes in which the conveyance of information is the goal, use of lower synchronicity media will lead to better communication performance.

Media Capabilities

We define media capabilities as the *potential* structures provided by a medium which influence the manner in which individuals can transmit and process information (see also Rice, 1987; Rice & Steinfield, 1993). Depending on the configuration of media capabilities, media will vary in their ability to support information transmission and information processing, which ultimately determines their capability to support synchronicity.

To identify media capabilities that may influence information transmission and processing, we turn to Shannon and Weaver's (1949) theory of communication. It states that the transmission of a message begins with a *source* (the sender) who creates a *message* for transmission. The source uses a *transmitter* (software and/or hardware) to encode or translate the message into a signal (e.g., text, voice, and video) that is sent over a communication *channel* (medium). The channel carries the signal to a *receiver* (software and/or hardware) which is used by the *destination* (recipient) to decode or convert the signal back into the message. See Figure 15.2. In this depiction of a communication system, encoding and decoding processes are important as they represent the processing required by the source and destination to make use of the medium to transmit and receive messages. These processes impact the relative ease with which individuals use the medium.

Media will vary in their capability to support the transmission and subsequent processing of the information contained in a message. Although there are many media capabilities that could plausibly influence communication performance, our goal is to select a relevant set of capabilities that may be used to assess a medium's ability to support information transmission and processing, and subsequently synchronicity. Shannon and Weaver's theory, which is engineering focused, identifies three capabilities that impact the ability of a channel to transmit information: the capacity of the channel (in bits per second), the number of frequencies that can be simultaneously used in the channel, and the types of symbols that can be sent. They also identify that many of the inefficiencies in communication come from the processes of encoding and decoding messages sent in the channel, which we view as relevant to information processing.

We believe that three primary media capabilities are important in deriving a medium's ability to support information transmission: transmission velocity (Shannon and Weaver's channel capacity), parallelism (analogous to Shannon

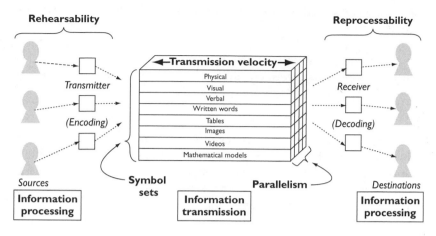

Figure 15.2 Communication system and media capabilities.

and Weaver's number of frequencies), and symbol sets (Shannon and Weaver's symbol types). Two capabilities build on Shannon and Weaver's encoding and decoding processes and are important for information processing: rehearsability (encoding) and reprocessability (decoding). While these two capabilities do not necessarily impact information transmission, we include them because they affect individuals' information processing of messages sent over the medium. In the sections below, we assume that media provide the same capabilities to all users (e.g., symbol variety), although this is not always the case; for example, email clients have different capabilities so that a sender may have the ability to include audio-video attachments that a receiver, using a different client, may not be able to access.

Transmission Velocity

Transmission velocity, derived from Shannon and Weaver's capacity concept, is the speed at which a medium can deliver a message to intended recipients. While not expressly identified in prior theories of media, transmission velocity is generally alluded to in terms of *immediate* or *rapid* (as in feedback, Burgoon et al., 1999–2000; Daft & Lengel, 1986) and *interactivity* (Te'eni, 2001; Zack, 1994).

Media high in transmission velocity allow messages to reach the recipients as soon as they are sent. Faster transmission velocity also allows a message to be responded to faster, meaning that the communication can approach continuous exchange with improved coordination and quicker feedback between individuals, resembling conversation (Goffman, 1967; Rogers, 1986). Higher transmission velocity supports synchronicity as it enables improved behavior

coordination and shared focus to exist between individuals working together
Therefore:

P2: Transmission velocity improves shared focus which will have a positive impact on a medium's capability to support synchronicity.

Parallelism

Parallelism, derived from Shannon and Weaver's number of frequencies, is the number of simultaneous transmissions that can effectively take place—which we depict as the width of the medium in Figure 15.2 (cf. multiple addressability: Rice, 1987; Sproull & Kiesler, 1991; Valacich, Paranka, George, & Nunamaker, 1993). Parallelism is the extent to which signals from *multiple senders* can be transmitted over the medium simultaneously. In traditional media such as the telephone, fewer transmissions can effectively take place over the medium at the same time, limiting the quantity of information transmitted per time period. In contrast, many of the new media can be structured to enable many concurrent transmissions to occur, increasing the volume of information that can be transmitted in a given time period (Burgoon et al., 1999–2000).

By allowing for multiple simultaneous transmissions, parallelism reduces some of the losses that can occur due to the need to transmit sequentially (Dennis et al., 1997; Gallupe et al., 1992; Nunamaker et al., 1991; Valacich, Dennis, & Nunamaker, 1992). Therefore, messages can be transmitted when desired, at any moment, without having to wait for the channel to clear or open. Likewise, multiple transmissions can be received simultaneously, reducing the time necessary to receive such transmissions as compared to receiving transmissions serially, or one at a time.

Parallelism impacts the synchronicity of a medium by increasing the number of concurrent transmissions and by supporting multidirectional communication (e.g., simultaneous sending of messages to multiple recipients, simultaneous receipt of messages from multiple senders) (Burgoon et al., 1999–2000; Goffman, 1981). By enabling multi-directional, multi-party transmissions, parallelism enables multiple simultaneous conversation threads (Herring, 1999). It allows for multiple, simultaneous discussions that can become intertwined, so that rather than focusing on one topic at a time, a discussion interleaves messages. Parallelism therefore reduces the interactional coherence of the discussion and impairs the ability of the users to develop a shared focus (Erickson, Herring, & Sack, 2002; Herring, 1999, 2003; Simpson, 2005). Thus parallelism acts to reduce synchronicity by reducing the shared focus. Therefore:

P3: Parallelism lowers shared focus which will have a negative impact on a medium's capability to support synchronicity.

Symbol Sets

Symbol sets, derived from Shannon and Weaver's types of symbols, are the number of ways in which a medium allows information to be encoded for communication—which we depict as the height of the medium in Figure 15.2—and subsumes Daft and Lengel's (1986) multiplicity of cues and language variety (cf. channel capacity: Te'eni, 2001). The essence of communication and language is symbols (Littlejohn, 1983; Sitkin et al., 1992). Humans can use a myriad of different types of symbols to communicate (Mead, 1934; Rogers, 1986; Short et al., 1976). At the most fundamental level, we can communicate in physical ways, from a handshake to a gentle touch on a shoulder of a friend, which can communicate volumes. We can communicate in visual ways by raising a hand, nodding a head, or closing our eyes. We can communicate verbally by speaking. We can use symbols, such as words, tables, images, video, mathematical models, etc.

Many media allow multiple symbol sets to be transmitted simultaneously (e.g., in a face to face conversation, we can speak words using different vocal tones, and make physical gestures). Symbol sets may affect the synchronicity supported by a medium in two fundamental ways.

First, the time and effort required to encode and to decode a message using a specific symbol set may impose production costs (Clark & Brennan, 1991) and processing delay costs (Reinsch & Beswick, 1990). These costs can alter the way in which the sender encodes messages and can impede the decoding and processing of these messages by the receiver, resulting in inefficient transmission and processing of messages. For example, it may be more efficient to transmit agreement with visual symbols such as a head nod than by typing "I agree with you."

Certain symbol sets can affect overall information transmission and processing efficiencies because of the time it takes to encode and decode using that symbol set. Some symbol sets are fast to encode and decode due to their naturalness (Kock, 2004). Other symbol sets are slower to encode; for example, an email message takes longer to encode than a verbal message because it takes more time to type than to speak (Williams, 1977). Some symbol sets are slower to decode; for example, a written message is faster to decode than a voice mail because reading is usually faster than listening (Williams, 1977). Physical, visual, and verbal symbol sets are fast to encode, facilitating turn-taking and coordination and making interactions faster (Goffman, 1967; Williams, 1977). Thus media incorporating these symbol sets have greater capability to support synchronicity as compared to media with written or typed symbol sets that are slower to encode (and decode). Therefore:

P4a: Media with more natural symbol sets (physical, visual, and verbal) have a greater capability to support synchronicity as compared to media with less natural symbol sets (written or typed).

Second, some information may be more precisely encoded and decoded in one symbol set than another. Physical gestures (e.g., touch), visual gestures (e.g., nods, smiles) and vocal tone can be used to amplify meaning beyond the words themselves far more efficiently and effectively than expressing those same meanings in spoken or written words (Williams, 1977). Conversely, some written or digital symbol formats (e.g., image and textual) can emphasize the same information in different ways (e.g., spatially or symbolically) such that outcomes differ according to the symbol set (Jarvenpaa, 1989; Vessey, 1991). Some symbol sets, while easy to encode, may have detrimental effects for decoding as they may add unintentionally to the message. For example, stating that everyone should calm down while simultaneously pounding one's fist might impair decoding and information processing due to the inconsistencies in the symbols used. Thus, some symbol sets facilitate precise encoding by allowing the sender more control in the application of the symbols used in a message, others may inhibit precise encoding, and others may induce the encoding of unintended messages, especially if the participants are from different cultures.

The inability to transmit certain symbol sets (e.g., physical, visual, and verbal symbols) may have some effect on the development of social perceptions (Daft & Lengel, 1986; Williams, 1977). In general, when physical, visual, and verbal symbols are removed, there is a reduction in social presence (Rice, 1993; Short et al., 1976), such that the people with whom one is communicating may become less like real people and more like objects, influencing what and how information is communicated (Postmes, Spears, & Lean, 2000; Sproull & Kiesler, 1991; Williams, 1977). These impacts may be temporary, or apply only to initial encounters, because over the long term deep personal relationships can develop over media lacking these symbol sets (Walther 1982).

Individuals can more effectively and efficiently encode and decode information when the symbol set matches the needs of the message. Symbol sets can be thought of as similar to a "hygiene factor" in the terminology of Herzberg, Mausner, & Synderman (1953): there is nothing inherently important or satisfying about a particular symbol set, but if the medium does not provide a particular symbol set when it is needed, then communication will be impaired (Farmer & Hyatt, 1994). For example, imagine that you are trying to describe how to perform a physical activity on a website. A verbal description alone is likely to be less effective than a visual demonstration and a verbal description or a series of annotated screen shots with a written description. Therefore:

P4b: Using a medium with a symbol set better suited to the content of the message will improve information transmission and information processing, and therefore will have a greater capacity to support synchronicity.

Rehearsability

Rehearsability is the extent to which the media enables the sender to rehearse or fine tune a message during encoding, before sending (cf. editability: Rice, 1987). Media that support rehearsability enable the sender to carefully craft a message before transmission to ensure that the intended meaning is expressed precisely, thus improving a recipient's subsequent decoding and information processing. Rehearsability is less important for individuals who have common experiences or shared mental models as they can communicate using expected protocols or with known symbols on a familiar subject (Carlson & Zmud, 1999; Kock, 2004; Zack, 1994). However, for new or complex information (e.g., transmissions among individuals without prior shared knowledge), rehearsability is important because it enables the sender to consider the context and possible interpretations of the message and encode it for more accurate decoding and understanding by the recipient (Cornelius & Boos, 2003; Kock, 1998).

Rehearsability can create delays in the transmission of messages because senders can take longer to compose messages. This is not specifically an impediment of the transmission velocity of the medium itself; rather it is due to the way in which senders appropriate and use the medium to send messages. This delay in message transmission, particularly if a fast response is expected, may reduce synchronicity as it impairs the development of coordinated behavior and focus. The impact of this delay may be offset if the sender takes extra care to attend to and craft a message to better integrate his or her comments with those of others(s), but there is nothing inherent in rehearsability that will *necessarily* induce this increased attention. Therefore:

P5: Rehearsability lowers shared focus, which will have a negative impact on a medium's capability to support synchronicity.

Reprocessability

Reprocessability is the extent to which the medium enables a message to be reexamined or processed again, during decoding, either within the context of the communication event or after the event has passed (cf. Rice, 1987; externally recorded memory: Sproull & Kiesler, 1991). Reprocessability affects information processing by allowing a recipient to spend more time decoding messages, revisiting prior messages for additional consideration, and by providing a memory that can help new participants understand past activities (Nunamaker et al., 1991). The reprocessability of a medium can impact the transmission of information since it enables both senders and recipients to reread and reconsider prior messages before engaging in communication.

Reprocessability is especially important for transmissions of new, complex or large volumes of information. The availability and use of reprocessability allows individuals to revisit messages to support information processing and understanding development (Weick & Meader, 1993). In general, reprocessability is more important for conveyance processes because they have greater needs for processing. Convergence, on the other hand, has a lesser need for reprocessability as the focus is on the mutual construction and adjustment for shared meaning development. While reprocessability could help convergence by supporting information processing (revisiting a discussion after the fact), it is not critical due to the importance of shared focus and interaction.

However, reprocessability can create delays in the transmission of messages because receivers can take longer to review and deliberate on previously received messages. Like rehearsability, this is not specifically an impediment of the transmission velocity of the medium itself; rather it is due to the way in which receivers appropriate and use the medium to reprocess information before responding to messages. This may lead to delays in information transmission, to the benefit of information processing. As a result, reprocessability may reduce synchronicity as it impairs the development of coordinated behavior and focus. Therefore:

P6: Reprocessability lowers shared focus which will have a negative impact on a medium's capability to support synchronicity.

Conclusions About Media Capabilities

Table 15.2 compares several commonly used media on these five capabilities, and the resulting impact on information transmission, information processing, and synchronicity. In several cases, media are listed as having a range of capabilities because they are configurable and can be appropriated and used in different ways. Likewise, specific devices may be hard to categorize as they provide multiple capabilities: a blackberry, for example, provides telephone, email, text messaging, and so on, so the capability of a device and how it affects synchronicity will depend upon which communication medium is used (e.g., voice, email, text messaging) and how that medium is used. In these cases, it is necessary to examine the underlying media capabilities provided and used, rather than considering the device itself as a single entity.

This table does not suggest that individuals must use certain media in certain ways; it just presents conclusions about the capabilities when media are used in these ways. For example, we can choose to use email in a near-synchronous manner, which would provide a set of capabilities more similar to that of synchronous electronic conferencing. We can also combine media.

Table 15.2 reinforces two conclusions that are often overlooked when considering new, digital media. First, media are not monolithic. It is possible for one medium to possess different levels of a communication capability depending upon how it is configured and used (e.g., one instant messaging

Table 15.2 Comparison of Selected Media and their Capabilities

	Transmission velocity	Parallelism	Symbol sets	Rehearsability	Reprocessability	Information transmission	Information processing	Synchronicity
Face-to-face	High	Median	Few–Many	Low	Low	Fast	Low	High
Video conference	High	Medium	Few–Medium	Low	Low	Fast	Low	High
Telephone conference	High	Low	Few	Low	Low	Fast	Low	Medium
Synchronous instant messaging	Medium–High	Low–Medium	Few–Medium	Medium	Medium–High	Medium	Low–Medium	Medium
Synchronous electronic conferencing	Medium–High	High	Few–Medium	Medium	High	Medium	Medium	Low–Medium
Asynchronous electronic conferencing	Low–Medium	High	Few–Medium	High	High	Slow	High	Low
Asynchronous electronic mail	Low–Medium	High	Few–Medium	High	High	Slow	High	Low
Voice mail	Low–Medium	Low	Few	Low–Medium	High	Slow	Medium	Low
Fax	Low–Medium	Low	Few–Medium	High	High	Slow	High	Low
Documents	Low	High	Few–Medium	High	High	Slow	High	Low

system may be text only, while another includes video) (Bretz, 1983; Walther, 1992).

Second, there is an inherent paradox between information transmission and information processing (Robert & Dennis, 2005). Media that have strong capabilities to support information transmission typically lack strong capabilities to support information processing and vice versa. No one medium has the best values for both information transmission and information processing, so no single medium could be labeled as most appropriate. The "best" medium is that which best provides the set of capabilities needed by the situation: the individuals, the *communication processes,* and the social context. In the age of digital media, concluding that face-to-face communication is best suited to equivocal tasks is not appropriate (Bretz, 1983).

MST proposes that the "best medium" for a given situation may be a combination of media. For example, consider a convergence process conducted face-to-face versus one conducted using a virtual whiteboard system. Face-to-face communication is more capable of supporting synchronicity, and thus we could expect the development of shared understanding to proceed more effectively and efficiently using it. Now, consider adding a whiteboard (virtual or otherwise) to the face-to-face discussion. Although we argued in Proposition P4b that media with written or typed symbol sets are less capable of supporting synchronicity, the combination of face-to-face communication (with its ability to support synchronicity) and the whiteboard (with its ability to enable reprocessability) may be better able to support the development of shared understanding than either medium alone. By balancing the strengths and weaknesses of media we can improve communication performance. As a result, we would expect that individuals' preferences for how they appropriate media and expectations for performance will have an influence on how they select media:

> P7: Individual preferences for performance and appropriation will influence how they assess the fit of media capabilities to communication needs, influencing their choice of media.

Discussion

MST proposes that communication performance will improve when the needs of conveyance and convergence processes are matched to appropriate media with the transmission velocity, parallelism, symbol sets, rehearsability, and reprocessability needed by those processes. In this section, we briefly review notable published work based on the initial version of the theory, before drawing implications for future research and practice.

Empirical Research on Media Synchronicity Theory

The original version of MST has been used by 32 journal articles (according to ISI Web of Knowledge citation analysis[3]) and there are more than 70 citations to it by scholarly manuscripts available on the Web (Google scholar search). None of these studies, however, has tested the complete original version of MST; likewise, none has tested the complete revised version of MST. Although bits and pieces of the original and revised theory have been tested or built upon, much of this research is subject to some of the limitations of the original version of MST or have applied MST outside its boundary conditions.

For instance, Carlson and George (2004) use some of the concepts of MST to develop and test hypotheses about media choice when the intent is to deceive the other participants. Thus in contrast to the original intent of MST (to predict the ability of participants to develop shared understanding), this article uses the original MST concepts to predict media choice preferences when some participants are deliberately attempting to *not* develop shared understanding. Nonetheless, media synchronicity was found to play a role in media selection and perceptions of the ability to deceive and to detect deceptions.

Maruping and Argawal (2004) applied some concepts from the original version of MST in their development of a new task-technology fit theory. However, rather than using the MST concepts of conveyance and convergence, they develop a new theory about the developmental stages of teams and attempt to match the MST media capabilities to team's needs for conflict management, motivation, and affect management in different stages of team development. In their paper, the concept of task (in this case interpersonal process types) is treated as a monolithic entity that remains constant over time. Immediacy of feedback is considered a capability of media (following the arguments in the initial version of MST), which we now consider as a socially experienced outcome resulting from use, not a capability of the media itself. As such, the propositions presented in their paper would be strengthened with the new conceptualization of MST. The application of team development phases, media capabilities, and communication requirements of the interpersonal process types are theoretically consistent with this version of MST.

In prior research there are many examples where MST's concepts have been misinterpreted or misapplied, due to limitations in the original version of the theory. The constructs and definitions provided in this paper provide a much better theoretical conception of MST regarding media, communication tasks, and communication performance, that enhance its application in future research on media selection.

Implications for Future Research and Practice

The propositions and concepts underlying MST suggest several opportunities for future research. In any of the primary areas in Figure 15.1 communication processes, media capabilities, appropriation factors, and communication performance, there are opportunities to expand and test our propositions, to refine the model, and to test its boundary conditions. Future research could examine the relationship between media capabilities and communication processes and the degree to which specific configurations of media capabilities (both transmission and information processing oriented) are more or less beneficial for one or both processes.

Future research could also examine the degree to which various factors influence appropriation and use (as noted in another chapter in this book, von Pape). Given that these factors have the potential to moderate the relative benefits of media capabilities for supporting various processes, understanding their interplay would aid in better understanding how individuals choose to appropriate media for communication performance.

Future research needs to address the extent to which media capabilities will actually be selected and appropriated. For example, some individuals prefer polychronic interaction, and will be more comfortable using parallelism than others who prefer monochronic interaction and may choose to avoid it (Lee, 1999). Likewise culture may influence how individuals choose to interact; individuals from some cultures may take more time for reflection and deliberation, even when using media that do not encourage such reflection (Lewis, 1999). In addition to cultural issues, a vast array of individual factors will likely influence media appropriation and selection (e.g., absorptive capacity—Cohen & Levinthal, 1990; introversion/extraversion—Topi, Valacich, & Rao, 2002; cognitive ability—Valacich, Jung, & Looney, 2006, and others, von Pape, this volume).

MST also has implications for practice. Because most tasks require both conveyance and convergence, the use of a single medium will likely not lead to ideal communication performance. "Richer" is not "better." The use of multiple media, either concurrently or consecutively, will lead to better communication performance, because no one medium provides the ideal combination of capabilities for both conveyance and convergence. Therefore, we should study how and why individuals may choose to use several media simultaneously (e.g., talking on the phone while engaging in several IM chats).

In supporting remote workers or virtual teams, media must be considered in terms of the capabilities they provide since the communication processes needed for a task may require different media capabilities. Managers implementing communication technologies should understand the nature of the individuals and context in which they will work, as this may suggest differing requirements for media capabilities. While some contexts may benefit from media with higher synchronicity (novel contexts), for others (familiar contexts) high synchronicity may not be needed, and may even be detrimental. Understanding the context provides insight as to the appropriate selection of a mix of media. It is also important to note that these needs are likely to change over time, as teams move from the novel to the familiar, so choices of media for project initiation may not be ideal once the project is underway (Fuller & Dennis, in press).

Notes

1 All authors contributed equally. We would like to thank Manju Ahuja, Allen Lee, Ron Rice, Brad Wheeler, Youngjin Yoo and the reviewers and editors for particularly helpful comments in refining the concepts in this paper. We would also like to thank Allen Lee and Lynne Markus for sharing working papers that aided in the development of our ideas. A previous version of this paper was presented at the 32nd Hawaii International Conference on System Sciences, 1999 and published in *MIS Quarterly* in 2008.
2 It is critical to understand that we are not matching task to media, but rather the lower level construct of communication processes to media.
3 Web of Knowledge does not report all citations to articles, just those in selected journals. For example, Carlson and George (2004), which we discuss in the text, is not listed among the articles.

References

Ballard, D. I. & Seibold, D. R. "Communication-Related Organizational Structures and Work Group Temporal Experiences: The Effects of Coordination Method, Technology Type, and Feedback Cycle on Members' Construals and Enactments of Time," *Communication Monographs* (71:1), 2004, pp. 1–27.

Bretz, R. *Media For Interactive Communication*, Sage Publications, Beverly Hills, CA, 1983.

Burgoon, J. K., Bonito, J. A., Bengtsson, B., Ramirez, Jr., A., Dunbar, N. E., & Miczo, N. "Testing the Interactivity Model: Communication Processes, Partner Assessments, and the Quality of Collaborative Work," *Journal of Management Information Systems* (16:3), Winter 1999–2000, pp. 33–56.

Burke, K. & Chidambaram, L. "How Much Bandwidth is Enough? A Longitudinal Examination of Media Characteristics and Group Outcomes," *MIS Quarterly* (23:4), December 1999, pp. 557–580.

Campbell, D. J. "Task Complexity—a Review and Analysis," *Academy of Management Review* (13:1), January 1988, pp. 40–52.

Carley, K. "The Value of Cognitive Foundations for Dynamic Social Theory," *Journal of Mathematical Sociology* (14:2–3), 1989, pp. 171–208.

Carlson, J. R. & George, J. F. "Media Appropriateness in the Conduct and Discovery of Deceptive Communication: The Relative Influence of Richness and Synchronicity," *Group Decision and Negotiation* (13:2), 2004, pp. 191–210.

Carlson, J. R. & Zmud, R. W. "Channel Expansion Theory and the Experiential Nature of Media Richness Perceptions," *Academy of Management Journal* (42:2), 1999, pp. 153–170.

Carnevale, P. J. D., Pruitt, D. G., & Seilheimer, S. D. "Looking and Competing:

Accountability and Visual Access in Integrative Bargaining," *Journal of Personality and Social Psychology* (40:1), 1981, pp. 111–120.

Christie, B., *Human Factors of Information Technology in the Office*, John Wiley and Sons, New York, 1985.

Clark, H. H. *Arenas of Language Use*, University of Chicago Press, Chicago, IL, 1992.

Clark, H. H. & Brennan, S. E. "Grounding in Communication," in *Perspectives on Socially Shared Cognition*, Resnick, L. B., Levine, J. M, & Teasley, S. D. (Eds.), American Psychological Association, Washington DC, 1991, pp. 127–149.

Clark, H. H. & Wilkes Gibbs, D. "Referring as a Collaborative Process," *Cognition* (22), 1986, pp. 1–39.

Cohen, W. C. & Levinthal, D. A. "Absorptive Capacity: A New Perspective on Learning and Innovation," *Administrative Science Quarterly*, (35:1), 1990, pp. 128–152.

Cornelius, C. & Boos, M. "Enhancing Mutual Understanding in Synchronous Computer-Mediated Communication by Training," *Communication Research* (30:2), 2003, pp. 147–177.

Daft, R. L. & Lengel, R. H. "Organizational Information Requirements, Media Richness and Structural Design," *Management Science* (32:5), 1986, pp. 554–571.

Daft, R. L., Lengel, R. H., & Trevino, L. K. "Message Equivocality, Media Selection and Manager Performance: Implications for Information Systems," *MIS Quarterly* (11:3), 1987, pp. 355–366.

DeLuca, D. C., Gasson, S., & Kock, N. "Adaptations that Virtual Teams Make so that Complex Tasks can be Performed Using Simple e-Collaboration Technologies," *International Journal of e-Collaboration* (2:3), 2006, pp. 64–85.

Dennis, A. R. & Kinney, S. T. "Testing Media Richness Theory In The New Media: Cues, Feedback, and Task Equivocality," *Information Systems Research* (9:3), 1998, pp. 256–274.

Dennis, A. R. & Reinicke, B. "Beta vs. VHS and the Acceptance of Electronic Brainstorming Technology," *MIS Quarterly* (28:1), 2004, 28:1, 1–20.

Dennis, A. R. & Valacich, J. S. "Rethinking Media Richness: Towards a Theory of Media Synchronicity," 32nd Hawaii International Conference on System Sciences, 1999.

Dennis, A. R., Valacich, J. S., Carte, T. A., Garfield, M. J., Haley, B. J., and Aronson, J. E. "Research Report: the Effectiveness of Multiple Dialogues in Electronic Brainstorming," *Information Systems Research* (8:2), June 1997, pp. 203–211.

Dennis, A. R., Wixom, B. H., & Vandenberg, R. J. "Understanding Fit and Appropriation Effects in Group Support Systems Via Meta-Analysis," *MIS Quarterly* (25:2), 2001, pp. 167–193.

DeSanctis, G. & Gallupe, R. B. "A Foundation for the Study of Group Decision Support Systems," *Management Science* (33:5), May 1987, pp. 589–609.

DeSanctis, G. & Poole, M. S. "Capturing the Complexity in Advanced Technology Use—Adaptive Structuration Theory," *Organization Science* (5:2), 1994, 121–147.

Eisenberg, E. M. "Jamming: Transcendence Through Organizing," *Communication Research* (17), 1991, 139–164.

El-Shinnawy, M. M. & Markus, M. L. "Media Richness Theory and New Communication Media: A Study of Voice Mail and Electronic Mail," *Proceedings of the International Conference on Information Systems*, Dallas, TX, 1992, pp. 91-105.

Erickson, T. Herring, S., & Sack, W. "Discourse Architectures: Designing and Visualizing Computer Mediated Communication," presented at *CHI 2002: Changing the World, Changing Ourselves*, 2002.

Farmer, S. M. & Hyatt, C. W. "Effects of Task Language Demands and Task Complexity on Computer Mediated Work Groups," *Small Group Research* (25:3), 1994, pp. 331–336.

Fulk, J. & Boyd, B. "Emerging Theories of Communication in Organizations," *Journal of Management* (17:2), 1991, pp. 407–446.

Fulk, J., Schmitz, J., & Steinfield, C. W., "A Social Influence Model of Technology Use," in Fulk, J. & Steinfield, C. W., (Eds.) *Organizations and Communication Technology*, Sage, Newbury Park, CA, 1990, pp. 117–140.

Fulk, J., Steinfield, C. W., Schmitz, J., & Power, J. G. "A Social Information Processing Model of Media Use in Organizations," *Communication Research* (14:5), 1987, pp. 529–552.

Fuller, R. M. & Dennis, A. R. "Does Fit Matter? The Impact of Task-Technology Fit and Appropriation on Team Performance in Repeated Tasks," *Information Systems Research*, in press.

Gallupe, R. B., Dennis, A. R., Cooper, W. H., Valacich, J. S., Basianutti, L. M., & Nunamaker, Jr. J. F. "Electronic Brainstorming and Group Size," *Academy of Management Journal* (35:2), 1992, pp. 350–369.

Gersick, C. J. G. & Hackman, J. R. "Habitual Routines in Task-Performing Groups," *Organizational Behavior and Human Decision Processes* (47:1), 1990, pp. 65–97.

Goffman, E. *Interaction Ritual*, Aldine Publishing, Chicago, IL, 1967.

Goffman, E. *Forms of Talk*, University of Pennsylvania Press, Philadelphia, PA, 1981.

Graetz, K. A., Boyle, E. S., Kimble, C. E., Thompson, P., & Garloch, J. L. "Information Sharing Face-to-Face, Teleconferencing, and Electronic Chat Groups," *Small Group Research* (29:6), 1998, pp. 714–743.

Habermas, J. *The Theory of Communicative Action: Reason and Rationalization of Society*, Beacon Press, Boston, MA, 1984.

Habermas, J. & Nielsen, T. H. "Jurgen Habermas: Morality, Society and Ethics: An Interview with Torbin Hvuud Nielson," *Acta Sociologica* (33:2), 1990, pp. 114.

Harrison, D. A., Mohammed, S., McGrath, J. E., Floret, A. T., & Vanderstoep, S. W. "Time Matters in Team Performance: Effects of Member Familiarity, Entrainment, and Task Discontinuity on Speed and Quality," *Personnel Psychology*, 56, pp. 2003.

Herring, S. "Interactional Coherence in CMC," *Journal of Computer-Mediated Communication*, vol. 4, 1999.

Herring, S. "Dynamic Topic Analysis of Synchronous Chat." Paper presented at the New Research for New Media: Innovative Research Methodologies Symposium. Minneapolis, MN: University of Minnesota School of Journalism and Mass Communication, 2003.

Herzberg, F., Mausner, B., & Synderman, B. *The Motivation to Work*, John Wiley, New York, 1953.

Hollingshead, A. B., McGrath, J. E., & O'Connor, K. M. "Group Task Performance and Communication Technology: A Longitudinal Study of Computer-mediated Versus Face-to-face Work Groups," *Small Group Research* (24:3), 1993, pp. 307–333.

Huang, W. W. & Wei, K. K. "An Empirical Investigation of the Effects of Group Support Systems and Task Type on Group Interactions from an Influence Perspective," *Journal of Management Information Systems* (17:2), Fall 2000, pp. 181–206.

Jarvenpaa, S. L. "The Effect of Task Demands and Graphical Format on Information Processing Strategies," *Management Science* (35:3), March 1989, pp. 285–303.

Jasperson, J., Carter, P., & Zmud, R. "A Comprehensive Conceptualization of

Post-Adoptive Behaviors Associated with Information Technology Enabled Work Systems," *MIS Quarterly* (29:3), September 2005, pp. 525–557.

Kanawattanachai, P. & Yoo, Y. "The Impact of Knowledge Coordination on Virtual Team Performance Over Time," *MIS Quarterly* (31:4), 2007, pp. 783–808.

King, R. C. & Xia, W. D. "Media Appropriateness: Effects of Experience on Communication Media Choice," *Decision Sciences* (28:4), 1997, pp. 877–910.

Kinney, S. T. & Watson, R. T. "The Effect of Medium and Task on Dyadic Communication," *Proceedings of the International Conference on Information Systems*, Dallas, TX, 1992, pp. 107-117.

Kock, N. "Can a Leaner Medium Foster Better Group Outcomes? A Study of Computer-Supported Process Improvement Groups" in *Effective Utilization and Management of Emerging Information Technologies*, Khosrowpour, M. (Ed.), Idea Group Publishing, Hershey, PA, 1998, pp. 22–31.

Kock, N. "The Psychobiological Model: Towards a New Theory of Computer-Mediated Communication Based on Darwinian Evolution," *Organization Science* (15:3), 2004, pp. 327–348.

Lee, A. S. "Electronic Mail as a Medium for Rich Communication: An Empirical Investigation Using Hermeneutic Interpretation," *MIS Quarterly* (18:2), 1994, pp. 143–157.

Lee, H. "Time and Information Technology: Monochronicity, Polychronicity and Temporal Symmetry," *European Journal of Information Systems*, (8:1): 1999, pp. 16–26.

Lewis, R. *When Cultures Collide*, Nicholas Brealey Publishing, London, 1999.

Lind, M. R. & Zmud, R. W. "The Influence of a Convergence in Understanding Between Technology Providers and Users on Information Technology Innovativeness," *Organization Science* (2:2), 1991, pp. 195–217.

Littlejohn, S. W. *Theories of Human Communication*, Wadsworth Publishing. Belmont, CA, 1983.

Majchrzak, A., Rice, R. E., Malhotra, A., & King, N., "Technology Adoption: The Case of a Computer-Supported Inter-Organizational Virtual Team," *MIS Quarterly* (24:4), 2000, pp. 569–600.

Markus, M. L. "Electronic Mail as Medium of Managerial Choice," *Organization Science* (5:4), 1994, pp. 502–527.

Maruping, L. M. & Argawal, R. "Managing Team Interpersonal Processes Through Technology: A Task-Technology Fit Perspective," *Journal of Applied Psychology* (89:6), 2004, pp. 975–990.

Maznevski, M. L. & Chudoba, K. M. "Bridging Space Over Time: Global Virtual Team Dynamics and Effectiveness," *Organization Science* (11), 2000, pp. 473–492.

McGrath, J. E. *Groups: Interaction and Performance*, Prentice-Hall, Englewood Cliffs, NJ, 1984.

McGrath, J. E. "Time, Interaction, and Performance (TIP): A Theory of Groups," *Small Group Research* (22:2), 1991, pp. 147–174.

McGrath, J. E. & Hollingshead, A. B. "Putting the 'Group' Back in Group Support Systems: Some Theoretical Issues About Dynamic Processes in Groups with Technological Enhancements," in *Group Support Systems: New Perspectives*, L. M. Jessup and J. S. Valacich (Eds.), Macmillan, New York, NY, 1993, pp. 78–96.

McGrath, J. E. & Hollingshead, A. B. *Groups Interacting with Technology*, Sage, Newbury Park, CA, 1994.

McGrath, J. E. & Kelly, J. E., Jr. *Time and Human Interaction: Toward a Social Psychology of Time*, Guilford, New York, NY, 1986.

Mead, G. H. *Mind Self and Society from the Standpoint of a Social Behaviorist*, University of Chicago Press, Chicago, IL, 1934.

Mennecke, B. E., Valacich, J. S., & Wheeler, B. C. "The Effects of Media and Task on User Performance: A Test of the Task-Media Fit Hypothesis," *Group Decision and Negotiation* (9:6), 2000, pp. 507–529.

Minsky, M. *The Society of Mind*, Simon and Schuster, New York, NY, 1986.

Miranda, S. M. & Saunders, C. S. "The Social Construction of Meaning: An Alternative Perspective on Information Sharing," Information Systems Research, 14:1, 2003, pp. 87–106.

Moscovici, S. "Toward a Theory of Conversion Behavior," in *Advances in Experimental Social Psychology* (13), L. Berkowitz (Ed.), Academic Press, New York, NY, 1980, pp. 209–239.

Murthy, U. S. & Kerr, D. S., "Decision Making Performance of Interacting Groups: An Experimental Investigation of the Effects of Task Type and Communication Mode," *Information & Management* (40), 2003, pp. 351–360.

Nunamaker Jr., J. F., Dennis, A. R., Valacich, J. S., Vogel, D. R., & George, J. F. "Electronic Meeting Systems to Support Group Work," *Communications of the ACM* (34:7), 1991, pp. 40–61.

Ngwenyama, O. K. & Lee, A. S. "Communication Richness In Electronic Mail: Critical Social Theory and Contextuality of Meaning," *MIS Quarterly* (21:2), 1997, pp. 145–167.

Petty, R. E. & Cacioppo, J. T. *Communication and Persuasion*, Springer-Verlag, New York, NY, 1986.

Postmes, T., Spears, R., & Lea, M. "The Formation of Group Norms in Computer-Mediated Communication," *Human Communication Research* (26:3), July 2000, pp. 341–371.

Putnam, L. L., Phillips, N., & Chapman, P. "Metaphors of Communication and Organization," in S. R. Clegg, C. Hardy, & W. R. Nord (Eds.), *Handbook of Organizational Studies*, Sage, London, 1996, pp. 375–408.

Random House. *Random House Dictionary of the English Language*, 2nd edition, Random House, New York, NY, 1987.

Reinsch, N. L. & Beswick, R. W. "Voice Mail Versus Conventional Channels: A Cost Minimization Analysis of Individuals' Preferences," *Academy of Management Journal* (33:4), 1990, pp. 801–816.

Rice, R. "Computer-mediated Communication and Organizational Innovation," *Journal of Communication* (37:4), 1987, pp. 65–94.

Rice, R. E. "Task Analyzability, Use of New Media, And Effectiveness: A Multi-Site Exploration of Media Richness," *Organization Science* (3:4), 1992, pp. 475–500.

Rice, R. E. "Media Appropriateness: Using Social Presence Theory To Compare Traditional And New Organizational Media," *Human Communication Research* (20:2), 1993.

Rice, R. E. & Shook, D. "Relationships of Job Categories and Organizational Levels to Use of Communication Channels, Including Electronic Mail: A Meta-analysis and Extension," *Journal of Management Studies* (27:2), 1990, pp. 195–229.

Rice, R. E. & Steinfield, C. "Experiences with New Forms of Organizational Communication Via Electronic Mail and Voice Messaging," in *Telematics and Work*,

J. H. Andriessen & R. Roe (Eds.), Lawrence Erlbaum and Associates, London, 1993.

Robert, L. & Dennis, A. R. "The Paradox of Richness: A Cognitive Model of Media Choice," *IEEE Transactions on Professional Communication*, (48:1), 2005, pp. 10–21.

Rogers, E. M. *Communication Technology: The New Media in Society*, The Free Press, New York, NY, 1986.

Schmitz, J. & Fulk, J. "Organizational Colleagues, Media Richness, and Electronic Mail," *Communication Research* (18:4), 1991, pp. 487–523.

Schultze, U. & Vandenbosch, B. "Information Overload in a Groupware Environment: Now You See It, Now You Don't," *Journal of Organizational Computing and Electronic Commerce* (8:2), 1998, 127–148.

Shannon, C. E. & Weaver, W. *The Mathematical Theory of Communication*, University of Illinois Press, Urbana, IL, 1949.

Shaw, W. E. *Group Dynamics*, 3rd edition, McGraw Hill, New York, 1981.

Sheer, V. C. & Chen, L. "Improving Media Richness Theory: A Study of Interaction Goals, Message Valence, and Task Complexity in Manager-Subordinate Communication," *Management Communication Quarterly* (18:1), 2004, pp. 76–93.

Short, J., Williams, E., & Christie, B. *The Social Psychology of Telecommunications*, Wiley, New York, 1976.

Simpson, J. "Conversational Floors in Synchronous Text-Based CMC Discourse," *Discourse Studies*, vol. 7, 2005, pp. 337–361.

Sitkin, S. B., Sutcliffe, K. M., Barrios-Choplin, J. R. "A Dual-Capacity Model of Communication Media Choice in Organizations," *Human Communication Research* (18:4), 1992, pp. 563–598.

Sproull, L. & Kiesler, S. *Connections: New Ways of Working in the Networked Organization*, MIT Press, Cambridge, MA, 1991, pp. 177–184.

Straus, S. G. "Technology, Group Process, and Group Outcomes: Testing the Connections in Computer-Mediated and Face-to-Face Groups," *Human–Computer Interaction* (12:3), 1997, pp. 227–266.

Straus, S. G. & McGrath, J. E. "Does the Medium Matter? The Interaction of Task Type and Technology on Group Performance and Member Perceptions," *Journal of Applied Psychology* (79:1), 1994, pp. 87–97.

Suh, K. S. "Impact of Communication Medium on Task Performance and Satisfaction: an Examination of Media-Richness Theory," *Information and Management* (35:5), 1999, pp. 295–312.

Te'eni, D. "Review: A Cognitive-Affective Model of Organizational Communication for Designing IT," *MIS Quarterly* (25:2), June 2001, pp. 251–312.

Topi, H., Valacich, J. S., & Rao, M. T. "The Effects of Personality and Media Differences on the Performance of Dyads Addressing a Cognitive Conflict Task," *Small Group Research*, 33(6), 2002, pp. 667–701.

Trevino, L. K., Lengel, R. H., & Daft, R. L. "Media Symbolism, Media Richness, and Media Choice in Organizations: A Symbolic Interactionist Perspective," *Communication Research* (14), 1987, pp. 553–574.

Trevino, L. K., Lengel, R. H., Bodensteiner, W., Gerloff, E., & Muir, N. K. "The Richness Imperative and Cognitive Style: The Role of Individual Differences in Media Choice Behavior," *Management Communication Quarterly* (4:2), 1990, pp. 176–197.

Valacich, J. S., Dennis, A. R., & Nunamaker, J. F. "Group-Size and Anonymity Effects on Computer-Mediated Idea Generation," *Small Group Research* (23:1), February 1992, pp. 49–73.

Valacich, J. S., Jung, J. H., & Looney, C. A. "The Effects of Individual Cognitive Ability and Idea Stimulation on Individual Idea Generation Performance," *Group Dynamics* (10:1), 2006, pp. 1–15.

Valacich, J. S., Paranka, D., George, J. F., & Nunamaker Jr., J. F. "Communication Parallelism and the New Media: A New Dimension for Media Richness," *Communication Research* (20:2), 1993, pp. 249–276.

Vessey, I. "Cognitive Fit: A Theory-Based Analysis of the Graphs Versus Tables Literature," *Decision Sciences* (22:2), 1991, pp. 219–240.

Vickery, S. K., Droge, C., Stank, T. P., Goldsby, T. J., & Markland, R. E. "The Performance Implications of Media Richness in a Business-to-Business Service Environment: Direct Versus Indirect Effects," *Management Science*, (50:8), 2004, pp. 1106–1119.

von Pape, T. "Media Adoption and Diffusion," in *Media Choice: A Theoretical and Empirical Overview*, T. Hartmann and P. Vorderer (Eds.), forthcoming.

Warkentin, M. E., Sayeed, L., & Hightower, R. "Virtual Teams Versus Face-to-Face Teams: An Exploratory Study of a Web-Based Conference System," *Decision Sciences* (28:4), 1997, pp. 975–996.

Walther, J. B. "Interpersonal Effects in Computer-Mediated Interaction," *Communication Research* (19:1), 1992, pp. 52–90.

Walther, J. B. "Computer Mediated Communication: Impersonal, Interpersonal, and Hyperpersonal Interaction," *Communication Research* (23:1), February 1996, pp. 3–41.

Watson-Manheim, M. B. & Belanger, F. "Communication Media Repertoires: Dealing with the Multiplicity of Media Choices," *MIS Quarterly* (31:2), June 2007, pp. 239–265.

Weick, K. E. *The Social Psychology of Organizing*, Addison Wesley, Reading MA, 1979.

Weick, K. E. "Cosmos vs. Chaos: Sense and Nonsense in Electronic Contexts," *Organizational Dynamics* (14:2), 1985, pp. 51–64.

Weick, K. E. & Meader, D. K. "Sensemaking and Group Support Systems," in *Group Support Systems: New Perspectives*, L. M. Jessup & J. S. Valacich (Eds.), Macmillan, New York, 1993, pp. 230–252.

Williams, E. "Experimental Comparisons of Face-to-face and Mediated Communication: A Review," *Psychological Bulletin* (84:5), 1977, pp. 963–976.

Yoo, Y. & Alavi, M. "Media and Group Cohesion: Relative Influences on Social Presence, Task Participation, and Group Consensus," *MIS Quarterly* (25:3), 2001, pp. 371–390.

Zack, M. H. "Electronic Messaging and Communication Effectiveness in an Ongoing Work Group," *Information and Management* (26:4), 1994, pp. 231–241.

Zigurs, I. & Buckland, B. K. "A Theory of Task Technology Fit and Group Support Systems Effectiveness," *MIS Quarterly*, (12:4), 1998, pp. 313–334.

Zmud, R. W., Lind, M. R., & Young, F. W. "An Attribute Space for Organizational Communication Channels," *Information Systems Research* (1:4), 1990, pp. 440–457.

Chapter 16

Media Adoption and Diffusion

Thilo von Pape

Users have lately been confronted with an increasing number of new media for both interpersonal and mass communication, namely in the context of the World Wide Web and mobile communication devices and services. To investigate why users choose a specific new medium for the first time, how these choices spread within a social system, and which choices follow in the course the implementation process, this chapter draws on *Diffusion of Innovations Theory*.

After an introductory overview of this approach's historical evolution, central elements of diffusion research are explained, and their strengths and drawbacks are discussed. The critique leads to three recent advances, namely 1) the integration of *Social Network Analysis* (*SNA*) to describe diffusion, 2) the complementation by social-psychological behavior theories on individual adoption decisions, and 3) the complementation by *Uses-and-Gratifications Approach* (*UGA*), *Cultural Studies* and *Sociology of Technology* as analytic responses to the discovery that users actively reinvent innovations. The following empirical overview gives insights into relevance and findings on the adoption and diffusion processes involving media choice. Finally, prospects on the approach's further development will be outlined.

Evolution of an Approach

The evolution of diffusion theory so far can be described in three partially overlapping stages:

1. arising from various sources from the end of the nineteenth century on until the 1960s,
2. consolidation into one comprehensive research tradition from the 1960s to the 1980s, and
3. theoretical and methodological deepening of specific elements also beginning in the 1960s, but still gaining momentum today.

Arising From Various Sources (1890–1960s)

Rogers (2003, pp. 44–45) lists nine independent origins of diffusion research, from anthropology (Wissler, 1914) and rural sociology (Ryan & Gross, 1943) to public health and medical sociology (Menzel & Katz, 1955), most of which originated between 1900 and 1950 (cf. Katz, Levin, & Hamilton, 1963). Two initiatives stand out among these equals.

The French sociologist Gabriel de Tarde (1843–1894) was the first to consider innovation as a general phenomenon over a wide spectrum of domains. Using data from public and economic statistics as well as observations ranging from Parisian street life to ancient art, Tarde (1962 [1890]; 1902) already evoked some of the phenomena constitutive of diffusion research up to today such as, for example, the role of opinion leaders and the S-shaped course of the diffusion curve. Also, he considered media as objects of diffusion, such as telegraphs, printing, and the Phoenician alphabet.

The agricultural sociologists Ryan and Gross (1943) largely shaped diffusion methodology with their study of the diffusion of hybrid corn among Iowa farmers (Rogers, 2003; Meyer, 2004; Lowery & deFleur, 1995). Meyer (2004, p. 59) resumes this methodology in five points: "1. quantitative data, 2. concerning a single innovation, 3. collected from adopters, 4. at a single point in time, 5. after widespread diffusion had already taken place."

A Comprehensive Research Tradition (1960s–1980s)

Everett Rogers (1931–2004) consolidated the diverse threads of diffusion theory in his seminal work *Diffusion of Innovations* (1962), giving an overview of more than 400 diffusion publications he found at the time. Rogers positioned his book with four subsequent editions (Rogers & Shoemaker, 1971; Rogers, 1983; 1995; 2003) not only as a "summary of past results," but also as a "research map for future studies" (Rogers & Shoemaker, 1971, p. 131). Thus, studies kept accumulating up to the number of 5,200 taken into account in the 2003 edition (Rogers, 2003, p. xviii). While media were considered primarily as channels for the communication of innovations (Rogers, 2003, p. 18), they also played a role as objects of diffusion. Studies have traced the diffusion of the Greek alphabet (Cook & Woodhead, 1959; McCarter, 1974; Warner, 1980), printing (Eisenstein, 1969), early radio technology (Lochte, 2000), the landline telephone (Fischer & Carroll, 1988), television (Brown, Malecki, Gross, Shrestha, & Semple, 1974; Loboda, 1974; Gurevitch & Loevy, 1972; Singhal, Doshi, Rogers, & Rahman, 1988), video cassette recorders (Ohashi, 2003; Ironmonger, Lloyd-Smith, & Soupourmas, 2000), and the fax machine (Straub, 1994; Weerahandi & Dalal, 1992; Holmlöv & Warneryd 1990). Also, specific media contents and formats have been the object of diffusion studies, such as telenovelas (Singhal, Rogers, & Brown, 1993).

The core assumptions of this "traditional diffusion theory" (Dearing & Meyer, 2006, p. 30) will be presented in the respective section below.

Deepening of Specific Elements (1960s to present)

From about the 1960s on, specific questions have been deepened through concepts from outside diffusion theory:

- Through which channels do innovations spread within interpersonal networks? This question was addressed by *Social Network Analysis* (*SNA*, Coleman, Katz, & Menzel, 1957, cf. Valente, 2006).
- Which factors determine the individual adoption decision? *Behavioral theories* from social psychology such as the *Theory of Reasoned Action* (*TRA*, cf. Fishbein & Ajzen, 1975), and the *Theory of Planned Behavior* (*TPB*, cf. Ajzen, 1985) have brought up models for this question.
- In which ways do users modify innovations in the course of their implementation? While the concept of *reinvention* (Rogers, 1983) is a first response to this question from within diffusion theory, various external approaches such as *Uses-and-Gratifications (UGA)*, *Cultural Studies* and *Sociology of Technology* have come up with further concepts.

Core Assumptions of Traditional Diffusion Theory

The classical theoretical corpus of *Diffusion of Innovations Theory* as it was laid down by Rogers can be considered as a bundle of elements containing hypotheses, heuristics and methods from two sources: One is the rather inductive generalization of existing approaches, and the other is the theoretical foundation of the Lasswell formula from communication theory (Lasswell 1948), which Rogers adapted as for structuring the findings.

Rogers describes his proceeding to generalize findings as a "meta- research," i.e. "the synthesis of empirical research results into more general conclusions at a theoretical level" (1983, p. 130). A maximum number of studies is revised in content analysis, focusing exclusively on the question of whether they have significant evidence to support specific generalizations, such as, for example, "Earlier adopters have higher social status than later adopters" (Rogers & Shoemaker, 1971, p. 357). As a result of this analysis, the 1971 edition of "Diffusion of Innovations" contains a "propositional inventory" of 103 generalizations in terms of bivariate correlations, listing for each generalization the number of studies supporting and not supporting it. A high number of empirical evidence combined with a high proportion of support permit us to judge this generalization as "valid" and eventually to consider it as a "principle" or even a "law" (Rogers & Shoemaker, 1971, p. 130).

In addition, Rogers and Shoemaker borrow from communication studies to structure their generalizations: They consider diffusion as a parallel to the communication process as expressed in the Lasswell formula (1948) and the corresponding "SMCRE"—model (Source → Message → Channel → Receiver → Effect): The inventor replaces the "source," the innovation the "message," diffusion channels the "channels," the adopter the "receiver" and adoption the "effects" (Rogers & Shoemaker, 1971, p. 20).

Combining literature review and communication theory, Rogers proposes a definition of diffusion structuring the core elements of diffusion theory: "Diffusion is the process in which an *innovation* is communicated through certain *channels* over *time* among the members of *a social system*" (Rogers, 2003, p. 5). The central dependent variable to most diffusion studies is *time*, i.e. the rapidity in which an innovation is adopted. The *innovation*'s characteristics, the *communication channels* applied and the characteristics of potential *adopters*[1] as well as the overall *social system* are primarily considered as factors influencing the time passing until adoption.

Time

Rogers reflects on "time" both on an individual and on a system's level, applying two heuristics to describe the process on each level.

The evolution leading to individual adoption—the *innovation decision process*—is considered as a consecution of five stages: *knowledge* of an innovation's existence and of its characteristics, *persuasion* about the adoption decision, the *decision* to adopt or reject, *implementation* as the process of putting the innovation into use, and *confirmation* through reinforcement of the adoption decision or—in case of discontent—discontinuity (Rogers, 2003, pp. 168–218).

The *diffusion* of a successful innovation in a social system is a process which Rogers describes in terms of the number and the consecutive segments of adopters (Figure 16.1). For successful innovations, the number of adopters can be described in terms of a bell curve, with the cumulative number of adopters representing an S-shaped diffusion curve. Thus, Rogers (2003, p. 280) characterizes the evolution of adoption decisions as a series of individual adoption decisions determined by a normal distribution of the potential adopters' determining characteristics. On this basis, Rogers (2003, pp. 267–299) discriminates five categories of adopters, characterizing each one of them through one dominant general value: *innovators* (venturesome), *early adopters* (respectful), *early majority* (deliberate), *late majority* (skeptical), and *laggards* (traditional). The partition is made on a purely statistical basis, by marking standard deviations (sd) from the average time of adoption ($\bar{\chi}$) (Figure 16.1).

Rogers acknowledges that other factors may influence adoption decisions beyond what is modeled in the normal distribution—by making an innovation more observable, more usable through direct network effects (as is the case for telecommunications innovations; cf. Gurbaxani, 1990; Rice, Grant,

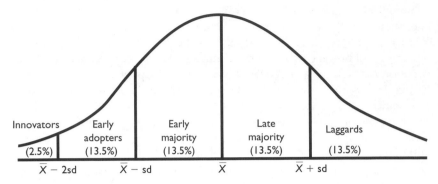

Figure 16.1 Adoption curve (Rogers, 2003, p. 281).

Schmitz, & Torobin, 1990; Allen, 1988) or more affordable through indirect network effects such as scaling effects permitting the producer to reduce the innovation's price (cf. Rogers, 2003, pp. 343–362; Mahler & Rogers, 1999). However, he does not present mathematical models for this dynamic.[2]

To identify factors influencing both the individual innovation decision process and the diffusion, Rogers (2003) proposes to analyze characteristics of the *innovation*, the *communication channels*, the *social system, and* the *adopters*.

Innovation

Five perceived attributes of innovations influence the rate of adoption: *relative advantage* compared to the status quo, *compatibility* with existing values, past experiences and needs, *trialability* as the degree to which the innovation can be tested without further engagement to use, *observability* and *complexity*, the latter having a negative influence on the adoption decision (Rogers, 2003, pp. 219–266).

Communication Channels

While mass media transmit awareness of the existence of an innovation, interpersonal communication is more relevant for the decision to adopt or reject it (Rogers, 2003, pp. 168–175). Corresponding to this generalization, Rogers also states that cosmopolite communication (interpersonal communication with others strange to the local network) rather influences the knowledge of an innovation while localite communication affects the decision itself (Rogers, 2003, pp. 207–208).

Adopter Attributes

The "innovativeness" is "the degree to which [a] unit of adoption is relatively earlier in adopting" (Rogers, 2003, p. 22). Thus, "early adopters" are, by definition, more innovative than "laggards." Rogers (2003, pp. 267–299) proposes 22 generalizations on social and personal characteristics correlating with innovativeness, such as a "high socioeconomic status" and a "more active and diverse communication behavior."

Social System

Finally, the social system as the context to adoption determines the paths of diffusion through its structure. A structural factor influencing diffusion is the degree of *homophily* within a social system, i.e. the tendency to communicate among actors with similar characteristics (cf. McCroskey, McCroskey, & Richmond, 2006): innovations are likely to spread within homophilous networks. Meanwhile, a certain degree of *heterophily* is necessary to permit innovations to enter into these networks: While people resembling each other usually don't offer each other anything new, contact with persons outside homophilous networks—also denoted as *weak ties* (Granovetter, 1973)— makes contact with innovation more likely. Overall, it is the socially more established *opinion leaders* who influence others on their adoption decision (Rogers, 2003, pp. 300–364).

The concepts outlined above make up a large part of traditional diffusion theory. Its current state can be summarized in the following words by Katz (1999, p. 147), indicating at the same time the need for further research: "I think that the best we can say about the state of diffusion theory today is that there is a more or less agreed paradigm—better, an accounting scheme—that allows for the classification of the wide variety of available case studies. True, there is the general S curve in the adoption of innovations and its more sophisticated elaborations; there is the general rule of trickle-down from higher to lower status; and there is the apparent need for reinforcement from peers prior to adoption. But the serious work of theorizing is still undone."

Critique and Recent Advances

Critique has addressed normative issues, theoretical and methodological issues and the very meta-theoretical approach with which Rogers has consolidated the diffusion tradition.

Normative Bias for Innovation and Diffusion

The normative critique is most emphasized by Rogers himself. He denounces a too optimistic view of innovations ("pro-innovation bias," Rogers, 2003, pp. 106–118) throughout many studies. Rogers (2003, pp. 130–133) also reproaches that many studies neglect the risks of social divides. These biases may be due to the fact that diffusion studies are often realized on behalf of organizations trying to promote diffusion of "their" innovation.

Theoretical and Methodological Stagnation

Moreover, critics denounce that "the number of diffusion studies continues at a high rate while the growth of appropriate theory is at an apparent standstill" (Katz, 1999, p. 145). Rogers himself notes in the preface of his standard work's last edition (2003, p. xxi): "we do not need more-of-the-same diffusion research." Specifically, the low degree of elaboration of diffusion theory's generalizations is criticized, which are almost completely restricted to two-variable correlations and omit considering interrelations and moderating effects between variables (Schmidt, 1976).

As a further symptom of stagnation, Meyer (2004) diagnoses that the methods are still confined to what Ryan and Gross had done in 1943. Also, the degree of standardization is very low. A lack of established scales for such constructs as "observability"—as an innovation attribute—or "social status"—as an adopter's characteristic—thus prevents comparison of different studies' outcomes. Meyer (2004, p. 69) resumes: "One cannot help but wonder whether the research questions asked over time have limited the methods selected, or rather if the methods established early on have restricted the research questions asked." The origin of both shortcomings may lie on a deeper level in the very epistemological proceeding which Rogers had chosen to integrate the various approaches into one comprehensive diffusion theory.

Inductive Epistemology

Rogers describes his proceeding to review a maximum number of studies in order to gain generalizations about innovation as a whole as "meta-research" (Rogers & Shoemaker, 1971). This approach has been contested for both the way data are accumulated and the interpretation of these accumulations.

Rogers collects evidence by a simple "vote taking" (Glass, 1976, p. 6) among existing findings, i.e. counting how many studies show significant support for a certain assertion and how many do not. This may be biased because neither sample size nor the size of effects nor the actual operationalization of constructs are considered in this method (Glass, 1976; Downs & Mohr, 1976). Also the *publication bias*—i.e., a tendency to prefer publications with significant outcomes in submission and acceptance—may cause an overestimation of hypotheses' confirmations. In sum, you cannot tell if a certain quota of confirmation is due to variance in respect to the theoretical generalization or in respect to differences between studies in operationalization, sample size or other methodological artifacts (Downs & Mohr, 1976).

Moreover, Rogers interprets the number and proportion of confirmative findings as indicators for a theoretical assumption's degree of "validity," insisting that 70 percent confirmation represents satisfactory validity (Rogers, 19831, p. 132). From a critical rationalist point of view, such an interpretation is problematic: If studies show that a general assumption does not account for all innovations, this assumption cannot be held up at all, but needs to be revised, confined in its range, or replaced by alternative assumptions. Attributing this importance to falsification of hypotheses would—according to Popper (1975)—have furthered the diffusion paradigm's evolution both theoretically and methodologically. As the following sections show, such an evolution seems to be on the way today due to the integration of new elements from outside diffusion theory.

Recent Theoretical and Methodological Advances in the Approach

As conceptual advances in diffusion theory, the integration of elements from social-psychological theories of behavior and from *SNA* will be presented, as well as the discovery of reinvention and potential approaches to enhance research on this phenomenon.

Social Network Analysis (SNA)

The concept of social networks was latent in the very first diffusion studies, insisting on the interpersonal influence between adopters (Ryan & Gross, 1943), but was only explicated and differentiated as *SNA* matured. Valente (2006) describes the evolution in four steps: First, interpersonal influence was discovered as an important factor influencing the adoption decision, notably by Coleman, Katz, and Menzel (1957) in their groundbreaking study on the diffusion of innovations among physicians. As a second step, structural models were integrated during the 1970s, permitting researchers to determine which channels transmit innovations in a network, and affirming the role of opinion leaders, but also the importance of weak ties as bridges for innovation (Granovetter, 1973). These efforts were soon appreciated by Rogers (Rogers and Kincaid, 1981) and accounted for in traditional diffusion research (Rogers, 1983). The third step is marked by a focus on critical points in the diffusion process such as the take-off of an innovation, when it has been adopted by a critical mass of members of a social system (Markus, 1987, cf. Schelling, 1978, Mahler & Rogers, 1999) or simply reached a threshold value within the personal network of a specific adopter (Valente, 1996). As a fourth step, the dynamic evolution of diffusion within networks is analyzed over time through event history analysis (Marsden & Podolny, 1990). This approach enables consideration of the specific distribution of influential actors and of those susceptible to adopt a behavior at any given point in time (Myers, 2000).

In general, the major contribution of *SNA* to diffusion theory is that this framework offers an extremely sharp set of empirical and analytical instruments permitting to differentiate, measure and predict interpersonal influence in the diffusion process.

Social-psychological Theories of Behavior

To better describe individual adoption decisions from a potential user's point of view, diffusion theory has been complemented by behavioral theories considering beliefs and evaluations towards adoption. While *TRA* by Fishbein and Ajzen (1975) was the first approach applying this concept to explain behavior, most empirical studies today rely on the enhanced *TPB* (Ajzen, 1985), presented in detail in Hartmann (this volume). Other related concepts are the *Technology Acceptance Model* (*TAM*, Davis, 1989) and, as the latest, the *Unified Theory of Adoption and Use of Technology* (*UTAUT*, Venkatesh, Morris, Davis, & Davis, 2003). These approaches have also explicitly integrated elements from *Diffusion of Innovations* theory, especially innovation attributes (Moore & Benbasat, 1991; Venkatesh, Morris, Davis, & Davis, 2003).

Thus came studies on the adoption and diffusion of home computers (Dickerson & Gentry, 1983; Davis, Bagozzi, & Warshaw, 1989; Lin, 1998; Dutton, Rogers, & Suk-Ho, 1987; Moore & Benbasat, 1991; 1996), videotext (Mayer, 1998; Bolton, 1981), e-mail (Gefen & Straub, 1997; Straub, 1994; Dimmick, Kline, & Stafford, 2000), the Internet with its different services such as e-learning (Lu, Liu, Yuan, & Liao, 2005), e-commerce (Pavlou & Chai, 2002) and instant messaging (Strader, Ramaswani, Sridhar, & Houle, 2007), mobile telephones and handheld devices (Ling, 1999, 2000; Schenk, Dahm, & Sonje, 1997; Leung & Wei, 1999; Davis & Venkatesh, 1996; Kshetri & Cheung, 2002; Sarker & Wells, 2003) and the different services accessible through these devices (Pedersen, Nysveen, & Thorbjornsen, 2002; Hung, Ku, & Chan, 2003).

These studies' contribution to diffusion theory is twofold: They have brought elaborated models on the causes of adoption, allowing differentiation between factors, and interrelations beyond simple two-variable-generalizations to be empirically identified. They have also led to standardization of empirical instruments, permitting competition and evolution of models.

Cultural Studies, Uses-and-gratifications, Sociology of Technology

A third element of diffusion theory that has been deepened recently is the question of how innovations are being actively implemented. Evidence has shown that users do not simply adopt innovations, but often reinvent them in the course of their implementation (Charters & Pellegrin, 1972; cf. Rice

& Rogers, 1980). Rogers (1983) has only partially responded to this evidence by underlining that communication of innovations is not a one-way process, by conceding that innovations can be reinvented by users in the course of their implementation, and by including four generalizations on reinvention. However, the large majority of generalizations remain focused on the binary adoption decision and a linear diffusion process. Thus, diffusion theory is still bound to the linear logic of the Lasswell formula with a relatively clear allocation of roles between a limited number of very active people who design innovations, and the large majority whose role is to take the binary adoption decision later (Dearing & Meyer, 2006).

Meanwhile, both cultural studies and mass communication theory have replaced this communication model by evoking the more creative activities of media users in "decoding" (Hall 1980) and seeking gratifications (Katz, Blumler, & Gurevitch, 1973).

In *Cultural Studies*, Silverstone established the *Domestication* approach, analyzing how users "tame" the "wild" communication technology in their everyday life (Silverstone & Haddon, 1996). This approach has since been applied to a number of media such as personal computers (Lehtonen, 2003; Venkatesh, 2001), Internet (Bakardjieva, 2005), mobile telephones (Haddon, 2003; Lehtonen, 2003), and "video on demand" (Ling, Nilsen, & Granhaug, 1999) (for an overview, see Berker, Harmann, Punie, & Ward, 2006).

The analysis of new media uses has also led to a "revival" of *UGA* (Ruggiero 2000, p. 20). Coming from innovations in television such as the remote control (Walker & Bellamy, 1991), cable TV (Atkin, 1993; Heeter & Greenberg, 1985; Jacobs, 1995), video recorders (Lin, 1993) and video text (Cowles, 1989), the approach was extended to personal computers (Perse & Dunn, 1998), computer games (Sherry, Lucas, Greenberg, & Lachlan, 2006), electronic bulletin boards (James, Wotring, & Forrest, 1995), websites (Eighmey & McCord, 1998), e-mail (Dimmick, Kline, & Stafford, 2000) and chat (Leung, 2001) as well as mobile telephones, personal digital assistants (Trepte, Ranné, & Becker, 2003; Peters & ben Allouch, 2005), mp3 players (Ferguson, Greer, & Reardon, 2007) and mobile multimedia applications (Wei, 2008).

Other approaches mainly from the *Sociology of Technology* describe how innovations are "framed" (Goffman, 1974; Taylor & Harper, 2003; Ling, 2004), "socially constructed" (Pinch & Bijker, 1984) or "socially shaped" (MacKenzie & Wajman, 1985).

These perspectives have contributed to the understanding that the adoption of a new medium is not a single decision to use a clearly defined object but rather a process of consecutive choices concerning the meaning and the functions attributed to an innovation by users—which may change the very face of the innovation in the course of the diffusion process (Wirth, von Pape, & Karnowski, 2008). This idea can be traced back to Tarde (1962,

1902), who describes the diffusion of innovations as a radiance of waves which may interfere and refract when entering different users' "lifeworlds" and thus change the innovations' character.

Conclusion and Future Directions

Diffusion of Innovations Theory is today a well established research perspective offering a large spectrum of heuristics and generalizations to understand and predict the choice to first use a new medium. Although centennial in age, it is undergoing major theoretical and methodological evolutions. These are driven by influences from *SNA*—as the complementary approach most considered within *Diffusion of Innovations Theory* so far—but also from social psychological behavior theories, *Cultural Studies, Uses-and-Gratifications* and *Sociology of Technology*.

Whether the choice to use a specific medium can be sufficiently explained by traditional diffusion theory or only with the additional support of one of the advances outlined above, depends largely on the medium in question. This can be illustrated by one concluding example: Apple's "iPhone" is on first sight a very clearly defined innovation, materialized in a specific artifact which is distributed in a linear way from licensed agents to consumers—a process clearly accounted for in the producer's sales figures. In this case, traditional diffusion theory holds many helpful concepts in store. For example, a high rate of adoption can be explained by the product's relatively low complexity and its high observability as a status symbol (Rogers, 2003, p. 266). Further, the fact that Apple cut prices by 33 percent after only six weeks on the market seems like a logical move to keep the innovation affordable as the adoption curve moves onwards from the innovators to less pecunious segments—just as described by classical diffusion theory (Rogers, 2003, p. 298). In terms of diffusion, this move also gave momentum to the technology, which is important in order to achieve network effects critical to this innovation (cf. Markus, 1987). However, both the individual users' preferences and the network effects can only roughly be considered on the basis of diffusion theory's bivariate generalizations, while behavioral theory and *SNA* permit considering these factors in much more detail: Studies on the diffusion of software and mobile Internet services show that different innovation attributes are salient for different adopters (Venkatesh, Morris, Davis, & Davis 2003; Hsu, Lu, & Hsu 2007). *SNA* shows that network effects occur—for some innovations—rather in the immediate personal network than in the overall social system (Valente, 1996), and it helps identify centrally positioned actors who influence diffusion within their networks (Valente & Davis, 1999).

Finally, when looking beyond the simple media devices, the question of what consumers do with them becomes more relevant: Apple gains not only through selling stylish devices, but also through various services available from these devices ranging from entertainment to Internet and telephony

(Fraser, 2007). The question thus becomes critical which services adopters will choose to use in the course of implementation. Also, Apple proposes a developer kit with which technologically sophisticated users can themselves create new services. Finally, hackers are busy developing entirely new applications undesired by the producer (e.g. bypassing commitments to providers). But which services will users—legally or illegally—develop and institutionalize? To respond to these questions, the formerly clear line between developers and users, conception and implementation needs to be lifted.

Potential users will always be confronted with media innovations of varying dynamic and complexity. Consequently, diffusion theory needs to propose a comprehensive toolkit from which researchers can pick the instruments which best apply to the adoption and implementation choices in question. To provide this option, two integrative steps seem necessary for the progress of diffusion research:

- Integration of *TPB* and *SNA* to describe diffusion: It seems evident that social norms, which play a determining role in *TPB*, are distributed along specific network structures that could be analyzed via *SNA*. On the other hand, individual actors' perspectives may permit us to understand factors critical to *SNA* such as individual adoption thresholds, which are arguably related to factors such as "attitude" and "subjective norm."
- Integration of approaches on implementation. This demands that we question the linear structure of diffusion and adoption processes, and emphasizes the users' creative contribution to the construction of innovations (Meyer, 2004). Here, *UGA*, Cultural Studies and Sociology of Technology are promising approaches (Wirth et al., in press).

Notes

1. While Rogers considers adopter characteristics as a part of the element "time," we will treat them independently here, to underline that they are a factor potentially influencing "time," as are "innovation," "the social system," and "communication"; (see also Katz et al., 1963, who discriminate between seven elements).
2. The most popular and most comprehensive alternative is the "Bass"-curve, comprising in its function both a logistic model and an exponential model of diffusion and any combination of both (Bass, 1969, for an overview, see Meade & Islam, 2006).

References

Agarwal, R. & Prasad, J. (1997). The role of innovation characteristics and perceived voluntariness in the acceptance of information technologies. *Decision Sciences*, 28 (3), 557–582.

Ajzen, I. (1985). From intentions to actions: A theory of planned behavior. In J. Kuhl & J. Beckman (Eds.), *Action-control: From Cognition to Behavior* (pp. 11–39). Heidelberg: Springer.

Allen, D. (1988). New telecommunications services: Network externalities and critical mass. *Telecommunications Policy*, 12 (3), 257–271.

Atkin, D. J., Jeffres, L. W., & Neuendorf, K. A. (1998). Understanding Internet adoption as telecommunications behavior. *Journal of Broadcasting & Electronic Media*, 42(4), 475–490.

Bakardjieva, M. (2005). *Internet Society: The Internet in Everyday Life*. London: Sage.

Bass, F. (1969). A new product growth model for consumer durables. *Management Science*, 15(5), 215–227.

Berker, T., Hartmann, M., Punie, Y., & Ward, K. (Eds.). (2006). *Domestication of Media and Technology*. New York: McGraw-Hill.

Bolton, W. T. (1981). The perception and potential adoption of channel 2000: Implications for diffusion theory and videotex technology. *Journal of Broadcasting*, 27(1), 141–153.

Bonfadelli, H. (2002). The Internet and knowledge gaps. *European Journal of Communication*, 17(1), 65–84.

Brown, L. A., Malecki, E. J., Gross, S. J., Shretha, M. N., & Semple, R. K. (1974). The diffusion of cable television in Ohio: A case study of diffusion agency location patterns and processes of the polynuclear type. *Economic Geography*, 50(4), 285–299.

Carey, J. W. (1977). Mass communication research and cultural studies: An American View. In J. Curran, M. Gurevitch, & J. Woolacott (Eds.), *Mass Communication and Society*. London: Edward Arnold.

Cestre, G. & Darmon, R. (1998). Assessing consumer preferences in the context of new product diffusion. *International Journal of Research in Marketing*, 15, 123–135.

Charters, W. W. Jr. & Pellegrin, R. S. (1972). Barriers to the innovation process: four case studies of differentiated staffing. *Educational Administration Quarterly*, 9, 1, 3–14.

Chin, W. W. & Marcolin, B. (2001). The future of diffusion research. *ACM SIGMIS Database*, 32 (3), 7–12.

Coleman, J. S., Katz, E., & Menzel, H. (1957). The diffusion of an innovation among physicians. *Sociometry*, 20 (4), 253–270.

Cook, R. M. & Woodhead, A. G. (1959). The diffusion of the Greek alphabet. *American Journal of Archeology*, 63(2), 175–178.

Cowles, D. (1989). Consumer perceptions of interactive media. *Journal of Broadcasting & Electronic Media*, 33(1), 83–89.

Davis, F. & Venkatesh, V. (1996). A critical assessment of potential measurement biases in the technology acceptance model: Three experiments. *International Journal Of Human–Computer Studies*, 45(1), 19–45.

Davis, F. D. (1989), Perceived usefulness, perceived easy of use, and user acceptance of information technology. *MIS Quarterly*, 13, 319–339.

Davis, F. D., Bagozzi, R. P., & Warshaw, P. R. (1989). User acceptance of computer technology: A comparison of two theoretical models. *Management Science*, 35(8), 982–1003.

Dearing, J. W. & Meyer, G. (2008). Revisiting diffusion theory. In A. Singhal & J. W. Dearing (Eds.), *Communication of Innovations: A Journey with Ev Rogers* (pp. 29–60). New Delhi: Sage.

Dearing, J. M. & Singhal, A. (2006). Communication of innovations: A journey with

Ev Rogers. In A. Singhal & J. Dearing, (Eds.), Communication *of Innovations: A Journey with Ev Rogers* (pp. 15–28). London: Thousand Oaks, New Delhi: Sage Publications.

Dickerson, M. D. & Gentry, J. W. (1983). Characteristics of adopters and non-adopters of home computers. *The Journal of Consumer Research*, 10(2), 225–235.

Dimmick, J., Kline, S., & Stafford, L. (2000). The gratification niches of personal e-mail and the telephone: Competition, displacement and complementarity. *Communication Research*, 27(2), 227–248.

Downs, G. W. & Mohr, L. B. (1976). Conceptual issues in the study of innovation. *Administrative Science Quarterly*, 21(4), 700–714.

Dutton, W. H., Rogers, E. M., & Suk-Ho, J. (1987). Diffusion and social impacts of personal computers. *Communication Research*, 14(2), 219–250.

Eighmey, J. & McCord, L. (1998). Adding value in the information age: uses and gratifications of sites on the World Wide Web. *Journal of Business Research*, 41(3), 187–194.

Eisenstein, E. L. (1969). The advent of printing and the problem of the Renaissance. *Past and Present*, 45, 19–89.

Ferguson, D. A., Greer, C. F., & Reardon, M. E. (2007) Uses and gratifications of MP3 players among college students: are Ipods more popular than radio? *Journal of Radio Studies*, 14(2), 102-121.

Fischer, C. S. (1992). *America Calling: A Social History of the Telephone to 1940.* Berkeley: University of California Press.

Fischer, C. S. & Carroll, G. R. (1988). Telephone and automobile diffusion in the United States, 1902–1937. *The American Journal of Sociology*, 93(5), 1153–1178.

Fishbein, M. & Ajzen, I. (1975). *Belief, Attitude, Intention and Behavior: An Introduction to Theory and Research.* Reading, MA: Addison-Wesley.

Flichy, P. (1995). *L'innovation technique. Récents développements en sciences sociales vers une nouvelle théorie de l'innovation.* Paris: La Découverte.

Fraser, H. M. (2007). The practice of breakthrough strategies by design. *Journal of Business Strategy*, 28(4), 66–74.

Gefen, D. & Straub, D. W. (1997). Gender differences in the perception and use of e-mail: An extension to the technology acceptance model, *MIS Quarterly*, 21(4), 389–400.

Glaser, G. V. (1976). Primary, secondary, and meta-analysis of research. *Educational Researcher*, 5(10), 3–8.

Goffman, E. (1974). Frame Analysis: An Essay on the Organization of Experience. New York: Harper and Row.

Granovetter, M. S. (1973). The strength of weak ties. *American Journal of Sociology*, 78(6), 1361–1380.

Gurevitch, M. & Loevy, Z. (1972). Diffusion of television as an innovation: The case of the Kibbutz. *Human Relations*, 25, 181–197.

Gurbaxani, V. (1990). Diffusion in computing networks: The use of BITNET. *Communications of the ACM*, 33(12), 65–75.

Haddon, L. (2003). Domestication and mobile telephony. In J. Katz (Ed.), *Machines That Become Us: The Social Context of Personal Communication Technology* (pp. 43–56). New Brunswick: Transaction Publishers.

Hall, S. (1980). Encoding/decoding. In S. Hall, D. Hobson, A. Lowe, & P. Willis (Eds.), *Culture, Media, Language* (pp. 128–138). London: Hutchison.

Heeter, C. & Greenberg, B. (1985). Cable and program choice. In D. Zillman & J. Bryant (Eds.), *Selective Exposure to Communication* (pp. 203–224). Hillsdale: Lawrence Erlbaum Associates.

Holak, S. (1988). Determinants of innovative durables adoption an empirical study with implications for early product screening. *Journal of Product Innovation Management*, 5(1), 50–69.

Holak, S. & Lehmann, D. (1990). Purchase intentions and the dimensions of innovation: an exploratory model. *Journal of Product Innovation Management*, 7(1), 59–73.

Holmlöv, P. G. & Warneryd, K.-E. (1990). Adoption and use of fax in Sweden. In M. Carnevale, M. Lucertini, & S. Nicosia (Eds.), *Modeling the Innovation: Communications, Automation and Information Systems* (pp. 95–102). Amsterdam: Elsevier Science.

Hsu, C.-L., Lu, H.-P., & Hsu, H.-H. (2007). Adoption of the mobile Internet: An empirical study of multimedia message service (MMS). *Omega*, 35, 715–726.

Hung, S.-Y., Ku, C.-Y., & Chan, C.-M. (2003). Critical factors of WAP services adoption: An empirical study. *Electronic Commerce Research an Applications*, 2(1), 42–60.

Ironmonger, D. S., Lloyd-Smith, C. W., & Soupourmas, F. (2000). New products of the 1980s and 1990s: The diffusion of household technology in the decade 1985–1995. *Prometheus*, 18(4), 403–415.

Jacobs, R. (1995). Exploring the determinants of cable television subscriber satisfaction. *Journal of Broadcasting & Electronic Media*, 39(2), 262–274.

James, M. L., Wotring, C. E., & Forrest, E. J. (1995). An exploratory study of the perceived benefits of electronic bulletin board use and their impact on other communication activities. *Journal of Broadcasting & Electronic Media*, 39(1), 30–50.

Karahanna, E., Straub, D., & Chervany, N. L. (1999). Information technology adoption across time: A cross-sectional comparison of pre-adoption and post-adoption beliefs. *MIS Quarterly*, 23 (2), 183–213.

Karnowski, V., von Pape, T., & Wirth, W. (2006). Zur Diffusion Neuer Medien: Kritische Bestandsaufnahme aktueller Ansätze und Überlegungen zu einer integrativen Diffusions- und Aneignungstheorie Neuer Medien. *Medien- und Kommunikationswissenschaft*, 54 (1), 56–74.

Katz, E. (1999). Theorizing diffusion: Tarde and Sorokin revisited. *Annals of the American Academy of Political and Social Science*, 566 (1), 144–155.

Katz, E., Levin, M. L., & Hamilton, H. (1963). Traditions of research on the diffusion of innovation. *American Sociological Review*, 28(2), 237–252.

Katz, E., Blumler, J. G., & Gurevitch, M. (1973). Uses and gratifications research. *The Public Opinion Quarterly*, 37 (4), 509–523.

Kshetri, N. & Cheung, M. K. (2002). What factors are driving China's mobile diffusion? *Electronic Markets*, 12(1), 22–26.

Lasswell, H. D. (1948). The structure and formation of Communication in Society. In L. Bryson (Ed.), *The Communication of Ideas*. New York: Harper and Brothers.

Lehtonen, T. (2003). The domestication of new technologies as a set of trials. *Journal of Consumer Culture*, 3(3), 363–385.

Leung, L. (2001). College student motives for Chatting on ICQ. *New Media & Society*, 3(4), 483–500.

Leung, L. & Wei, R. (1999). Who are the mobile have-nots? Influences and consequences. *New Media & Society*, 1(2), 209–226.

Lin, C. A. (1998). Exploring the personal computer adoption dynamics. *Journal of Broadcasting & Electronic Media*, 41(1), 95–112.

Lin, C. A. (2003). An interactive communication technology adoption model. *Communication Theory*, 13 (4), 345–365.

Ling, R. (1999). "I am happiest by having the best." The adoption and rejection of mobile telephony, R&D report 15/99. Kjeller, Norway: Telenor.

Ling, R. (2000). The adoption of mobile telephony among Norwegian teens, May 2000. Telenor notat, 57.

Ling, R. (2004). *The Mobile Connection: The Cell Phone's Impact on Society*. San Francisco, Oxford: Elsevier/Morgan Kaufmann.

Ling, R., Nilsen, S., & Granhaug, S. (1999). The domestication of video-on-demand: folk understanding of a new technology. *New Media & Society*, 1(1), 83–10.

Loboda, J. (1974). The diffusion of television in Poland. *Economic Geography*, 50(1), 70–82.

Lochte, R. H. (2000). Invention and innovation of early radio technology. *Journal of Radio Studies*, 7(1), 93–115.

Loges, W. E. & Jung, J.-Y. (2001). Exploring the digital divide: Internet connectedness and age. *Communication Research*, 28(4), 536–562.

Lowery, S. A. & DeFleur, M. L. (1995). The Iowa study of hybrid seed corn. Milestones in mass communication research: Media effects. In S. A. Lowery & M. L. DeFleur (Eds.), *Milestones in Mass Communication Research: Media Effects* (pp. 115–133). White Plains, NY: Longman.

Lu, H.-P., Liu, S.-H., Yuan, C., & Liao, H.-L. (2005). Factors influencing the adoption of e-learning websites: An empirical study. *Issues in Information Systems*, 6(1), 190–196.

MacKenzie, D. & Wajcman, J. (eds.) (1985) *The Social Shaping of Technology: How the Refrigerator Got Its Hum*. Milton Keynes: Open University Press.

Mahler, A. & Rogers, E. M. (1999). The diffusion of interactive communication innovations and the critical mass: the adoption of telecommunications services by German banks. *Telecommunications Policy*, 23, 719–747.

Markus, M. L. (1987). Toward a critical mass theory of interactive media: Universal access, interdependence and diffusion. *Communication Research*, 14, 491–511.

Markus, M. L. (1990). Toward a critical mass theory of interactive media: Universal access, interdependence and diffusion. In J. Fulk & C. Steinfield (Eds.), *Organizations and Communication Technology* (194–218). Newbury Park, CA: Sage.

Marsden, P. & Podolny, J. (1990). Dynamic analysis of network diffusion processes. In J. Weesie & H. Flap (Eds.), *Social Networks Through Time* (pp. 197–214). Utrecht: ISOR.

Mayer, R. N. (1998). The growth of the French videotex system and its implications for consumers. *Journal of Consumer Policy*, 11(1), 55–83.

McCarter, P. K. (1974). The early diffusion of the alphabet. *Biblical Archeologist*, 37(3), 54–68.

McCroskey, L. L., McCroskey, J. C., & Richmond, V. P. (2006). Analysis and improvement of the measurement of interpersonal attraction and homophily. *Communication Quarterly*, 54, 1–31.

Meade, N. & Islam, T. (2006). Modelling and forecasting the diffusion of innovation —a 25-year review. *International Journal of Forecasting*, 22(3), 519–545.

Menzel, H. & Katz, E. (1955). Social relations and innovation in the medical profession: The epidemiology of a new drug. *Public Opinion Quarterly*, 19, 337–353.

Meyer, G. (2004). Diffusion methodology: Time to innovate? *Journal of Health Communication*, 9 (Supplement 1), 59–69.

Moore, G. C. & Benbasat, I. (1991). Development of an instrument to measure the perceptions of adopting an information technology innovation. *Information Systems*, 2(3), 192–222.

Moore, G. C. & Benbasat, I. (1996). Integrating diffusion of innovations and theory of reasoned action models to predict utilization of information technology by end-users. In K. Kautz & J. Pries-Heje (Eds.), *Diffusion and Adoption of Information Technology* (pp. 132–146). London: Chapman and Hall.

Morris, M. G. & Venkatesh, V. (2000). Age differences in technology adoption decisions: Implications for a changing work force. *Personnel Psychology*, 53(2), 375–403.

Musmann, K. & Kennedy, W. H. (1989). *Diffusion of Innovations: A Select Bibliography*. Westport, CT: Greenwood Press.

OECD. (2001). *Understanding the Digital Divide*. Paris: OECD.

Myers, D. J. (2000). The diffusion of collective violence: infectiousness, susceptibility, and mass media networks. *American Journal of Sociology*, 106(1), 173–208.

Ohashi, H. (2003). The Role of Network Effects in the US VCR Market. *Journal of Economics & Management Strategy*, 12(4), 447–494.

Pavlou, P. A. & Chai, L. (2002). What drives electronic commerce across cultures? A cross-cultural empirical investigation of the theory of planned behavior. *Journal of Electronic Commerce Research*, 3(4), 240–253.

Pedersen, P. E., Nysveen, H., & Thorbjornsen, H. (2002). *The Adoption of Mobile Services: A Cross Service Study*. Bergen, Norway: Foundation for Research in Economics and Business Administration.

Perse, E. M. & Dunn, D. G. (1998). The utility of home computers and media use: implications of multimedia and connectivity. *Journal of Broadcasting & Electronic Media*, 42(4), 435–456.

Peters, O. & Ben Allouch, S. (2005). Always connected: A longitudinal field study of mobile communication. *Telematics & Informatics*, 22(3), 239–256.

Pinch, T. J. & Bijker, W. E. (1984). The social construction of facts and artefacts: Or how the sociology of science and the sociology of technology might benefit each other. *Social Studies of Science*, 14, 399–441.

Popper, K. R. (1975), *Objective Knowledge—An Evolutionary Approach*, 4th ed. Oxford: Clarendon.

Rice, R. E. & Katz, J. E. (2003). Comparing internet and mobile phone usage: digital divides of usage, adoption and dropouts. *Telecommunication Policy*, 27, 597–623.

Rice, R. E., Grant, A., Schmitz, J., & Torobin, J. (1990). Individual and network influences on the adoption and perceived outcomes of electronic messaging. *Social Networks*, 12, 27–55.

Rice, R. E. & Rogers, E. M. (1980). Reinvention in the innovation process. *Knowledge: Creation, Diffusion, Utilization*, 1(4), 499–514.

Rogers, E. M. (1962). *Diffusion of Innovations*. New York: Free Press.

Rogers, E. M. (1983). *Diffusion of Innovations: A Cross-Cultural Approach* (3 ed.). New York: Free Press.

Rogers, E. M. (2000a). *Diffusion of Printing and the Internet*. Conference on the Printing Press and Internetted Computers. Santa Monica, California.

Rogers, E. M. (2000b). The digital divide. *Convergence*, 7(4), 96–111.

Rogers, E. M. (2003). *Diffusion of Innovations* (5th ed.). New York: Free Press.

Rogers, E. M. & Kincaid, D. L. (1981). *Communication Networks: Toward a New Paradigm for Research*. New York: Free Press.

Rogers, E. M. & Shoemaker, F. (1971). *Communication of Innovations: A Cross-cultural Approach* (2nd ed.). New York: Free Press.

Ryan, B. & Gross, N. C. (1943). The diffusion of hybrid seed corn in two Iowa communities. *Rural Sociology*, 8(1), 15–24.

Sarker, S. & Wells, J. D. (2003). Understanding mobile handheld device use and adoption. *Communications of the ACM*, 46(12), 35–40.

Schelling, T. (1978). *Micromotives and Macrobehavior*. New York, London: W. W. Norton.

Schenk, M., Dahm, H., & Sonje, D. (1997). Die Bedeutung sozialer Netzwerke bei der Diffusion neuer Kommunikationstechniken. *Kölner Zeitschrift für Soziologie und Sozialpsychologie*, 49(1), 35–52.

Schmidt, P. (1976). *Innovation*. Hamburg: Hoffmann und Campe.

Sherry, J. L., Lucas, K., Greenberg, B. S. & Lachlan, K. (2006). Video game uses and gratifications as predictors of use and game preference. In P. Vorderer & J. Bryant (Eds.), *Playing Video Games: Motives, Responses, and Consequences* (pp. 213–224). Mahwah: Lawrence Erlbaum Associates.

Silverstone, R. & Haddon, L. (1996). Design and the domestication of information and communication technologies: Technical change and everyday life. In R. Silverstone & R. Mansell (Eds.), *Communication by Design: The Politics of Information and Communication Technologies* (pp. 44–74). Oxford: Oxford University Press.

Singhal, A., Doshi, J. K., Rogers, E. M., & Rahman, S. A. (1988). The diffusion of television in India. *Media Asia*, 15(4), 222–229.

Singhal, A., Rogers, E. M., & Brown, W. J. (1993). Harnessing the potential of entertainment-education telenovelas *International Communication Gazette*, 51(1), 1–18.

Soule, S. A. (1999). The diffusion of an unsuccessful innovation. *Annals of the American Academy of Political and Social Science*, 566, 120–131.

Strader, T. J., Ramaswami, S. N., & Houle, P. A. (2007). Perceived network externalities and communication technology acceptance. *European Journal of Information Systems*, 16, 54–65.

Strang, D. & Soule, S. A. (1998). Diffusion in organizations and social movements: From hybrid corn to poison pills. *Annual Review of Sociology*, 24, 265–290.

Straub, D. W. (1994). The effect of culture on IT diffusion: E-mail and fax in Japan and the U.S. *Information Systems Research*, 5(1), 23–47.

de Tarde, G. (1962 (1890)). *The Laws of Imitation* (Les lois de l'imitation). Gloucester, MA: P. Smith.

de Tarde, G. (1902). L'invention considérée comme moteur de l'évolution sociale. *Revue Internationale de Sociologie*, 7, 561–574.

Taylor, A. S. & Harper, R. (2003). The gift of the gab: a design oriented sociology of young people's use of mobiles. *Journal of Computer Supported Cooperative Work*, 12(3), 267–296.

Tornatzky, L. G. & Klein, R. J. (1982). Innovation characteristics and innovation adoption-implementation: A meta-analysis of findings. *IEEE Transactions on Engineering Management*, 29(1), 28–45.

Trepte, S., Ranné, N., & Becker, M. (2003). "Personal digital assistants": Patterns of user gratifications. *Communications: European Journal of Communication Research*, 8(4), 457–473.

Valente, T. (2006). Communication network analysis and the diffusion of innovations. In A. Singhal & J. W. Dearing (Eds.), *Communication of Innovations: A Journey with Ev Rogers* (pp. 61–82). New Delhi: Sage.

Valente, T. W. (1996). Social network thresholds in the diffusion of innovations. *Social Networks*, 18, 69–89.

Valente, T. W. & Davis, R. L. (1999). Accelerating the diffusion of innovations using opinion leaders. *Annals of the American Academy of Political and Social Science*, 566, 55–67.

Venkatesh, A. (2001). The home of the future: an ethnographic study of new information technologies in the home. *Advances in Consumer Research*, 28, 88–96.

Venkatesh, V., Morris, M. G., Davis, G. B., & Davis, F. (2003). User acceptance of information technology: Toward a unified view. *MIS Quarterly*, 27(3), 425–478.

Vishwanath, A. & Goldhaber, G. M. (2003). An examination of the factors contributing to adoption decisions among late-diffused technology products. *New Media & Society*, 5(4), 547–572.

Walker, J. R. & Bellamy, R, V. (1991). Gratifications of grazing: an exploratory study of remote control use. *Journalism Quarterly*, 68(3), 422–431.

Warner, S. (1980). The alphabet: An innovation and its diffusion. *Vetus Testamentum*, 30(1), 81–90.

Weerahandi, S. & Dalal, S. R. (1992). A choice-based approach to the diffusion of a service: Forecasting fax penetration by market segments. *Marketing Science*, 11(1), 39–53.

Wissler, C. (1914). The influence of the horse in the development of plains culture. *American Anthropologist*, 16, 1–25.

Wirth, W., von Pape, T., & Karnowski, V. (2008). An integrative model of mobile phone appropriation. *Journal of Computer-Mediated Communication (JCMC)*, 13(1), 593–617.

Index